KATHY SLOANE

# RETHINKING OUR CLASSROOMS

## Teaching for Equity and Justice

A *Rethinking Schools* Publication

# TABLE OF CONTENTS

## INTRODUCTION

**Creating Classrooms for Equity and Social Justice**
by the editors ............................... 4

**"Lions"**
by Langston Hughes ................... 6

## POINTS OF DEPARTURE

Points of Departure includes a number of readings that exemplify the teaching principles we outline in the Introduction.

**Unlearning the Myths That Bind Us**
by Linda Christensen ................... 8

**Rethinking "The Three Little Pigs"**
by Ellen Wolpert ............................. 11

**10 Quick Ways to Analyze Children's Books**
by The Council on Interracial Books for Children ....................... 14

**Celebrating the Joy in Daily Events**
by Linda Christensen ................... 16

**"Ode to My Socks"**
by Pablo Neruda ........................... 17

**Taking Multicultural, Anti-racist Education Seriously**
an interview with Enid Lee ........ 19

## RETHINKING MY CLASSOOM

Rethinking My Classroom includes our "core" articles. At various grade levels and disciplines, five teachers offer concrete examples of how a social justice curriculum transformed their classroom practice.

**Race and Respect Among Young Children**
by Rita Tenorio ....................... 24

**"My Hair is Long"**
by Loyen Redhawk Gali ............. 29

**Teaching for Social Justice: One Teacher's Journey**
by Bob Peterson ....................... 30

**The Challenge of Classroom Discipline**
by Bob Peterson ....................... 34

**Songs that Promote Justice**
by Bob Peterson ....................... 38

**"Ballad of the Landlord"**
by Langston Hughes ................. 39

**The Complexities of Encouraging Social Action**
by Bob Peterson ....................... 40

**"Honeybees"**
by Paul Fleischman ...................... 42

**Tapping Into Feelings of Fairness**
by Karen Miller ........................... 44

**"Love's Gonna Get Us"**
by Damon Turner ....................... 49

**Building Community from Chaos**
by Linda Christensen ................ 50

**Discipline: No Quick Fix**
by Linda Christensen ................ 56

**Getting Off the Track**
by Bill Bigelow ........................... 58

**"what the mirror said"**
by Lucille Clifton ......................... 66

## TEACHING IDEAS

How do we prompt students to watch TV critically? How can we use math to unmask social inequities? Teaching Ideas provides a variety of class-room-tested activities that illus-trate themes woven throughout the book.

**Using Pictures to Combat Bias**
by Ellen Wolpert ........................ 68

**My Mom's Job Is Important**
by Matt Witt ............................... 70

**"My Father Was A Musician"**
by Dyan Watson .......................... 73

**There's More to Heroes Than He-Man**
by Marcie Osinsky ....................... 74

**Black Lies/White Lies**
by Nancy Schniedewind and Ellen Davidson ......................... 75

**Bringing the World into the Math Class**
by Claudia Zaslavsky ................. 76

**"Dream Voyage to the Center of the Subway"**
by Eve Merriam ............................ 79

**Coping With TV**
by Bob Peterson .......................... 80

**Talking Back to TV Commercials** ............................ 82

**Looking Pretty, Waiting for the Prince**
by Lila Johnson .......................... 83

**Math and Media: Bias Busters**
by Bob Peterson .......................... 84

**What Do We Say When We Hear 'Faggot'?**
by Lenore Gordon ...................... 86

**The Organic Goodie Simulation**
by Bill Bigelow and Norm Diamond ................. 88

# TABLE OF CONTENTS

"Questions from a
Worker Who Reads"
by Bertolt Brecht..........................91

World Poverty and
World Resources
by Susan Hersh
and Bob Peterson ...................... 92

Math, Equity,
and Economics..............................94

Taking the Offensive
Against Offensive Toys
by Lenore Gordon ....................... 96

"Forgiving My Father"
by Justin Morris .......................... 97

The Day Sondra Took Over
by Cynthia M. Ellwood...............98

"Little Things Are Big"
by Jesús Colón ........................... 102

What Can Teachers Do
About Sexual Harassment?
by Ellen Bravo
and Larry Miller..........................103

Flirting vs. Sexual Harassment:
Teaching the Difference
by Nan Stein
and Lisa Sjostrom ................... 106

"Rayford's Song"
by Lawson Inada ....................... 108

Celebrating the Student's Voice
by Linda Christensen .............. 109

Promoting Social Imagination
by Bill Bigelow
and Linda Christensen .............110

"Two Women"
Anonymous ...................................112

Role Plays: Show, Don't Tell
by Bill Bigelow .............................114

Testing, Tracking, and Toeing the
Line: A role play on the origins of
the modern high school
by Bill Bigelow .............................117

## RETHINKING OUR ASSUMPTIONS

The articles in Rethinking Our Assumptions are filled with insights from teachers, scholars, and researchers on issues ranging from cultural differences between students and teachers to biases in children's literature.

Expectations and 'At-Risk' Children
by L.C. Clark.................................. 126

Teachers and Cultural Styles
by Asa G. Hilliard III.................. 127

The Pigs: When Tracking Takes Its Toll
by Molly Schwabe........................129

Seeing Color:
A Review of White Teacher
by Lisa Delpit ............................130

"Face the Facts: We're Not That Bad"
by Felícitas Villanueva ............. 133

I Won't Learn From You!
by Herbert Kohl ......................... 134

"Rebellion Against the North Side"
by Naomi Shihab Nye .............. 136

The Politics of Children's Literature
by Herbert Kohl ......................... 137

"The Funeral of
Martin Luther King, Jr."
by Nikki Giovanni ....................... 141

Whose Standard?
Teaching Standard English
by Linda Christensen ...............142

Thoughts on Teaching
Native American Literature
by Joseph Bruchac...................146

Why Students
Should Study History
an interview with
Howard Zinn .............................. 150

"In Memory of Crossing
the Columbia"
Elizabeth Woody........................ 157

Students as Textbook Detectives
by Bill Bigelow
and Bob Peterson .....................158

"To the Young Who Want to Die"
by Gwendolyn Brooks.............. 160

## BEYOND THE CLASSROOM

Beyond the Classroom connects innovations in classroom practice with strategies for broader change, drawing on examples from around the country to identify possibilities and dangers.

Why We Need to Go
Beyond the Classroom
by Stan Karp ............................. 162

"Gurl"
by Mary Blalock..........................167

Forging Curriculum Reform
Throughout a District
by David Levine ..........................168

Why Standardized Tests Are Bad
by Terry Meier .............................. 171

Detracking Montclair High
by Stan Karp ............................. 176

Tracking: Why Schools Need
To Take Another Route
by Jeannie Oakes ....................... 178

"Lineage"
by Margaret Walker ..................182

## TEACHING GUIDE/ RESOURCES

The Teaching Guide/Resources section includes curricula, books, videos, journals, and organizations that have been useful in constructing classrooms for social justice. Here, we also offer teaching ideas for using the poetry included in this volume.

Poetry Teaching Guide .............. 184

Videos with a Conscience
by Bill Bigelow
and Linda Christensen ............187

Books to Empower
Young People................................. 191

Other Resources ........................ 196

# Creating Classrooms for Equity and Social Justice

*Rethinking Our Classrooms* begins from the premise that schools and classrooms should be laboratories for a more just society than the one we now live in. Unfortunately, too many schools are training grounds for boredom, alienation, and pessimism. Too many schools fail to confront the racial, class, and gender inequities woven into our social fabric. Teachers are often simultaneously perpetrators and victims, with little control over planning time, class size, or broader school policies — and much less over the unemployment, hopelessness, and other "savage inequalities" that help shape our children's lives.

But *Rethinking Our Classrooms* is not about what we cannot do; it's about what we can do. Brazilian educator Paulo Freire writes that teachers should attempt to "live part of their dreams within their educational space." Classrooms can be places of hope, where students and teachers gain glimpses of the kind of society we could live in and where students learn the academic and critical skills needed to make it a reality. We intend the articles in *Rethinking Our Classrooms* to be both visionary and practical; visionary because we need to be inspired by each other's vision of schooling; practical because for too long teachers have been preached at by theoreticians, well removed from classrooms, who are long on jargon and short on specific examples.

We've drawn the articles, stories, poems, and lessons in *Rethinking Our Classrooms* from different academic disciplines and grade levels. Despite variations in emphasis, a common social and pedagogical vision unites this collection. This vision is characterized by several interlocking components that together comprise what we call a so-cial justice classroom. In *Rethinking Our Classrooms* we argue that curriculum and classroom practice must be:

• **Grounded in the lives of our students.** All good teaching begins with a respect for children, their innate curiosity and their capacity to learn. Curriculum should be rooted in children's needs and experiences. Whether we're teaching science, mathematics, English, or social studies, ultimately the class has to be about our students' lives as well as about a particular subject. Students should probe the ways their lives connect to the broader society, and are often limited by that society.

• **Critical**. The curriculum should equip students to "talk back" to the world. Students must learn to pose essential critical questions: Who makes decisions and who is left out? Who benefits and who suffers? Why is a given practice fair or unfair? What are its origins? What alternatives can we imagine? What is required to create change? Through critiques of advertising, cartoons, literature, legislative decisions, military interventions, job structures, newspapers, movies, agricultural practices, or school life, students should have opportunities to question social reality. Finally, student work must move outside the classroom walls, so that scholastic learning is linked to real world problems.

• **Multicultural, anti-racist, pro-justice.** In our earlier publication, *Rethinking Columbus*, we used the Discovery myth to demonstrate how children's literature and textbooks tend to value the lives of Great White Men over all others. Traditional materials invite children into Columbus's thoughts and dreams; he gets to speak, claim land, and re-name the ancient homelands of Native Americans, who appear to have no rights. Implicit in many traditional accounts of history is the notion that children should disregard the lives of women, working people, and especially people of color — they're led to view history and current events from the standpoint of the dominant groups. By contrast, a social justice curriculum must strive to include the lives of all those in our society, especially the marginalized and dominated. As anti-racist educator Enid Lee points out (see interview, p. 19), a rigorous multiculturalism should engage children in a critique of the roots of inequality in curriculum, school structure, and the larger society — always asking: How are we involved? What can we do?

• **Participatory, experiential.** Traditional classrooms often leave little room for student involvement and initiative. In a "rethought" classroom, concepts need to be experienced first-hand, not just read about or heard about. Whether through projects, role plays, simulations, mock trials, or experiments, students need to be mentally, and often physically, active. Our classrooms also must provoke students to develop their democratic capacities: to question, to challenge, to make real decisions, to collectively solve problems.

• **Hopeful, joyful, kind, visionary.** The ways we organize classroom life should seek to make children feel significant and cared about — by the teacher and by each other. Unless students feel emotionally and physically safe, they won't share real thoughts and feelings. Discussions will be tinny and dishonest. We need to design activities where students learn to trust and care for each other. Classroom life should, to the greatest extent possible, pre-figure the kind of democratic and just society we envision and thus contribute to building that society. Together students and teachers can create a "community of conscience," as educators Asa Hilliard and Gerald Pine call it.

• **Activist.** We want students to come to see themselves as truth-tellers and change-makers. If we ask children to critique the world but then fail to encourage them to act, our classrooms can degenerate into factories for cynicism. While it's not a teacher's role to direct students to particular organizations, it is a teacher's role to suggest that ideas should be acted upon and to offer students opportunities to do just that. Children can also draw inspiration from historical and contemporary efforts of people who struggled for justice. A critical curriculum should be a rainbow of resistance, reflecting the diversity of people from all cultures who acted to make a difference, many of whom did so at great sacrifice. Students should be allowed to learn about and feel connected to this legacy of defiance.

• **Academically rigorous.** A social justice classroom equips children not only to change the world but also to maneuver in the one that exists. Far from devaluing the vital academic skills young people need, a critical and activist curriculum speaks directly to the deeply rooted alienation that currently discourages millions of students from acquiring those skills.

A social justice classroom offers more *to* students than do traditional classrooms and expects more *from* students. Critical teaching aims to inspire levels of academic performance far greater than those motivated or measured by grades and test scores. When children write for real audiences, read books and articles about issues that really matter, and discuss big ideas with compassion and intensity, "academics" starts to breathe. Yes, we must help students "pass the tests," (even as we help them analyze and critique the harmful impact of test-driven education). But only by systematically reconstructing classroom life do we have any hope of cracking the cynicism that lies so close to the heart of massive school failure,

> *Rethinking Our Classrooms begins from the premise that schools and classrooms should be laboratories for a more just society than the one we now live in.*

and of raising academic expectations and performance for all our children.

• **Culturally sensitive.** Critical teaching requires that we admit we don't know it all. Each class presents new challenges to learn from our students and demands that we be good researchers, and good listeners. These days, the demographic reality of schooling makes it likely that white teachers will enter classrooms filled with children of color. As African-American educator Lisa Delpit writes in her review of the book *White Teacher* (see p. 130), "When teachers are teaching children who are different from themselves, they must call upon parents in a collaborative fashion if they are to learn who their students really are." They must also call upon culturally diverse colleagues and community resources for insights into the communities they seek to serve. What can be said about racial and cultural differences between teachers and students also holds true for class differences.

\* \* \* \*

We're suspicious of the "inspirational speakers" administrators bring to faculty meetings, who exhort us to become super-teachers and classroom magicians. Critical teaching requires vision, support, and resources, not magic. We hope the stories, critiques,

and lesson ideas here will offer useful examples which can be adapted in classrooms of all levels and disciplines and in diverse social milieus. Our goal is to provide a clear framework to guide classroom transformation.

But as vital as it is to re-imagine and re-organize classroom practice, ultimately it's insufficient. Teachers who want to construct more equitable, more meaningful, and more lively educational experiences for children must also concern themselves with issues beyond the classroom walls. For example, if a school uses so-called ability grouping to sort students, then no matter how successful we are in our efforts to remake classroom life, many students will still absorb negative messages about their capacity to achieve. We need to confront tracking and standardized testing, the funding inequalities within and between school districts, and the frequent unwillingness of teacher unions to address issues of quality education. Rethinking our classrooms requires rethinking the role of teacher unions and inventing strategies so that teachers can make alliances with parents and community organizations who have an interest in equity. Toward this end we've offered a chapter, "Beyond the Classroom."

As we go to press with this special edition of *Rethinking Schools*, there are many reasons to be discouraged about the future: Districts continue to slash budgets across the country; violence in our schools shows no signs of abating; attempts to privatize the schools have not slowed; and the country's productive resources are still used to make zippier video games, smarter smart bombs, and fancier athletic shoes, rather than used in less profitable arenas like education and affordable housing.

There is a Zulu expression: "If the future doesn't come towards you, you have to go fetch it." We hope *Rethinking Our Classrooms* will be a useful tool in the movement to go fetch a better future: in our classrooms, in our schools, and in the larger society. There are lots of us out there. Critical and activist teachers work all across the country. Let's make our voices heard. ❑

— *the editors*

# Lions

## By Langston Hughes

*Lions in zoos*
*Shut up in a cage*
*Live a life of smothered rage.*
*Lions in the forest*
*Roaming free*
*Are happy as ever*
*Lions can be.*

Langston Hughes is probably the most famous poet of the Harlem Renaissance. He chose to write about ordinary people — as he said, "workers, roustabouts, and singers, and job hunters...people up today and down tomorrow...beaten and baffled, but determined not to be wholly beaten." (See p. 184 for lesson ideas.)

RETHINKING OUR CLASSROOMS

KATHY SLOANE

# POINTS OF DEPARTURE

Although the one-room schoolhouse is a relic of the past, certain patterns within American education have proven stubbornly durable: the dominance of the teacher's voice, reluctance to accept cultural diversity, and uncritical acceptance of the social and political order.

The articles in this introductory chapter show how teachers can challenge these patterns through classroom alternatives which deepen learning and enrich interactions between students and teachers.

# Unlearning the Myths That Bind Us
## Critiquing Fairy Tales and Films

By Linda Christensen

I was nourished on the milk of American culture: I cleaned the dwarves' house and waited for Prince Charming to bring me life; I played Minnie Mouse to Mickey's flower-bearing adoration, and, later, I swooned in Rhett Butler's arms — my waist as narrow and my bosom every bit as heaving as Scarlett's. But my daddy didn't own a plantation; he owned a rough and tumble bar frequented by loggers and fishermen. My waist didn't dip into an hourglass; in fact, according to the novels I read, my thick ankles doomed me to be cast as the peasant woman reaping hay while the heroine swept by with her handsome man in hot pursuit.

Our students suckle the same pap. They learn that women are passive, men are strong, and people of color are either absent or evil. Our society's culture industry colonizes their minds and teaches them how to act, live, and dream. The "secret education," as Chilean writer Ariel Dorfman dubs it, delivered by children's books and movies instructs students to accept the world as it is portrayed in these social blueprints. And often that world depicts the domination of one sex, one race, one class, or one country over a weaker counterpart. My student Omar wrote, "When we read children's books, we aren't just reading cute little stories, we are discovering the tools with which a young society is manipulated."

More than social primers, these tales, filled with ducks and mice and elephants in green suits, inhibit the ability of older students to question and argue with the texts they read. Children's literature is perhaps the most influential genre read. As my colleague Bill Bigelow noted, young people, unpro-

tected by any intellectual armor, hear these stories again and again, often from the warmth of their mother's or father's lap. The messages, or "secret education," linked with the security of their parents' arms, underscore the power these texts deliver. The stereotypes and world view embedded in these stories become accepted knowledge.

Too often, my high school students read novels, history texts, and the daily paper as if they were watching a baseball game — they keep track of who's up, who's out, and the final score. They are consumers. Many students don't know how to read. I don't mean they are illiterate. They can read the words. They can answer multiple choice questions about who said "to be or not to be" and who wore a scarlet letter under his vest. But they just "walk on the words," as Brazilian educator Paulo

> 'Have you ever seen a Black person, an Asian, a Hispanic in a cartoon? Did they have a leading role or were they a servant? The hero or the villain?'

Freire says, instead of wrestling with the words and ideas presented.

My goal is to give students the tools to critique every idea that encourages or legitimates social inequality — every idea that teaches them they are incapable of imagining and building a fundamentally equal and just society. Children shouldn't be taught that domination is normal or nice or funny. That's why we watch *The Little Mermaid* and read *The Ugly Duckling* in my high school English classes.

### Exposing the Myths: How to Read Cartoons

We begin by reading the preface and first chapter of Ariel Dorfman's book *The Empire's Old Clothes*, subtitled, "What the Lone Ranger, Babar, and other innocent heroes do to our minds." I ask students to read Dorfman and keep track of their responses in a dialogue journal which consists of a paper folded in half from the top to the bottom. They quote or paraphrase Dorfman on the left side of the paper and argue, agree, or question him on the right. Dorfman writes in his book:

"Industrially produced fiction has become one of the primary shapers of our emotions and our intellect in the twentieth century. Although these stories are supposed to merely entertain us, they constantly give us a secret education. We are not only taught certain styles of violence, the latest fashions, and sex roles by TV, movies, magazines, and comic strips; we are also taught how to succeed, how to love, how to buy, how to conquer, how to forget the past and suppress the future. We are taught more than anything else, how not to rebel."

Thus, according to Dorfman, children's and popular literature function to maintain existing power relations in society and to undercut the possibility of greater democracy and equality.

I ask students if they agree with Dorfman's notion that children receive a "secret education." Do they remember any incidents from their own childhood that support his allegations? This is difficult for some students. The dialogue journal spurs them to argue, to talk back, to create a conversation with the writer. Dorfman is controversial. He gets under their skin. Many of them don't want to believe that they have been manipulated by children's books or advertising. As Dorfman writes:

"There has also been a tendency to avoid scrutinizing these mass media products too closely, to avoid asking the sort of hard questions that can yield disquieting answers. It is not strange that this should be so. The industry itself has declared time and again with great forcefulness that it is innocent, that no hidden motives or implications are lurking behind the cheerful faces it generates."

Dorfman's desire "to dissect those dreams, the ones that had nourished my childhood and adolescence, that continued to infect so many of my adult habits" bothered Justine, a senior in my Contemporary Literature and Society class a few years ago. In her dialogue journal she responded:

"Personally, handling the dissection of dreams has been a major cause of depression for me. Not so much dissecting — but how I react to what is found as a result of the operation. It can be overwhelming and discouraging to find out my whole self image has been formed mostly by others or underneath my worries about what I look like is years (17 of them) of being exposed to TV images of girls and their set roles given to them by TV and the media. It's painful to deal with. The idea of not being completely responsible for how I feel about things today is scary. So why dissect the dreams? Why not stay ignorant about them and happy? The reason for me is that those dreams are not unrelated to my everyday life. They

WALT DISNEY CO.

The jealous stepmother in *Snow White*.

influence how I behave, think, react to things. ... My dreams keep me from dealing with an unpleasant reality."

In looking back through this passage and others in Justine's dialogue with Dorfman, Justine displayed discomfort with prying apart her ideals, with discovering where she received her ideas, and yet she also grudgingly admitted how necessary this process was if she wanted to move beyond where she was at the time. Her discomfort might also have arisen from feeling incapable of changing herself or changing the standards by which she is judged in the larger society. In a later section of her journal, she wrote, "True death equals a generation living by rules and attitudes they never questioned and producing more children who do the same."

Justine's reaction is typical of many students. She was beginning to peel back the veneer covering some of the injustice in our society. She appreciated the importance of constructing a more liberatory set of possibilities for girls and women, but at the same time was overwhelmed by the hugeness of this task — unsure if she would have anything to hang on to after she began dismantling her old values.

### Charting Stereotypes

To help students both dismantle those old values and reconstruct more just ones, I carry twin objectives with me when we begin this study of children's culture: first, to critique portrayals of hierarchy and inequality, but also to enlist students in imagining a better world, characterized by relationships of mutual respect and equality. We start by watching cartoons and children's movies — Bugs Bunny,

Popeye, Daffy Duck, and Heckle and Jeckle videos in one class; in my freshman class we also watch Disney's *The Little Mermaid*. On first viewing, students sometimes resist critical analysis. Kamaui said, "This is just a dumb little cartoon with some ducks running around in clothes." Later they notice the absence of female characters in many of the cartoons. When women do appear, they look like Jessica Rabbit or Playboy centerfolds. We keep track of the appearance of people of color in classic children's movies — Cinderella, Sleeping Beauty, Snow White. We look at the roles women, men, people of color, and poor people play in the same films. We also cover men's roles. As they view each episode, they fill in a chart. Here is a partial sample from the ninth grade class evaluation of *The Little Mermaid*.

**Women's Roles:**

Ariel: Pretty, white, shapely, kind. Goal: Marry the prince.

Ursula: Fat, white, mean. Goals: Get back at Triton, power.

Maid: Chubby, confused, nice, white. Goals: Meals on time, clean clothes.

**People of Color**: None, although Sebastian the crab is Jamaican and the court musician.

**Poor People**: Servants. No poor people have major roles.

After filling in a couple of charts, collectively and on their own, students write about the generalizations children might take away from these tales. The ninth graders are quick to point out the usual stereotypes on their own, "Look, Ursula the sea witch is ugly and smart. The young, pretty ones only want to hook their man; the old, pretty ones are mean because they are losing their looks." Kenneth noticed that people of color and poor people are either absent or servants to the rich, white, pretty people. Tyler pointed out that the roles of men are limited as well. Men must be virile and wield power or be old and the object of "good-natured" humor.

Both the freshmen and the seniors write critiques of the cartoons, targeting parents or teachers as an audience. Mira, a senior two years ago, attacked the racism in these Saturday morning

The Ugly Duckling

rituals. Because of her familiarity with Native American cultures, her analysis was more developed:

"Indians in Looney Tunes are also depicted as inferior human beings. These characters are stereotypical to the greatest degree, carrying tomahawks, painting their faces, and sending smoke signals as their only means of communication. They live in tipis and their language reminds the viewer of Neanderthals. We begin to imagine Indians as savages with bows and arrows and long black braids. There's no room in our minds for knowledge of the differences between tribes, like the Cherokee alphabet or Celilo salmon fishing."

## A Black Cinderella?

Kenya, a freshman, scolded parents in her essay, "A Black Cinderella? Give Me A Break." "Have you ever seen a Black person, an Asian, a Hispanic in a cartoon? Did they have a leading role or were they a servant? What do you think this is doing to your child's mind?" She ended her piece, "Women who aren't White begin to feel left out and ugly because they never get to play the princess." Kenya's piece bristled with anger at a society that rarely acknowledges the wit or beauty of women of her race. But she wasn't alone in her

feelings. Sabrina W. wrote, "I'm not taking my kids to see any Walt Disney movies until they have a Black woman playing the leading role." They wanted the race of the actors changed, but they didn't challenge the class or underlying gender inequities that also accompany the lives of Cinderella, Ariel, and Snow White.

Kenya's and Sabrina's anger is justified. There should be more women of color who play the leads in these white-on-white wedding cake tales. But I want them to understand that if the race of the main character is the only thing changing, injustice will remain. We read Mary Carter Smith's delightful retelling of Cinderella, "Cindy Ellie, A Modern Fairy Tale," which reads like laughter — bubbly, warm, spilling over with infectious good humor and playful language. In Smith's version, Cindy Ellie, who lives in East Baltimore, was "one purty young black sister, her skin like black velvet." Her father, "like so many good men, was weak for a pretty face and big legs and big hips." Her step-mother "had a heart as hard as a rock. The milk of human kindness had curdled in her breast. But she did have a pretty face, big legs, and great big hips. ... Well, that fool man fell right into that woman's trap." Cindy Ellie's step-sisters were "two big-footed, ugly gals" who made Cindy Ellie wait on them hand and foot. When the "good white folks, the good Asian folks, and the good black folks all turned out and voted for a good black brother, running for mayor" there was cause for celebration, and a chance for Cindy Ellie to meet her Prince Charming, the mayor's son. With the help of her godma's High John the Conqueror Root, Cindy Ellie looked like an "African Princess." "Her rags turned into a dazzling dress of pink African laces! Her hair was braided into a hundred shining braids, and on the end of each braid were beads of pure gold! ... Golden bracelets covered her arms clean up to her elbows! On each ear hung five small diamond earrings. On her tiny feet were dainty golden sandals encrusted with dazzling jewels!

Cindy Ellie was laid back!"

The students and I love the story. It is well told and incorporates rich details that do exactly what Sabrina, Kenya, and their classmates wanted — it celebrates the beauty, culture, and language of African Americans. It also puts forth the possibility of cross-race alliances for social change.

But, like the original tale, Cindy Ellie's main goal in life is not working to end the plight of the homeless or teaching kids to read. Her goal, like Cinderella the First's, is to get her man. Both young women are transformed and made beautiful through new clothes, new jewels, new hairstyles. Both have chauffeurs who deliver them to their men. Cindy Ellie and Cinderella are nicer and kinder than their step-sis-

ters, but the Prince and Toussant, the mayor's son, don't know that. Both of the C-girls compete for their men against their sisters and the rest of the single women in their cities. They "win" because of their beauty and their fashionable attire. Both of these tales leave African American and white women with two myths: happiness means getting a man, and transformation from wretched conditions can be achieved through new clothes and a new hairstyle.

I am uncomfortable with those messages. I don't want students to believe that change can be bought at the mall, nor do I want them thinking that the pinnacle of a woman's life is an "I do" that supposedly leads them to a "happily ever after." I don't want my women stu-

# Rethinking 'The Three Little Pigs'

### By Ellen Wolpert

There's scarcely a parent or young child who isn't familiar with "The Three Little Pigs." It has a simple plot line, is easily remembered, and it's so much fun imitating the big bad wolf as he huffs and puffs and "blo-o-ws" the house down.

I find the story is also useful to talk about the stereotypes in so many of our favorite tales.

I first became aware of the story's hidden messages when we were doing a unit on housing several years ago at my daycare center. As part of the unit, we talked about different homes and the many approaches to solving a basic human need: a place to live.

### An Interesting Question

During the discussion I suddenly thought to myself, "Why are brick homes better than straw homes?"

To this day, I'm not completely sure why that question popped into my mind. I do know, however, that I had been sensitized by the movement for a multicultural curriculum, which

**Why are brick homes better than straw homes?**

had taught me to take a questioning approach to even the most seemingly innocuous materials and to look beneath the surface for hidden assumptions.

After thinking about it, I realized that one of the most fundamental messages of "The Three Little Pigs" is that it belittles straw and stick homes and the "lazy types" who build them. On the other hand, the story extols the virtues of brick homes, suggesting that they are built by serious, hard-working people and strong enough to withstand adversity.

Is there any coincidence that brick homes tend to be built by people in

Western countries, often by those with more money? That straw homes are more common in non-European cultures, particularly Africa and Asia?

Once I realized some of these hidden messages, the question became what to do about it. In my experience, the best approach is not to put-down such beloved tales and refuse to read them, but to use them to pose questions for children. One might explain, for example, that in many tropical areas straw homes are built to take best advantage of cooling breezes. In some areas, straw homes are on stilts as protection from insects and animals or to withstand flooding.

Such a perspective then becomes part of a broader process of helping children to understand why homes are different in different parts of the world — and that just because something is different doesn't mean it's inferior. ❑

*Ellen Wolpert is director of the Washington-Beech Community Preschool in Boston.*

dents to see their "sisters" as competition for that scarce and wonderful commodity — men. As Justine wrote earlier in her dialogue journal, it can be overwhelming and discouraging to find our self-images have been formed by others, but if we don't dissect them, we will continue to be influenced by them.

## Writing as a Vehicle for Change

I hoped the essays they wrote critiquing cartoons would force students to look deeper into the issues — to challenge the servant/master relationships or the materialism that makes women appealing to their men. For some students the cartoon unit exposes the wizardry that controls our dreams and desires — our self images — but others shrug their shoulders at this. It's OK for some people to be rich and others poor; they just want to see more rich people of color or more rich women. Or better yet, be rich themselves. They accept the inequalities in power and economic relationships. Their acceptance teaches me how deep the roots of these myths are planted and how much some students, in the absence of visions for a different and better world, need to believe in the fairy tale magic that will transform their lives.

Mira and her classmates wrote their most passionate essays of the year on this topic. But venting their frustrations with cartoons — and even sharing it with their class — seemed an important, but limited task. Yes, they could write articulate essays. Yes, they honed their arguments and sought the just-right examples from their viewing. Through critiques and the discussions that followed they were helping to transform each other — each comment or observation helped expose the engine of our society, and they were both excited and dismayed by their discoveries. But what was I teaching them if the lesson ended there? Ultimately, I was teaching that it was enough to be critical without taking action, that we could quietly rebel in the privacy of the classroom while we were practicing our writing skills, but we didn't really have to do anything about the problems we uncovered, nor did we need to create

Aladdin

Jessica Rabbit from Looney Tunes.

anything to take the place of what we'd expelled. And those were not the lessons I intended to teach. I wanted to develop their critical consciousness, but I also hoped to move them to action.

But for some students — especially the seniors — the lesson didn't end in the classroom. Many who watched cartoons before we started our study say they can no longer enjoy them. Now instead of seeing a bunch of ducks in clothes, they see the racism, sexism, and violence that swim under the surface of the stories. Pam and Nicole swore they would not let their children watch cartoons. David told the class of coming home one day and finding his nephews absorbed in Looney Tunes. "I turned that TV off and took them down to the park to play. They aren't going to watch that mess while I'm around." Radiance described how she went to buy Christmas presents for her niece and nephew. "Before, I would have just walked into the toy store and bought them what I knew they wanted — Nintendo or Barbie. But this time, I went up the clerk and said, 'I want a toy that isn't sexist or racist.'"

Students have also said that what they saw in cartoons, they see in advertising, on prime time TV, on the news, in school. Turning off the cartoons didn't stop the sexism and racism. They couldn't escape, and now that they'd started analyzing cartoons, they couldn't stop analyzing the rest of the world. And sometimes they wanted to stop. During a class discussion Sabrina S. said, "I realized these problems weren't just in cartoons. They were in everything — every magazine I picked up, every television show I watched, every billboard I passed by on the street." As Justine wrote earlier, at times they would like to remain "ignorant and happy." The following year it became more evident than ever that if we stayed with critique and didn't move to action students might slump into cynicism.

## Taking Action

To capture the passion and alleviate the pain, Tim Hardin, a Jefferson English teacher, and I decided to get the students out of the classroom with their anger — to allow their writing and their learning to become vehicles for change. Instead of writing the same classroom essays students had written the years before, we asked students to think of an audience for their cartoon analysis. Most students chose parents. A few chose their peers. Then they decided how they wanted to reach them. Some wanted to create a pamphlet which could be distributed at PTA meetings throughout the city. That night they went home with assignments they'd given each other — Sarah would watch Saturday morning cartoons; Sandy, Brooke, and Carmel would watch after-school cartoons; and Kristin and Toby were assigned before-school cartoons. They ended up writing a report card for the various programs. They graded each show A-F and wrote a brief summary of their findings:

"DUCK TALES: At first glance the precocious ducks are cute, but look closer and see that the whole show is based on money. All their adventures revolve around finding money. Uncle Scrooge and the gang teach children that money is the only important thing in life. Grade: C-

"TEENAGE MUTANT NINJA TURTLES: Pizza-eating Ninja Turtles.

> I don't want my students to believe that change can be bought at the mall.

What's the point? There isn't any. The show is based on fighting the 'bad guy,' Shredder. Demonstrating no concern for the townspeople, they battle and fight, but never get hurt. This cartoon teaches a false sense of violence to kids: fight and you don't get hurt or solve problems through fists and swords instead of words. Grade: D

"POPEYE: This show oozes with horrible messages from passive Olive Oyl to the hero 'man' Popeye. This cartoon portrays ethnic groups as stupid. It is political also — teaching children that Americans are the best and conquer all others. Grade: F."

On the back of the pamphlet, they listed some tips for parents to guide them in wise cartoon selection.

Most of the other students wrote articles they hoped to publish in various local and national newspapers or magazines. (See p. 83) Catkin wrote about the sexual stereotyping and adoration of beauty in children's movies. Her article describes how she and other teenage women carry these messages with them still:

"Women's roles in fairy tales distort reality — from Jessica Rabbit's six-mile strut in *Who Framed Roger Rabbit?* to Tinkerbelle's obsessive vanity in *Peter Pan*. These seemingly innocent stories teach us to look for our faults. As Tinkerbelle inspects her tiny body in a mirror only to find that her minute hips are simply too huge, she shows us how to turn the mirror into an enemy. ...And this scenario is repeated in girls' locker rooms all over the world. ...Because we can never look like Cinderella, we begin to hate ourselves.

The Barbie syndrome starts as we begin a life-long search for the perfect body. Crash diets, fat phobias, and an obsession with the materialistic become commonplace. The belief that a product will make us rise above our competition, our friends, turns us into addicts. Our fix is that Calvin Klein push-up bra, Guess jeans, Chanel lipstick, and the latest in suede flats. We don't call it deception; we call it good taste. And soon it feels awkward going to the mailbox without makeup."

Catkin hopes to publish her piece in a magazine for young women so they will begin to question the origin of the standards by which they judge themselves.

The writing in these articles is tighter and cleaner because it has the potential for a real audience beyond the classroom walls. The possibility of publishing their pieces changed the level of students' intensity for the project. Anne, who turned in hastily written drafts last year, said, "Five drafts and I'm not finished yet!"

But more importantly, students saw themselves as actors in the world; they were fueled by the opportunity to convince some parents of the long-lasting effects cartoons impose on their children or to enlighten their peers about the roots of some of their insecurities. Instead of leaving students full of bile, standing around with their hands on their hips, shaking their heads about how bad the world is, we provided them the opportunity to make a difference. ❑

*Linda Christensen (lchrist@aol.com) is language arts coordinator for Portland Public Schools and a* Rethinking Schools *editor.*

Works Cited:
Anderson, Hans Christian (retold by Lilian Moore), (1987). *Ugly Duckling.* New York: Scholastic.
Dorfman, Ariel, (1983). *The Empire's Old Clothes.* New York: Pantheon.
Shor, Ira and Paulo Freire, (1987). *A Pedagogy for Liberation.* South Hadley, MA: Bergin & Garvey.
Smith, M.C. (1989). "Cindy Ellie, A Modern Fairy Tale." *Talk That Talk.* New York: Simon and Schuster, 396-402.

# 10 Quick Ways to Analyze Children's Books for Racism and Sexism

## By the Council on Interracial Books for Children

Both in school and out, young children are exposed to racist and sexist attitudes. These attitudes — expressed over and over in books and in other media — gradually distort their perceptions until stereotypes and myths about minorities and women are accepted as reality. It is difficult for a librarian or teacher to convince children to question society's attitudes. But if a child can be shown how to detect racism and sexism in a book, the child can proceed to transfer the perception to wider areas. The following ten guidelines are offered as a starting point in evaluating children's books from this perspective.

### 1. Check the Illustrations

**Look for Stereotypes.** A stereotype is an oversimplified generalization about a particular group, race, or sex, which usually carries derogatory implications. In addition to blatant stereotypes, look for variations which in any way demean or ridicule characters because of their race or sex.

**Look for Tokenism.** If there are non-white characters in the illustrations, do they look just like whites except for being tinted or colored in? Do all minority faces look stereotypically alike, or are they depicted as genuine individuals with distinctive features?

**Who's Doing What?** Do the illustrations depict minorities in subservient and passive roles or in leadership and action roles? Are males the active "doers" and females the inactive observers?

### 2. Check the Story Line

The Civil Rights Movement led publishers to weed out many insulting passages, particularly from stories with Black themes, but the attitudes still find expression in less obvious ways. The following checklist suggests some of the subtle (covert) forms of bias to watch for.

**Standard for Success.** Does it take "white" behavior standards for a person of color to "get ahead"? Is "making it" in the dominant white society projected as the only ideal? To gain acceptance and approval, do people of color have to exhibit extraordinary qualities — excel in sports, get A's, etc.? In friendships between white children and children of color, is it the child of color who does most of the understanding and forgiving?

**Resolution of Problems.** How are problems presented, conceived, and resolved in the story? Are people of color considered to be "the problem?" Are the oppressions faced by people of color and women represented as causally related to an unjust society? Are the reasons for poverty and oppression explained, or are they just accepted as inevitable? Does the story line encourage passive acceptance or active resistance? Is a particular problem that is faced by a person of color resolved through the benevolent intervention of a white person?

**Role of Women.** Are the achievements of girls and women based on their own initiative and intelligence, or are they due to their good looks or to their relationship with boys? Are sex roles incidental or critical to characterization and plot? Could the same story be told if the sex roles were reversed?

### 3. Look at the Lifestyles

Are people of color and their setting depicted in such a way that they contrast unfavorably with the unstated norm of white middle-class suburbia? If the non-white group is depicted as "different," are negative value judgments implied? Are people of color depicted exclusively in ghettos, barrios, or migrant camps? If the illustrations and text attempt to depict another culture, do they go beyond oversimplifications and offer genuine insights into another lifestyle? Look for inaccuracy and inappropriateness in the depiction of other cultures. Watch for instances of the "quaint-natives-in-costume" syndrome (most noticeable in areas like costume and custom, but extending to behavior and personality traits as well).

### 4. Weigh the Relationships Between People

• Do the whites in the story possess the power, take the leadership, and make the important decisions? Do people of color and females function in essentially supporting roles?

• How are family relationships depicted? In African-American families, is the mother always dominant? In Latino families, are there always lots of children? If the family is separated, are societal conditions — unemployment, poverty — cited among the reasons for the separation?

### 5. Note the Heroes

For many years, books showed only "safe" non-white heroes — those who avoided serious conflict with the white establishment of their time. People of color are insisting on the right to define their own heroes (of both sexes) based on their own concepts and struggles for justice.

• When minority heroes do appear, are they admired for the same qualities that have made white heroes famous or because what they have done has benefited white people? Ask this question: "Whose interest is a particular figure really serving?"

### 6. Consider the Effects on a Child's Self Image

• Are norms established which limit the child's aspirations and self-concepts? What effect can it have on African-American children to be continuously bombarded with images of the color white as the ultimate in beauty, cleanliness, virtue, etc., and the color black as evil, dirty, menacing, etc.? Does the book counteract or reinforce this positive association with the color white and negative association with black?

• What happens to a girl's self-esteem when she reads that boys perform all of the brave and important deeds? What about a girl's self-esteem if she is not "fair" of skin and slim of body?

• In a particular story, is there one or more person with whom a child of color can readily identify to a positive and constructive end?

### 7. Consider the Author or Illustrator's Background

Analyze the biographical material on the jacket flap or the back of the book. If a story deals with a multicultural theme, what qualifies the author or illustrator to deal with the subject? If the author and illustrator are not members of the group being written about, is there anything in their background that would specifically recommend them as the creators of this book? The same criteria apply to a book that deals with the feelings and insights of women or girls.

### 8. Check Out the Author's Perspective

No author can be wholly objective. All authors write out of a cultural as well as personal context. Children's

Choosing good books is a key step in anti-bias teaching.

KATHY SLOANE

books in the past have traditionally come from white, middle-class authors, with one result being that a single ethnocentric perspective has dominated American children's literature. With the book in question, look carefully to determine whether the direction of the author's perspective substantially weakens or strengthens the value of his/her written work. Are omissions and distortions central to the overall character or "message" of the book?

### 9. Watch for Loaded Words

A word is loaded when it has insulting overtones. Examples of loaded adjectives (usually racist) are "savage," "primitive," "conniving," "lazy," "superstitious," "treacherous," "wily," "crafty," "inscrutable," "docile," and "backward."

• Look for sexist language and adjectives that exclude or ridicule women. Look for use of the male pronoun to refer to both males and females. The following examples show how sexist language can be avoided: "ancestors" instead of "forefathers;" "firefighters" instead of "firemen;" "manufactured" instead of "manmade;" the "human family" instead of the "family of man."

### 10. Look at the Copyright Date

Books on "minority" themes — usually hastily conceived — suddenly began appearing in the mid-1960s. There followed a growing number of "minority experience" books to meet the new market demand, but most of these were still written by white authors, edited by white editors, and published by white publishers. They therefore reflected a white point of view. Only recently has the children's book world begun to even remotely reflect the realities of a multiracial society or the concerns of feminists.

The copyright dates, therefore, can be a clue as to how likely the book is to be overtly racist or sexist, although a recent copyright date is no guarantee of a book's relevance or sensitivity. The copyright date only means the year the book was published. It usually takes a minimum of a year — and often much more than that — from the time a manuscript is submitted to the publisher to the time it is actually printed and put on the market. This time-lag meant very little in the past, but in a time of rapid change and changing consciousness, when children's book publishing is attempting to be "relevant," it is increasingly significant. ❑

# Celebrating the Joy in Daily Events

## By Linda Christensen

In a classroom where students and I critique everything from Donald Duck to U.S. foreign policy, I also need to prompt kids to celebrate the ordinary, the common daily events they take pleasure in. I want to find ways to coax joy back into the room, especially when students feel down about the ways of the world. One look at the number of Doc Martens and Reeboks or whichever shoe happens to be the fashion of the hour tells me that students are still seduced by consumerism. They are bombarded with messages that their route to happiness is a Diet Pepsi, a new deodorant, or a shampoo that will make them irresistible. At times, students and I explicitly examine ads and their messages, but I also use odes, a traditional poetic form, to help students re-see the beauty in the world outside the mall.

I stumbled across odes a few years ago when I fell in love with Pablo Neruda's poetry. Students read Neruda's "Ode to Socks," in which he praises a pair of socks given him by a friend. The odes allow students to find the positive in their daily lives. Neruda's odes also push students to use concrete details and imagery in their pieces. I use *Selected Odes of Pablo Neruda,* which has the original Spanish as well as the English translation.

1. Students read the poem in both languages. (This validates students who speak Spanish as well as locating writing in the broader linguistic world. I encourage students who speak more than one language to write in either or both languages.)

2. We discuss how Neruda describes the socks: "two woolen /fish, /two long sharks /of lapis blue /shot /with a golden thread, /two mammoth blackbirds." The more time we examine the imagery in Neruda's poem, the more students attempt daring, outrageous imagery. We also note how he talks about both the gift and the giver.

3. Then I ask students to make a list of objects they might praise — a gift, an everyday object, something that has meaning for them even though it might not seem important to anyone else. A few students share their ideas helping to dislodge memories for their classmates.

4. I turn off the lights and ask students to take a few deep breaths and close their eyes. (They hate this at first. They're afraid other people might look at them. It takes patience to get this to work in my classes.) Then I ask students to think about what they are going to praise. I do this part slowly — 30 to 60 seconds for each question. There's a tendency to rush because the class is silent, but it takes a while to get a visual image. I ask students to remember what the object looks like, smells like, sounds like, what else it reminds them of, how they came to get it. I find the guided visualization helps students remember more detail. When I turn the lights back on, I again ask students to write in silence.

5. With classes of younger students, I sometimes begin by asking them to write a paragraph describing the object and a paragraph about how they came to have the object. They can use these details in their poems.

Students have written odes to the Spanish language, their skin, their weight, lesbians, a mother's hands, animal cookies, ham, a grandfather's hat, tap dance, coffee, Jefferson High School, chocolate chip cookies, the color red, writing, and more. The ode became a form they returned to frequently in their writing.

Sarah Scofield, whose beautiful reading of Neruda's poetry in Spanish allowed her to share her linguistic talent with classmates, wrote this poem:

*Ode to Spanish*

*A language*
*As beautiful as music:*
*Melodious verbs*
*Harmonious adjectives*
*Rhythmic nouns*
*Intertwine as I speak.*
*An orchestra of words*
*Conducted by my tongue.*
*I compose*
*A new song*
*As those around me listen.*
*Musical sentences*
*Rich with the notes*
*Of culture.*
*A romance language*
*stirring the hearts*
*of its listeners.*
*The music plays on*
*As I watch with wonder how*
*My untrained yet experienced tongue*
*conducts the orchestra,*
*and the music pleases me.*

I don't want to exaggerate the importance of this lesson. It is a small weapon in my fight against cynicism and despair. But I do believe that if I want my students to imagine a more just society, I must spend time teaching them how to find what's good as well as to find what's bad. My classroom provides a small space to help students not only construct a critique, but also to build a community that can laugh and share joy. (See p. 186 for suggestions on organizing read-arounds.) ❏

This article is adapted from Linda Christensen's teaching guide to *Rites of Passage,* an award-winning literary magazine produced by students at Jefferson High School in Portland, Oregon.

# Ode to My Socks • Oda a los calcetines

By Pablo Neruda

Maru Mori brought me
a pair
of socks
knitted with her own
shepherd's hands,
two socks soft
as rabbits.
I slipped
my feet into them
as if
into
jewel cases
woven
with threads of
dusk
and sheep's wool.

Audacious socks,
my feet became
two woolen
fish,
two long sharks
of lapis blue
shot
with a golden thread,
two mammoth blackbirds,
two cannons,
thus honored
were
my feet
by
these
celestial
socks.
They were
so beautiful
that for the first time
my feet seemed
unacceptable to me,
two tired old
fire fighters
not worthy
of the woven
fire

Me trajo Maru Mori
un par
de calcetines
que tejió con sus manos
de pastora,
dos calcetines suaves
como liebres.
En ellos
metí los pies
como en
dos
estuches
tejidos
con hebras del
crepúsculo
y pellejo de ovejas.

Violentos calcetines,
mis pies fueron
dos pescados
de lana,
dos largos tiburones
de azul ultramarino
atravesados
por una trenza de oro,
dos gigantescos mirlos,
dos cañones:
mis pies
fueron honrados
de este modo
por
estos
celestiales
calcetines.
Eran
tan hermosos
que por primera vez
mis pies me parecieron
inaceptables
como dos decrépitos
bomberos, bomberos,
indignos
de aquel fuego
bordado,

| | |
|---|---|
| of those luminous | de aquellos luminosos |
| socks. | calcetines. |
| | |
| Nonetheless, | Sin embargo |
| I resisted | resistí |
| the strong temptation | la tentación aguda |
| to save them | de guardarlos |
| the way schoolboys | como los colegiales |
| bottle | preservan |
| fireflies, | las luciérnagas, |
| the way scholars | como los eruditos |
| hoard | coleccionan |
| sacred documents. | documentos sagrados, |
| I resisted | resistí |
| the wild impulse | el impulso furioso |
| to place them | de ponerlos |
| in a cage | en una jaula |
| of gold | de oro |
| and daily feed them | y darles cada día |
| birdseed | alpiste |
| and rosy melon flesh. | y pulpa de melón rosado. |
| Like explorers | Como descubridores |
| who in the forest | que en la selva |
| surrender a rare | entregan el rarísimo |
| and tender deer | venado verde |
| to the spit | al asador |
| and eat it | y se lo comen |
| with remorse, | con remordimiento, |
| I stuck out | estiré |
| my feet | los pies |
| and pulled on | y me enfundé |
| the | los |
| handsome | bellos |
| socks, | calcetines |
| and | y |
| then my shoes. | luego los zapatos. |
| | |
| So this is | Y es ésta |
| the moral of my ode: | la moral de mi oda: |
| twice beautiful | dos veces es belleza |
| is beauty | la belleza |
| and what is good is doubly | y lo que es bueno es doblemente |
| good | bueno |
| when it is a case of two | cuando se trata de dos calcetines |
| woolen socks | de lana |
| in wintertime. | en el invierno. |

### translated by Margaret Sayers Peden

Pablo Neruda was born on July 12, 1904, in a small frontier town of southern Chile, the son of a railroad worker. He was active in the struggle for social justice for his entire adult life. He received the Nobel Prize for Literature in 1971 and died in 1973. (See p. 184 for lesson ideas.)

# Taking Multicultural, Anti-racist Education Seriously

## An Interview with Educator Enid Lee

*The following is condensed from an interview with Enid Lee, a consultant in anti-racist education and organizational change, and author of* Letters to Marcia: a Teachers' Guide to Anti-Racist Education. *Based in Toronto, Lee is the former supervisor of race/ethnic relations for the North York Board of Education in metropolitan Toronto. She was born and raised in the Caribbean, and has been working in the field of language, culture and race for more than 15 years in Canada and the United States. She was interviewed by Barbara Miner of* Rethinking Schools.

### What do you mean by a multicultural education?

The term "multicultural education" has a lot of different meanings. The term I use most often is "anti-racist education."

Multicultural or anti-racist education is fundamentally a perspective. It's a point of view that cuts across all subject areas, and addresses the histories and experiences of people who have been left out of the curriculum. Its purpose is to help us deal equitably with all the cultural and racial differences that you find in the human family. It's also a perspective that allows us to get at explanations for why things are the way they are in terms of power relationships, in terms of equality issues.

So when I say multicultural or anti-racist education, I am talking about equipping students, parents, and teachers with the tools needed to combat racism and ethnic discrimination, and to find ways to build a society that includes all people on an equal footing.

It also has to do with how the school is run in terms of who gets to be involved with decisions. It has to do with parents and how their voices are heard or not heard. It has to do with who gets hired in the school.

If you don't take multicultural education or anti-racist education seriously, you are actually promoting a monocultural or racist education. There is no neutral ground on this issue.

### Why do you use the term "anti-racist education" instead of "multicultural education?"

Partly because, in Canada, multicultural education often has come to mean something that is quite superficial: the dances, the dress, the dialect, the dinners. And it does so without focusing on what those expressions of culture mean: the values, the power relationships that shape the culture.

I also use the term anti-racist education because a lot of multicultural education hasn't looked at discrimination. It has the view, "People are different and isn't that nice," as opposed to looking at how some people's differences are looked upon as deficits and disadvantages. In anti-racist education, we attempt to look at — and change — those things in school and society that prevent some differences from being valued.

Oftentimes, whatever is white is treated as normal. So when teachers choose literature that they say will deal with a universal theme or story, like childhood, all the people in the stories are of European origin; it's basically white culture and civilization. That culture is different from others, but it doesn't get named as different. It gets named as normal.

Anti-racist education helps us move that European perspective over to the side to make room for other cultural perspectives that must be included.

### What are some ways your perspective might manifest itself in a kindergarten classroom, for example?

It might manifest itself in something as basic as the kinds of toys and games that you select. If all the toys and games reflect the dominant culture and race and language, then that's what I call a monocultural classroom even if you have kids of different backgrounds in the class.

I have met some teachers who think

> If you don't take multiculturalism seriously, you are promoting a monocultural or racist education. There is no neutral ground on this issue.

that just because they have kids from different races and backgrounds, they have a multicultural classroom. Bodies of kids are not enough.

It also gets into issues such as what kind of pictures are up on the wall? What kinds of festivals are celebrated? What are the rules and expectations in the classroom in terms of what kinds of language are acceptable? What kinds of interactions are encouraged? How are the kids grouped? These are just some of the concrete ways in which a multicultural perspective affects a classroom.

## How does one implement a multicultural or anti-racist education?

It usually happens in stages. Because there's a lot of resistance to change in schools, I don't think it's reasonable to expect to move straight from a monocultural school to a multiracial school.

First there is this surface stage in which people change a few expressions of culture in the school. They make welcome signs in several languages, and have a variety of foods and festivals. My problem is not that they start there. My concern is that they often stop there. Instead, what they have to do is move very quickly and steadily to transform the entire curriculum. For example, when we say classical music, whose classical music are we talking about? European? Japanese? And what items are on the tests? Whose culture do they reflect? Who is getting equal access to knowledge in the school? Whose perspective is heard, whose is ignored?

The second stage is transitional and involves creating units of study. Teachers might develop a unit on Native Americans, or Native Canadians, or people of African background. And they have a whole unit that they study from one period to the next. But it's a separate unit and what remains intact is the main curriculum, the main menu. One of the ways to assess multicultural education in your school is to look at the school organization. Look at how much time you spend on which sub-

jects. When you are in the second stage you usually have a two- or three-week unit on a group of people or an area that's been omitted in the main curriculum.

You're moving into the next stage of structural change when you have elements of that unit integrated into existing units. Ultimately, what is at the center of the curriculum gets changed in its prominence. For example, civilizations. Instead of just talking about Western civilization, you begin to draw on what we need to know about India, Africa, China. We also begin to ask different questions about why and what we are doing. Whose interest is it in that we study what we study? Why is it that certain kinds of knowledge get hidden? In mathematics, instead of studying statistics with sports and weather numbers, why not look at employment in light of ethnicity?

Then there is the social change stage, when the curriculum helps lead to changes outside of the school. We actually go out and change the nature of the community we live in. For example, kids might become involved in how the media portray people, and start a letter-writing campaign about news that is negatively biased. Kids begin to see this as a responsibility that they have to change the world.

I think about a group of elementary school kids who wrote to the manager of the store about the kinds of games and dolls that they had. That's a long way from having some dinner and dances that represent an "exotic" form of life.

In essence, in anti-racist education we use knowledge to empower people and to change their lives.

**If we don't make it clear that some people benefit from racism, we are being dishonest.**

Teachers have limited money to buy new materials. How can they begin to incorporate a multicultural education even if they don't have a lot of money?

We do need money and it is a pattern to underfund anti-racist initiatives so that they fail. We must push for funding for new resources because some of the information we have is downright inaccurate. But if you have a perspective, which is really a set of questions that you ask about your life, and you have the kids ask, then you can begin to fill in the gaps.

Columbus is a good example. It turns the whole story on its head when you have the children try to find out what the people who were on this continent might have been thinking and doing and feeling when they were being "discovered," tricked, robbed and murdered. You might not have that information on hand, because that kind of knowledge is deliberately suppressed. But if nothing else happens, at least you shift your teaching, to recognize the native peoples as human beings, to look at things from their view.

There are other things you can do without new resources. You can include, in a sensitive way, children's backgrounds and life experiences. One way is through interviews with parents and with community people, in which they can recount their own stories, especially their interactions with institutions like schools, hospitals and employment agencies. These are things that often don't get heard.

I've seen schools inviting grandparents who can tell stories about their own lives, and these stories get to be part of the curriculum later in the year. It allows excluded people, it allows humanity, back into the schools. One of the ways that discrimination works is that it treats some people's experiences, lives, and points of view as though they don't count, as though they are less valuable than other people's.

I know we need to look at materials. But we can also take some of the

Anti-racist education celebrates diversity.

existing curriculum and ask kids questions about what is missing, and whose interest is being served when things are written in the way they are. Both teachers and students must alter that material.

## How can a teacher who knows little about multiculturalism be expected to teach multiculturally?

I think the teachers need to have the time and encouragement to do some reading, and to see the necessity to do so. A lot has been written about multiculturalism. It's not like there's no information. If you want to get specific, a good place to start is back issues of the *Bulletin* of the Council on Interracial Books for Children.

You also have to look around at what people of color are saying about their lives, and draw from those sources. You can't truly teach this until you reeducate yourself from a multicultural perspective. But you can

begin. It's an ongoing process.

Most of all, you have to get in touch with the fact that your current education has a cultural bias, that it is an exclusionary, racist bias, and that it needs to be purged. A lot of times people say, "I just need to learn more about those other groups." And I say, "No, you need to look at how the dominant culture and biases affect your view of non-dominant groups in society." You don't have to fill your head with little details about what other cultural groups eat and dance. You need to take a look at your culture, what your idea of normal is, and realize it is quite limited and is in fact just reflecting a particular experience. You have to realize that what you recognize as universal is, quite often, exclusionary. To be really universal, you must begin to learn what Africans, Asians, Latin Americans, the aboriginal peoples and all silenced groups of Americans have had to say about the topic.

## How can one teach

**multiculturally without making white children feel guilty or threatened?**

Perhaps a sense of being threatened or feeling guilty will occur. But I think it is possible to have kids move beyond that.

First of all, recognize that there have always been white people who have fought against racism and social injustice. White children can proudly identify with these people and join in that tradition of fighting for social justice.

Second, it is in their interest to be opening their minds and finding out how things really are. Otherwise, they will constantly have an incomplete picture of the human family.

The other thing is, if we don't make it clear that some people benefit from racism, then we are being dishonest. What we have to do is talk about how young people can use that from which they benefit to change the order of things so that more people will benefit.

If we say that we are all equally discriminated against on the basis of racism or sexism, that's not accurate. We don't need to be caught up in the guilt of our benefit, but should use our privilege to help change things.

I remember a teacher telling me last summer that after she listened to me on the issue of racism, she felt ashamed of who she was. And I remember wondering if her sense of self was founded on a sense of superiority. Because if that's true, then she is going to feel shaken. But if her sense of self is founded on working with people of different colors to change things, then there is no need to feel guilt or shame.

## What are some things to look for in choosing good literature and resources?

I encourage people to look for the voice of people who are frequently silenced, people we haven't heard from: people of color, women, poor people, working-class people, people with disabilities, and gays and lesbians.

I also think that you look for materials that invite kids to seek explanations beyond the information that is before them, materials that give back to people the ideas they have developed, the music they have composed, and all those things which have been stolen from them and attributed to other folks. Jazz and rap music are two examples that come to mind.

I encourage teachers to select materials that reflect people who are trying and have tried to change things to bring dignity to their lives, for example Africans helping other Africans in the face of famine and war. This gives students a sense of empowerment and some strategies for making a difference in their lives. I encourage them to select materials that visually give a sense of the variety in the world.

Teachers also need to avoid materials that blame the victims of racism and other "isms."

In particular, I encourage them to look for materials that are relevant. And relevance has two points: not only where you are, but also where you want to go. In all of this we need to ask what's the purpose, what are we trying to teach, what are we trying to develop?

Multicultural literature encourages multicultural respect.

## What can school districts do to further multicultural education?

Many teachers will not change curriculum if they have no administrative support. Sometimes, making these changes can be scary. You can have parents on your back and kids who can be resentful. You can be told you are making the curriculum too political.

What we are talking about here is pretty radical; multicultural education is about challenging the status quo and the basis of power. You need administrative support to do that.

In the final analysis, multicultural or anti-racist education is about allowing educators to do the things they have wanted to do in the name of their profession: to broaden the horizons of the young people they teach, to give them skills to change a world in which the color of a person's skin defines their opportunities, where some human beings are treated as if they are just junior children.

Maybe teachers don't have this big vision all the time. But I think those are the things that a democratic society is supposed to be about.

When you look at the state of things in the United States and Canada, it's almost as if many parts of the society have given up on decency, doing the right thing and democracy in any serious way. I think that anti-racist education gives us an opportunity to try again.

Unfortunately, I feel that this educational movement is going to face a serious challenge. The 1980s were marked by very conservative attitudes, and some of the gains of the social change movements in the 1960s and 1970s were rolled back.

A major struggle is taking place in the 1990s to regain those victories of the 1960s and 1970s. I think that anti-racist education can help us do that. But the conservative forces are certainly not going to allow this to happen without a battle. We'd better get ready to fight. ❑

CLEO

# Rethinking My Classroom

Theoretical recipes for changing the classroom are many; practical examples are few.

In this chapter, classroom teachers at varying grade levels share their personal struggles to transform their teaching. They explain how they work with young people to confront and transcend key dilemmas such as tracking, student passivity, and social injustice.

# Race and Respect Among Young Children

## By Rita Tenorio

When Angela came to talk to me, she was close to tears. With a sympathetic "witness" on each side, she said, "Matt called me a name. I don't like it."

Matt was summoned for a quiet conference. "What did he call you?" I asked Angela. "Brownski," she said, "He's making fun of me."

Matt came to his own defense. "Well, I was just teasing," he said. "I mean, I wasn't talking about her color or anything."

Unfortunately, blond, blue-eyed Matt *was* talking about Angela's skin color. When he didn't get his way with the puzzle they were sharing, he used this seemingly innocent word as a put-down. He knew he'd get a reaction from Angela and counted on the power of his light skin to win the argument. He hadn't counted on Angela speaking out.

In my 20 years of teaching I have learned that, contrary to what adults often believe, young children are not "colorblind." Instead, they have an unstated but nonetheless sophisticated understanding of issues of race and power. One of our most important roles as teachers, I believe, is to recognize racism's effect on children, address the issue directly, and give students the beginning skills and strategies they will need to combat racism in their lives.

In this instance I encouraged Angela to tell Matt why she was angry. I also reminded Matt of our classroom rules and our prohibition against name-calling and put-downs. Matt apologized, both seemed satisfied, and they went back to their puzzle.

The issue was resolved — for the moment. Questions remained, however. Would Matt react differently the next time he wanted his way? Had Angela become more assertive in responding to insults? While I felt that Matt's put-

> Dealing with issues of race is perhaps the most complicated problem I have encountered as a kindergarten teacher.

down reflected a deeper problem, I had handled it the same way I would have handled any squabble. Most importantly, I hadn't resolved more fundamental questions: What was my role in exploring these issues with young children? What should be my next step?

Dealing with issues of race is perhaps the most complicated problem I have encountered as a kindergarten teacher. For many years, the problem didn't seem to "exist," and was glossed over as part of the view that "all children are the same, black, white or brown." In the last eight years, coinciding with my development as a teacher and exploration of issues such as "whole language" and heterogeneous grouping, I've struggled to develop a better understanding of anti-racist teaching. Some of the factors that have been crucial in my development have been the support of my colleagues, a districtwide curriculum reform, and my involvement in a new two-way bilingual school that embraces an anti-rac-

ist teaching philosophy.

As Janet Brown McCracken states in her book *Valuing Diversity*, "curriculum is what happens" in the classroom every day. What may seem innocent "pretend" play among young children is actually a rehearsal for later activities in life. Thus, I've learned to observe children's play and intervene when necessary to counteract discriminatory behaviors. Interactions where children put each other down or where children reflect the discrimination that is so prevalent in our world provide opportunities for strong lessons in counteracting stereotypes and racism. They are as much a part of the curriculum as teaching a science lesson or reading a story.

In the first year of my teaching I came across a quote that asked, "How much must a child trust himself, others, and the world in order to learn?" Throughout the 20 years I've worked with children and their families, I've always felt that trust was a key component to success. The changes I've made in designing the curriculum in my class have deepened my respect for the notion of trust. I've come to understand that feeling "safe" in school includes the students knowing that the teacher understands and respects their experience and background.

### The 'Best' Environment

As a kindergarten teacher I had been trained to provide a nurturing environment in my classroom. I wanted to provide a safe place where children could believe in themselves, become more independent and organized, plan and think through a task, and acquire the social skills needed for success in school.

As I began my career, I gathered ideas and activities; attended workshops on art, music, games, and stories; and planned a variety of lessons. I thought I was giving students the best curriculum possible. Even in those early years, multicultural education was part of this curriculum. Moving from holiday to holiday, we learned about cultures all over the world. I changed bulletin boards and literacy activities to correspond to the holidays, and proudly integrated the activities into our daily lessons. We learned about our "differences" and celebrated our "similarities." I insisted that "we can all live together" and forbade words or actions that would "hurt" anyone.

My message was that everyone would be treated fairly and equally in our classroom. I made sure we were all going to be the same.

It worked. At least I thought it worked.

My classroom was filled with active, playful, well-disciplined children. I held high expectations for all the children and by all obvious measures they were growing and learning in ways that pleased both me and their parents. Yet over the years I became uncomfortable with my approach.

## Seeing the Flaws

In the late 1980's I, like many teachers, was influenced by the whole language philosophy and research on the benefits of heterogeneous groupings.

Whole language helped me understand that my curriculum, while framed in a multisensory approach that included both academics and play, lacked choices. My plan was just that, mine. The day's activities were only minimally influenced by my students' interests and talents. Further, writing was not an integral part of the literacy process. And while we had many fine children's books in the classroom, I was still locked into the district's basal reading program.

As I learned about heterogeneous grouping, I saw other flaws. I still had students "tracked" for math and reading instruction, with children grouped according to their skills. While all chil-

Young children are aware of race and prejudice.

dren improved, the "top" group got furthest ahead while the "low" group struggled.

Most importantly, even in my fair and "equal" classroom environment, I still had frustrating conflicts such as the conflict between Matt and Angela. Sometimes it centered around a verbal put-down, other times it involved body language; white or lighter-skinned children would get up and move if a brown Latino or African-American child sat next to them. Life on the playground could be even rougher, and certain students would be isolated or ridiculed if they were different.

Even the children's "make believe" stories were at times defined by race. Comments like, "You can't be the queen; there are no Black queens," caught me off-guard. Equally disturbing, more often than not the children accepted these hierarchies without complaint.

While I knew that kindergarten chil-

dren were too young to intellectually understand the complexities of issues such as racism or prejudice, their behaviors showed the influence of societal stereotypes and biases. Throughout my career, I have had children who vehemently believed that Indians all live in "teepees" or, even worse, that there were no more Indians "cause the cowboys killed them all."

I had wanted to believe that children arrived in kindergarten with an open mind on all subjects. But the reality is different. Children mirror the attitudes of society and of their families.

Researchers have found that between the ages of 2 and 5, children not only become aware of racial differences but begin to make judgments based on that awareness. Having watched on average over 5,000 hours of TV by age 5, it is no wonder that some children believe all Indians are dead. Television's influence is further compounded by the segregated lives many children lead prior to coming to school.

### Taking the First Steps

I began to reshape my kindergarten to be less teacher-centered and more heterogeneously grouped. It felt good to get rid of the workbooks and replace them with quality literature and the children's own stories. I was particularly amazed at how much the children liked to write in their journals and how quickly they learned to read the familiar stories they helped to choose.

Issues of bias, the children's personal interactions, and multicultural education were more complicated. When it came to changing the curriculum and countering tracking, the key to success was reinforcing and building upon the knowledge students brought with them to school. Yet on issues of race, if I merely supported the children's natural "instincts" and knowledge, I would end up reinforcing stereotypes and prejudice. I wasn't sure how to resolve this contradiction. I only knew that the transition in this area would not be so easy.

In the early childhood area where "color blindness" was the prevailing attitude, there were few resources for dealing with racism and bias. I did not have broad personal experience in dealing with these issues, especially in deciding what was appropriate for young children.

Many colleagues shared my concern as we, like others in urban districts in the late 1980s, struggled with systemwide curriculum reform. I found necessary support and ideas from networking with other teachers. Further, my individual transition was supported by systemwide changes as the Milwaukee Public Schools initiated a curriculum and adopted as their first of 10 goals that "students will project anti-racist, anti-biased attitudes through their participation in a multilingual, multiethnic, culturally diverse curriculum."

### A New School

Other developments helped spur my thinking. In a unique opportunity, I was part of the founding staff of a new two-way, English/Spanish bilingual school called La Escuela Fratney. The language component, while important in its own right, was part of a broader framework that had at its core a multicultural, "anti-racist" curriculum. We wanted our students to not only learn about the history and culture of the major ethnic groups, but to also understand racism's influence on all of us. Here was my chance to forge an entirely new kindergarten curriculum.

I found several important resources to help in this transition. One was the opportunity to work with Enid Lee, an African-Canadian educator who specializes in anti-racist education. Her insights helped me redefine multicultural education and try to incorporate an anti-racist perspective into every subject. Another valuable resource was *The Anti-Bias Curriculum* by Louise Derman-Sparks and the ABC Task Force, which includes not only curriculum ideas but also concrete examples of ways to deal with interactions among students.

Both Lee and *The Anti-Bias Curriculum* taught me an important lesson: it is not the awareness of racial and cultural differences that leads to prejudice and racism, but how people respond to those differences. I realized I needed to do two things. First, I had to immediately respond to unacceptable behavior by the children, such as racist put-downs or slurs. Second, I had to develop a curriculum that included anti-bias lessons that help students recognize and respond to stereotypes and prejudice.

# Dealing with Prejudice

**Do** deal with the situation immediately.

**Do** confirm that the particular type of abuse is hurtful and harmful and will not be tolerated.

**Do** value the feelings of others by active, sensitive listening.

**Do** take steps to support the victim and enable him or her to develop a stronger sense of self.

**Do** take those involved aside to discuss the incident.

**Do** explain to students why such incidents occur and undertake ongoing, long-term (pro-active) strategies with the class for combating stereotyping, prejudice, and negative attitudes to differences.

**Do** apply consequences to the attacker in accordance with the school rules, code of behavior, and race/ethnocultural relations policy.

**Don't** ignore it, let it pass unchallenged, or let intangible fears block your ability to act.

**Don't** overreact with another put-down of the offender.

**Don't** impose consequences before finding out exactly what happened from those involved.

**Don't** focus entirely on applying consequences to the offender while ignoring the feelings of the victim.

**Don't** embarrass either party publicly.

**Don't** assume that the incident is an isolated occurrence divorced from the overall context in which it occurred.

**Don't** humiliate the attacker when imposing consequences. Remember that the attacker may feel like a victim too.

Reprinted from *Unity in Diversity: A Curriculum Resource Guide for Ethnocultural Equity and Anti-racist Education*, Ontario Ministry of Education, April, 1991.

## Taking a Stance

My goal of an anti-bias curriculum was helped by our vision at Fratney, where we have adopted schoolwide themes that give teachers a chance to proactively address issues of race. For example, during the first theme ("We Respect Ourselves and Others") we strive to build the kindergarten community by learning about each other's lives and families. Our reading lessons include literature that reflects the culture and experience of the students. A favorite activity is making a big puzzle on which each piece has the name of a student and describes "something that I'm very good at." Because the makeup of our kindergarten population includes Latino, African-American and white children, the value of various cultures is underscored.

Together we define our classroom rules and discuss what "fairness" means to each of us. Playground problems become the topics for class discussions or role plays during which students hear from each other how they might more peacefully resolve their disputes. We learn about people who have worked for fairness and equality. We practice the use of I-messages to respond to name calling. A student might say, "I feel bad when you call me names so please stop," rather than responding with another put-down.

The other themes, "We Send Messages When We Communicate," "We Make a Difference on Planet Earth," and "We Share the Stories of the World," offer the same potential for development.

I find such an approach helps to increase children's awareness of themselves and of their peers. Much more difficult has been the process of immediately intervening when children are mean to each other or say stereotypical or inappropriate things. It's much easier to let a remark slide, rationalizing that the children don't really understand what they've said or that it might lead to a discussion with which we as teachers are not entirely comfortable. During the Gulf War, for instance, many students used very negative terms when referring to the Iraqis. Another year, cer-

Kindergartners at La Escuela Fratney.

tain children used the word "fag" as a deliberate put-down.

For me, some of the most "teachable moments" in multicultural/anti-racist teaching have come in responding to children's negative remarks. First, I put a stop to the behavior and make clear that it is inappropriate. Then I try to explain why it is inappropriate and acknowledge the "victim's" feelings.

Often the remark is unrelated to the conflict at hand, and I try to help the parties focus on the real problem. The child who told her classmate that "there are no Black queens," for instance, needs to understand not only that her remark is incorrect, but also that she has insulted her friend. Next, she had to see the real issue was that she wanted to wear the rhinestone crown and sequin dress which were part of the playhouse scenario. Beyond that moment, it's good to have discussions of the queens throughout African history, perhaps using a piece of literature like *Mufaro's*

*Beautiful Daughters*, by John Steptoe, or *Ashanti to Zulu*, by Margaret Musgrove.

Some of the stereotypes at Fratney are related to our two-way bilingual program and the fact that some students are hearing Spanish for the first time. For example, I remember when an English-speaking student named Sean referring to Miguel, a Spanish-speaking student said, "I don't want to sit next to him. He talks funny."

One response might have been, "Miguel is very nice Sean. In our room we take turns sitting next to all the kids." But such a response would not have addressed Sean's nervousness or curiosity about a different language. It may have merely caused Sean to be less verbal about his feelings while still avoiding Latino classmates. In my view, Sean's remark was really a question to the adults as he tried to understand and get used to an unfamiliar situation

A more appropriate response might be, "Miguel doesn't talk funny, Sean. He's speaking Spanish like the other people in his family. You and I are speaking English. In our classroom, we'll be learning a lot about both languages. It's fine for you to ask questions about what Miguel is saying, or say that you don't understand. But it's not OK to say that he talks funny. That's a put-down to all of us who speak Spanish."

Another constant source of comments is skin color. A child may say, for instance, "Jonathan is too brown. I'm glad I'm lighter than him." One response from the teacher might be, "We're all the same. It doesn't matter what color you are." While meant to promote equality, it doesn't address the child's view that "being lighter is better." In addition, it might send Jonathan a very negative message. Such a comment from a child indicates that they are quite aware that we are *not* all the same.

I've found it difficult to respond to these types of insults, particularly because an historical explanation of slavery and why society views light skin more positively is inappropriate for this age. Yet it's important that the teacher

**Understanding grows through sharing.**

intervene immediately to contradict the notion of "brown as bad." It's also appropriate to give Jonathan a chance to share his feelings. The teacher might use this incident as the basis for a unit of study about skin color and people's perceptions related to this issue.

Most important, dismissing or ignoring negative remarks confuses students and sends them the message that the teacher doesn't really believe their stated view that "everyone is equal."

## The Journey Continues

My role as teacher continues to be one of providing that safe, nurturing environment and preparing students for their experiences ahead. I strive to move children from the extremes of, on one hand, being afraid to do much of anything, or, on the other, being completely impulsive in their behavior. I want them to view kindergarten as a place where they can take risks and feel success. All of this remains a challenge. And at times I'm discouraged by the enormous

influence that the larger society has on their awareness and biases.

I know that I must also be willing to take risks and make mistakes. I must be open to the experiences of our children and their families. I must recognize and respond to the students' negative behaviors. It's a struggle, but I believe it's a worthwhile one. We must provide each of our children a world where they are truly valued.

Early childhood educators hold an incredible amount of influence over the minds of the children they teach. As the popular cliché goes, "All I really need to know I learned in kindergarten." For today's students, "all they need to know" goes beyond the traditional formula of playing fair and putting things back in their place. It includes developing the skills and strategies to counteract the racism in their lives. ❑

*Rita Tenorio (RMMT@aol.com) is a 1st grade teacher at La Escuela Fratney in Milwaukee and a* Rethinking Schools *editor.*

# My Hair Is Long

By Loyen Redhawk Gali


*My hair is as long as a pony's tail*
*and as shiny as a river.*
*My skin is as brown as a bear*
*getting up in the sunlight.*
*My eyes are as big as berries*
*but as dark as buffalo hide.*
*My ears are like pears cut in half*
*ready to eat.*
*My heart is like the drum beat as*
*I dance in the arbor.*
*My hands are soft as a rabbit's fur*
*in the forest.*
*My legs are as long as a baby deer's legs*
*as they run along the edge of the river.*
*My stomach is as big as a buffalo's*
*as it grazes through the land.*
*My voice is like the scream of an eagle*
*but can be as quiet as a mouse.*
*When I laugh, it sounds like*
*a woodpecker getting some food.*
*And my smile is as big as a lake.*


Loyen Redhawk Gali, age 11, is a student in Oakland, California. (See page 184 for lesson ideas.)

# Teaching for Social Justice: One Teacher's Journey

## By Bob Peterson

It's November and a student brings in a flyer about a canned food drive during the upcoming holiday season. The traditional teacher affirms the student's interest — "That's nice and I'm glad you care about other people" — but doesn't view the food drive as a potential classroom activity.

The progressive teacher sees the food drive as an opportunity to build on students' seemingly innate sympathy for the down-trodden, and, after a class discussion, has children bring in cans of food. They count them, categorize them, and write about how they feel.

The critical teacher does the same as the progressive teacher — but more. The teacher also uses the food drive as the basis for a discussion about poverty and hunger. How much poverty and hunger is there in our neighborhood? Our country? Our world? Why is there poverty and hunger? What is the role of the government in making sure people have enough to eat? Why isn't it doing more? What can we do in addition to giving some food?

Participating in a food drive isn't the litmus test of whether one is a critical teacher. But engaging children in reflective dialogue is.

Unfortunately, a lack of reflective dialogue is all too common in American schools. Less than 1% of instructional time in high school is devoted to discussion that requires some kind of response involving reasoning or an opinion from students, according to researcher John Goodlad in his study of American schooling. A similar atmosphere dominates all too many elementary classrooms, where worksheets and mindless tasks fill up children's time.

Divisions between traditional, progressive, and critical teaching are of-ten artificial and many teachers use techniques common to all three. As I attempt to improve my teaching and build what I call a "social-justice classroom," however, I have found it essential to draw less on traditional methods and more on the other two.

Lots of literature has been written on progressive methods — the process approach to writing, whole language, activity-based mathematics, and so forth. But there is little written about critical/social-justice approaches to teaching, especially for elementary teachers. What follows is an outline of lessons that I have learned as I have tried, sometimes more successfully than others, to incorporate my goal of critical/social-justice teaching into my classroom practice over the past 15 years.

There are five characteristics that I think are essential to a critical/social-justice classroom:

- A curriculum grounded in the lives of our students.
- Dialogue.
- A questioning/problem-posing approach.
- An emphasis on critiquing bias and attitudes.
- The teaching of activism for social justice.

A well organized class based on collaboration and student participation is a prerequisite for implementing such a program (see article, p. 34). I'd also like to add that such "characteristics" are actually goals — never quite reached by even the best teachers, but always sought by all good teachers.

## Curriculum Grounded in the Lives of Our Students

A teacher cannot build a community of learners unless the voices and lives of the students are an integral part of the curriculum. Children, of course, talk about their lives constantly. The challenge is for teachers to make connections between what the students talk about and the curriculum and broader society.

I start the year with a six-week unit on the children's families and backgrounds. To begin the unit I have students place their birthdates on the class timeline — which covers nearly 600 years (an inch representing a year), and which runs above the blackboard and stretches around two walls. Students write their names and birthdates on 3x5 cards and tie the cards with yarn to the hole in the timeline that corresponds to their year of birth. On the second day we place their parents' birthdates on the

> A teacher cannot build a community of learners unless the voices and lives of the students are an integral part of the curriculum.

timeline, on the third day those of their grandparents or great-grandparents. Throughout the year, students add dates that come up in our study of history, literature, science, and current events. The timeline provides students with a visual representation of time, history, and sequence, while fostering the understanding that everything is interrelated.

The weekly writing homework assignment during this family background unit consists of children collecting information about their families — how they were named, stories of family trips, favorite jokes, an incident when they were young, a description of their neighborhood. Students share these writings with each other and at times with the whole class. They use these assignments as rough drafts for autobiographies which are eventually bound and published. The assignments also inspire classroom discussion and further study. For example, one of my students, Faviola Perez, wrote a poem about her neighborhood, which led to discussions about violence and what we might do about it. The poem goes:

### My Street at Night

*My mom says, "Time to go to bed."*
*The streets at night*
*are horrible*
*I can't sleep!*
*Cars are passing*
*making noise*
*sirens screaming*
*people fighting*
*suffering!*
*Suddenly the noise goes away*
*I go to sleep*
*I start dreaming*
*I dream about people*
*shaking hands*
*caring*
*caring about our planet*
*I wake up*
*and say*
*Will the world be*
*like this some day?*

In the discussion that followed, many students shared similar fears and gave examples of how family members or friends had been victims of violence.

Students at La Escuela Fratney.

Others offered ways to prevent violence.

"We shouldn't buy team jackets," said one student.

"The police should keep all the criminals in jail forever," was another suggestion. Needless to say, the students don't have a uniform response, and I use such comments to foster discussion. When necessary or appropriate, I also interject important questions that might help the students deepen or reconsider their views. I also try to draw connections between such problems and issues of conflict that I witness daily in the class. When a student talks about a killing over a mundane argument or a piece of clothing, for instance, I ask how these differ from some of the conflicts in our school and on our playground, and how we might solve them.

Focusing on problems in writing and discussion acknowledges the seriousness of a child's problem; it also fosters community because the students recognize that we share common concerns. Ultimately, it can help students to re-examine some of their own attitudes that may in fact be a part, albeit small, of the problem.

Throughout the rest of the year I try to integrate an examination of children's lives and their community into all sections of the curriculum. In reading groups, children relate both contemporary and classic children's books to their own lives. For example, in one activity I have students divide their paper vertically: on one side they copy an interesting sentence from a book they are reading; on the other side they write how that reminds them of something in their own lives. The students then share and discuss such reflections.

In math we learn about percentages,

fractions, graphing, and basic math through using numbers to examine their own lives. For example, my fifth-grade class keeps logs of the time that they spend watching television, graph it, and analyze it in terms of fractions and percentages. As part of our school's nine-week, schoolwide theme called "We Send Messages When We Communicate" they surveyed all the classes in the school to see how many households had various communication equipment, from telephones to computers to VCRs.

Such activities are interesting and worthwhile but not necessarily critical. I thus tried to take the activity a step further — not only to affirm what's going on in the children's lives, but to help them question if watching television is always in their best interests. As we looked at television viewing, for instance, we found that some of our students could save over 1,000 hours a year by moderating their TV watching.

"I can't believe I waste so much time watching TV," one girl stated during a discussion.

"You're not wasting it," replied one boy. "You're learning what they want you to buy!" he said sarcastically.

Similar discussions helped children become more conscious of the impact of television on their lives and minds, and even led a few to reduce the number of hours they watched.

One problem, however, that I have encountered in "giving voice" to students is that the voices that dominate are sometimes those of the more aggressive boys or those students who are more academically skilled. I try to overcome this problem by using structures that encourage broader participation. During writing workshop, for example, I give timed "free writes" where children write about anything they want for a set period of time. Afterward they immediately share their writing with another student of their choice. Students then nominate classmates to share with

the entire class, which often has the effect of positive peer pressure on those who don't normally participate in class. By hearing their own voices, by having other students listen to what they have to say, children become more self-confident in expressing their own ideas, and feel more a part of the classroom community.

## Dialogue

The basic premise of traditional teaching is that children come to school as empty vessels needing to be filled with information. "Knowledge" is something produced elsewhere, whether by the teacher or the textbook company, and then transferred to the student.

This approach dominates most schools. "Reform" usually means finding more effective ways for children to remember more "stuff" or more efficient ways to measure what "stuff" the students have memorized.

Homeless people sleep under blanket-covered park benches across the street from the White House. By making transparencies of news photos such as this, teachers can spark discussion about contemporary social issues.

RETHINKING OUR CLASSROOMS

I agree that children need to know bunches of "stuff." I cringe any time one of my fifth graders confuses a basic fact like the name of our city or country. But I also know that the vast bulk of "stuff" memorized by children in school is quickly forgotten, and that the "empty vessel" premise is largely responsible for the boring, lecture-based instruction that dominates too many classrooms.

The curricular "stuff" that I want the children to learn will be best remembered if it relates to what they already know, if they have some input into what "stuff" is actually studied, and if it is studied through activities rather than just listening. All three approaches depend on dialogue and on making students an integral part of their own learning.

To initiate dialogue I may use a song, poem, story, news article, photo, or cartoon. These dialogue "triggers" are useful for both classroom and small-group discussion. I often use them as starting points in social studies, writing, or math lessons. I have a song, word, poster, and quotation of the week which, whenever possible, are related to our curriculum topics.

For example, during the study of the American Underground Railroad earlier this year, I used the song "New Underground Railroad," written by Gerry Tenney and sung by Holly Near and Ronnie Gilbert. The song compares the Underground Railroad of the mid-1800s in the United States to that of the movement to save Jews during World War II and to the sanctuary movement to help "illegal" Salvadoran refugees in the 1980s. My student from El Salvador connected immediately to the song. She explained to the class the problems of violence and poverty that her family had faced because of war in El Salvador. This one song raised many more questions, for example: Why did the Nazis kill people? What is anti-Semitism? Who runs El Salvador? Why does the United States send guns to El Salvador? Why are people from El Salvador forced to come to the United States secretly?

Another trigger that I use is overhead transparencies made from provocative newspaper or magazine photographs. For example, for a poetry lesson during writing workshop, I used a *New York Times* photograph taken during a winter cold spell that showed piles of snow-covered blankets and cardboard on park benches near the White House. (See photo, p. 32.) Many students initially thought the piles were trash. When I told them that they were homeless people who had been snowed upon while asleep, my students were angry. The discussion ranged from their own experiences seeing homeless people in the community to suggestions of what should be done by the president.

"That's not fair," one student responded.

"Clinton said he'd take care of the homeless people if he got elected and look what he's done," said a second student. "Nothing."

"I didn't vote for him," said a third. "Us kids never get to do anything, but I know that if we were in charge of the world we'd do a better job."

"Like what?" I asked.

"Well, on a day that cold he should have opened up the White House and let them in," responded one student. "If I were president, that's what I'd do."

One of my students, Jade Williams, later wrote a poem:

*Homeless*

*I walk to the park*
*I see homeless people laying*
*on a bench I feel sad*
*to see people sleeping outside*
*nowhere to go I felt*
*to help them let them stay*
*in a hotel*
*give them things*
*until they get*
*a job and*
*a house to stay*
*and let them*
*pay me back*
*with their love*

## A Questioning/ Problem-posing Approach

Lucy Calkins, director of the Teachers College Writing Project at Columbia University, argues that teachers must allow student viewpoints to be part of the classroom curriculum. "We can't give children rich lives, but we can give them the lens to appreciate the richness that is already there in their lives," she writes in her book, *Living Between the Lines*.

But even that approach is not enough. We should also help students to probe the ways their lives are both connected to and limited by society. This is best done if students and teachers jointly pose substantive, challenging questions for the class to try to answer.

Any time a student poses a particularly thoughtful or curious question in my class we write it down in the spiral notebook labeled "Questions We Have" that hangs on the board in front of the room. It might be during a discussion, at the beginning of a day, or during a reflection on another student's writing. Not every question is investigated and thoroughly discussed, but even the posing of the question helps students to consider alternative ways of looking at an issue.

In a reading-group discussion, for example, the question arose of how it must have felt for fugitive slaves and free African Americans to fear walking down the street in the North during the time of slavery. One student said, "I sort of know how they must have felt." Others immediately doubted her statement, but then she explained.

"The slaves, especially fugitive slaves, weren't free because they couldn't walk the streets without fear of the slave masters, but today are we free?" she asked. "Because we can't walk the streets without fear of gangs, violence, crazy people, drunks, and drive-bys."

In reading groups a common assignment is to pose questions from the literature that we read. For example, while reading *Sidewalk Story* by Sharon Bell Mathis, a children's novel in which the main protagonist, a young girl, struggles to keep her best friend from being evicted, my students posed questions about the ethics of eviction, failure to pay rent, homelessness, discrimination, and the value of material possessions over friendship.

**Continued on page 35**

# The Challenge of Classroom Discipline

By Bob Peterson

One of the most challenging tasks in any elementary classroom is to build a community where students respect one another and value learning. Too often, children use put-downs to communicate, resolve conflicts violently, and have negative attitudes toward school and learning. These problems often are based in society. How can one tell students not to use put-downs, for example, when that is the predominant style of comedy on prime-time television?

But schools often contribute to such problems. Approaches based on lecturing by teachers, passive reading of textbooks, and "fill-in-the-blank" worksheets keep students from making decisions, from becoming actively involved in their learning, and from learning how to think and communicate effectively.

## Involving Students in Decision-making

If a teacher wants to build a community of learners, a number of things have to happen. Students need to be involved in making decisions. They need to work regularly in groups. They need a challenging curriculum that involves not only listening but actually doing. They need to understand that it is OK to make mistakes, that learning involves more than getting the "right" answer.

At the same time, teachers need to make sure that students are not set up for failure. Teachers need to model what it means to work independently and in groups so that those who have not learned that outside of school will not be disadvantaged. Teachers need to be clear about what is and what is not within the purview of student decision-making. And teachers need to learn to build schoolwide support for this kind of learning and teaching.

The parameters of students' deci-

> Each year I have students discuss their vision of an ideal classroom.
> I let kids know I am willing to negotiate certain rules. But things don't always go smoothly.

sion-making range from choosing what they write, read, and study, to deciding the nature of their collaborative projects, to helping establish the classroom's rules and curriculum.

Each year I have students discuss their vision of an ideal classroom and the rules necessary in such a classroom. I explain how certain rules are made by the state government, by the school board, by the school itself, and by the classroom teacher. I let kids know that I will be willing to negotiate certain rules, but that my willingness to agree to their proposals (because ultimately I hold authority in the classroom) is dependent on two things: the soundness of their ideas and their ability as a group to show that they are responsible enough to assume decision-making power. I also tell kids that if they disagree with rules made outside of the classroom, they should voice their concerns.

Things don't always go smoothly. One year while discussing school rules the kids were adamant that anybody who broke a rule should sit in a corner with a dunce cap on his or her head. I refused on the grounds that it was humiliating. Eventually we worked out other consequences including time-outs and loss of the privilege to come to the classroom during lunch recess.

The cooperative learning technique of the "T-Chart" is helpful in getting kids to understand what a community of learners looks like during different activities. The teacher draws a big "T" on the board and titles the left side "looks like" and the right side "sounds like." Kids brainstorm what an outside visitor would see and hear during certain activities. For example, when we make a "T-chart" about how to conduct a class discussion, students list things like "one person talking" under "sounds like" and "kids looking at the speaker" and "children with their hands raised" under "looks like." We hang the T-chart on the wall; this helps most children remember what is appropriate behavior for different activities.

Classroom organization is another essential ingredient in building a community of learners. The desks in my class are in five groups of six each, which serve as "base groups." I divide the students into these base groups every nine weeks, taking into account language dominance, race, gender, and special needs, creating heterogeneous groups to guard against those subtle forms of elementary school "tracking."

## Dividing Students into Base Groups

Throughout the day children might work in a variety of cooperative learning groups, but their base group remains the same. Each group has its own bookshelf where materials are kept and homework turned in. Each group elects its own captain who makes sure that materials are in order and that his or her group members are "with the program." For example, before writing workshop, captains distribute writing folders to all students and make sure that everyone is prepared with a sharpened pencil.

Sometimes the group that is the best prepared to start a new activity, for example, will be allowed to help in dramatization or be the class helpers for that lesson. This provides incentive for team captains to get even the most recalcitrant students to join in with classroom activities.

By organizing the students this way, many of the management tasks are taken on by the students, creating a sense of collective responsibility. Arranging the students in these base groups has the added advantage of freeing up classroom space for dramatizations or classroom meetings where kids sit on the floor.

When students use their decision making power unwisely, I quickly restrict that power. During reading time, for example, students are often allowed to choose their own groups and books. Most work earnestly, reading cooperatively, and writing regularly in their reading response journals. If a reading group has trouble settling down, I intervene rapidly and give increasingly restrictive options to the students. Other students who work successfully in reading groups model how a reading group should be run: the students not only conduct a discussion in front of the class, but plan in advance for a student to be inattentive and show how a student discussion leader might respond.

A well-organized class that is respectful and involves the students in some decision-making is a prerequisite for successful learning. Cooperative organization and student involvement alone won't make a class critical or even build a community of learners, but they are essential building blocks in its foundation. ❑

Student involvement is key to a successful class.

## Teaching Social Justice

continued from page 33

"Is it better to have friends or money?" a student asked, which formed the basis of a lengthy discussion in the reading circle.

Other questions that students have raised in our "Questions We Have" book include: Who tells the television what to put on? Why do geese fly together in an angle? Did ministers or priests have slaves? How many presidents owned slaves? Why haven't we had a woman president? Why are the faces of the presidents on our money? How do horses sweat? If we are free, why do we have to come to school? When did photography start? Who invented slavery? Why are people homeless? What runs faster, a cheetah or an ostrich? Did any adults die in the 1913 massacre of 73 children in Calumet County, Michigan? (in reference to the Woody Guthrie song about a tragedy that grew out of a labor struggle).

Some questions are answered by students working together using reference materials in the classroom or school library. (Cheetahs can run up to 65 miles an hour while ostriches run only 40 mph.) Other questions are subjects of group discussion; still others we work on in small groups. For example, the question "What is the difference between the master/slave relationship and the parent/child relationship?" developed one afternoon when a child complained that his parent wouldn't allow him out in the evening for school story hour. A girl responded that we might as well all be slaves, and a third student posed the question. After a brief group discussion, I had children work in groups of 3 or 4 and they continued the debate. They made two lists, one of similarities and one of differences, between the master/slave relationship and the parent/child relationship. They discussed the question in the small groups, then a spokesperson from each group reported to the class.

The fascinating thing was not only the information that I found about their lives, but also how it forced children to reflect on what we had been studying in our unit on slavery and the Underground Railroad. When one student said, "Yeah, it's different because masters whipped slaves and my mom doesn't whip me," another student responded by saying, "All masters didn't whip their slaves."

When another student said that their mothers love them and masters didn't love their slaves, another girl gave the example of the slave character Izzie in the movie *Half Free, Half Slave* that we watched, in which Izzie got special privileges because she was the master's girlfriend. Another girl responded that that wasn't an example of love; she was just being used.

In this discussion, students pooled their information and generated their own understanding of history, challenging crude generalizations typical of children this age. Students also started evaluating what was fair and just in their own lives. It was clear to all that the treatment of slaves was unjust. Not so clear was to what extent and how children should be disciplined by their parents. "That's abuse!" one student remarked after hearing about how one child was punished.

"No, it's not. That's how my mom treats me whenever I do something bad," responded another.

While no "answers" were found, the posing of this question by a student, and my facilitating its discussion, added both to kids' understanding of history and to their sense of the complexity of evaluating what is fair and just in contemporary society.

## Emphasis on Critiquing Bias

Raising questions about bias in ideas and materials — from children's books to school texts, fairy tales, news reports, song lyrics, and cartoons — is another key component of a social justice classroom. I tell my fifth graders it's important to examine "the messages that are trying to take over your brain" and that it's up to them to sort out which ones they should believe and which ones promote fairness and justice in our world.

To recognize that different perspectives exist in history and society is the first step toward critiquing materials and evaluating what perspectives they represent or leave out. Ultimately it helps children see that they, too, can have their own values and perspectives independent of what they last read or heard.

We start by examining perspective and voice. "Whose point of view are we hearing?" I ask.

One poem that is good to initiate such a discussion is Paul Fleischman's dialogue poem, "Honeybees," from *Joyful Noise: Poems for Two Voices*. (See p. 42.) The poem is read simultaneously

Education must provoke reflection.

*Susan Lina Ruggles*

by two people, one describing the life of a bee from the perspective of a worker, and one from the perspective of a queen. Children love to perform the poem and often want to write their own. They begin to understand how to look at things from different perspectives. They also start to identify with certain perspectives.

After hearing the song of the week, "My Country 'Tis of Thee My People Are Dying," by Buffie Saint Marie, one of my students wrote a dialogue poem between a Native American and a U.S. soldier about smallpox-infected blankets the U.S. government traded for land. In another instance, as part of a class activity when pairs of students were writing dialogue poems between a master and a slave, two girls wrote one between a field slave and a house slave, further deepening the class's understanding about the complexity of slavery. During writing workshop six weeks later, three boys decided to write a "Triple Dialogue Poem" that included the slave, a slave master, and an abolitionist.

Students also need to know that children's books and school textbooks contain biases and important omissions. I find the concept of "stereotypes" and "omission" important to enhance children's understanding of such biases.

For example, around Thanksgiving time I show my students an excellent filmstrip called "Unlearning Native American Stereotypes" produced by the Council on Interracial Books for Children. It's narrated by Native American children who visit a public library and become outraged at the various stereotypes of Indians in the books. One year after I showed this, my kids seemed particularly angry at what they had learned. They came the next day talking about how their siblings in first grade had come home with construction paper headdresses with feathers. "That's a stereotype," my kids proudly proclaimed. "What did you do about it?" I asked. "I ripped it up," "I slugged him," came the chorus of responses.

After further discussion, they decided there were more productive things they could do than to hit their siblings. They scoured the school library for books with Indian stereotypes and found few. So they decided to investigate the first-grade room. Two of the students wrote a letter to the teacher asking permission and then went in. They found a picture of an Indian next to letter I in the alphabet strip on the wall. They came back excited, declaring that they had "found a stereotype that everybody sees every day!" They decided they wanted to teach the first graders about stereotypes. I was skeptical, but agreed, and after much rehearsal they entered the first-grade classroom to give their lesson. Returning to my classroom, they expressed frustration that the first-graders didn't listen as well as they had hoped, but nonetheless thought it had gone well. Later the two students, Paco Resendez and Faviola Alvarez, wrote in our school newspaper:

"We have been studying stereotypes of Native Americans. What is a stereotype? It's when somebody says something that's not true about another group of people. For example, it is a stereotype if you think all Indians wear feathers or say "HOW!" Or if you think that all girls are delicate. Why? Because some girls are strong."

The emphasis on critique is an excellent way to integrate math into social studies. Students, for example, can tally numbers of instances certain people, viewpoints, or groups are presented in a text or in mass media. One year my students compared the times famous women and famous men were mentioned in the fifth-grade history text. One reaction by a number of boys was that men were mentioned far more frequently because women must not have done much throughout history. To help facilitate the discussion, I provided background resources for the students, including biographies of famous women. This not only helped students better understand the nature of "omission," but also generated interest in reading biographies of women.

In another activity I had students tally the number of men and women by occupation as depicted in magazine and/or TV advertisements. By comparing their findings to the population as a whole, various forms of bias were uncovered, not only in how the media portrays the population, but in the structure of jobs that helps segregate women into occupations such as office worker or waitress. Another interesting activity is having students tally the number of biographies in the school library and analyze them by race, gender, and occupation.

One of my favorite activities involves comparing books. I stumbled on this activity one year when my class read a story about inventions in a reading textbook published by Scott Foresman Co. The story stated that the traffic light was invented by an anonymous policeman. Actually it was invented by the African-American scientist Garrett A. Morgan. I gave my students a short piece from an African-American history book and we compared it with the Scott Foresman book. We talked about which story we should believe and how one might verify which was accurate. After checking out another book about inventions, the students realized that the school text was wrong.

## The Teaching of Activism for Social Justice

The underlying theme in my classroom is that the quest for social justice is a never-ending struggle in our nation and world; that the vast majority of people have benefited by this struggle; that we must understand this struggle; and that we must make decisions about whether to be involved in it.

I weave the various disciplines around this theme. When I read poetry and literature to the children, I often use books that raise issues about social justice and, when possible, in which the protagonists are young people working for social justice. In math, we will look at everything from the distribution of wealth in the world to the percentage of women in different occupations. The class songs and posters of the week also emphasize social struggles from around the world. I also have each student make what I call a "people's textbook" — a three-ring binder in which they put handouts and some of their own work, particularly interviews that they conducted. There are sections for geography, history, current events, songs, poetry, and mass media. I also have a gallery of freedom fighters on the wall — posters of people we have studied in social studies and current events.

In addition to studying movements for social justice of the past, students discuss current problems and possible solutions. One way I do this is by having students role-play examples of discrimination and how they might respond.

I start with kids dramatizing historical incidents such as Sojourner Truth's successful attempt to integrate street cars in Washington, D.C. after the Civil War, and Rosa Parks' role in the Montgomery, Alabama, bus boycott. We brainstorm contemporary problems where people might face discrimination, drawing on our current events studies and interviews children have done with family members and friends about types of discrimination of which they are aware.

One day in the spring of 1993, my class was dramatizing contemporary examples. Working in small groups, the students were to choose a type of discrimination — such as not being allowed to rent a house because one receives welfare, or not getting a job because one is a woman — and develop a short dramatization. Afterward, the kids would lead a discussion about the type of discrimination they were acting out.

After a few dramatizations, it was Gilberto, Juan, and Carlos' turn. I had no clue as to what they were going to dramatize.

It was a housing discrimination example — but with a twist. Gilberto and Juan were acting the part of two gay men attempting to rent an apartment, and Carlos was the landlord who refused to rent to them. I was surprised, in part because in previous brainstorming sessions on discrimination none of my students had mentioned discrimination against gay people. Further, as is often unfortunately the case with fifth graders, in the past my students had shown they were prone to uncritically

Fratney students collaborate on a project.

accept anti-gay slurs and stereotypes. But here, on their own initiative, were Gilberto, Juan, and Carlos transferring our class discussion of housing discrimination based on race to that of sexual orientation.

The dramatization caused an initial chorus of laughs and jeers. But, I noticed, the students also listened attentively. Afterwards, I asked the class what type of discrimination had been modeled.

"Gayism," one student, Elvis, yelled out.

It was a new word to me, but it got the point across. The class then went on to discuss "gayism." Most of the kids who spoke agreed that it was a form of discrimination. During the discussion, one student mentioned a march on Washington a week earlier, demanding gay rights. (Interestingly, Gilberto, Juan, and Carlos said they were unaware of the march.)

Elvis, who coined the term "gayism," then said: "Yeah, my cousin is one of those lesi... lesi..."

"Lesbians," I said, completing his sentence.

"Yeah, lesbian," he said. He then added enthusiastically: "And she went to Washington to march for her rights."

"That's just like when Dr. King made his dream speech at the march in Washington," another student added.

Before long the class moved on to a new role play. But the "gayism" dramatization lingered in my memory.

One reason is that I was pleased that the class had been able to move beyond the typical discussions around gay issues — which had in the past seemed to center on my explaining why students shouldn't call each other "faggot." More fundamentally, however, the incident reminded me of the inherent link between the classroom and society, not only in terms of how society influences the children who are in our classrooms for six hours a day, but also in terms of how broader movements for social reform affect daily classroom life.

It's important not only to study these progressive social movements and to dramatize current social problems, but to encourage students to take thoughtful action. By doing this they see themselves as actors in the world, not just things to be acted upon.

One of the best ways to help students in this area is by example — to expose

> It's important that children see themselves as actors in the world, not just things acted upon.

them to people in the community who are fighting for social justice. I regularly have social activists visit and talk with children in my classes. I also explain the activities that I'm personally involved in as an example of what might be done. (See article, p. 40.)

I tell students they can write letters, circulate petitions, and talk to other classes and children about their concerns. My students have gone with me to marches that demanded that M.L. King's birthday be made a national holiday and that there be an end to the nuclear arms race. Two of my students testified before the City Council, asking that a Jobs With Peace referendum be placed on the ballot. Another time students at our school testified with parents in front of the City Council that special monies should be allocated to rebuild our school playground.

If we neglect to include an activist component in our curricula, we cut students off from the possibility of social change. We model apathy as a response to the world's problems.

Such apathy is not OK. At a time when cynicism and hopelessness increasingly dominate our youth, helping students understand the world and their relationship to it by encouraging social action may be one of the few antidotes. Schools are a prime place where this can take place. Teachers are a key element in it happening. Teaching for social justice is a necessary priority as we approach the new century. ❑

*Bob Peterson teaches 5th grade at La Escuela Fratney in Milwaukee and is an editor of* Rethinking Schools.

# Songs that Promote Justice

*Following are a few of the songs that I use in my classroom.*

"Bread and Roses," by Judy Collins.

"Deportee," by Woody Guthrie.

"Follow the Drinking Gourd," by the Kim and Reggie Harris Group.

"Happy Birthday, Martin Luther King," by Stevie Wonder.

"The Harder They Come," by Jimmy Cliff.

"Harriet Tubman," by Holly Near and Ronnie Gilbert.

"I Cried," by Holly Near.

"Lawless Avenue," by Jackson Browne.

"Lives in the Balance," by Jackson Browne.

"On Monday," by Leadbelly.

"My Country 'Tis of Thee My People Are Dying," by Buffy St. Marie.

"Mr. Wendal," by Speech and Arrested Development.

"The Letter," by Ruben Blades.

"New Underground Railroad," by Holly Near and Ronnie Gilbert.

"1913 Massacre," by Woody Guthrie and Jack Elliott.

"Samba Lando," by Seves/Manns.

"Sister Rosa," by The Neville Brothers.

"The Secret Life of Plants," by Stevie Wonder.

"There But for Fortune," by Phil Ochs.

"Unite Children," by The Children of Selma.

"We Are the Champions," by Queen.

"Where have All the Buffalo Gone?" by Buffy St. Marie.

"Why?" by Tracy Chapman.

"You Can Get It If You Really Want," by Jimmy Cliff.

# Ballad of the Landlord

By Langston Hughes

Landlord, landlord,
My roof has sprung a leak.
Don't you 'member I told you about it
Way last week?

Landlord, landlord,
These steps is broken down.
When you come up yourself
It's a wonder you don't fall down.

Ten Bucks you say I owe you?
Ten Bucks you say is due?
Well, that's Ten Bucks more'n I'll pay you
Till you fix this house up new.

What? You gonna get eviction orders?
You gonna cut off my heat?
You gonna take my furniture and
throw it in the street?

Um-huh! You talking high and mighty.
Talk on — till you get through.
You ain't gonna be able to say a word
If I land my fist on you.

Police! Police!
Come and get this man!
He's trying to ruin the government
And overturn the land!

Copper's whistle!
Patrol bell!
Arrest.

Precinct Station.
Iron cell.
Headlines in press:

MAN THREATENS LANDLORD

TENANT HELD NO BAIL

JUDGE GIVES NEGRO 90 DAYS
IN COUNTY JAIL

Langston Hughes is probably the most famous poet of the Harlem Renaissance. He chose to write about ordinary people — as he said, "workers, roustabouts, and singers, and job hunters...people up today and down tomorrow beaten and baffled, but determined not to be wholly beaten." (See p. 184 for lesson ideas.)

# The Complexities of Encouraging Social Action

*By Bob Peterson*

Most teachers believe that politics should be kept out of the classroom. But it never is. Even a teacher who consciously attempts to be politically "neutral" makes hundreds of political decisions — from the posters on the wall to attitudes toward holidays. Is Valentine's Day celebrated, but not International Women's Day?

It's not only a case of what the teacher does, but what the teacher doesn't do. If a teacher decides not to discuss social movements, such as the movement against the War in Vietnam or labor organizing during the Great Depression, the subtle yet clear message is that social activism is not worthy of study, let alone something that students should consider a civic responsibility. It also disequips children from understanding that ordinary people make a difference in shaping events.

The most difficult dilemma arises not in studying social issues but in encouraging students to be socially active. The fear is that if teachers promote social activism, they are indoctrinating their students and promoting a "pied-piper" syndrome. But in a society that professes democratic ideals, one of the key purposes of the public school system is to foster participation in civic life. Further, not to take a deliberate stance against problems such as racism is in actuality a stance of indifference that helps perpetuate injustice.

At the same time, safeguards are necessary. First, in discussing social issues, various points of view must be examined. At the elementary level, this usually is the teacher's responsibility.

Second, teachers shouldn't hide their personal opinions on controversial subjects, but opinions should be labeled as such. It must also be absolutely clear that a student's grade does not depend on agreeing with the teacher.

For a teacher to pretend to have no opinion on controversial topics, however, is not only unbelievable but sends a message that it's OK to be opinionless and apathetic toward key social issues.

Recognizing such safeguards is the easy part. More difficult is applying them. To help illustrate the complexities, I'll share a classroom example.

Several years ago the Sanctuary movement was a vibrant force protecting Central Americans fleeing political persecution and entering this country without legal papers. At the time, my fifth-grade students and I were studying the anti-slavery Underground Railroad. The comparisons between the two movements were striking. To help make the links between historical and contemporary events, and to make the issues of flight and persecution come

> **Even a teacher who consciously attempts to be politically 'neutral' makes hundreds of political decisions — from the posters on the wall to attitudes toward holidays.**

alive, I invited a speaker who had spent five years in El Salvador. As part of the presentation about U.S. policies in Central America, the speaker showed some slides. At first, some of the students laughed nervously at the distended bellies of starving Salvadoran children. But their nervousness turned to horror and then anger as they began to understand that U.S. bombs were being dropped on these children.

In a follow-up discussion, the kids asked, "Why? Why is the U.S. doing this? Why does Reagan do it?"

The speaker and I responded, "Why do you think?"

"Because Reagan supports the rich," said one, with others murmering "yeah" in agreement.

But others were not satisfied. "Why? Why does he support the rich?" they asked.

Finally the speaker responded, "Because it is the job of the President in this country to support the rich."

Paco's hand shot up. "If that's the case, what about Kennedy?" he demanded. The bell rang before the speaker could answer.

In a group meeting the next day, we struggled to understand the two ways in which the U.S. was involved — supporting the government in El Salvador and the Contras in Nicaragua. I read some excerpts from a Reagan speech defending the U.S. role, and the late Archbishop Romero's plea to stop U.S. arm shipments to El Salvador. The children didn't understand Reagan's worry about "communism," but in discussion, indicated that they felt the horrors of hunger and war were the greatest danger.

The children decided to write letters to our congressional representatives and to the President about U.S. military involvement in El Salvador and Nicaragua. The next day one boy, Michael, came in and said, "Mr. Peterson, we have to send weapons to Central America or else the Russians will take over and no one will believe in God anymore."

"Michael, you've been talking to your mom," I said. "Great. Keep it up. We'll talk about that later." But we ran out of time that day, so as he left I gave him some short readings produced by Food First on hunger and land distribution in Central America. I asked him to read them with his mom. The following day he didn't show up, and I was concerned.

At a class meeting a week later, another student, Emma, announced that we had to discuss the letters we wrote to the President. "They won't do any good," she lamented, "I bet he just tore them up." She then proposed we go on a field trip to Washington, D.C., to meet the President and that I, the teacher, finance it. I politely declined.

At that point I offered an alternative. I said that sometimes people protest in Washington, D.C., but often people protest here in Milwaukee. I cited as a current example protests held regularly by the Milwaukee chapter of the Pledge of Resistance, a group that promotes human rights in Central America. The kids immediately said that they wanted to go to one of the protests. Caught up in their enthusiasm, I sent home permission slips to parents explaining that though it was not part of the official curriculum, for those with parents' permission, I would supervise a public bus trip after school to the Federal Building. There we would join the protest against aid to the "Contras," U.S.-sponsored guerrillas fighting the government in Nicaragua. Half the class, 12 children, brought back permission slips. The next Monday those students stayed after school and made signs. (Careful not to use school supplies, I used my own money to buy tag board and markers.) At first the students asked me what they should say. I said that if they were going on a protest march, they had better know what they were protesting.

So they wrote their own slogans: Let them run their land; Support the poor — not the freedom fighters — they're the rich; Give Nicaragua their Freedom; Help Central America, Don't Kill Them; Give Nicaragua Some Food Instead of Weapons; We want Freedom and Peace; and Stop Spending Money to Make Bombs.

After we made the signs, we walked to the bus stop (our optimistic spirits only slightly dampened by a steady drizzle) and headed for the Federal Building. My students, who were overwhelmingly Latino, were welcomed with open arms. Along with 150 others, we walked, marched, chanted and finally went home, wet and exhausted.

The next day during class, some of those who were at the protest led a discussion about the event and about U.S. policies in Central America. The kids talked and listened — and generally acted as if they were on top of the world.

One student, Paula Martinez, wrote the following in our magazine, *Kid Power*:

"On a rainy Tuesday in April some of the students from our class went to protest against the Contras. The people in Central America are poor and being bombed on their heads. When we went protesting it was raining and it seemed like the Contras were bombing us. A week before we had a visitor, Jim Harney. He had been to El Salvador. He talked to our class about what was going on in El Salvador. He said it was terrible. A lot of people are dying. He showed us slides of El Salvador and told us it's bad to be there. He hoped that our government will give them food and money and not bombs."

Michael, the boy who had come back from home concerned about the Russians and God, didn't go to the march. He said he had to baby-sit. Parent conferences were a week later and I was a bit apprehensive to see Michael's mother, fearing she might be upset with our protest march.

She walked in the room and sat down. "Mr. Peterson, I want to thank you," she said. "Michael has become interested in everything. He watches the news; he talks to me about what's going on; he knows more about things than me, sometimes. I don't know what you did. But thanks."

As we talked, it was clear that her views on Central America hadn't changed. But our differences were secondary. What was most important to both of us was that her son had started to read the world. □

Milwaukee protest sparked by the beating of Rodney King by L.A. police.

SUSAN LINA RUGGLES

# Honeybees

## By Paul Fleischman

The following is a dialogue poem, to be read by two people. The first person reads down the left column, the second person, down the right. Capitalized phrases are to be read in unison.

| | |
|---|---|
| *BEING A BEE* | *BEING A BEE* |
| | *is a joy.* |
| *is a pain.* | |
| | *I'm a queen* |
| *I'm a worker* | |
| *I'LL GLADLY EXPLAIN.* | *I'LL GLADLY EXPLAIN.* |
| | *Upon rising, I'm fed* |
| | *by my royal attendants,* |
| *I'm up at dawn, guarding* | |
| *the hive's narrow entrance* | |
| | *I'm bathed* |
| *then I take out* | |
| *the hive's morning trash* | |
| | *then I'm groomed.* |
| *then I put in an hour* | |
| *making wax,* | |
| *without two minutes' time* | |
| *to sit and relax.* | |
| | *The rest of my day* |
| | *is quite simply set forth:* |
| *Then I might collect nectar* | |
| *from the field* | |
| *three miles north* | |
| | *I lay eggs,* |

or perhaps I'm on
larva detail

by the hundred.

feeding the grubs
in their cells,
wishing that I were still
helpless and pale.

I'm loved and I'm lauded,
I'm outranked by none.

Then I pack combs with
pollen — not my idea of fun.

When I've done
enough laying

Then, weary, I strive

I retire

to patch up any cracks
in the hive.

for the rest of the day.

Then I build some new cells,
slaving away at
enlarging this Hell,
dreading the sight
of another sunrise,
wondering why we don't
all unionize.
TRULY, A BEE'S IS THE
WORST
OF ALL LIVES.

TRULY, A BEE'S IS THE
BEST
OF ALL LIVES.

Paul Fleischman writes books for young children — prose and poetry. (See p. 184 for lesson ideas.)

# Tapping into Feelings of Fairness

## By Karen Miller

When I tell people I've been teaching social studies for 10 years in middle school, I often see a vacant look on their face. Teaching social studies they understand. But middle school?

They know the term, but you can tell that many are just not sure what this neither fish-nor-fowl, neither elementary-nor-high-school phenomenon is all about. On the other extreme, you get those who confidently act as if they understand middle school — why, it's just like elementary school, only the kids are a year or two older.

If only it were that simple.

Over the years I've come to realize that to effectively teach middle school in general, and to teach about social justice issues in particular, it's helpful to understand some of the specific characteristics of this age group.

Some of the critical issues are the same as with any age group. The curriculum, for example, has to relate to the students' lives, lessons have to be interactive, students have to be involved, and students must have choices, whether in choosing writing topics or interdisciplinary projects. With middle school, however, it's essential to realize that the kids are embarking on a precarious transition from child to adult. Their peers are more important than anything else in their lives, and a successful teaching strategy must involve a high degree of peer interaction. It's their friends, not the teacher, who provide the positive feedback the students are looking for as they cope with the insecurities and questions they face in their lives.

There is also a healthy questioning among most middle school kids. It's an age when many kids are just starting to discover that it's OK to disagree not only with mom and dad, but also with the teacher. From there it's easy to suggest that it's OK to disagree with history books or the president. Once the students have discovered it's OK to disagree with authorities, then my role as a teacher is to help them learn how to form opinions, to understand what those opinions are based on, and, I hope, have them act on those opinions.

Furthermore, social justice issues are a natural for middle school students. The kids seem to have an inherent concern with being treated unfairly and they are quick to voice that concern. In general, they haven't yet developed the cynicism that unfortunately helps poison the atmosphere in some high school classrooms. If I can tap into those emotions over fairness, it's a short leap to helping them understand how somebody else might feel when they are treated unfairly, whether it's African Americans, or workers in a factory, or immigrants. The key is to approach the kids at their level and then nurture a broader understanding.

## Prejudice Toward Immigrants

My approach to teaching is shaped by the specifics of my school, a predominantly white, working-class school in Portland, Ore. If I had to pick one main social problem in the school, it would be prejudice and racism toward other students. I feel it is my responsibility as a teacher to address this issue, and to try to mold my curriculum accordingly.

In my school, the tensions focus on immigrants who have moved to Portland in recent years, predominantly from Asia. About 12% of our students are in our English as a Second Language program; over 70% of the ESL students are Asian American, mostly from Vietnam, and another 25% are Russian. A few are Latin American. Our white students are not immune to the anti-immigrant sentiment increasing in this country, and a small minority take out those sentiments on fellow students.

Two years ago a Russian girl named Tatyana came to my class in tears. A normally quiet student who never complained, Tatyana said, "I just can't do it anymore. I'm not coming back to the school because of the constant teasing."

Partly it was a language question, she said. When a teacher called on her and she had to answer a question, she could hear kids giggle. Out in the hall, she said, kids would imitate her speech and accent. Kids also taunted her because she didn't "dress right" — she wore skirts and blouses instead of jeans. Tatyana stayed in school, but she was only there about half the time. When I called home to ask why she was absent, I was told she was baby-sitting. This was probably true. But I also knew that her school experience was very painful to her and that this contributed to her absence.

I remember another incident several years ago, this one involving Mia, a Vietnamese girl. Mia had written a very moving story, published in a local book of short stories, about her experience living on the streets in Vietnam and selling gum in order to survive. The story also recounted how Mia was picked up by police, placed in an orphanage and ultimately adopted by a family in the United States.

Because her story had already been published, Mia gave permission to have it read aloud to the class. It was an emotionally powerful story, and many students were quite moved. However, we also have some "skinhead" wannabes in our school, who go out of their way to prove their "skinhead" political credentials. Mia later told me how two of the "skinhead" wannabes later said to her in the halls, "Hey Mia, want some gum?"

I knew I had to get the kids to deal with this growing problem of "skinheads," racism, prejudice, and stereotypes. And I knew it couldn't be just during the cracks of the school day but had to be a core part of my teaching.

## Immigration and Discrimination

So what does this mean in practice?

There's not a quick answer, and perhaps the best way to explain is to go through a particular unit on immigration I have done with eighth graders in recent years as part of a history/language arts block.

As is true for many teachers throughout the country, I am not free to completely mold my own curriculum. The immigration unit was given to me as part of a team-teaching decision by teachers of 8th grade U.S. history.

Although I was handed the task of doing a 3-month unit on immigration starting with the 1880s, within that I was able to develop my own approach.

One of the advantages of classroom practice being ignored in most policy discussions about school reform is that teachers sometimes have a fair amount of freedom once they close their classroom doors.

I also have many of my U.S. history students in a separate reading block, where issues can be tied in to the history/language arts block. During the unit on immigration, for example, our reading block may be discussing *Roll of Thunder, Hear My Cry,* a book by Mildred Taylor about Cassie, a young African-American girl in the 1930s. In the book, Cassie's understanding of racism grows and she stands up for her beliefs. Another book I have used in this context is *Lyddie,* by Katherine Paterson, which deals with an immigrant girl working in a textile factory who must decide whether to join other workers organizing for better conditions. Although I don't necessarily tie either reading into the immigration unit, since not all the students are in both blocks or in the history class, those who are often make the connections on their own.

My main approach in the immigration unit was to forgo a "just the facts" approach and to pick out themes that ultimately would connect with the students' lives and the issues of racism and discrimination. I also knew that a lecture approach wouldn't work, but that somehow I would have to tap into the kids' emotional feelings toward such issues.

My co-teacher and I decided to first approach the issues historically, to have the students experience issues of immigration in a safe way, and then to bring the curriculum to current issues. But before that, we began by breaking the students into groups of four and asking them to answer the question, "What is an American?" A seemingly simple question, it is fraught with complexities. Is a recent immigrant from Russia an American? What about people who emigrate but don't become citizens? Can one be both a Vietnamese and an American? My main purpose in this exercise, however, was not to provide a definitive answer but to get kids to think about the assumptions they brought to the question. The lists, for

Latinos are one of the fastest-growing immigrant groups.

S. Beth Atkin from Voices from the Fields

instance, tended to include things like white, speaks English, born in America — definitions which left out a lot of the students and families at our school.

After the "What is an American" exercise, my co-teacher and I started a month-long project under which students would assume and develop the identity of an immigrant. First, the kids were divided into groups of four or five and assigned to a pretend-family from a particular country. Their first assignment was to come up with names from that country, their ages (they must represent three different generations), occupations, religion, and a history of their family experience. Because we started with the late 1800s, we focused on countries of that era, which tended to be mostly European. In addition to providing some historical background, this also kept the majority of students within a manageable comfort zone when they began the project. They weren't immediately forced to deal with current animosity toward Asians, Russians, or Latinos, so their defenses were down because, after all, this was just history.

Using different resources and providing ample time for research, the kids began developing a family history and scrapbook. They kept a journal written by their new character. Entries dealt with issues such as how it feels to leave home for a new country, the type of dinner they have their last night at home, why they are leaving, what they think they might find in America, and so forth. Many students recreated birth certificates for the scrapbook, or drew maps of their homeland, described traditions and customs, or listed favorite foods. While kids developed new family histories and scrapbooks, we read stories of immigrants from various novels, watched appropriate movies, and so forth. Each time I teach this unit, I am surprised at how quickly the kids adopt their new identities, many calling each other by their new names. One of the most interesting parts of the unit, however, is what comes next.

It takes about a week for the kids to develop their family histories. After that, we have them go through a role play about entering Ellis Island. (The

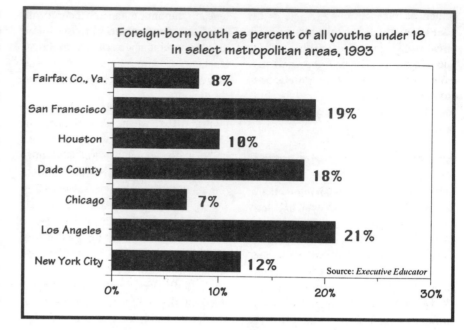

**Foreign-born youth as percent of all youths under 18 in select metropolitan areas, 1993**

| Metropolitan Area | Percent |
|---|---|
| Fairfax Co., Va. | 8% |
| San Franscisco | 19% |
| Houston | 10% |
| Dade County | 18% |
| Chicago | 7% |
| Los Angeles | 21% |
| New York City | 12% |

Source: *Executive Educator*

first year I used the packaged simulation mentioned at the end of this article.)

## Ellis Island Simulation

We had trained students from another class to come in and play the role of officials at Ellis Island, and my co-teacher and I also played the role of officials. We pronounced the immigrants' names incorrectly, we were impatient with them, we pushed and shoved them, we deported a few for "health" reasons, and we grilled them on their occupations, education, English abilities, and plans in America.

The "immigrant" students, needless to say, became upset, angry, and hurt. We actually had some kids in tears, one because one of the officials repeatedly kept pronouncing her Italian family's name wrong. In frustration, she changed her name from Marticelli to Martin because it was easier to say and sounded more American. (I can guarantee you that the students in the Marticelli "family" had a new understanding of what was and wasn't an "American" name.)

After the Ellis Island simulation, the students continued in their role for about three weeks, again combining historical research, readings from novels, and development of their family histories. They had to look for a city to live in, a home or apartment, their first

job, and so forth. They also maintained their journals during this time. For their final project for this section, each family finished the scrapbook they had already started: they rewrote their journal entries, took family photos (a lot of the kids dressed up in historical dress and took pictures), made pretend tickets from their voyage, passports, and birth certificates. Many of the students in the various "families" became quite attached to each other.

That was the first phase. The next phase jumped a bit, historically.

As a history teacher, I am not overly concerned about teaching chronologically. Instead, I tend to teach thematically. I find this strategy works with middle school students. Timelines and facts are not particularly important to them. What sticks in their heads are dramatic events, issues that tap into their emotions, that make sense to them personally. Emotions, not logic, rule.

As a transition, we had a panel of immigrants come and talk to the class to show the range of immigrants currently coming to this country. Members of the panel included a student's mother from Norway, a teacher at the school who had emigrated from Canada, a student's grandparent from Russia, and an 8th-grade Korean student. When the students interviewed the panel, it was clear that the extended role playing from the previous three weeks had influenced their thinking. Some of the questions included: How did people treat you when you first came here? Do people pronounce your name wrong? Why did you come here? Was it hard to learn English?

After this transition, we wanted to start dealing with immigration issues that would more closely touch on the current discrimination and prejudice in our school. But we knew that topic was a bit too close to jump into immediately. So first we had the students write about a time when they experienced discrimination — whether it was based on race, religion, or age (adolescents all seem to have stories about how they were treated unfairly just because they were teenagers). Students took the assignment seriously and wrote from the heart. While there were a number of moving essays, the class was particularly struck by the experiences of Amber, an African-American girl.

"People get discriminated against all of the time because of their race," Amber wrote. "Sometimes it's just some name calling or teasing. Other times it can be as bad as personal harm. I can remember once I almost got my hair set on fire because I am black. I have also been assaulted a number of times in the past three years."

We shared the essays while sitting in a circle. Those students who wanted were allowed to pass. If students write something they feel is too personal, they are encouraged to write another essay that is less emotionally loaded to share. The key in any exercise of this sort is to help the students to open up, but also to ensure that there is ample support and flexibility. As with the extended role play on the immigrant families, the exercise helps build a sense of community in the class: students see each other as an integral part of the group — a very important concept at the middle school age.

While the students read their essays, I took notes and wrote down what emotions came up (anger, discouragement, cynicism) and how the students coped with such emotions (talking back, walking away). We then came up with a list of emotions and strategies that we pasted on the wall. This was a concrete way to continue to tap into the students' feelings about discrimination as we started talking about current issues.

## Need for Collective Action

As useful as this exercise is, I also learned that we need to deepen the student's sense of discrimination and what to do about it. My students tended to approach discrimination as an individual problem that needed only an individual response. There was little sense of the need to take collective action to change attitudes, or laws, or practices — whether through petitions, meetings, or lobbying.

One of the changes I have made over the years to instill a sense of activism is to bring in people who are combating discrimination. Speakers, for example, have ranged from a woman from Cascade AIDS Project to speakers from a local shelter for street youth. I have also started clipping news articles or collecting stories about activists, especially teenagers, in order to provide concrete examples.

Another activity that has helped students deal with current issues is pairing students in my class with students from an English as a Second Language class. They ask the ESL students about their personal interests, hobbies, why they moved to this country, what it was like. My students then write a biography-poem about the ESL student. Often we display the poems on the walls, complete with photos of the partners.

> Instilling a sense of activism and collective responsibility is one of the most difficult aspects of teaching for social justice.

Another successful activity involves a "Pledge of Appreciation of Cultural Diversity." For this assignment, each student is asked to write and sign an individual pledge showing their commitment to respect all people, and outlining specific activities they plan to do to make a difference. To underscore the seriousness of the pledge, students have a witness also sign their pledge.

Many of the pledges noted that it was important for kids to know who you are and what your background is — an understanding that for many students sheds a new light on things such as Black pride or the Vietnamese students speaking Vietnamese at lunch. Other examples of pledges included:
• I will not make fun of people whose language is different from my own.
• I will learn to correctly pronounce three names of ESL students.
• I will learn to say hello in three different languages.
• I will invite two ESL students to have lunch with me.
• I will tutor a student who is learning English.

In the big scheme of life such pledges may not seem profound. But for students who began the year wondering whether you had to be white to be an American, my kids had come a long way.

Perhaps our most interesting final project involved a mural the kids designed and painted. (That year we had a grant to work with a muralist.) The kids wanted to tie in the mural with immigration, discrimination, prejudice, and social problems, and the muralist worked with the kids on designing and painting the mural. The kids voted to divide the mural into three parts: past, present, and future. For the past, they depicted characters like Harriet Tubman and Martin Luther King. The present wasn't too hard to figure out — the themes revolved around gangs, drugs, deterioration of our neighborhoods, and so forth. The most difficult part was deciding what to do for the "future" panel.

The kids decided to have an intersection with two roads right before the "future" panel: One road led to a world filled with gangs and violence and poverty and segregation. The other was a kind of yellow brick road to utopia, where people and animals lived in harmony.

We asked the students how they could let people know they have a choice about which road to follow? So the students decided to paint a trash dumpster at the intersection where one could choose whether to throw off gang jackets, drugs, and guns.

The kids were thrilled with their ideas, and the mural turned out to be both beautiful and provocative. To this day, it remains in our school. But in retrospect, I also feel I missed an opportunity. I too was caught up in the excitement of designing and painting a mural and didn't encourage the students to reflect a bit more on its message and assumptions. We made it seem that everything was just an individual decision, and that individual decisions alone were enough.

I have found that instilling a sense of activism and collective responsibility is one of the most difficult aspects of teaching for social justice. Partly this is because our society discourages collective action and instead encourages the view that people are individual consumers and workers who need only concern themselves with their individual careers, lifestyles, and families. I don't have any pat answers and, as I mentioned earlier, one solution I have used is to bring in a number of speakers who talk about their activism.

Another area that I still struggle with is trying to move the students beyond viewing discrimination as an individual problem and helping them understand there are issues such as institutional racism and sexism. With middle school students, however, there's not as much latitude as with high school students. Plus, there are limited resources for these grade levels. When I find high school materials that address such issues, I try to rewrite or modify them for middle school students. My main goal, however, is to encourage students to understand that stereotypes exist, that they are learned and passed along, and that the students need to question their assumptions about other groups of

Helping students understand the difference between individual and institutional bias is difficult but necessary.

people. Thus my students may not understand the institutional intricacies of who is served by discrimination and racism, but at least they understand that such "isms" exist, and they are better equipped to recognize them.

Another issue, complicated in part by the unit's focus only on immigration issues beginning with the late 19th century, is helping students understand that, contrary to the view of most textbooks, the United States is not "a nation of immigrants." Such an approach ignores Native Americans, the African-Americans who were brought here as slaves, and the Chicanos who found themselves living in the United States only because the U.S. conquered roughly one-third of Mexico during the Mexican-American war in 1846-48.

While trying to address such issues, I also try to be careful not to spend all our time looking at injustice, racism, and prejudice. I think it's critical with middle school students to develop a classroom community. Helping my students develop a democratic community emphasizing equality and caring may be the most effective result of my classroom practice.

There are times that it is easy to be discouraged by what I realize are the many shortcomings in my curriculum. I try to improve, but I also try to remember that change is a constant struggle. Just because I have not yet reached the state of perfect teacherhood doesn't mean I should abandon the few gains I have been able to make with my students.

I, along with my students, am on a discovery process of teaching and learning for social justice. ❐

*Karen Miller teaches at Kellogg Middle School in Portland, Oregon.*

An essential resource is "We Left Our Homeland, a Sad, Sad, Day," by Nora Elegreet-DeSalvo and Ronald Levitsky, *The English Journal*, October 1989. Many of my ideas were based on suggestions from this article, which provides a good overview of how to do an immigration unit.

Another good resource is *Ellis Island*, a simulation by INTERACT, PO Box 997, Lakeside, CA, 92040, 619-448-1474. The simulation is easily adaptable and is a good starting point for those who have never done a simulation before.

For other books dealing with these issues see the resource guide on p. 187.

# Love's Gonna Get Us
# (Material Love)

By Damon Turner

Hey, Mr. Smooth! Mr. Ladies' Man!
Yeah, I'm talking to you, Man.
I see those threads you have on.

Yeah, I see the Reebok Pumps,
Avia sweats, and Nike cross trainers
you wearin',
And you're not even an athlete,
brothaman.

I know what these David Robinson,
Michael Jordan, Bo Jackson commercials
do for you.
Now you seem to think
that you can go out
There and do it all.

What do they tell you?
Oh, yeah,
they tell you to 'Just Do It.'
That is, just do it wearing your Nike,
Your Reebok, your Adidas,
and your Converse.

Who are you trying to be
wearing that
Mars Blackmon/Michael
Jordan t-shirt?
Do you think wearing that
shirt
Allows you to defy the forces
Of gravity as we know it?

Hell no! I don't think so.
What Nike, Reebok, Adidas,
Avia, and Converse
Don't care about is you.
What they 'care' about
Is yo' money, yo' money,
and mo' of yo' money.

Next time you wear your athletic attire
Endorsed by those million dollar brothers,
Think about the economic dividends
Taken out of your community
And placed into their greedy little hands.

Yeah, when you jump another brother
For his NFL or NBA endorsed starter,
Think about what good it does your people.

Yeah, brothaman. Mr. Nike, Mr. Adidas,
Mr. Reebok pump you up.
Just think about it.

Damon Turner, a graduate of Jefferson High School in Portland, Oregon, is currently attending Clark College in Atlanta. His play "The Fellas" was recently produced in a young minority playwrights' forum. (See p. 184 for teaching ideas.)

# Building Community from Chaos

By Linda Christensen

Over winter break, I read a book on teaching that left me feeling desolate because the writer's vision of a joyful, productive classroom did not match the chaos I faced daily. My students straggled in, still munching on Popeye's chicken, wearing Walkmen, and generally acting surly because of some incident in the hall during break, a fight with their parents, a teacher, a boyfriend or girlfriend. This year, more than ever, they failed to finish the writing started in class or read the novel or story I assigned as homework. Too often, they were suffering from pains much bigger than I could deal with: homelessness, pregnancy, the death of a brother, sister, friend, cousin due to street violence, the nightly spatter of guns in their neighborhoods, the decay of a society.

For too many days during the first quarter, I felt like a prison guard trying to bring order and kindness to a classroom where students laughed over the beating of a man, made fun of a classmate who was going blind, and mimicked the way a Vietnamese girl spoke until they pushed her into silence.

Each September I have this optimistic misconception that I'm going to create a compassionate, warm, safe place for students in the first days of class because my recollection is based on the final quarter of the previous year. In the past, that atmosphere did emerge in a shorter time span. But the students were more homogeneous, and we were living in somewhat more secure and less violent times. While students shared the tragedies of divorce and loss of friendships, their class talk was less often disrupted by the pressure cooker of society — and I was more naive and rarely explored those areas. We were polite to each other as we kept uncomfortable truths at bay.

Now, I realize that classroom community isn't always synonymous with warmth and harmony. Politeness is often a veneer mistaken for understanding, when in reality it masks uncovered territory, the unspeakable pit that we turn from because we know the anger and pain that dwells there. At Jefferson High School in Portland, Oregon, where the interplay of race, class and gender creates a constant background static, it's important to remind myself that real community is forged out of struggle. Students won't always agree on issues, and the fights, arguments, tears, and anger are the crucible from which a real community grows.

Still, I hate discord. When I was growing up, I typically gave up the fight and agreed with my sister or mother so that a reconciliation could be reached. I can remember running to my "safe" spot under my father's overturned rowboat whenever anger ran loose in our house.

Too often these days I'm in the middle of that anger, and there's no safe spot. My first impulse is to make everyone sit down, be polite, and listen to each other, a great goal that I've come to realize doesn't happen easily. Topics like racism and homophobia are avoided in most classrooms, but they seethe like open wounds. When there is an opening for discussion, years of

> For too many
> days during
> the first quarter,
> I felt like
> a prison guard.

anger and pain surface. But students haven't been taught how to talk with each other about these painful matters.

I can't say that I've found definitive answers, but as the year ended, I knew some of the mistakes I made. I also found a few constants: To become a community, students must learn to live in someone else's skin, understand the parallels of hurt, struggle, and joy across class and culture lines, and work for change. For that to happen, students need more than an upbeat, supportive teacher; they need a curriculum that teaches them how to empathize with others.

## Sharing Power and Passion

Before I could operate on that level, I had to find a way to connect with my students. Ironically, violence was the answer. This year none of the get-acquainted activities that I count on to build a sense of community worked in my fourth block class. Students didn't want to get up and interview each other. They didn't want to write about their names. They didn't want to be in the class, and they didn't want any jive-ass let's-get-to-know-each-other games or activities. Mostly, our 90-minute blocks were painfully long as I failed daily to elicit much response other than groans, sleep or anger. It's hard to build community when you feel like you're "hoisting elephants through mud" as my friend Carolyn says. I knew it was necessary to break through their apathy and uncover something that made these students care enough to talk, to read, to write, to share — even to get angry.

My fourth block class first semester was Senior English, a tracked class where most of the students were short on credits to graduate — as TJ said, "We're not even on the five year plan"

— but long on humor and potential. They came in with their fists up and their chins cocked. They had attitudes. Many of them already had histories with each other.

To complicate matters, our year opened with a storm of violence in the city. The brother of a Jefferson student was shot and killed. Two girls were injured when random bullets were fired on a bus. A birthday party at a local restaurant was broken up when gunfire sprayed the side of the restaurant. So violence was on the students' minds. I learned that I couldn't ignore the toll the outside world was exacting on my students. Rather than pretending that I could close my door in the face of their mounting fears, I needed to use that information to reach them.

In the first days, the only activity that aroused interest was when they wrote about their history as English students — what they liked, what they hated, and what they wanted to learn this year. Many of these students skulked in the low track classes and they were angry — not against tracking, because they weren't aware that another kind of education might be possible, but against the way their time had been wasted on meaningless activity. "The teacher would put a word on the board and then make us see how many words we could make out of the letters. Now what does that prepare me for?" Larry asked. But they also hated reading novels and talking about them because novels "don't have anything to do with our lives." The other constant in many of their written responses was that they felt stupid.

For the first time, they got excited. I knew what they didn't want: worksheets, sentence combining, reading novels and discussing them, writing about "stuff we don't care about." But I didn't know what to teach them. I needed to engage them because they were loud, unruly, and out of control otherwise. But how? I decided to try the "raise the expectations" approach and use a curriculum I designed for my Contemporary Literature and Society class which receives college credit.

During those initial days of listening to these seniors and trying to read

In order to build community, teachers need to build on students' strengths.

KATHY SLOANE

the novel *Thousand Pieces of Gold*, by Ruthann Lum McCunn, I discovered that violence aroused my students. Students weren't thrilled with the book; in fact they weren't reading it. I'd plan a 90 minute lesson around the reading and dialogue journal they were supposed to be keeping, but only a few students were prepared. Most didn't even attempt to lie about the fact that they weren't reading and clearly weren't planning on it.

In an attempt to get them involved in the novel, I read aloud an evocative passage about the unemployed peasants sweeping through the Chinese countryside pillaging, raping, and grabbing what was denied them through legal employment. Suddenly students saw their own lives reflected back at them through Chen whose anger at losing his job and ultimately his family led him to become an outlaw. Chen created a new family with this group of bandits. Students could relate: Chen was a gang member. I had stumbled on a way to interest my class. The violence created a contact point between the literature and the students' lives.

This connection, this reverberation across cultures, time and gender challenged the students' previous notion

*Kids need to feel they belong.*

that reading and talking about novels didn't have relevance for them. They could empathize with the Chinese but also explore those issues in their own lives.

This connection also created space to unpack the assumption that all gangs are bad. Chen wasn't born violent. He didn't start out robbing and killing. Lalu, the novel's main character, remembered him as a kind man who bought her candy. He changed after he lost his job and his family starved.

Similarly, kids in gangs don't start out violent or necessarily join gangs to "pack gats" and shoot it out in drive-bys. Because the tendency in most schools is to simultaneously deny and outlaw the existence of gangs, kids rarely talk critically about them.

A few years ago, scholar Mike Davis wrote an article analyzing the upsurge of gang activity in L.A. He found it linked to the loss of union wage jobs. I hadn't explored Portland's history to know whether our situation is similar to L.A.'s, but I suspected economic parallels. When I raised Davis's research, kids were skeptical. They saw other factors: the twin needs of safety and belonging.

Our discussion of gangs broke the barrier. Students began writing about violence in their own lives and their neighborhoods. TJ explained his own brushes with violence:

"[T]he summer between my sophomore and junior years, some of my friends were getting involved in a new gang called the Irish Mob. ... My friends were becoming somebody, someone who was known wherever they went. The somebody who I wanted to be. ... During the next couple of weeks we were involved in six fights, two stabbings, and one drive-by shooting. We got away on all nine cases. The next Saturday night my brother was shot in a drive-by. The shooters were caught the same night."

Kari wrote that she joined a gang when she was searching for family. Her father lost his job; her mother was forced to work two jobs to pay the rent. Kari assumed more responsibility at home: cooking dinner, putting younger brothers and sisters to bed, and cleaning. While at middle school, Kari joined the Crips. She said at first it was because she liked the "family" feel. They wore matching clothes. They shared a language and nicknames. In a neighborhood that had become increasingly violent, they offered her protection. She left the gang after middle school because she was uncomfortable with the violence.

Students were surprised to learn that Hua, a recent immigrant from Vietnam, was also worried about her brother who had joined a gang. Her classmates were forced to reevaluate their initial assessments of her. While she had seemed like an outsider, a foreigner, her story made a bond between them.

At first, I worried that inviting students to write about violence might glorify it. It didn't turn out that way. Students were generally adamant that they'd made poor choices when they were involved in violent activities. As TJ states in his essay, "I wanted to be known wherever I went. ... But I went about it all wrong and got mixed in. ... It was nothing I had hoped for. Sure I was known and all that, but for all the wrong reasons."

More often students shared their fears. Violence was erupting around them and they felt out of control. They needed to share that fear.

Through the topic of violence I captured their interest, but I wanted them to critique the violence rather than just describe it. I had hoped to build a community of inquiry where we identified a common problem and worked to understand it by examining history and our lives. That didn't happen. It was still early in the year, and students were so absorbed in telling their stories and listening to others it was difficult to pull them far enough away to analyze the situation. I didn't have enough materials that went beyond accusations or sensationalism, but the topic itself also presented practical and ethical problems, especially around issues of safety and confidentiality.

I want to be clear: bringing student issues into the room does not mean giving up teaching the core ideas and skills of the class; it means I need to use the energy of their connections to drive us through the content.

For example, students still had to write a literary essay. But they could use their lives as well as Lalu's to illustrate their points. Students scrutinized their issues through the lens of a larger vision as James did when he compared the violence in his life to the violence in Lalu's:

"Lalu isn't a gang member, but some of the folks, or should I say, some of the enemies she came in contact with reminded me of my enemies. Bandits in the story represented the worst foes of my life. In some ways bandits and gangs are quite similar. One would be the reason for them turning to gang life. Neither of them had a choice. It was something forced upon them by either educational problems or financial difficulties. It could have been the fact that their families were corrupt or no love was shown. Whatever the reasons, it was a way of survival."

Finding the heartbeat of a class isn't always easy. I must know what's happening in the community and the lives of my students. If they're consumed by the violence in the neighborhood or the lack of money in their house, I'm more likely to succeed in teaching them if I intersect their preoccupation.

Building community means taking

into account the needs of the members of that community. I can sit students in a circle, play getting-to-know-each-other games until the cows come home, but if what I am teaching in the class holds no interest for the students, I'm just holding them hostage until the bell rings.

## A Curriculum of Empathy

As a critical teacher I encourage students to question everyday acts or ideas that they take for granted (see "Unlearning the Myths," p. 8 and "Standard English: Whose Standard?" p. 142). But I also teach them to enter the lives of characters in literature, history or real life whom they might dismiss or misunderstand. I don't want their first reaction to difference to be laughter or withdrawal. I try to teach them how to empathize with people whose circumstances might differ from theirs. Empathy is key in community building.

I choose literature that intentionally makes students look beyond their own world. In the class I teach with Bill Bigelow, we used an excerpt from Ronald Takaki's *A Different Mirror* about Filipino writer Carlos Bulosan. Bulosan wrote, "I am an exile in America." He described the treatment he received, good and bad. He wrote of being cheated out of wages at a fish cannery in Alaska, being refused housing because he was Filipino, being tarred and feathered and driven from town.

We asked students to respond to the reading by keeping a dialogue journal. Dirk, who is African-American, wrote, "He's not the only one who feels like an exile in America. Some of us who were born here feel that way too." As he continued reading, he was surprised that some of the acts of violence Bulosan encountered were similar to those endured by African Americans. In his essay on immigration, he chose to write about the parallels between Bulosan's life and the experiences he's encountered:

"When I was growing up I thought African Americans were the only ones who went through oppression. In the reading, 'In the Heart of Filipino

America' I found that Filipinos had to go through a lot when coming to America. I can relate with the stuff they went through because my ancestors went through sort of the same thing."

Dirk went on to describe the parallels in housing discrimination, lynching, name calling, being cheated out of wages that both Filipinos and African Americans lived through.

Besides reading and studying about "others," we wanted students to come face to face with people they usually don't meet as a way of breaking down their preconceived ideas about people from other countries. For example, during this unit, we continued to hear students classify all Asians as "Chinese." In the halls, we heard students mimic the way Vietnamese students spoke. When writing about discrimination, another student confessed that she discriminated against the Mexican students at our school. Our students were paired with English-as-Second-Language students who had emigrated from another country — Vietnam, Laos, Cambodia, Eritrea, Mexico, Guatemala, Ghana. They interviewed their partner and wrote a profile of the student to share in class. Students were moved by their partners' stories. One student whose brother had been killed at the beginning of the year was paired with a student whose sister was killed fighting in Eritrea. He connected to her loss and was amazed at her strength. Others were appalled at how these students had been mistreated at *their* school. Many students later used the lives of their partners in their essays on

immigration.

Besides making immigration a contemporary rather than a historical topic, students heard the sorrow their fellow students felt at leaving "home." In our "curriculum of empathy," we forced our class to see these students as individuals rather than the ESL students or "Chinese" students, or an undifferentiated mass of Mexicans.

A curriculum of empathy puts students inside the lives of others. By writing interior monologues (see "Promoting Social Imagination," p. 110), acting out improvisations, taking part in role plays (see "Role Plays: Show Don't Tell," p. 114), and creating fiction stories about historical events, students learn to develop understanding about people whose culture, race, gender or sexual orientation differs from theirs.

"Things changed for me this year," Wesley wrote in his end-of-the-year evaluation. "I started respecting my peers. My attitude has changed against homosexuals and whites." Similarly, Tyrelle wrote, "I learned a lot about my own culture as an African American but also about other people's cultures. I never knew Asians suffered. When we wrote from different characters in movies and stories I learned how it felt to be like them."

## Sharing Personal Stories

Building community begins when students get inside the lives of others in history, literature or down the hallway, but they also learn by exploring their own lives and coming to terms with the people they are "doing time" with in the classroom. Micere Mugo, a Kenyan poet, recently said, "Writing can be a lifeline, especially when your existence has been denied, especially when you have been left on the margins, especially when your life and process of growth have been subjected to attempts at strangulation." For many of our students their stories have been silenced in school. Their histories have been marginalized to make room for "important" people, their interests and worries passed over so I can teach Oregon history or *The Scarlet Letter*.

To develop empathy, students need

> Building community begins when students get inside the lives of others in history, literature or down the hallway.

to learn about each others' lives as well as reflect on their own. When they hear personal stories, classmates become real instead of cardboard stereotypes: rich white girl, basketball-addicted black boy, brainy Asian. Once they've seen how people can hurt, once they've shared pain and laughter, they can't so easily treat people as objects to be kicked or beaten or called names. When students' lives are taken off the margins, they don't feel the same need to put someone else down.

Any reading or history lesson offers myriad opportunities for this kind of activity. I find points of conflict, struggle, change, or joy and create an assignment to write about a parallel time in their lives. We've had students write about times they've been forced to move, been discriminated against or discriminated against someone else, changed an attitude or action, worked for change, lost a valuable possession. Obviously, losing a treasured item does not compare to the Native Americans' loss of their land, but telling the story does give students a chance to empathize with the loss as well as share a piece of themselves with the class.

When I was a child, my mother took me to the pond in Sequoia Park on Sundays to feed the ducks. They'd come in a great wash of wings and waves while I broke the bread into pieces to throw to them. I loved to watch them gobble up the soggy loaf, but I began noticing how some ducks took more than others. In fact, some ducks were pushed to the side and pecked at. I've noticed the same thing happens in classrooms. Students find someone who they think is weak and attack them. In my fourth block class, the victim was Jim. He'd been in my class the year before. I'd watched him progress as a writer and thinker. In his end of the year evaluation, he drew a picture of himself as a chef; his writing was the dough. In an essay, he explained how writing was like making bread. He was proud of his achievements as a writer.

In both classes, Jim was a victim. He was going blind because of a hereditary disease. It didn't happen overnight, but he struggled with terror at his oncoming blindness. Because he was steadily losing his eyesight, he was clumsy in the classroom. He couldn't see where he was going. He knocked into people and desks. He accidently overturned piles of books. Students would respond with laughter or anger. Some days he cried silently into the fold of his arms. He told me, "I know the darkness is coming." Several male students in the class made fun of him for crying as well. One day, Amber was in a typically bad mood, hunched inside her too-big coat and snarling at anyone who came near. When Jim bumped her desk on the way to the pencil sharpener and her books and papers tumbled on the floor, she blew up at him for bumbling around the room. Jim apologized profusely and retreated into his shell after her attack.

A few days later I gave an assignment for students to write about their ancestors, their people. First, they read Margaret Walker's poems, "For My People" and "Lineage" and others. I told them they could imagine their people as their immediate ancestors, their race, their nationality or gender. Jim wrote:

### To My People With Retinitis Pigmentosa

*Sometimes I hate you*
*like the disease*
*I have been plagued with.*
*I despise the "sight" of you*
*seeing myself in your eyes.*
*I see you as if it were you*
*who intentionally*
*damned me to darkness.*
*I sometimes wish*
*I was not your brother;*
*that I could stop*
*the setting of the sun*
*and wash my hands of you forever*
*and never look back*
*except with pity,*
*but I cannot.*
*So I embrace you,*
*the sun continues to set*
*as I walk into darkness*
*holding your hand.*

**Building community is a year-long process.**

Students were silenced. Tears rolled. Kevin said, "Damn, man. That's hard." Amber apologized to Jim in front of the class. At the end of the year she told me that her encounter with Jim was one of the events that changed her. She learned to stop and think about why someone else might be doing what they're doing instead of immediately jumping to the conclusion that they were trying to annoy her.

My experience is that, given a chance, students will share amazing stories. Students have told me that my willingness to share stories about my life — my father's alcoholism, my family's lack of education, my poor test scores, and many others, opened the way for them to tell their stories. Students have written about rape, sexual abuse, divorce, drug and alcohol abuse. And through their sharing, they make openings to each other. Sometimes a small break. A crack. A passage from one world to the other. And these openings allow the class to become a community.

### Students as Activists

Community is also created when students struggle together to achieve a common goal. Sometimes the opportunity spontaneously arises out of the conditions or content of the class, school, or community. During Bill's and my first year teaching together, we exchanged the large student desks in our room with another teacher's smaller desks without consulting our students. We had forty students in the class, and not all of the big desks fit in the circle. They staged a "stand in" until we returned the original desks. One year our students responded to a negative article in a local newspaper by organizing a march and rally to "tell the truth about Jefferson to the press." During the Columbus quincentenary, my students organized a teach-in about Columbus for classes at Jefferson. Of course, these "spontaneous" uprisings only work if teachers are willing to give over class time for the students to organize, and if they've highlighted times when people in history resisted injustice, making it clear that solidarity and courage are val-

Given a chance, students will share amazing stories.

ues to be prized in daily life, not just praised in the abstract and put on the shelf.

But most often I have to create situations for students to work outside of the classroom. I want them to connect ideas and action in tangible ways. Sometimes I do this by asking students to take what they have learned and create a project to teach at nearby elementary or middle schools. Students in Literature and U.S. History write children's books about Abolitionists, the Nez Perce, Chief Joseph, and others. After students critique the media (see "Unlearning The Myths That Bind Us," p. 8), they are usually upset by the negative messages children receive, so I have them write and illustrate books for elementary students. They brainstorm positive values they want children to receive, read traditional and contemporary children's books, critique the stories, and write their own. They develop lesson plans to go with their books. For example, before Bev read her book about John Brown she asked, "Has anyone here ever tried to change something you thought was wrong?" After students shared their experiences, she read her book. Students also created writing assignments to go with their books so they could model the writing process.

Students were nervous before their school visits. As they practiced lesson plans and received feedback from their peers, there was much laughter and anticipation. They mimicked "bad" students and asked improper questions that have nothing to do with the children's book: Is she your girlfriend? Why are your pants so baggy? Why does your hair look like that?

When they returned, there were stories to share: children who hugged their knees and begged them to come back;

kids who wouldn't settle down; kids who said they couldn't write. My students proudly read the writings that came out of "their" class. They responded thoughtfully to each student's paper.

James, a member of my English 12 class, was concerned by the number of young children who join gangs. He and several other young men wrote stories about gang violence and took them to our neighborhood elementary school. He strode into the class, wrote "gangs" in big letters on the board and sat down. The fifth grade class was riveted. He and his teaching mates read their stories and then talked with students about gangs. As James wrote after his visit:

"For a grown person to teach a kid is one thing. But for a teenager like myself to teach young ones is another. Kids are highly influenced by peers close to their age or a little older. I'm closer to their age, so they listen to me. ... Some of these kids that I chatted with had stories that they had been wanting to get off their chest for a long time. ... When I came to class with my adventures of being a gangster, that gave them an opportunity to open up. Spill guts. [No one] should object to me teaching these shorties about gang life, telling them that it's not all fun and games. It's straight do or die. Kill or be killed."

The seriousness with which the students understand their lives was in sharp contrast to the seeming apathy they displayed at the year's beginning. Through the year, I came to understand that the key to reaching my students and building community was helping students excavate and reflect on their personal experiences, connecting it to the world of language, literature, and society. We moved from ideas to action, perhaps the most elusive objective in any classroom.

Community and activism: these are the goals in every course I teach. The steps we take to reach them are not often in a straight path. We stagger, sidestep, stumble, and then rise to stride ahead again. ❑

*Linda Christensen (lchrist@aol.com) is language arts coordinator for Portland Public Schools and a* Rethinking Schools *editor.*

# Discipline: No Quick Fix

## By Linda Christensen

*Idea*

*concept*

Creating a climate of respect is easy to talk about and hard to practice. Ideally, we want a space where students listen respectfully and learn to care about each other. A sign in our hallway reads: No Racist or Sexist Remarks. I've often said, "I just don't tolerate that kind of behavior." But this year, it was like saying, "I don't tolerate ants." I have ants in my kitchen. I can spray chemicals on them and saturate the air with poison and "not tolerate" them, or I can find another solution that doesn't harm my family or pets in the process. If I just kick kids out of class, I "don't tolerate" their actions, but neither do I educate them or their classmates. And it works about as well as stamping out a few ants. I prepare them for repressive solutions where misbehavior is temporarily contained by an outside authority, not really addressed. Sometimes, I am forced to that position, but I try not to be.

### Dealing with Name-calling

This year, students in the class Bill Bigelow and I co-teach were often rude to each other. Their favorite put down was "faggot." (This in a class where a young woman came out as a lesbian.) During the first weeks, several young women complained that they had been called names by boys in class. They felt the hostility and wanted to transfer out. They didn't feel comfortable sharing their work or even sitting in the class because they were pinched, hit, or called names when our backs were turned. As one of the main, but certainly not the only, instigators, "Wesley," wrote in his end of the year evaluation, "I started the year off as I finished the last year: bad, wicked and obnoxious. I was getting kicked out of class and having meetings with the deans about my behavior every other day."

> I have yet to discover a quick fix for out of control behavior. Perhaps it's just letting students know we care enough to talk outside of school.

For critical teachers trying to build community, this creates a serious problem. Do we eliminate this student? When, after trying time outs, calling his home, talking with his coach, and keeping him after class, we finally kicked him out — his friends said, "They're picking on him." Which wasn't true. But it set us up as the bad guys and divided us from the students we wanted to win over.

Increased police presence in the area has created situations where students gain honor by taunting the cops in front of peers. This carries over to class, where we represent the same white authority as the police until students get to know us. While Wesley was not skilled academically, in other respects he was brilliant. He was an artist at toeing the line theoretically and creating total chaos in the process. He'd raise his hand and make perfectly nice comments about someone's paper in such a way that the entire class knew he was mocking the whole procedure. Even with two of us in the classroom, he defeated us at every turn. Clearly, we were playing on his terrain, and he knew the game better than we did even if we'd

taught longer than he'd been alive.

Here we were teaching about justice, tolerance, equality, and respect, and yet when we had a problem with a talented student who didn't want to go along, we turned him over to the deans. Ultimately, what lesson does that teach our students? That we talk a good game, but when pushed, we respond like other traditional teachers? It's a complex issue. I don't want to keep the class from progressing because of one or two students, but I don't want to "give up" on students either. On bad days, I threw him out. On good days, I tried to look behind his behavior and figure out what motivated it.

In teaching critical literacy, I tell students to look behind the words to discover what the text is really saying; in working with "problem" students in class, I need to look behind the students' behavior. What is motivating this? How can I get to the root of the problem? In my experience, the more negative students feel about themselves and their intellectual ability, the more cruel or withdrawn they are in the classroom.

Tyrelle, Wesley's classmate, wrote early in the year that he felt stupid. "My problem is I don't like to read out loud because I don't think the class would like it. Every time I try to write or do something my teachers told me that's stupid, you did it wrong, or you can't spell. My friends [who were classmates] say it too. I don't say anything. I just act like I don't hear it, but I really do."

One day I overheard his friends teasing him about his spelling. After class I talked with him about it. I arranged for him to come in so we could work privately and I would teach him how to write. Because so many of his friends were in the class, he was afraid to ask for help. His way of dealing with the problem was to close down — put his head on his desk and sleep — or make fun of people who were trying to do their work. This did not totally stop, but once he found a way into his writing he would usually settle down and work.

During the second semester he wrote, "You guys have helped me become a better person because you were always after me, 'Tyrelle, be quiet. Tyrelle, pay attention.' After a while I learned how to control myself when it was time to." He'd also learned to separate himself from his friends so he could work.

Wesley who admitted to being "bad, wicked and obnoxious" was also a victim of poor skills and low academic self esteem. He'd sneak in after school for help with his writing, or I'd go over the homework readings and teach him how to "talk back" to the author. Sometimes he'd call me at home when he was stuck. At the end of the year his mother said, "He told me that he didn't think he could write. Now he says he knows how." With both of these students, recognizing the cause of the behavior — embarrassment over poor skills — and helping them achieve success helped to change their behavior. Once the withdrawn or antisocial actions stopped, they contributed to the community rather than sabotaging it. This was not a miraculous, overnight change. On some days, the behavior backslid to day one, but most times there was steady improvement.

I have yet to discover a quick fix for out of control behavior. I try calling my students' homes in September to establish contact and expectations. I usually ask, "Is there anything you can tell me that will help me teach your child more effectively?" Parents know their child's history in schools and can give important insights. When my daughter didn't turn in a project, her teacher called me. I discovered that her class had long term work that students needed to complete at home. I appreciated the call because Anna insisted that she didn't have homework. Her teacher made me realize how much parents need to hear from teachers — not only for keeping track of homework, but so we can work in tandem.

Often working with a coach or ac-

There is no miraculous cure for discipline problems.

tivities advisor helps because they've established strong one-on-one relationships. They also have access to an area where the student feels successful. One coach, for example, told me that "Jeremy" just realized that he would play high school ball, maybe college ball, but he'd never be pro. He'd turned from gangs to sports in the 7th grade, and the vision that fueled him was the NBA. Suddenly, that dream came against reality. He practiced hours every day, but he knew he wouldn't make it. His attitude had been sour and nasty for weeks. He needed a new vision. This information helped me to understand Jeremy and allowed me to get out the college guide and talk about choices. His final essay was "Life After Sports."

Mostly, I call students at night and talk with them after the day is over, their friends are no longer around, and both of us have had a chance to cool down. Students joke about how they can't get away with anything because Bill and I call their homes. I overheard one student say, "Man, I got to go to class today otherwise they'll call my uncle tonight." Perhaps it's just letting them know we care enough to take our time outside of school that turns them around. ❐

# Getting Off the Track: Stories from an Untracked Classroom

By Bill Bigelow

In school, I hated social studies. My U.S. history class was, in the words of critical educator Ira Shor, a memory Olympics, with students competing to see how many dates, battles and presidents we could cram into our adolescent heads. My California history class was one long lecture, almost none of which I remember today, save for the names of a few famous men — mostly scoundrels. This marathon fact-packing was interrupted only once, as I recall, by a movie on raisins. *Social* studies — ostensibly a study of human beings — was nothing of the kind. "Poor History," writes Eduardo Galeano, "had stopped breathing: betrayed in academic texts, lied about in classrooms, drowned in dates, they had imprisoned her in museums and buried her, with floral wreaths, beneath statuary bronze and monumental marble."

Today, students who prove unresponsive to similar memory games are often labeled "slow learners," — or worse — and find themselves dumped in a low-track class, called "basic" or "skills," understood by all as "the dumb class." This is classic victim-blaming, penalizing kids for their inability to turn human beings into abstractions, for their failure to recall disconnected factoids. And it's unnecessary. Tracking is usually advocated with good intentions; but its only educational justification derives from schools' persistence in teaching in ways that fail to reach so many children, thus necessitating some students' removal to less demanding academic pursuits.

Untracking a school requires untracking instruction. Unfortunately, many of those who argue against tracking offer only the vaguest hints of what an effective untracked class could look like. Hence their critique that tracking

> **Many who argue against tracking offer only the vaguest hints of what an effective untracked class could look like.**

delivers inferior instruction to many students, lowers self-esteem, reproduces social hierarchies, reinforces negative stereotypes, etc. may have ironic consequences. Compelled by these and other arguments, schools that untrack without a thoroughgoing pedagogical transformation can end up simply with a system of tracking internal to each classroom. I've seen this in more than one "untracked" school: students who come to class able to absorb lectures, write traditional research papers, memorize discrete facts — and stay awake — succeed; those who can't, sit in the back of class and sleep, doodle, or disrupt — and fail. Those of us critical of tracking need to offer a concrete and viable vision of an untracked classroom. Otherwise, the results of untracking will replicate the results of tracking, and many educators will lean back in their chairs and say, "I told you so."

## Components of an Untracked Classroom

As a classroom teacher, I've found that an anti-tracking pedagogy has several essential and interlocking components. And while the examples I'll use are drawn from my high school social studies classes, these components remain as valid in other content areas or can be adapted.

• **Show, don't tell.** Through role plays, improvisations, and simulations students need to *experience*, not simply hear about, social dynamics.

• **Assignments need to be flexible enough to adjust to students' interests or abilities.** Teachers can assign projects, poetry, personal writing, critiques, etc. which allow students to enter and succeed at their own levels of competence and creativity. This is not a suggestion to give easy assignments, but to adopt a flexible academic rigor. And in no way should this detract from students developing traditional scholastic skills they will need to pursue higher education.

• **The curriculum needs to constantly draw on students' lives as a way of delving into broader social themes.** Knowledge needs to be both internal and external; history, government, sociology, literature is always simultaneously about "them" *and* us.

• **The classroom environment needs to be encouraging, even loving.** All students need to know that their potential is respected, that they are included in a community of learners. A rhetoric of caring is insufficient. Both the form and content of the class must underscore every child's worth and potential.

• **What we teach has to matter.** Students should understand how the information and analytic tools they're developing make a difference in their lives, that the aim of learning is not just a grade, simple curiosity, or "because you'll need to know it later."

• **An anti-tracking pedagogy should explicitly critique the premises of tracking.** Students need to examine the history and practice of tracking in order to become aware of and expel doubts about their capacity to think and achieve. We cannot merely untrack our classrooms; we have to engage students in a dialogue about *why* we untrack our classrooms. More than this, the curriculum needs to critique the deeper social inequities and hierarchies that were the original stimulus for tracking and continue today to breed unjust educational practices.

• **Finally, the method of evaluating students in an untracked class should embody the flexibility and caring described above.** We can't advocate creating flexible assignments that adjust to students' interests and abilities and then hold youngsters accountable to rigid performance criteria. Evaluation needs to be guided by principles of equity rather than efficiency.

The power of an anti-tracking approach lies in the interrelationship of these components, not in merely applying them checklist fashion. Lest my examples sound too self-congratulatory or facile, I should begin by confessing that all this is easier said than done, and my classroom is rarely as tidy as my written descriptions. My students, just like everyone else's, get off task, hold distracting side conversations, and often fail to complete their homework. The aim here is not to provide a cookbook of tried and true educational recipes but to contribute to a broader discussion about how we can teach for justice in an unjust society, and to explore how such a commitment can contribute to successful classroom practice.

## Bringing the Curriculum to Life

Role plays, simulations, and improvisations allow students to climb into history and social concepts and to explore them from the inside. It's a first-person approach to society that gives each student an equal shot at grasping concepts and gaining knowledge. Students who are advanced in traditional academic terms are not held back with this more experiential approach, but neither are they privileged by their facility with, say, Standard English or their stamina in reading and memorizing textbookspeak. Just about every unit I teach includes at least one role play, simulation, or set of improvisations.

For example, in a unit on U.S. labor history, students role play the 1934 West Coast longshore strike (see *The Power in Our Hands*, pp.74-77 and 148-163.) In five groups — longshoremen, waterfront employers, farmers, unemployed workers and representatives of the central labor council — students confront the choices that confronted the original strike participants. From each group's respective standpoint students propose solutions to the strike, decide whether they want the governor to call in the national guard to protect strikebreakers, and determine how they will respond if the guard is called upon. Not all groups have clear positions on the questions and so students have to use their creativity to design potential resolutions and their per-

Bill Bigelow listens to social studies students.

suasive powers to build alliances with members of other groups.

The dynamics of the strike are lived in the classroom, experienced firsthand by students, instead of being buried in the textbook. Longshoremen negotiate with farmers to support the strike, waterfront employers seek to entice the unemployed with offers of work, and more than one group threatens violence if the governor calls in the guard. Students must master lots of information in order to effectively represent their positions, but it's not just a memory olympics — they have to *use* the information in the heat of deal-making and debate.

Most students have a great time, running around the room negotiating and arguing with recalcitrant peers; often, students remain engaged after the bell rings. But the role play is not simply play. As Paulo Freire says, "Conflict is the midwife of consciousness," and the simulated conflict in role plays like this allows students to reflect on much larger issues: When are alliances between different social groups possible? What role does the government play, and should it play, in labor disputes? Is violence or the threat of violence justified in class conflict? Can people be out for themselves, but also support each other? These are big and tough questions, but because they draw on an experience every student watched and helped create, they are concrete rather than abstract. Regardless of past academic achievement, the activities and discussion challenge every student.

These and other questions can also lead us to explore the contemporary relevance of the 60 year-old-strike. Often students-as-longshoremen cobble together an alliance including farmers, the unemployed, and the central labor council. What do you think happened in real life? I ask. "Sure we can get together," many a student has responded. "But we're just in a role play in a classroom. It's easy to get together in here. I don't think it could happen in real life." Most students are surprised to learn that it *did* happen in real life — working people in 1934 maintained a remarkable degree of solidarity. And from this knowledge we discuss when people can

and cannot get together. Students also reflect on their own cynicism about people's capacity to unite for worthy goals.

After the role play I sometimes ask students to relate our discussion to their lives, and to write about a time when they were able to stick together with a group for a common objective. In our class read-around the next day I encourage students to take notes on common themes they hear in each other's stories. Here, too, we can continue to pursue theoretical questions about unity, but it's a pursuit rooted in our experience, not one imposed on a class as an abstract academic inquiry. It is serious academic work, democratized through students' in-class experience and its connection to their lives.

## Improvisation and Equal Access to the Curriculum

Improvisation is another kind of "leveling" role play that seeks to give all students equal access to information and theoretical insight. In a unit on U.S. slavery and resistance to slavery, I provide students with a set of first person roles for different social groups in the South, which supplements information already gleaned from films, a slide-lecture, poetry, a simulation, readings, and class discussions. They read these roles and in small groups select from a list of improvisation choices. They can also create their own improv topic or combine some of mine to form something new.

The topics are bare-bones descriptions requiring lots of student initiative

> Role plays, simulations and improvisations allow students to climb into history and explore it from the inside.

to plan and perform. For example:

• A plantation owner tells a mother and father, who are enslaved, that he's going to sell their children. He needs the money.

• An enslaved person encounters a poor white farmer on the road. The farmer accuses the slave of looking him directly in the eye, which is illegal.

• An enslaved person asks an owner if she/he can buy her or his freedom.

There's an obvious danger that students' performances of these and any role plays can drift toward caricature. Caricature may allow students to distance and insulate themselves from the enormity of the subject, but it can also allow them to trivialize one of the most horrendous periods in human history. However, the alternative of students remaining outside, removed from a subject like the enslavement of African people, seems to me a greater danger. So we talk about how we can't possibly know what people experienced, but through our performance, imagination, writing, and discussion we're going to do the best we can. And students have responded with passionate skits that have moved many in the class to tears — that have, in Toni Morrison's words, given "voice to the 'unspeakable.'"

As students perform the improvs I ask them to take notes on powerful lines or situations, as they'll be writing from the perspective of one or more of the characters. After each skit we discuss the problem posed, and how students handled it. As we progress, I draw on their improvs to teach about laws, different forms of resistance, how certain practices varied from region to region or in different time periods. It's a series of mini-lectures, but accessible to all students because they are linked to a shared experience.

Afterward I ask students to write an interior monologue — the inner thoughts — from the point of view of one of the characters in an improv. People have the freedom to write from the point of view of a character they represented or one they watched. I encourage students to "find your passion," as my teaching partner, Linda Christensen, likes to say — so they're free to rearrange and massage the as-

Strikers battle police during San Francisco general strike, July 1934.

signment to fit their interest. Most students write the assigned interior monologue, but some prefer poems, dialogue poems, or letters. This, too, is a vital part of an anti-tracking pedagogy: students need sufficient freedom to enter an assignment at a point of their choosing; they must be able to reconstruct the task according to their interests and abilities.

For example, after one set of improvisations, "Diane," a young woman with a low track academic history, wrote a dialogue poem about childbirth. The paired perspectives are from the wife of a white plantation owner and an enslaved African American woman. It reads in part:

My man is not here to hold my hand.
*My man is not here to hold my hand.*

He's out in the field.
*He's out in the field.*

with a whip in his hand.
*with a whip at his back.*

I lay here on my feather bed.
*I lay here on the blanketed floor.*

The pain comes. I push.
*The pain comes. I push.*

Someone, please come and help.
*Someone, please come and help.*

The midwife comes, the doctor, too.
*The midwife comes, no doctor.*

Silk sheets in my mouth.
*A wood stick in my mouth.*

To halt the screams.
*To halt the screams.*

I push some more.
*I push some more.*

I sigh relief. The child is born.
*I sigh relief. The child is born.*

Strong lungs scream.
*Silence.*

It squirms there, full of life.
*It lies there, cold and blue.*

It is a boy.
*It was a boy.*

Another born to be big and strong.
*Another one born to be laid in the ground.*

A babe suckling at my breast.
*This babe lying in my arms.*

Tomorrow I will plan a party.
*Tomorrow I will go to the field. ...*

None of the improvs had been about childbirth, but this was where Diane found her passion.

There are no wrong answers here. Virtually every interior monologue or poem is plausible, even if students approach the same character's thoughts in very different ways. Chaunetta writes from the point of view of a woman whose children are sold off, Eric from that of a man contemplating escape, Monica from that of a plantation owner reflecting on his dissatisfaction with his overseers. Some of the pieces, like Diane's, are publishable, some not even close. But each student gains an insight with validity, and together their portraits form an emotional and empathic patchwork quilt. And again, the assignment challenges all students, regardless of supposed skill levels.

## Untracking the Big Questions

Before students begin the read-around I ask them to take notes on three questions: 1) In what ways were people hurt by slavery? 2) How did people resist slavery? and 3) Explain why you think slavery could or could not have ended without a violent struggle. We circle-up for the read-around. I encourage, but don't require, everyone in class to share his or her writing. As students read their pieces they compliment each other, offer "aha's," and take notes on the questions. This is not an editing session, so critical remarks aren't allowed — thus students know they'll only hear positive comments if they choose to share. The read-around, or sharing circle, builds community as youngsters applaud each other's efforts and insights. The medium is the message: we all count here.

Afterward, people look over their notes and write on the questions. Unlike textbook questions, these encourage students to make meaning themselves, not to parrot back the meaning decided by some publishing company. The third question is a difficult one, calling for students to reflect on the obstacles to social change. It's a question that ordinarily might be set aside for the "advanced" class, but because of an anti-tracking pedagogy it can be approached by everyone: they all watched the improvs, they all participated, they heard my mini-lectures, they discussed their questions and insights, they climbed inside someone's head to write from his or her point of view and they listened to the "collective text" created by the entire class.

Wrestling with a question like this is simply the next step. Everyone can succeed, and everyone is intellectually challenged. And because theory is grounded in students' in-class experience, the assignment doesn't privilege those students who may be more prac-

Students discuss a role play in Bill Bigelow's class

*JAMES WHITNEY*

ticed at abstract thinking.

If we want our classes to be accessible to students regardless of academic background and confidence we have to discover ways of bringing concepts alive. Simulations are another show-don't-tell strategy. For example, in exploring the history of work in the United States, particularly "scientific management" or "Taylorization" — owners studying and then chopping up the labor process into component parts and assigning workers one repetitive task — a simple lecture would reach some students. But using paper airplanes and students as skilled workers to simulate changes in the production process provides all students access to a vital piece of history that can help them reflect on their own work lives.

We can tape off the floor and offer pieces of chocolate to simulate land and wealth distribution in different societies; unsharpened and sharpened pencils can represent raw materials and manufactured products to help us show the dynamics of colonialism; and with balls of cotton, shirts, wheat, "guns," and

bank notes, we can walk students through pre-Civil War sectional conflicts. An untracked classroom can be both more playful and more rigorous than a traditional read-this/listen-to-this/write-this approach.

We can also allow kids to get out of the classroom and into the community, both as social investigators and change-makers. Students can visit a senior citizens' center to interview people about a particular time period. They might tour a factory to learn about working conditions, or travel to a Native American community to meet and talk with activists. Often, I conclude a major unit or a semester by encouraging students to become "truth-tellers" — to take their knowledge about an issue beyond the classroom walls. One year, a student of Linda's and mine choreographed and performed for a number of classes a dance on the life of Ben Linder, the Portlander murdered by the Contras in Nicaragua. Numbers of students re-write children's books from a multicultural standpoint and use them to lead discussions at elementary schools. One group produced a videotape, cablecast city-wide, about the erosion of Native American fishing rights on the Columbia River. One year, a student in a global studies class wrote and recorded "The South Africa Rap," questioning why corporations leave communities in the United States and invest in apartheid; it was subsequently played by several community radio stations around the country. A real-world curriculum aims to give students an equal opportunity to understand society — and to change it.

## A New Teacher-Student Covenant

An anti-tracking pedagogy needs to offer alternatives to traditional teaching methods and critique these methods as well. The traditional teacher-student covenant proposes to rehearse students for alienation: I give you an assignment over which you have no or little control. It's not about you, it's about subject *x*. I think it up — or, more often, a textbook company thinks it up — I design it, you perform it, and I evaluate it. In exchange for successfully carrying out your part of the bargain I give you a reward: your grade. Neither the work nor the grade has any intrinsic value, but the grade has exchange value that can be banked and spent later for desired ends. Conception and execution are separate, and this dichotomy prepares young people for a life of essential powerlessness over the conditions of their labor and the purposes towards which that labor is used. An anti-tracking pedagogy needs to offer a new covenant, one that promises students an education rooted in their lives, with much greater initiative and participation.

In Linda Christensen's and my Literature and History course we constantly draw on students' lives as a way of illuminating both history and literature, and in turn draw on the history and literature as a way of illuminating students' lives. In the slavery and slave resistance unit, mentioned above, we read an excerpt from Frederick Douglass' autobiography in which a teenage Douglass defies and physically confronts his overseer (*Narrative of the Life of Frederick Douglass*, pp. 68-75.) We discuss the conditions in Douglass' life that propelled him into this confrontation, and growing out of the discussion ask students to write about a time in their lives when they stood up for what was right. The assignment gives a framework for students' writing but offers them lots of room to move, and as with the other assignments described, this one adjusts to a student's skill level. Some students may be able to write a personally probing, metaphorical piece while others may struggle to write a couple paragraphs — but the assignment offers all students a point of entry.

The read-around celebrates the diversity of students' experience, and in some cases their bravery or self-sacrifice: Nate writes about confronting a racist and abusive police officer, Stephanie about attending an anti-nuclear power demonstration, Josh about challenging a teacher's unfairness, Zeneda about interrupting an incident of sexual harassment. But the stories also give us the raw material to reflect on when and why people resist, and the relative effectiveness of some forms of resistance over others. And we can test our findings against Frederick Douglass' experiences.

In a unit on the history and sociology of schooling, students write about an encounter with inequality in education, and at a different point, about a positive learning experience. In a lesson on the Cherokee Indian Removal, they write about a time their rights were violated. After reading a Studs Terkel interview with C.P. Ellis, who quit his leadership position in the Klan and became a civil rights advocate and union organizer, students write about a significant change they made in their lives.

The personal writing and sharing undercuts a curriculum designed to inure students to alienated work, as the assignment also equalizes students' opportunity for academic success and theoretical insight. Moreover, it is a key part of creating a classroom discourse that in both form and content tells each student: you matter; your life and learning are important here. That's another

> **Ultimately, an anti-tracking pedagogy needs to engage students in an explicit critique of tracking. The unequal system of education must be examined.**

aim of breaking from a curriculum that is traditionally male dominated, and extols the lives of elites over working people and people of color. Unless we reorient the content of the curriculum to better reflect the lives of all our students, we implicitly tell young people, "Some of you are better than others, some of you are destined for bigger things."

## An Explicit Critique of Tracking

Ultimately, an anti-tracking pedagogy needs to engage students in an explicit critique of tracking. As Jeannie Oakes and others have shown, one of the by-products of tracking, even one of its aims, is that low-tracked students blame themselves for their subordinate position in the scholastic hierarchy; students come to believe that they are defective and the system is OK. Consequently, the unequal system of education, of which tracking is an important part, needs a critical classroom examination so that students can expose and expel the voices of self-blame and can overcome whatever doubts they have about their capacity for academic achievement. (Also see Role Play on Tracking, p. 117.)

In our unit on the history and sociology of schooling, students look critically at their own educations. We start with today and work backwards in time to understand the origins of the structures that now seem as natural as the seasons. From David Storey's novel, *Radcliffe*, we read a short excerpt that poignantly describes the unequal treatment received by students of different class backgrounds and, as mentioned earlier, ask students to recall an episode of unequal schooling from their own lives. We use the novel excerpt and students' stories to talk about the hidden curricula embedded in school practices — the lessons students absorb about democracy, hierarchy, power, solidarity, race, social class, resistance, etc. Students make observations on their own educational experiences, both past and present, and informally inventory the building's resources: who gets what kinds of equipment, facilities, class sizes and why? Our students' research is subversive in the best sense of the term as they engage in a critical inquiry that subverts the apparent legitimacy of a system of privilege that benefits some at the expense of others.

We read excerpts of Jean Anyon's 1980 *Journal of Education* article, "Social Class and the Hidden Curriculum of Work," which attempts to demonstrate that schools' expectations of students vary depending on the social position of students' parents. For example, through her research Anyon found that schools in working class communities value rote behavior and following directions; "affluent professional schools" value creativity and student initiative. The article, written for an academic journal, is a real stretch for a lot of students and might stay beyond their reach if we confined our conceptual exploration to reading and discussion. Instead, we test Anyon's theory by traveling to a wealthier, suburban school to make observations on classroom and school dynamics. We return to compare these to their observations of our own Jefferson High, a school in the center of a predominantly African American, working class community. Their first-hand experience makes theory student-friendly, and allows everyone to participate in the discussion as we evaluate Anyon's argument.

> "Fair grading" is an oxymoron and I'd prefer not to give letter grades at all.

We read excerpts from the second chapter of Jeannie Oakes' *Keeping Track* on the history of tracking and a chapter on the history of the SAT test, "The Cult of Mental Measurement," from David Owens' *None of the Above*. From Paul Chapman's *Schools as Sorters*, we review a 1920 survey (p. 126) conducted by Stanford University that found high school students had aspirations that were too high for the jobs available: over 60% of them wanted professional careers, whereas fewer than 5% of jobs were in the professions. Concluded Stanford psychologist William V. Proctor: "For [students'] own best good and the best good of the nation a great many of them should be directed toward the agricultural, mechanical, and industrial fields." Could the "problem" of students' high expectations help explain some social groups' commitment to intelligence testing and tracking? My students react with some anger at this conscious attempt to deflate children's dreams.

Providing new information and ways to question the character of schooling is a vital component of untracking any school or classroom. As I've suggested, tracking is not just a bad idea, but is a practice linked to the legitimation and maintenance of deep social inequality. Undercutting the legitimacy of unfair privilege is thus another necessary piece in an anti-tracking strategy. As indicated in the classroom examples provided, the curriculum can offer students permission and encouragement to critique social inequities and to think about alternatives. Further, introducing into the classroom

a legacy of resistance to injustice helps nurture an ethos of hope and possibility. Learning from individuals and movements working for democratic social change, both past and present, provides inspiration that not only can societies change for the better, but so can we. Because tracking rests on a premise that people's intellectual capabilities and potential for achievement are fixed, an anti-tracking curriculum needs to demonstrate a more hopeful — and realistic — view of human possibility.

## Grades and Equity

At the end of the first quarter Linda and I taught together, Alphonso came to complain about his grade. "I don't think I deserve a C," he argued. "Maybe I can't write as well as Katy. But she came in writing like that, and I've worked really hard. Compare what I'm doing now to what I wrote when the year began. I think I deserve at least a B." Alphonso's complaint illustrates a dilemma of evaluating or, more precisely, grading students in an untracked class. Alphonso was right: Katy knew more history, wrote with more detail and clarity, and had a firmer grasp of course concepts. But Alphonso had worked hard, made important strides in his writing and comprehension, and regularly shared his insights with the class. Still, were we to grade on a curve or based on some fixed standard of achievement, a C would have been fair, even generous. However, we had told the class we wouldn't grade this way, but that their grades would be based on effort, openness, growth, consistency of written and oral participation, respect for one another, as well as clarity of analysis. Thus we gladly changed Alphonso's grade and confessed our mistake.

"Fair grading" is an oxymoron and I'd prefer not to give letter grades at all. I attended an ungraded college, Antioch, where professors wrote students end of the term letters indicating academic strengths and areas needing work. Students responded with self-evaluations that commented on teachers' assessments. It all seemed to make

An untracked class needs an egalitarian grading system.

more sense. Of course, Antioch professors didn't see 150 students a day. Nor were they ordered by school or state authorities to sum up a student's performance with a single letter grade.

An anti-tracking pedagogy needs a system of student evaluation that does not reward students based primarily on the knowledge with which they begin a class. A system of fixed criteria from the outset benefits some and penalizes others largely on the basis of class, race, gender or nationality. An untracked class needs an egalitarian evaluation system that lets all students know they can succeed based on what they do in class, not on what they have or have not accomplished in the past.

Linda and I do not assign letter grades on individual assignments during the term. Instead, we write comments on students' papers indicating our evaluation and keep track of in-class participation and completion of written work. Students maintain folders of their work and at the end of each term write extensive self-evaluations analyzing all aspects of their achievement in class and present a case for a

particular letter grade. Linda and I read their evaluations, review their folders, discuss their overall progress and conference with students. Only then do we assign letter grades.

As in Alphonso's case, sometimes we blow it. But students are always free to challenge us, call our criteria into question and draw our attention to factors we may have overlooked. Every year we tell students about Alphonso to underscore our fallibility and to encourage their vigilance.

Ours is obviously not the only way to grade. But whatever system teachers adopt should derive from a broader anti-tracking philosophy and strategy. In evaluation, as with everything else, we must be bound by considerations of equity, not tradition or efficiency.

## An Anti-tracking Pedagogy

An anti-tracking pedagogy is more than just a collection of good teaching ideas strung together in a classroom with kids of different social backgrounds and educational histories. That may be a step in the right direction, but

we still need to ask: towards what? Is it enough to offer quality education in a heterogeneous setting, as some untracking proponents suggest? I don't think so. Once out of school, our students will still be "tracked" by jobs that require little decision-making and initiative, by high unemployment, by racism and sexism. We can't truly untrack schools without untracking society. Thus an anti-tracking pedagogy should equip educators and students to recognize and combat all inequity. Its organizing principle should be justice — in the classroom, in school, and in society at large. ❐

*Bill Bigelow (bbpdx@aol.com) teaches at Franklin High School in Portland, Oregon and is a* Rethinking Schools *editor.*

Some of the anti-tracking lessons mentioned here, and others, are described in greater detail in his curricula *Strangers in Their Own Country* (South Africa), *The Power in Our Hands* (U.S. labor history), and *Inside the Volcano* (U.S. foreign policy in Central America), available from Teaching for Change, 800-763-9131, www.teachingforchange.org.

# what the mirror said

By Lucille Clifton


*listen,*

*you a wonder.*

*you a city*

*of a woman.*

*you got a geography*

*of your own.*

*listen,*

*somebody need a map*

*to understand you.*

*somebody need directions*

*to move around you.*

*listen,*

*woman,*

*you not a noplace*

*anonymous*

*girl;*

*mister with his hands on you*

*he got his hands on*

*some*

*damn*

*body!*


Lucille Clifton is the former Poet Laureate of Maryland. She is a professor of literature and creative writing at the University of California at Santa Cruz. (See p. 184 for teaching ideas.)

# Teaching Ideas

Drop in to any large teachers' convention and you're likely to find hundreds of publishers' representatives selling textbooks, manuals, and software which they insist will promote foolproof teaching techniques. You are unlikely to find resources to help you confront the corporate and political forces that shape students' attitudes and beliefs.

This chapter explores practical ways young people can critique powerful influences such as racism, sexism, and homophobia — and celebrate personal struggles to reclaim their full humanity.

# Using Pictures to Combat Bias

### By Ellen Wolpert

For many years, I separated my political work and my education work. Politics was something I did before and after work. Education was what I did at my job at the daycare center.

One of the benefits of the women's movement and educational awareness around multiculturalism is that they helped me bridge those worlds and better understand the politics of our everyday lives.

I gravitated toward pictures because I'm a visually oriented person and because young children are particularly sensitive to pictures: during the time they struggle to understand first the spoken word and then the written word, they spend their lives "reading" images to understand the world. Through visual images, I wanted to integrate cultural diversity and challenge the dehumanizing images that children receive.

At first I thought about using visual displays such as bulletin boards. But I found such displays unbearably passive. I wanted to create something the kids could play with, something that would become a part of their everyday activities. I began collecting pictures — from magazines, rummage-sale books, photographs taken by myself of the children's families, newspapers, discarded library books — you name it. Then I used those photos and pictures to make games that were the same kind of games the kids already knew and enjoyed: bingo, lotto, rummy, memory/matching games.

Catalogs are filled with such card games, generally using zoo animals, endangered species, numbers, or stylized graphics. I decided to save the money I spent on such games and use it toward my own picture collection.

In order to make this project more real, let me go through the steps of collecting and using the photos.

First, I've developed three basic

GLORIA FEARN

**Young children are particularly receptive to visual images.**

sizes of photos: 5x7, 7.5x8.5, and 7.5x11 (a full-page picture from *National Geographic*, for example.) The smaller photos lend themselves to games such as concentration and rummy, while the bigger ones are good for sorting and counting games.

Second, I try to collect two of each. I then mount the photos on mat board and cover with clear contact paper. While two copies are essential for games such as concentration, rummy and puzzle-type games can be done with single copies.

Third, I try to organize the pictures around various themes: families, housing, sports, work, African Americans, Native Americans, women, food, transportation, ways of carrying things, and so forth. The more photos I collect, the better I am able to mix and match and develop a variety of possibilities.

Here's an example of how I use the picture cards for a concentration/memory game using pictures of Native Americans. For a good game of con-

centration with young children, it is best to have two copies of at least 10 different images. I go through my card collection and pick out 10 sets of pictures that counteract the usual stereotypes of Native Americans, for example, wearing feathers and living in teepees. Some of the pictures I have: a young girl playing football, a man getting on a subway in New York, a man in a pin-stripe suit who heads a corporation, a family playing lacrosse, a young boy watching TV in a Seminole chikee, some kids who had set up a lemonade stand, and so forth. (For this collection, I was greatly helped by copies of *National Geographic* that showed Native Americans in contemporary situations.)

I don't permanently separate my collection into discrete groups. For instance, I also use some of the Native American photos in a concentration game with other themes. I might, for instance, use the picture of the man and the New York subway during a game with a transportation theme, or the picture of the girl playing football in a sports theme.

The most important thing is to use the cards to spark discussion. I find this is particularly easy during some of the sorting games, such as a form of rummy.

To make the rummy game, I use about 40 different images. I deal out three to a player, with a draw pile and a discard pile. The idea is to find something in common on three different cards. The players can determine the common attributes — whether it's food, men taking care of babies, women workers, people protesting injustice, housing, and so forth. As we play the game, I try to get the kids talking about what is in the picture and how they determined the common attribute. This not only develops specific language skills, but also forces the children to focus on what is in the picture.

Because I concentrate on images that counter bias, this also indirectly challenges stereotypes. But I also interject comments. For example, one of my children once kept referring to "sitting Indian style" whenever I asked children to sit in a circle on the floor. When we played with my Native American cards, I specifically pointed out cards showing Native Americans sitting on couches, chairs, and so forth.

It's important that teachers create activities that elicit children's comments in order to pick up on stereotypes and assumptions mentioned in casual conversations. I use those everyday comments as the basis for a game. For instance, if a boy repeatedly mentions that girls can't play baseball, I might pull out pictures that show girls playing sports.

Similarly, when the movie *Aladdin* came out, I decided to collect photos of Arabs doing various things, whether an Arab father reading to his daughter, or an Arab doctor, or an Arab businessman in a "Western" suit. I used these cards to counter the movie's stereotypes of Arabs as hook-nosed, knife-wielding, turban-wearing, Jafar-like "bad guys."

Finally, I think it's important to add your own photographs to such collections. I've taken pictures of kids on the

CLEO

**Pictures can be a useful tool in anti-bias education.**

playground, taking special care to show girls playing sports and climbing, and boys playing with dolls or playing "dress-up." I've also encouraged children to bring in pictures, which is particularly useful when we do a unit on families. I have found that such photos are the most "real" to kids and the most valuable part of my picture collection. They also provide a way for children to readily connect their family lives with their learning.

Pictures alone won't transform a classroom. But they can become a key element in a classroom that encourages tolerance, understanding, and self-respect. As children play with the pictures — as their own images are reflected back at them in positive ways, as their ideas and analytical thinking are encouraged, as they begin to understand that diversity exists everywhere — they will begin to develop pride, self-confidence, and respect for others. ❐

*Ellen Wolpert has been working in daycare for over 20 years. She is currently director of the Washington-Beech Community Preschool in Boston.*

# Sources for Pictures

*National Geographic* is a great source of photos, as are news magazines such as *Time* and *Newsweek*. With *National Geographic*, make sure not to overemphasize the "exotic" photos of people of color; the magazine is perhaps best known for such photos, but has a much wider variety. Be careful when using magazines because these often are saturated with stereotypical middle class images.

Photographic essay books are often available at terrific discounts, particularly after the Christmas season. There

are also a few books worth buying:

*In America* by Eve Arnold, Knopf. A diverse collection of photos.

*Songs of My People: African Americans, A Self-Portrait*, Eric Easter, et al., eds., Little Brown. An excellent source of photographs of African Americans.

*Family Portraits in Changing Times* by Helen Nestor, New Sage Press. Excellent collection of photos from diverse families.

*Generations: A Universal Family Album*, by Anna Cohn and Lucinda Leach, Pantheon. Wonderful photos of women and men with children.

# My Mom's Job Is Important

## By Matt Witt

"My mother is a cashier. She works at Zayre's. My mom said to be a good cashier you should be punctual, courteous, broad-minded, honest and accurate."

So begins fifth grader Antonia Guzman's account of her mother's job at a discount department store. But Antonia's account does not stop with the usual recitation of the skills and attitudes people need to fit into the world of work which so often emerge from classroom units on employment. Instead, Antonia goes on to explore her mother's dreams and reflects on the importance of her mother's contribution:

"My mom said that the job she wants if she could change her job right away is to become an entrepreneur. She would like to own a retail business like a gift shop. She would like to be an entrepreneur because she would like to be her own boss, and your income is not limited and you can work at your own pace.

"I think my mom's job is important

> **Why study work? Because it is a central aspect of our lives and of our society.**

because if there's no cashier no one would keep track of the prices when a customer buys an item or a product."

Antonia is a student at Oyster Bilingual Elementary School in Washington, D.C., a public school whose students come from a wide variety of racial, ethnic, and economic backgrounds. Parents and teachers at Oyster organized a year long "Program on Work," which demonstrated some exciting approaches to teaching and learning about work.

In the Oyster program, children critically examined slides of work situations, interviewed their parents, explored probing questions, entertained controversy, invited parents and other adults into the classroom to talk (and in one case, sing) about work, and constructed a display for parents featuring stories, poems, and drawings they had created. An understanding and respect for their parents' jobs was combined in the unit with the exploration of legal and historical issues. Slides and a discussion guide developed in the program are available to teachers or parents interested in adapting any of the ideas.

Why study work? First, because it is a central aspect of our lives and our society. If a goal of education is to teach students to think critically about how our society is organized, their study of work-related issues cannot be limited to learning the difference between "goods" and "services," memorizing a few names like Samuel Gompers or George Meany, and soaking up donated corporate propaganda that paints an incomplete picture of the country's economic life.

## Connecting with the Community

Second, studying work is a good way to encourage interaction between students, parents, community residents, and teachers — either by bringing people from the community into the classroom to talk about their work or by sending students out to investigate.

Third, studying work provides stimulating subject matter with which to develop skills such as writing, interviewing, debating, drawing, and singing.

The program at Oyster School began with discussions about work in each class from second grade through sixth, conducted by teachers and parent vol-

Age 7 Name Phyllis Owens.

My mom is the Boss of culumbia direk marketing.

**Drawings by students from Oyster Bilingual Elementary School.**

unteers. To begin with a subject students could relate to easily, they were shown slides of child labor taken in the U.S. in the early years of this century.

"What are these children doing?" students were asked. When they established that the children in the slides were working — in coal mines, cotton fields, textile mills, and other industries — students were asked, "Why are they working and not in school?"

## Exploring Child Labor

Through further discussion, students discovered that as recently as when their grandparents were children, many young people were employed in child labor. This led to many questions: "Why did child labor exist? Who benefited from it, and who opposed it? What did working people do to get it outlawed?"

Slides of modern-day child labor in other countries provoked comments from students from recent immigrant families. "They still don't have any laws against children having to work," said a student who came to the United States from Guatemala. "Children have to do a lot of hard work, especially on the farms."

Students were then asked whether children have a right to get an education instead of going to work, which provoked a discussion about who decides what is a right and what is not.

They were shown slides of people of different races, ages, and genders, and were asked whether they thought it would be legal for an employer looking to hire someone to pick among those people based on those differences. They also saw a slide of a pregnant woman and were asked whether it would be legal to fire her if she refused to do a task that might threaten the health of her unborn child.

After students gave their views, they learned that laws establishing what they considered to be obvious rights had been passed just since their parents were born. Asked how they thought workers got those laws passed, students drew on what they learned during a school-wide program honoring Martin Luther King, Jr., and the Civil Rights Movement.

"Boycotts," they suggested. "Sit-ins. Strikes. Marches."

Historical slides showed some of these tactics being used, including sit-down strikes in the 1930s and equal-rights rallies in the 1960s. Rights, students learned, are not given but won, and change with time as new social movements emerge.

Next, students saw slides of men doing traditionally "male" jobs — doctor, factory worker, coal miner—and women doing traditionally "female" jobs such as secretary, flight attendant, and homemaker. That prompted a discussion about whether both men and women could do those jobs.

The next slides showed men and women doing the jobs that are stereotyped as being only for the opposite sex. Discussion followed on whether all people should be able to choose jobs that suit them, or whether, as a few boys in each class would argue, "the only work women should do is at home."

Another discussion in all classes, including pre-k, kindergarten, and first grade, was based on slides of various Oyster parents doing their jobs. Construction workers and housekeepers are more common among the school's families — but the range is wide including a lawyer, a reporter, a dancer, a furniture maker, a cab driver, and aides to government officials. The occupations were discussed from many points of view. "What does the person shown actually do in his or her job? What would be satisfying about the work, and what would make it difficult, stressful, or dangerous? What makes the job important to society?"

In all classes, students were able to identify a number of reasons that each job is valuable to society. In some cases, that led to new questions, such as, "If each job is important, why are some jobs paid more than others?"

## What Do You Do at Work?

When shown slides of homemakers and asked what job these people were doing, a few students answered, "They don't have a job. They just stay home." This provoked lively discussions about the duties of homemakers and both the strains and satisfactions of child rearing.

With these classroom discussions as background, students were assigned to interview their parents or other adults about their work. "What do you do while I'm at school? What do you like about your job? What would you change if you could?"

What they learned from these interviews was as varied as the jobs their parents did. Many children learned that what their parents liked most about their jobs was a chance to meet or help people, while a common complaint was that customers or employers did not treat them with respect.

Some of the recent immigrants told their children they wished they had jobs like they had had in their native countries, instead of the less skilled work they were confined to in the United States.

My mom is a singer.

Other parents talked about problems with shift work, mandatory overtime, and being denied benefits that were due them.

All classes from pre-k to sixth grade had discussions about what they had learned. In the pre-k through first grade classes, a parent brought in a guitar and sang with the children, "What does your mama (or papa, grampa, etc.) do? What does your mama do? What does your mama do when you're in school, you're in school?" The song would stop as a student explained what she or he had found out, and pick up again when it was time to give someone else a chance.

After all students did drawings and the second through sixth grade classes wrote reports or poems using what they had learned, their work was put on display at the school and compiled in a booklet. Parents were invited to the school one evening to see the display, get copies of the booklet, and take part in a community forum about work along with teachers, students, local union leaders, and local labor scholars.

## Problems and Lessons

In carrying out the "Program on Work" teachers and parents at Oyster School encountered a number of problems. For example, when the program was first proposed, some of the white middle-class parents active in the PTA objected that "the poorer families are not going to want the fact that they are a housekeeper or a janitor plastered all over the walls." As it turned out, the opposite was true: parents with lower-status jobs greatly appreciated both the recognition they received and the open discussion of issues of equity in the work world.

Another obstacle was the desire of some teachers to narrowly define the program as "career education." It took a great deal of discussion to convince some that the role of the school was to prepare students not merely to fit into the world of work as it exists, but to be able to analyze it and critique it.

In adapting the program for other schools, certain omissions would have to be corrected and some program elements could be developed further. For example, children of the few parents at this particular school who were without work were simply told to interview them about jobs they used to have or would like to have, or to interview an older sibling, neighbor, friend, or worker at the school.

In retrospect, more time should have been spent in classroom discussion on unemployment, disability, retirement, and other issues related to people without work. Students could have been asked to think of all the reasons why someone might be unemployed or unable to work, to consider what obligation society has to such people, if any, and to discuss possible solutions. Perhaps someone active in a community organization working to win expanded jobs programs could have been invited to talk with students about the causes of unemployment and proposed remedies.

Particularly for older students, the chance to experience or at least observe one or more jobs would be an obvious complement to discussions and interviews about adults' views of work. Parents from a fourth grade class at Oyster demonstrated the potential for "work experience" activities by arranging for students to work as teacher's aides in a nearby nursery school. When each had had a turn, the students had a lengthy discussion about what they had learned, and prepared an oral report which was given to the rest of the school during an assembly.

Workplace visits are also recommended. They are most fruitful if a worker visits the school first and prepares students to think about the working conditions they will see, how conditions have changed over the years, how decisions are made when problems come up, and so on. Otherwise, such visits tend to focus almost exclusively on what tasks a worker performs at his or her job.

One final suggestion: schools that need extra funds for materials, transportation, or other expenses to incorporate the world of work into the curriculum might consider asking local unions for help. They also may be able to help set up workplace visits. ❐

*Matt Witt, an Oyster Bilingual School parent, was coordinator of the school's "Program on Work." He is currently communications director for the Teamsters Union.*

BY ALEXANDRA RUIZ
MY FATHER IS A PAINTER

# My Father Was A Musician

By Dyan Watson


*In the basement they played.*
*"Jam session" he called it,*
*halting only to mend a chord or two.*


*The house swayed from side to side*
*dancing freely, carelessly*
*while neighbors shut doors and windows.*


*Sometimes I would sneak into his bedroom*
*just to see it, touch It,*
*pluck a string or two.*


*At night, I dreamed*
*of concerts and demos.*


*I want to be just like him.*


Dyan Watson graduated from Jefferson High School in Portland, Oregon. She currently plays saxophone and studies at Willamette University in Salem, Oregon. (See p. 184 for lesson ideas.)

# There's More to Heroes than He-Man

## By Marcie Osinsky

As part of a yearlong folktale curriculum, I began a study of heroes and heroines with my first- and second-grade class. First the kids and I brainstormed about heroic characters. The Ninja Turtles and He-Man topped the list. The children's concept of heroism did not include people in their lives.

As a result, I decided to use oral history and storytelling techniques to highlight the heroism of people close to them. Children need to see models of strength and courage within their own families and communities in order to identify such qualities in themselves. I have also found that oral history and storytelling are wonderful ways to include parents in building a classroom community that respects differing perspectives and voices.

After making our own definitions of heroism using storybooks and folktales, we invited parents to a "story-sharing breakfast" to talk to us about people who were heroic in their lives. In phone conversations and informal chats, parents and I spoke about heroic people and role models in our lives.

To prepare the children, I modeled an interview where I made a lot of mistakes. I interrupted and asked questions out of the blue. The kids told me what I did wrong. We then did mini-interviews where I interviewed another adult about his or her heroic person.

Then we had our "story-sharing breakfast." The parents sat in groups with children and told stories and answered questions. The images of all the characters in the stories filled the room. One grandmother talked of how she stowed away on a ship to Europe in World War II to be a foreign correspondent. A man told how he delivered eggs early each day to put himself through college while raising his family.

As the stories progressed, the atmosphere became one of listening, telling, and questioning. Kids were involved in the conversation and learned what was dear to their parents. They learned the importance of listening and realized how experiences and values are passed down through generations.

Soon after the story-sharing breakfast, for example, Gabriel and Brent were chopping onions in class to make soup. Gabriel was having difficulty and Brent showed him his technique to cut onions, explaining: "This is how I chop onions. This is how my mom chops onions and my nana chops onions. This is how my whole family chops onions. We've been chopping onions like this since — since the cavemen."

## The Parents' Stories

The stories connected the kids to another time in history when people also faced everyday hardships and difficult decisions, as some of the kids do now.

While quite a few parents told dramatic stories about war and conflicts from their home countries, others told stories that showed the heroism of difficult decisions and everyday struggles.

One parent, Lynne, told how she wanted to be a dancer and moved from the West Coast to Boston. She explained how hard it was to be alone in a strange city and to try to make it in a career such as dancing. She told of another dancer who encouraged her and gave her confidence. "I will always remember her," Lynn said of the dancer, "because she gave me such strength to go after what I wanted to do."

One student said of Lynne's story, "She was her own hero." When I asked why, the child said, "Because it was a scary thing to move from California and to become a dancer and live here, and she did it."

One parent told of a man saving her mother's life when she was hit by a car in Haiti. The accident occurred during curfew at a time of political unrest, and the driver did not stop. An ambulance was called but did not come. People were afraid the woman might die. "Then a man walked to her, grabbed her and put her on his shoulder," the parent said. "He carried her to the hospital. If he had not carried my mother, I would not have a mother right now. That man was not afraid to get killed on the street."

The kids were upset after hearing the story. They asked questions like, "Why couldn't you go out in the street? Who would shoot you? Why would you get shot by police if you had not done anything wrong?"

Kids connected stories they had heard to events in Boston or Los Angeles. I felt it was important to give the children a forum to raise their concerns and know that there are adults who share those concerns. The story-telling became a sophisticated discussion of attitudes toward solving conflicts.

As we continued, I began to see how stories help connect the listener to a different time, place, and cultural context, giving the children a sense of belonging to a larger history. After learning that she had family roots in Africa and hearing more stories about the continent, Darlene said, "Oh yeah, I been to Africa, with my ancestors."

Through the project, I discovered the power of storytelling not only to create a curriculum respecting diverse perspectives but to allow parents and children to help shape that curriculum so that it reflects their realities.

The stories from our breakfast became an important part of life at our school. We illustrated and transcribed them and made a book. Throughout the year, the book was read over and over again by the kids and parents. ❑

*Marcie Osinsky teaches first and second grade at Martin Luther King, Jr. School in Cambridge, MA.*

# Black Lies/White Lies

By Nancy Schniedewind and Ellen Davidson

**Objective:**

To help students understand how connotations in our language perpetuate racism.

**Materials:**

Dictionaries, paper, pencils, chart paper, markers.

**Implementation:**

Tell students they will work on an activity to examine language. Teach the term "connotation." Divide students into groups of five. Give each group a large sheet of paper. They list all the words or phrases they can think of that have the word "white" or "black" in them. For example, "black lies," "black eye," "white as snow." After ten minutes the groups mark their lists as follows: "+" for a phrase with a positive connotation, "-" for one with a negative connotation, and "0" for one with a neutral connotation. Groups then look up the words "white" and "black" in their dictionaries and write down definitions. It is helpful if different groups have different dictionaries. Use dictionaries as advanced as they can handle.

The class joins together. Appoint a recorder to stand at the front of the room. Starting with "black," each group calls out a word or phrase with "black" in it. Record these along with their markings of "+," "-," and "0." Take turns until all the groups have their ideas listed. Then do the same for "white." Similarly, list dictionary definitions.

**Discussion:**

1. How many "black" words have positive connotations? How about "white" words? How many of each have negative connotations?

2. What reactions do you have as you look at this list?

3. How might black people feel hearing these words and phrases all the time? How about white people?

4. Many of our ideas are formed through language. Our feelings about ourselves often come from words we hear. What does our language imply about white people? About black people? ❒

**How does language about race influence perceptions?**

*Nancy Schniedewind and Ellen Davidson are teacher educators and writers.*

From Schniedewind, N. and Davidson, E., *Open Minds to Equality: A Sourcebook of Learning Activities to Promote Race, Sex, Class, and Age Equity* © 1983 by Allyn and Bacon. Reprinted by permission.

*Susan Lina Ruggles*

# Bringing the World into the Math Class

## By Claudia Zaslavsky

Children in our schools come from a multiplicity of ethnic, racial, and economic backgrounds. How can our teaching of mathematics respond to the diverse needs and learning styles of the school population?

Mathematics adapts readily to a multicultural context. Children learn how mathematics arose from the needs of the societies of the past and of today. Other cultures' numeration and measurement systems, games of chance and games of skill, and patterns in art and architecture are all sources of learning experiences.

Similarly, we can profitably relate the study of mathematics to other disciplines. Activities and games can correlate with social studies, language arts, fine arts, and industrial arts, encouraging students to appreciate the many aspects of mathematics.

Investigations into sex-role stereotyping reveal that boys are more likely than girls to receive exposure to such informal sources of mathematics learning as the construction of toys, puzzles, and sports, while girls are socialized to care more about people. By integrating mathematics education with the study of culture and history, we may motivate more girls to become involved in mathematics.

## Numbers in Other Languages

Ask your students whether any of them can count in languages other than English. These talented children can then take pride in their ability to teach the counting words to their classmates.

Comparison of the number words in a foreign language with the corresponding English words encourages analysis of the structure of the numeration systems. English and most other European languages base their systems on grouping by 10s and powers of 10. Why is 10 commonly used as the base? Is it because we have 10 fingers (digits)? But the French word for 80 means "four 20s!" And in the Mende language of Sierra Leone, the word for 20 means "a whole person" — all 20 fingers and toes — and 40 is expressed as "two whole persons."

Grouping by 20s is common among the peoples of West Africa and Middle America (Maya, Aztec, etc.) Perhaps they went barefoot in their warm climates, and therefore found it logical to count both fingers and toes. However, the Inuit Eskimos also have a numeration system based on 20.

In English we use a combination of multiplication and addition to form the higher numbers: 45 means "four times ten plus five." In some languages the construction of large numbers involves subtraction. The Yoruba (Nigeria) word for 45 means "take five and ten from three times twenty."

## Origins

Ask your students to imagine how and why people first found it necessary to use number words. Even the experts cannot agree on the origins of counting. Some theories are: to count one's private possessions; to keep track of the group's livestock; for ritual and religious purposes; to trade with other individuals or groups. Your students' theories may be just as valid as those of the experts.

The question of origin is sure to engender a lively discussion and to put across several useful ideas. Children will learn to appreciate that people invent new ways of doing things because of objective needs and that each group responds to these needs in its own unique manner.

Mathematical concepts are related to real life and develop as the society develops. Having recognized the need to count, people invented number words, and then organized them into systems with well-defined structures. Written symbols and computational methods became necessary, as well as systems of finger and body gestures. Children should begin to recognize that mathematics is a growing body of knowledge to which even they can contribute.

## Symbols

Students can investigate the number symbols (numerals) of ancient societies and compare them with the Hindu-Arabic system in use today. They might consider such aspects as the number of different symbols, the order in which they are written, the use of zero, positional notation and place value, and convenience in keeping records and carrying out calculations. Figure 1 shows some ways of expressing 2369.

Although thousands of different languages exist today, we would have little difficulty in reading examples of computation in almost any arithmetic textbook in the world. Most people now use the 10-digit place-value system originated by the Hindus in India and transmitted by the Arabs to Asia, Africa, and Europe. By the time northern Europe adopted it, about the year 1500, the system was almost 1000 years old. This cultural borrowing is typical of the way

> **Mathematical concepts are related to real life and develop as the society develops.**

in which ideas spread from one region to another.

Native American tribes speaking hundreds of different languages occupied the territory that later became the United States. The Indians of the Great Plains invented a sign language, including gestures for numbers, that enabled them to carry on complete conversations without having to say a word.

African peoples speak over 1000 different languages, and also use gestures for communication. Although two different ethnic groups live in adjoining areas, they might use entirely different systems of gesture counting. In some cases the finger signs are related to the number words, in other cases they are quite different.

Happily, teachers no longer go along with the taboo on finger counting imposed on previous generations of students. We recognize the value of "hands-on" materials in helping children to learn arithmetic operations. What materials are "handier" than the fingers?

After investigating some systems of gesture counting, children might also invent their own gesture system and number words, and try them out on their classmates. They can learn to compute with their fingers, as in Chisanbop (also called "Fingermath"), a system based on the Korean and Japanese abacus.

Shops in Asian countries and the Soviet Union often have an abacus and a calculator sitting side by side next to the cash register. Although the Chinese suan-pan differs somewhat from the Japanese and Korean soroban, both are based on calculation by groups of 5's and 10's. The Russian scet has 10 beads on each strand, with the two middle beads colored differently for convenience in counting. Children can make their own abaci, and use them for computation.

## Geometry and Measurement

An investigation of styles of housing in different cultures is a valuable source of experiences with shapes and sizes as well as with perimeter and area concepts. It can also develop skills in approximation and estimation. We are accustomed to right angles and straight sides in our homes and furniture. Can we imagine living with other shapes? Ask your students to draw floor plans of a simple home. What shapes do they envision?

Let students pretend that they are living in a society where they must produce almost everything by their own efforts and where a house must be constructed with as little material as possible. The task is to determine which shape will afford the greatest amount of floor space for a given investment of labor and materials.

They can test some of the possible shapes, to see which gives the largest area for a given perimeter, a given amount of material.

Distribute grid paper, and have them follow this procedure:

1. Choose a perimeter — for example, 32 units. Tear off a strip of graph paper at least 32 units in length to serve as a tape measure, or use a piece of string of the required length.

a. Form a circle with a circumference of 32 units, and sketch it on the graph paper.

b. Sketch several rectangles with a perimeter of 32 units, having different dimensions.

c. Draw several other shapes having a 32-unit perimeter.

2. Compute the area of each figure by counting the number of small squares enclosed by each perimeter.

3. Arrange the results in a table. Which figure has the greatest area? Which rectangle encloses the greatest area? What other conclusions can be drawn?

4. Compare the areas by constructing a bar graph.

Children will raise many questions: How can we make the circle perfect? How can we trace around the string when it keeps moving? How shall we count the fractions of small squares? Counting all these little squares is boring; isn't there a short cut?

As children carry out the activity and discuss their problems, they discover that the circle has the greatest area, and the square is the largest rectangle. To draw a circle, one need only mark a few points on the circumference while a classmate holds the string in place; then the circle can be drawn freehand. An adequate approximation of the area results from counting only those fractions of squares that exceed half the square, and ignoring the smaller fractions. Examining the symmetry of the shape allows one to avoid counting all the little squares. The number of squares in a rectangle is the product of the two dimensions, actually the area formula. Children learn the difference between area and perimeter, and when to use square units as distinct from units of length.

Students will conclude that people who build round houses achieve the

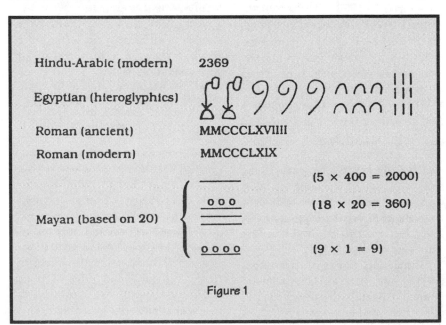

| Hindu-Arabic (modern) | 2369 |
| Egyptian (hieroglyphics) | |
| Roman (ancient) | MMCCCLXVIIII |
| Roman (modern) | MMCCCLXIX |
| Mayan (based on 20) | (5 × 400 = 2000) |
| | (18 × 20 = 360) |
| | (9 × 1 = 9) |

Figure 1

greatest possible floor space for a given amount of building material. Why, then, is the rectangle shape most common in our society?

This project can expand in many directions. Children can construct African-type compounds of round houses with conical roofs, decorated in geometric patterns of various colors — math, social studies, and art are all combined in one lesson. Students can investigate the influence of the environment and of technology on styles of homes in different cultures. They can estimate areas and perimeters of objects in the classroom, and then measure to check their estimates. Students will suggest other applications.

Examining the geometric forms of symbols, such as the ankh, the cross, the star, and the peace sign is another worthwhile activity. Children can look for symmetry of design and repeating motifs in decorated objects and cloth, and then produce their own versions. Geometric concepts have real meaning when they are presented in such a concrete and relevant form.

## Games of Chance and Skill

From time immemorial human beings have tried to divine the future. Some divining practices led to games of chance, and eventually to the important field of mathematical probability and statistics. A toss of a coin is the simplest form of gambling. Some societies used cowrie shells, others used nuts, still others threw knucklebones, which then developed into dice.

Two excellent games of chance are the Jewish Dreidel game associated with the Hannukah festival, and the Mexican game called Toma-Todo. Both are played with tops or spinners, a four-sided *dreidel* or a six-sided *topa*. Any number of children can try to predict the outcome before each spin and keep a record of success or failure, thus adding to the excitement of the game. Once they have mastered the rules, they can make up variations.

Three-in-a-row games can be traced as far back as 1300 B.C., when diagrams for the games were chiseled into the roof slabs of the temple to Seti I in ancient Egypt. Tic-tac-toe is the most popular form in the United States, and one of the simplest to play. Investigations into the versions that children play in other lands — Morris in England, Mill in other European countries, Shisima in Kenya, Nerenchi in Sri Lanka — have shown me that they help children improve their decision-making skills.

The ancient stone game is a good way to introduce a unit on African heritage and Africa's contributions to world culture. Known by its generic name Mancala, an Arabic word meaning "transferring," it is called Wari or Oware or Adi in Ghana, Ayo by the Yoruba people of Nigeria, and Giuthi by the Kikuyu of Kenya. Kalah is a commercial version. African captives brought the game to the New World, and social scientists have used the style of playing to trace the ancestry of black people now living in the Caribbean, the United States, and regions of Brazil and other countries of South America.

Playing the game depends entirely upon skill, not at all on luck, yet some versions are simple enough for first graders. The popular West African versions can be played with an egg carton as a gameboard and band beans for playing pieces. At the beginning it may be advisable to distribute sheets of paper on which the "board" has been drawn, so that children can see exactly what is going on. (For the game rules see Zaslavsky, 1973 or Dolber, 1980.) On the simplest level, the game affords practice in counting and reinforces the concept of one-on-one correspondence. At a more advanced stage, a child uses all the operations of arithmetic.

Games of strategy help children to acquire skills in logical inference and decision making, important training for solving problems in the technological society of the future. They can vary the method of play by changing the rules, the shape of the board or the number of counters, each version requiring a different strategy. After all, that's how new games are invented!

Through activities such as those described here, our students become aware of the role mathematics plays in all societies and of the need for math-

There's more to math than numbers.

ematical problem solving and decision making in real life.

Furthermore, children learn to appreciate the contributions of people all over the world. Geography and history take on new meaning as children learn other number systems, analyze styles in housing, and trace the dispersion of games. They can take pride in their own heritage, as they become familiar with other cultures. ❑

*Claudia Zaslavsky is a retired mathematics teacher who now works as an educational consultant giving inservice workshops and courses on multicultural and interdisciplinary applications of mathematics.*

Reprinted with permission of the author from *Curriculum Review*, January/February 1985, Vol. 24, #3.

References:
Dolber, Sam. *From Computation to Recreation Around the World*. San Carlos, CA: Math Aids, 1980.

*Feelings, Muriel. *Moja Means One: Swahili Counting Book*. NY: Dial, 1971.

*Lumpkin, Beatrice. *A Young Genius in Old Egypt*. Chicago: Dusable Press, 1979.

Zaslavsky, Claudia. *African Counts: Number and Pattern in African Culture*. Westport, CT: Lawrence Hill, 1979.

Zaslavsky, C. *Preparing Young Children for Math*. New York: Schocken, 1979.

*Zaslavsky, C. *Count on Your Fingers African Style*. New York: Crowell, 1980.

*Zaslavsky, C. *Tic-Tac-Toe and Other Three-in-a-Row Games, From Ancient Egypt to the Modern Computer*. New York: Crowell, 1982.

*Children's books.

# Dream Voyage
# to the Center of the Subway

By Eve Merriam


*One day*
*the billboards all implore*
*"BUY NOTHING"*

*In the broken vending machine*
*push the plunger*
*and pop out*
*a flower*
*sprung dewborn*
*fresh every hour.*

Eve Merriam (1916 - 1992) a poet, playwright, and writer inspires children with her writing.
(See p. 184 for lesson ideas.)

# Coping with TV: Some Lesson Ideas

## By Bob Peterson

"One thousand and ninety-five hours!" Elizabeth shook her head in disbelief as she announced to the class the amount of time she would "have for herself" each year if she reduced her TV watching from five to two hours a day.

"That's over 45 days of time!" added Dennis, as he quickly figured it out on the calculator.

The class brainstormed what a kid could do with that much time — learn to juggle or to play a musical instrument, read scores of books, write their own book, get good at a sport. Of course, several in the class proudly proclaimed that if they had that much extra time, they'd do what they liked best to do — watch TV.

For years I chose to ignore TV, on the one hand blaming it for many of my students' problems but on the other feeling it was beyond my control. Yet I came to realize that because of TV's negative impact on children, we must teach children how to cope with television. At La Escuela Fratney, the kindergarten through 5th grade school where I teach, the staff decided to tackle the problem head on and sponsor an annual No-TV Week. Our goal was not only to decrease the amount students watch television but to increase students' skills in critically analyzing television and other media.

### Limiting the Habit

Students need to recognize that TV watching can develop into an addiction. Students often are familiar with the word "addiction" and link it to drugs. The anti-TV addiction commercials available on video from the Media Foundation are useful for sparking discussion of TV addiction (see resources next page). The commercials show entranced children watching television,

> The average five-year old will have spent 5,000 hours in front of the TV before entering kindergarten — longer than the time it takes to get a college degree.

and explain how the child is addicted. In follow-up discussions, students can explore the meaning of addiction, different types, and how people overcome their addiction.

Statistics can be helpful. According to the Nielsen, Inc., children on the average watch about 24 - 28 hours of television per week. The average five-year old will have spent 5000 hours in front of the TV before entering kindergarten, more time than he or she will spend in conversation with his or her parents for the rest of their lives and longer than it would take to get a college degree.

Part of Fratney's success at reducing kids' TV watching was because we worked closely with our students' families. No-TV Week is not aimed just at students and staff but also at family members. During the week, everyone — staff, students, and family members — are asked to voluntarily pledge not to watch TV for a week.

To prepare students for the week, teachers try to raise the students' awareness of how much time they spend watching television. Students keep a week-long log of the TV they watch, including the names and times of the programs.

Some of the teachers then have each child tabulate the number of hours they watched TV, making comparisons and reflecting on the differences. Some classes rank their favorite shows and discuss why they are popular. For older students, the No-TV Week can be tied to math lessons. The students figure out the average hours of TV watched daily, weekly, annually, or from the time they were five years old to age 18.

Some classes prepare "No-TV Week Survival Kits" with alternative home activities such as playing games, going on a bicycle ride, making cookies, or reading a book. One year my class coordinated a schoolwide campaign to come up with 500 things to do instead of watching TV. Another year my fifth graders went to each class and surveyed the students about the types of media/communication devices in their homes — from TVs to computers, from phones to fax machines. They tallied the data, figured out the percentages, and made bar graphs to display the survey's results.

Because many children have difficulty conceptualizing "life before TV," I have children interview a family member or friend who grew up without television. Questions include: How did your life change after you got a television set? What did you do instead of watching TV?

Parent response to No-TV Week has ranged from wildly enthusiastic, to highly supportive, to nonchalant. Although most of the families fall in the middle, there are a number who tell wonderful stories about how the week forced them to reconsider their television habits. One parent, for example, explained how previously her family had always watched TV during dinner. While she didn't like the habit, she wasn't sure how to change it. After the No-TV Week, she said, she felt confident enough to ban the television during dinner and call for family conversation instead. Another parent said that after the week, she started a practice of telling her kids at breakfast several times a week that it would be a No-TV Day. A third parent said her children even ask for No-TV evenings because they like to play games with mom and dad.

## Critique

After the first No-TV week, parents suggested we put more emphasis on helping children critique and analyze television. They were concerned not only about the shows but the commercials.

The teachers started by focusing on commercials. On the average, children see 20,000 TV commercials a year — over 350,000 by the time they are 18, according to Action on Children's Television. One of my homework assignments asks students to "Add up the Ads" and to keep track of all the TV ads they saw in one night — both the number and the minutes. This gives the children an understanding of how commercials saturate our lives and gets them to begin thinking how the television industry rests on advertising dollars.

For one lesson plan on commercials, teachers videotaped certain commercials and later watched them with their students. Teachers posed the question, "What messages are sent by the commercial and why?" They also explained the difference between implicit and explicit messages. After watching and discussing various commercials, students wrote about the ads' explicit and implicit messages. As Maria noted, "You seem to be always happy if you eat that cereal." John concluded, "There always are pretty ladies next to new cars. It must be so men come in to look at them."

TV shows can be critiqued in the same way. I have taped segments of cartoons and sit-coms to show in class. We analyze the messages and ask: How are problems solved? Who does most of the talking? What race, gender and age are the characters in the shows — or commercials? How many instances of violence does one observe? How many put-downs are there? As a follow-up homework assignment, students interview a family member about the positive and negative messages of TV shows. One parent answered, "Children tend to believe that violence is the way to solve problems like in violent TV shows." Another responded, "TV has a bad effect because it absorbs much of the brain."

How much of our kids' brains TV will "absorb" is an open question. But media literacy projects like our No-TV Week present the question for discussion and allow collective reflection on one of the most powerful influences on our children's lives. ❒

*Bob Peterson teaches at La Escuela Fratney in Milwaukee, Wis. and is an editor of* Rethinking Schools.

## No-TV Resources

Winn, Marie, *Unplugging the Plug-In Drug* (New York: Penguin Books, 1987). Gives a detailed description of how to run a No-TV campaign.

Lappé, Frances Moore and family, *What to Do After You Turn Off the TV* (New York: Ballantine Books, 1989). Hundreds of great ideas.

The Media Foundation, 1243 West 7th Ave., Vancouver, British Columbia, V6H 1B7 Canada. (800) 663-1243. Produces a VHS video called "The 12 Minute Media Revolution," which includes startling commercials about TV addiction and overconsumption: $25/ individuals; $45/ schools and institutions.

Also publishes quarterly magazine, *Adbusters*, $18/year.

# Talking Back to TV Commercials: Questions to Ask

**1.** What is the product or service being sold?

**2.** What things should someone know about this product or service before deciding whether to buy it?

**3.** What images appear on the screen? What are the images designed to communicate? Do they supply specific information about the product/service? If so, what is it? (If the images don't provide information about the product/service, what does their purpose seem to be?)

**4.** Is music used in the commercial? How does the music make you feel?

**5.** Does the commercial have a male or a female announcer or a narrator? How does the voice sound?

**6.** Do people appear in the commercial? Are people of color included? How do the people behave? Are there any stereotypes?

**7.** Do the men in the commercial behave differently than the women? How?

**8.** What group does the commercial seem to be aimed at?

**9.** How might the commercial be different if the purpose were to give viewers information instead of to get them to buy something?

---

## Teaching ideas:

1. Watch the excellent film, *Killing Us Softly*, about images of women in advertising. Also watch, *Who's Calling the Shots?*, a provocative video about alcohol and advertising. (See page 188 for descriptions; page 190 for ordering information.) These are aimed at high school through adult audiences, but parts could be selected and shown to children of all ages.

Divide students into small groups and distribute several magazines to each group. Ask them to find ads that contain images of men and women. Using their own insights, and information from *Killing Us Softly*, students should analyze these ads for messages about men's and women's roles. Ask them to list all the characteristics of women and men in a number of ads — for example men: in control, looking away from women, upper class, rich, etc.; women: scantily clothed, conventional good looks, looking adoringly at men, etc. If you have access to an opaque projector, allow each group to present an ad and lead a discussion. Questions to raise: What is the typical male/female relationship portrayed in the ads? What insecurities/fears do the ads encourage?

2. Use a stop-watch to calculate the number of commercial minutes per half hour. Compare the total number of commercial minutes at different times. (For example, afterschool, primetime, Saturday morning.) Call the local TV station and ask for a rate sheet on costs of commercials for different times and days. Calculate ad revenues per half hour for different shows. Why do some cost more? What does that say about the values of those who buy commercials?

3. Look for evidence of the impact of commercials in your school or community. (For example, company logos on clothes, specific products bought by classmates or teachers, slogans or taglines adopted into student speech, commercial markings on posters, and "teaching" materials in schools.)

*Writing a Critique:*

Instructions for students:

"Use the information you've gathered to write a critique of advertising. Writing a critique is a little like advertising. Only in this case, you are trying to convince your reader to agree with your point of view by using evidence. Take whatever position you want. Are you upset with the way commercials manipulate people's feelings or use sex to sell products? Do you like the clever ways music or special effects are used or how some ads tell a little story? Use the evidence you've gathered to support your position." ❑

# Looking Pretty, Waiting for the Prince

## By Lila Johnson

*As a senior, Lila Johnson uncovered the "secret education" that cartoons, advertising, and the media slipped into her life. She wrote this article to educate others about the inaccurate visions Disney & Co. sell children.*

My two brothers and I lived for our daily cartoon fix. We hungered for the vibrant reds, blues, and yellows that raced around our screen for an insane hour or two.

When we were away from the tube, we assumed the roles of our favorite characters: Bugs Bunny, that wise-cracking, carrot-munching rabbit; Yosemite Sam, rough and tough shoot-'em-down cowboy; and Popeye, the all-American spinach-guzzling sailor. We took our adopted identities outside and to school where our neighbors and friends did the same.

Now, as a senior in high school, I see that cartoons are not just lighthearted, wacky fun. Animated material touches on such sensitive issues as roles of men and women in society, and people of color.

Cartoons are often the birthplace of the cultural stereotypes we learn and remember, as I do today: the idea that Indians are savages — tomahawks and moccasins, teepees and war paint — the bad guys who pursued my favorite cowboys, or the belief that Arabs have nothing better to do than to tear across deserts in robes while swinging fierce swords and yelping like alien creatures.

These notions didn't just occur to my brothers and me magically. We saw Indians in our afternoon cartoons and on some of our favorite Disney movies like *Peter Pan*. We witnessed villainous Arabs thieve their way through violent episodes of *Popeye*.

What is not seen in relation to people of different cultures can be as harmful as some of the things that are seen. People of color are rarely seen as the heroes of animated presentations. I can think of only one Disney classic where

Cartoons are often the birthplace of cultural stereotypes.

a person of color is the principal and heroic character — *The Jungle Book*. Not an impressive list.

Children search for personal identity. In first grade I adored Bonnie Bondell, a girl in my class. She wasn't a cartoon character, but she could have been. She had glossy blonde hair and blue eyes. She had a sparkly smile and a sweet voice. She could have been Cinderella's younger sister or Sleeping Beauty's long lost cousin. For those reasons, I longed to be just like her.

I look at old photos of myself now, and have decided that I was pretty cute. I wasn't a traditional cutie, and that's exactly what bothered me then. My father is African American and my mother is German and Irish. Put the two together and I'm the result. Olive complexion, dark curly hair, brown and green eyes. All wrong. At least according to the "Fairy Tale Book of Standards."

The pride that I had in myself as a person with a colorful heritage did not blossom before it was crushed. The pride that I had in myself as a female was following the same path.

Women's roles in cartoons lack the cleverness and depth of their male counterparts. Instead, they are laced with helplessness and ignorance. The women are often in need of rescue — they seem incapable of defending or helping themselves. When they aren't

busy being rescued, they spend their time looking pretty, waiting for a prince.

In first grade, these illustrations moved me to action. They influenced me to push aside my slacks and rustic bike and turn to dresses and dolls. I had to start practicing perfection if I was going to be happy. Weak, helpless, boring, I struggled to be all of those, then I could call myself a princess, an awkward one, but a princess nonetheless.

At the same time, my brothers swung guns and swords like they were attached to their hands. They tossed aside their piles of books and tubs of clay — heroes didn't read or create — they fought! So they flexed their wiry muscles and wrestled invisible villains. They dressed, ate, talked, became miniature models of their violent heroes.

Sometimes it was fun, like a game, playing our parts. But we began to feel unhappy when we saw that some things weren't quite right. As I said — I wasn't Bonnie Bondell or Cinderella. My brothers, never destined to be hulks, went to great lengths to grow big, but gallons of milk and daily measurements didn't help. It wasn't a game anymore.

I have some fond memories of those afternoons with my brothers, yet I know that I will also remember them for the messages I swallowed as easily as gum drops. My newfound awareness has enabled me to better understand those messages I absorbed and the ones I observe daily, whether on billboards, in movies, or in magazines. I see them in a new light. A critical one. I don't have to be a princess to be happy or pretty. I don't need to rely on characters to learn about real people.

I proudly perceive myself as an exuberant, creative, responsible, open-minded individual who will never be reduced to a carbon copy of a fictional being. ❑

*Lila Johnson wrote this while a senior at Jefferson High School, in Portland, Ore.*

# Math and Media: Bias Busters

### By Bob Peterson

Math, like language, is an essential tool to analyze and address social problems. This is particularly true when helping students critique the mass media for bias. Below are several teaching ideas that can be used in classrooms while integrating math into language arts and social studies.

## Photo Fairness

Fairness and Accuracy in Reporting (FAIR), a media watchdog group based in New York, looked at the front-page photos for one month in three major dailies, the *New York Times, USA Today*, and *Washington Post*, and found that women were dramatically slighted.

Between Aug. 15 and Sept. 15, 1991, FAIR found that in the *Washington Post*, only 13% of the front-page photo subjects were women. In the *New York Times* the percentage was 11%. *USA Today* featured more women (30%), but while 55% of white men seen on *USA Today's* front page were representatives of government or business, not a single woman was in those categories.

People of color in the three papers seemed to fit neat stereotypes. Thirty percent of all men of color in front page photos were athletes; another 14 percent were criminals. All the women of color pictured on the *Washington Post* front page were victims — of fire, poverty or homes destroyed by drugs.

Students can monitor newspapers or magazines in a similar fashion, keeping records in journals and making visual displays on bulletin boards. Math skills of simple computation, averages, percent, and graphing can be utilized. Students could take action against any inequities they might discover by writing to the newspaper and using their findings to teach younger children about the bias they detected.

Material for the above was taken from *Extra!*, — a publication of FAIR, Vol. 4 No. 7.

## Researching Bias in Newspapers

Discovering whose perspective is printed in newspapers is easy, and fun to tabulate. Using different color highlighters, have students mark every time certain people are quoted in the paper. Then analyze results by gender, race, government vs. non-government officials, celebrity status, and other categories of your choosing. For example, how often do newspapers quote grassroots activists opposed to governmental policies, especially on the federal level?

Students can do the same with entire stories. They can outline in one color all those stories about violence and crime, for example, and use another color to outline stories about people working for justice and peace. Similarly, one can highlight how many times people of color are featured in stories of crime or drug-addiction, and how many times they are portrayed positively.

A FAIR study of 2,850 articles in the *Washington Post* and the *New York Times* found that 78% of the stories were primarily based on the words of government officials. Another FAIR study found that only 13% of those quoted in front-page stories in the *Post* were women, and only 6% in the *Times'* front-page stories.

ABSOLUTE HANGOVER.

YOU'LL BE SWINGING WITH THE VERY FINEST, WHEN YOU LIFT YOUR GLASS IN THIS TOAST, FOR IT PROMISES TO ELEVATE YOUR SPIRIT, AS IT SO GENTLY CARESSES YOUR THROAT.

ADBUSTERS

Ten percent of North Americans are alcoholics. Nearly half of all automobile deaths are alcohol related. A teenager sees 100,000 alcohol ads before reaching legal drinking age. Above, consumer awareness poster by Adbusters.

UNPLUG, 360 Grand Ave., P.O. Box 385, Oakland, CA 94610. (510) 268-1100. Advocacy group opposing commercialism in education.

Center for Media Literacy, 1962 S. Shenandoah St., Los Angeles, CA 90034. Extensive catalog of critical media materials including curriculums promoting general analysis of advertising and others with a special emphasis on alcohol and tobacco ads.

ADBUSTERS, The Media Foundation, 1243 W. 7th Ave., Vancouver, BC V6H 1B7. (800) 663-1243. Journal aiming to "clean up advertising and consumerism's polluting effects on the mental and physical environment."

Center for Study of Commercialism, 1875 Connecticut Ave. NW, Suite 300, Washington, DC 20009. (202) 332-9110. National lobby and advocacy group promoting public and consumer interests in media.

Educational Video Center, 60 E. 13th St., New York, NY 10003. (212) 254-2848. Media project that trains and empowers young people to use media creatively. Student-made videos.

Project Censored, Sonoma State University, Rohnert Park, CA 94928. (707) 664-2500. Publishes a yearly list of unreported and under-reported stories of importance. Also co-published with Carl Jensen *Censored: The News that Didn't Make the News — and Why* (New York: Four Walls and Eight Windows, 1994). An extremely useful resource to engage students in thinking about the politics of daily papers and the nightly news. Much of the book can be used with students. (Write the publisher at 39 West 14th St., #503, New York, NY 10011.)

FAIR (Fairness and Accuracy in Reporting), 130 W. 25th St., New York, NY 10001. (212) 633-6700. Well-documented reports on media bias and imbalance. Publication *EXTRA!*, $30 for six issues plus 6 issues of *EXTRA! Update* newsletter. ❑

## Charting the Bias in Encyclopedias — CD ROMs and Book Sets

CD ROM encyclopedias are useful for student research, but are no less biased than the book-set encyclopedias they are based upon. When my fifth graders were studying famous people, for instance, two girls were concerned that the selection for Thomas Edison was much longer than that for Harriet Tubman. This led to a class project in which the children kept data on the length of the selections for many famous people, based on their gender, and race. After looking at about 40 people, the students calculated the average length of the entries according to race and gender. They then tabulated the results in a bar graph and wrote letters of protest to the software company that produced the CD ROM encyclopedia.

## Bias Detectors in the School Library

Teachers can also use the school library as the basis for anti-bias projects. One easy project is for children to analyze all the biographies in the school library on the basis of gender, race, class, or disability. They can then categorize them and use percentages and fractions to describe the collection. Working jointly with the librarian, school administration, and the PTA, the students might try to encourage a more diverse collection of books. ❑

# What Do We Say When We Hear 'Faggot'?

## By Lenore Gordon

Alice is eleven. She walks down the school halls with her arm around her best friend, Susan. During lunch, they sit on the floor holding hands or combing each other's hair. Lately, Alice has been called "dyke," and boys have been told not to be her friend.

Brian refuses to take part in a fight on his block. As he makes his way home, he hears cries of "faggot" and "sissy." Suddenly he begins to run, realizing that the other children may now attack him.

Carl is gifted musically; he would like to join the elementary school chorus. Although he hesitates for several weeks, the music teacher persuades him to join. One morning soon after, he enters the classroom tense and angry after chorus, muttering that several boys have called him "gay."

Some children play a "game" called "Smear the Queer," in which one child suddenly attacks another, knocking him to the ground. The attacker shouts "Fag!" and then runs away.

Homophobic name-calling is pervasive. Even first graders are now using such terms as "faggot" to ridicule others, and such name-calling is increasingly common in the older grades. Homophobic name-calling is devastating to young people experiencing homosexual feelings. For youngsters who are not gay, such name-calling creates or reinforces hostility towards the gay and lesbian population. And it forces all children to follow strict sex-role behaviors to avoid ridicule.

Because homosexuality is such a charged issue, teachers rarely confront children who use homophobic name-calling to humiliate and infuriate other children. Many teachers do not realize that this sort of name-calling can be dealt with in much the same way as other kinds of bigotry and stereotyping.

Teaching children to be critical of oppression is teaching true morality, and teachers have the right, indeed the obligation, to alert their students to all forms of oppression. Educating children not to be homophobic is one way to show the difference between oppressive and non-oppressive behavior.

Challenging homophobic name-calling by teaching children non-judgmental facts about homosexuality and by correcting myths is also intrinsically connected to anti-sexist educational values, since homophobia is used to reinforce rigid sex roles. Furthermore, if adults criticize other forms of name calling but ignore anti-gay remarks, children are quick to conclude that homophobia is acceptable.

Boys are far more likely to be the object of homophobic name-calling than girls, perhaps because sex roles for boys remain, to some extent, more rigidly defined. A boy involved in a traditional "female-only" activity such as sewing or cooking risks out-and-out contempt from his peers, as well as the possibility of being called "faggot" or "sissy." Girls are more able to partici-

> **Because homosexuality is such a charged issue, teachers rarely confront children who use homophobic name-calling to humiliate and infuriate others.**

pate in activities that have traditionally been for boys, such as sports or shop, without loss of peer approval.

At the late elementary and junior high school levels, physical affection between girls is far more acceptable than between boys, but a girl will be called a "dyke" if she does not express, by junior high, a real interest in pleasing boys or in participating with other girls in boy-centered discussions.

As an elementary school teacher, I have made an awareness of oppression and of the concept of "majority" and "minority" a focus of current events, history, and social studies. Throughout the year we discuss those who are not in the majority in this country: Native Americans, Puerto Ricans, Blacks, Chicanos, disabled people, older people, and many others. We also discuss women, a generally powerless majority.

If oppression is being discussed, it is impossible to ignore lesbians and gay men as a group that faces discrimination. Children in the middle grades have a strong sense of justice, and they can understand the basic injustice of people being abused because they are different from the majority. They can also identify with the powerlessness of oppressed groups because children themselves are often a verbally and sometimes a physically abused group.

### Types of Name-calling

When initiating a discussion of name-calling, teachers can explain that there are two kinds of name-calling. One kind of name-calling, unrelated to any particular group, is often scatological or sexual (i.e., the four-letter words). The other is group-biased; it uses the name of a group — "nigger," "chink," "polack," etc. — as the insult and implies that there is something wrong with being a member of that group.

Group-biased name-calling can be handled in a variety of ways. Sometimes children do not truly understand why a word is offensive. If a teacher simply takes the time to tell the class that a particular word insults or demeans a group of people, children will often stop using the word. (Occasionally, children do not even know what a term means. One New York City ten-year-old who frequently called others "faggot" told me that the word meant "female dog." A twelve-year-old said that a lesbian is a "Spanish Jew.")

Discussions about the meaning of homophobic words can often be quite consciousness-raising. When I hear a child use the word faggot, I explain that a "faggot," literally, is a stick used for kindling. I also explain that gay people used to be burned in medieval times simply for being gay, and they had to wear a bundle of sticks on their shirts to indicate that they were about to be burned. (At times, gay men were used as the kindling to burn women accused of witchcraft.) After the discussion that ensues from this revelation, I make it clear to my students that the word is not to be used again in my classroom, and it rarely is.

When I talk about the words "lesbian" and "gay men," there is always a stir of discomfort, so I ask what those words mean. I am also usually told that a gay man is an "effeminate" man. We discuss the stereotyping inherent in that myth, as well as the fact that "effeminate" means "behaving like a woman," and the class begins to realize that "behaving like a woman" is viewed negatively.

When asked what it really means to be called a "faggot" and why it is insulting for a boy to be called "gay," students will often respond that saying a boy is like a girl is the worst insult imaginable. At this point, girls are likely to sense that something unjust has been touched upon, and they will often take up their own defense, while simultaneously having their own consciousness raised.

Before we go on with the lesson plan, I usually attempt to reach a consensus on definitions. Here are some that have seemed acceptable: "Someone who loves someone of the same sex, but can be close to people of the opposite sex if they want to" and "Someone who romantically loves someone of the same sex." We added the word "romantically" in one class after a boy commented in a confused tone, "But I love my father ..." When discussing definitions, it is important to tell children that gays and lesbians are as different from one another as are heterosexual men and women. There is no such thing as a "typical" lesbian or gay man.

## Imagining Names

When we continue with the lesson plan and students are asked to imagine being called names as they walk with a close friend of the same sex, they describe feeling "different," "dumb," "weird," "afraid," and "embarrassed." (One very different response was, "I'd feel loved, because the main thing would be walking with someone I loved.") When asked how they would feel as one of the name-callers, children usually admit that they "would feel like part of the group."

Suggested responses to homophobic attacks have included, "It's my choice," "We like each other, and for your information, we're not homosexual," "I'm not ashamed," "I'm just as different as you are," "I don't care," and "So what!"

I have also used the music of Holly Near to teach about oppression. Songs are an effective tool in reaching children, who seem to retain information presented in this mode quite easily. Near sings about the oppression of many different groups and her songs help students make linkages between their struggles.

Another way to combat homophobia — particularly for older students — is to invite a speaker from a gay organization to talk to the class. Listening to a gay or lesbian who is also a living, breathing human being — someone who has parents, siblings, and looks a little nervous in front of a group — is often a decisive factor in breaking down homophobic stereotypes.

> Teachers have the obligation to alert students to all forms of oppression.

Homophobic attitudes can also be countered in discussions about sex roles. Students can be asked, "What does a boy have to do to 'act like a girl?'" (and vice versa). The stereotypic behaviors that are mentioned can usually be quickly discounted by asking children to consider their own home lives. Many children, particularly those with single or divorced parents, have seen their mothers working and their fathers cleaning the house.

Another classroom activity is to ask students to look in any standard dictionary or thesaurus for the definitions of "male" and "female," "masculine" and "feminine," "husband," "wife," etc. The definitions are often so blatantly offensive and stereotypic that they create a small sensation when read aloud, thus challenging children to rethink their own definitions.

Discussing homophobic concepts is one thing; enduring homophobic name-calling is an entirely different matter. The pressure to conform is especially overwhelming within the school/peer structure, and it is vital that teachers try to instill the courage needed to function independently when one is the object of ridicule.

I attempt to teach my students to be willing to defend not only their own rights but the rights of others. Because name-calling is so common among children, and because it embodies the bigotry learned from adults, it is a good place for educators to begin. □

*Lenore Gordon is a writer from the New York area.*

This article is adapted from *The Bulletin* of the Council on Interracial Books for Children, Vol. 14, Nos. 3 & 4.

# The Organic Goodie Simulation

## By Bill Bigelow and Norm Diamond

This activity is about power. Set in an imaginary society, it poses students a challenge: Can you overcome divisions and unite to create needed changes? If so, what circumstances encouraged this unity? If not, why not? Unfortunately, these days many students are cynical about their capacity to work together — for a better school, a better community, a better society. Without confronting that cynicism, students run the risk of dismissing much of the history from which they could draw hope for the future. This lesson lets them experience some of the pressures that lead workers to organize. Depending on what happens in class, students either glimpse the possibility of organizing and practice overcoming cynicism, or gain an experience out of which their attitudes can be directly discussed. It's also a lot of fun.

### Grade Level:
Middle school to adult

### Materials Needed:
One large machine-like object, e.g., a TV or an overhead projector.

### Time Required:
One class period (at least 45 minutes) to "play," and time for a follow-up discussion.

### Procedure:
1. Close the door and pull the blinds in the classroom. Tell students to imagine that we are going to have to live in this classroom for the rest of our lives (many groans). Explain that there is no soil for farming but we are in luck because we have a machine that produces food — organic goodies. Correct yourself, and point out that actually *you* own the machine. Put the projector or whatever machine you've selected in the front of the classroom.

2. Tell students that you need people to work for you producing organic goodies. Workers will receive money to buy enough food to live on — those not working will find it hard to survive. Ask for volunteers who want to work, eat, and survive. (On those occasions when additional coercion is necessary, we tell students that to receive credit for the activity they must not starve.) Choose only half the class as workers. The other half will be unemployed. Sit the two on opposite sides of the room, one group facing the other.

3. Now explain the economics of your society. Put the "Organic Goodie Economy" chart (see below) on the board. (You might want to have the chart up earlier, covered with a map or a screen.)

Explain that five organic goodies a day are necessary to survive in a fairly healthy manner. Those receiving less, the non-workers, will gradually get sick and starve. Go over the chart with students: Each worker *produces* eleven (11) goodies a day. All workers are *paid* $6.00 a day. A goodie costs $1. One dollar is deducted from the pay of each worker to make small welfare payments to the unemployed. So, after taxes, a worker can buy five goodies a day, enough to survive. Explain that as the owner, you of course deserve more because it's your machine, and without your machine everyone would starve.

4. Show the unemployed that, as the chart indicates, they only receive $2 a day in welfare payments. This means they can only buy two goodies a day

## Organic Goodie Economy

Production = 11 x number of workers

| | Workers | Unemployed | Owner |
|---|---|---|---|
| | | Per Day | |
| Wages | $6 x no. workers | Nothing | Nothing |
| Taxes | -$1 x no. workers | +$2 x no. unemployed | -$1 x no. unemployed (see note) |
| Consumption | 5 Organic Goodies x no. workers | 2 x no. unemployed | 6 Organic Goodies |
| Surplus | Nothing | Nothing | 4 x no. workers, minus 6 for daily consumption |

*Example*: If there were 10 workers and 10 unemployed, a total of 110 goodies would be produced. After taxes, the workers would be able to consume 50. From welfare payments, the unemployed would consume 20, leaving a total of 40 for the owner — 34 after consuming his or her six.

*Note*: Workers' and owner's tax needs to provide $2 to each unemployed person (taxes paid in Goodies).

— they are slowly starving to death. They desperately need work.

5. Make sure each student understands his/her position. Now the "game" begins. Your goal is to increase your profits — that's all you're after. The way you can do this is through cutting wages. *Note:* No money or goodies are actually exchanged. We generally begin by telling students to imagine that a number of weeks have elapsed and then ask members of each group how they have been eating, how they're feeling. (By the way, everyone *could* be employed to produce goodies — eleven a day, as mentioned — but we don't tell that to students unless they ask.)

6. There is no "correct" order in which to proceed, but here are some techniques that have worked for us:

• Ask which of the unemployed people wants to work. Offer someone $5.50 a day — less than other workers but more than the $2 they're getting now in welfare payments. After you have a taker, go to the workers and ask who is willing to accept $5.50. Fire the first person who refuses to accept the lower wage and send him or her across the room to sit with the unemployed. Hire the unemployed person who was willing to accept the lower wage. Continue this procedure, trying to drive down wages.

• Occasionally you might ask workers to repeat after you, "I am a happy worker." Fire those who refuse and hire someone who is unemployed.

• We often make derogatory comments about the "welfare bums" and invite workers to do the same. (Later we can talk about why the people were on welfare, and who was the real bum.)

• Anyone who mentions "union" or striking or anything disruptive should be fired immediately. Get all workers to sign "yellow dog" contracts promising never to join a union as long as they work for you.

FRED WRIGHT/UE NEWS

• Sometimes we hire a foreman (a spy), for a little more money, who will turn in "subversive" workers. Occasionally we whisper something in a worker's ear, to encourage suspicion and division among workers. Someone usually threatens to take over the machine. When this happens we hire a policeman or two to protect it. We explain that she or he is here to protect "all our property equally, not just my machine." Having someone physically protect the machine also alerts students to the fact that they could take it over.

• It's important to keep workers and unemployed from uniting to strike, or worse, to take control of your machine. You can offer privileges to people to prevent them from seeing their common interests — differential wages, shorter work days, perhaps even profit sharing.

• If they are successful in uniting and stopping production, you have a couple of options: 1. You can wait them out, indicating your surplus, and how quickly they will starve (use the chart to remind them how much you have left over everyday); or 2. Give in to their wage demands and a little later raise the price of organic goodies. After all, you can justify your need for more income to meet your higher costs.

• Sometimes we announce that every three minutes an unemployed person will die of starvation. This emphasizes to the entire class that should they fail to act there will be consequences.

7. The game is unpredictable, and a range of things has happened while playing it. What *always* happens, how-

ever, is that people try to get organized. The game ends when students have had ample opportunity to get together — successfully or otherwise. Participants may be totally demoralized or they may have taken over the machine and decided to run it collectively.

8. For homework, we ask students to write on the experience. Questions might include: What did you personally do to try to stop my efforts to divide people? How effective were you? Were there actions you considered, but didn't take? Why not? If we were to do this simulation again, what different actions would you take? We also ask students to comment on the Fred Wright cartoon, and how it relates to our activity.

Additional discussion and/or writing questions include:
• What methods did I use to try to keep people from getting together to oppose me? When was I successful? When unsuccessful?

• At which points were you most successful in getting together? When were you least successful?

• What kept you from immediately calling a meeting and demanding equal treatment, or simply walking over to the machine and taking it over? Here we try to get at students' preconceptions about people's capacity to stick together. Did they think that efforts to unite all workers and unemployed would eventually be betrayed? Why? We want to explore with students what in their lives would leave them hopeful or skeptical. Have they had experiences that convinced them that people could unite and act together for important goals?

• As the owner, what kind of attitudes would I want you to have about your ability to work together as a unified group? What attitude would I want you to have about property rights? About respect for authority?

As a follow up activity, sometimes we ask students to think of a time in their lives when they were able to work successfully with others toward a common objective. We ask them to write this up as a story. We then share our stories in class and take notes on the circumstances that allow people to unite — creating what we call a "collective text," the wisdom we can draw from each other's lives.

Does all this sound too complicated? It's not. A number of teachers have told us, "I didn't want to do that activity because I wasn't sure I could remember everything, and I didn't know if it would work." As they discover: It works. ❏

*Bill Bigelow (bbpdx@aol.com) teaches at Franklin High School in Portland, Oregon and is a* Rethinking Schools *editor. Norm Diamond was editor of the* Portland Alliance.

This article is adapted from Bigelow and Diamond's *The Power in Our Hands: A Curriculum on the History of Work and Workers in the United States* (Monthly Review Press, 1988) available from "Teaching for Change, 800-763-9131, www.teachingforchange.org. ($18 plus postage.) The inspiration for this lesson came from Mike Messner's article, "Bubblegum and Surplus Value," *The Insurgent Sociologist,* 6 #4 (Summer 1976): 51-56.

This article is reprinted by permission of Monthly Review Foundation.

# Questions From A Worker Who Reads

By Bertolt Brecht


Who built Thebes of the seven gates?
In the books you will find the names of kings.
Did the kings haul up the lumps of rock?
And Babylon, many times demolished
Who raised it up so many times? In what houses
Of gold-glittering Lima did the builders live?
Where, the evening that the Wall of China was finished,
Did the masons go? Great Rome
Is full of triumphal arches. Who erected them? Over whom
Did the Caesars triumph? Had Byzantium, much praised in song
Only palaces for its inhabitants? Even in fabled Atlantis,
The night the ocean engulfed it
The drowning still bawled for their slaves.

The young Alexander conquered India.
Was he alone?
Caesar beat the Gauls.
Did he not have even a cook with him?
Philip of Spain wept when his armada
Went down. Was he the only one to weep?
Frederick the Second won the Seven Years' War. Who
Else won it?

Every page a victory.
Who cooked the feast for the victors?
Every ten years a great man.
Who paid the bill?

So many reports.
So many questions.

Bertolt Brecht (1898-1956) was a major German playwright and poet known for his uncompromising anti-Nazism and his support of workers' struggles. (See p. 184 for lesson ideas.)

# Poverty and World Resources

## by Susan Hersh and Bob Peterson

Media stories of street children in Brazil, war-ravaged lives of children in Bosnia, and starving kids in Sudan occasionally give students in North America a glimpse of the ways many children live in other parts of the world. Such news reports are possible starting places for increasing students' understanding of global inequity and the need for justice. At times we will take a particularly poignant photo and make a transparency of it to use it as a trigger for discussion in our fifth grade classes.

Invariably the question kids ask is, "Why?" "Why don't the people in Sudan have enough food or water?" "Why are there so many street children in Latin America?" And most news reports or student newsweeklies offer shallow answers that rarely go beyond famine, drought, and war.

Schools need to help them understand the basic divisions between rich and poor in the world, and the reasons behind such inequity. Key terms include: resources, GNP, wealth, distribution, income, power, and colonialism.

Hunger may be a good place to start addressing the issue of world poverty, but it's important that even the youngest children have the issue placed in broader contexts. One way to help upper elementary and secondary students understand the unequal distribution of people and wealth is an activity that combines math, geography, writing, and social studies.

Depending on the sophistication of the students, this activity can be more or less teacher directed, with either the teacher providing most of the information or having the students take the data and arrange themselves accordingly.

### Procedure

*Materials:*

• 11x17 inch maps for each student or pair of students to write on

• 50 chips (25 of one color, and 25 of another) for each map

• 25 slips of paper with "I was born in [name of continent, based on chart]"

• 25 chocolate chip cookies

• playground map, or signs with names of continents and yarn to distinguish boundaries

• transparency of resource chart

• writing paper

*Implementation:*

• Give each student or pair of students a world map. Have them identify the continents and other places that you may have been studying.

• Ask students how many people they think are in the world. After students have guessed, show them an almanac with the current estimate. Ask: If we represent all the people in the world with 25 chips, how many people is each chip worth? (Each chip represents approximately 200 million people.)

• Give 25 chips to each student/

From a commercial on over-consumption, produced by the Media Foundation.

*ADBUSTERS*

## World Population and Wealth by Continent

| Continent | Population | | | Wealth | | |
|---|---|---|---|---|---|---|
| | (in billions) 1992 | % of world | # in class of 25 | per capita GNP in U.S. $ | % of world | # of treats out of 25 |
| Africa | .682 | 12.5% | 3 | 630 | 3 | 1 |
| Asia* | 3.334 | 61.0% | 17 | 1,680 | 22 | 5 |
| Australia | .027 | 0.5% | | 3,380 | 0.4 | 0 |
| Europe* | .695 | 13.0% | 3 | 12,990 | 39 | 10 |
| N. America | .283 | 5.0% | 1 | 21,580 | 30 | 7 |
| S. America | .458 | 8.0% | 2 | 2,170 | 6 | 2 |
| World Total | 5.479 | 100.0% | 25 | ———— | 100 | 25 |

Sources: Population figures are from the United Nations Population Fund, *The State of World Population 1993*, quoted in the *Universal Almanac, 1994*. GNP figures are from the World Bank, quoted in the *Universal Almanac, 1994*. GNP is defined as the total national output of goods and services. Percentage of world wealth is an estimate based on total GNP. (Not shown in the graph.)

* **Note:** The figures for Europe and Asia are estimates because the available data segregates data from the USSR. For purposes of this lesson the authors folded the figures from the former USSR into Europe and Asia based on a 2 to 1 ratio.

group and have them distribute them by continent where they think people live. Discuss student estimates and then tell them the accurate figures. Have them rearrange their chips to reflect the facts. Ask students to draw conclusions based on their differing stacks of chips.

• Explain to the students that you are now going to give them another 25 chips of a different color and that they represent all the wealth produced in the world. (The worth of all the goods and services produced every year — from health care to automobiles.) Tell them to put the chips on the continents to indicate their estimate of who gets this wealth. (Each chip represents 1/25 of the world's total amount of goods and services produced.)

• Discuss student estimates and record them on the chalkboard. Have students reflect on the size of the two different stacks of chips, population and resources. Collect the chips.

• Tell the students you are going to demonstrate how population and wealth are distributed by continent. Have each student pick a slip of paper from a container. (The "I was born ..." slips) They may not trade what continent they are from. (As you distribute the slips listen for any stereotypical reactions to the continents — these will indicate possibilities for future lessons.)

• Have students go to an area in the room that you have designated to represent that continent. (Playground maps work great for this!) After the students are in their areas, remind them that they each represent about 200 million people and that you are going to distribute the world's riches.

• Use a popular treat — rice crispy bars or chocolate chip cookies — and distribute them according to the percentages given in the chart. Announce the number of treats you are giving to each continent as you do so. Allow students to divide their share within the group. Don't encourage intra-group sharing, but don't forbid it.

• Ask each continental group to write down what they think of the wealth distribution.

• Bring the students back together and discuss their feelings. Have a report-back from the continents and individuals. Show students the information from the chart via a transparency or handout. Connect their emotions and feelings of fairness to the information on the chart.

• Some questions worth posing if the students don't ask them themselves:

"How did the distribution of wealth get to be so unequal?"

"Who do you think decides how wealth is distributed?"

"Should wealth be distributed equally?"

"Do you think that within a particular continent the wealth is distributed fairly?"

"How does the unequal distribution of wealth affect the power that groups of people hold?"

"Within our community is wealth distributed fairly?"

"What can be done about the unequal way wealth is distributed?"

"Who can we talk with to find out more information about these matters?"

• After the discussion, have students write an essay about their feelings, what they learned, and what they might want to do about world poverty.

• Students can do follow-up research on related topics, such as: the role colonialism played in the wealth disparity; how current policies of U.S. corporations and the U.S. government are affecting people in the poorer nations; the role government taxes and budgets play in distributing resources, and what different organizations and politicians are doing about world poverty. (See Resources section, pp. 183-201, for lists of groups and curricula for additional information.) ❑

*Susan Hersh developed this lesson while teaching 5th graders at La Escuela Fratney in Milwaukee, Wis.*
*Bob Peterson teaches 5th grade at La Escuela Fratney. He is an editor of Rethinking Schools.*

# Math, Equity, and Economics

*Using mathematics to look at economic realities of our communities can bring math alive for students and help them better understand social problems. There are many ways to use math to look at economics. One of the best is to survey local and national print media for statistics. Below is a sampling of data, with possible teaching ideas.*

## Unequal Earnings

Use the information to the right to have students figure the difference between categories. Have students make their own graphs using the data. Have students present this information to their families and members of the community and survey people as to why they think there are these inequities.

1. Elicit students' reactions to the wage data in the graph by asking: "How do these statistics make you feel?"

2. Ask students to list "hypotheses," possible explanations, for the dramatic inequality in earnings. Which of these seem most reasonable? How could we go about testing these hypotheses? Who could we interview? What historical information would we want to know?

3. How might these economic realities contribute to hostility between different racial groups? ❐

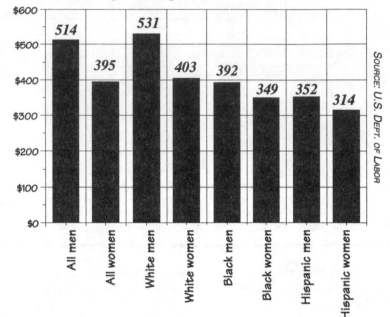

**Median Weekly Earnings of Full-Time Workers in 1993**

| | |
|---|---|
| All men | 514 |
| All women | 395 |
| White men | 531 |
| White women | 403 |
| Black men | 392 |
| Black women | 349 |
| Hispanic men | 352 |
| Hispanic women | 314 |

SOURCE: U.S. DEPT. OF LABOR

## Low Earnings

One in five full-time workers has low annual earnings, according to the U.S. Census Bureau. "Low earnings" are defined as annual earnings below the poverty level for a 4-person family with two children.

About 18% of the nation's 81 million year-round full-time workers earned less than $13,091 in 1992 — a 50% increase in the number of people with low earnings in 1979. Women are more likely than men to have low earnings. In 1992, 24% of all full-time women workers had low earnings, while 14% of men had low earnings.

Students might interview family and community members in order to estimate how much it costs a family of four to live, and compare the cost to the income of low-earnings workers. Basic services such as housing, child care, education, medical care, transportation, and food can be calculated.

For more information contact the U.S. Census Bureau Customer Services Office at (301) 763-4100. ❐

# Government Budgets

Local, state, and federal budgets are key factors in the quality of life for our communities. Unfortunately, they are usually complex and hard for even adults to understand. Nonetheless, with some coaching from teachers and the right materials, students can analyze such budgets, and see how they affect their lives. Teachers and students can get information on budgets from their elected officials or citizens' groups.

Some on the national level include:

• National Priorities Project, Inc., 160 Main St., Suite 6, Northampton, MA 01060. (413) 584-9556.

• Center for Defense Information, 1500 Massachusetts Ave. NW, Washington, DC 20036. (202) 862-0700.

• Friends Committee on National Legislation, 245 2nd St. NE, Washington, DC 20002. (202) 547-6000.

• Friends of the Earth, 218 D St. SE, Washington, DC 20003. (202) 544-2600.

• Children's Defense Fund, 25 E St. NW, Washington, DC 20001. (202) 628-8787.

• Citizens for Tax Justice, 1311 L St. NW, Suite 400, Washington, DC 20005. (202) 626-3780. ❐

# Inequalities of Wealth

Wealth is different than income. Income is the amount of money that comes into a household from varying sources during the course of the year. Wealth, on the other hand, is the monetary value (minus debt) of what a household owns: consumer durables (houses, cars, stereos, etc.) plus financial assets (stocks, bonds, savings accounts, property, life insurances, etc.). For most Americans the majority of their wealth comes from the equity value of their homes.

The distribution of wealth is less equal than income. As the figure shows, the 9% of the population worth more than $250,000 holds almost one-half the net wealth of this nation. If one were to focus solely on financial assets, the picture would be more skewed: in a study by the Fed-eral Reserve Board, fully 55% of all American households had no net financial assets. By contrast, the top 2% of wealth holders owned 54% of the country's financial assets; the top 10% owned 86%.

Questions that can be asked include: "What problems in our country would be eliminated or reduced if wealth were distributed more equally?"

A class project could have the students interviewing family and friends about their understanding of the concentration of wealth in this society. What is that understanding based on? ☐

The above information is taken from *Social Stratification in the United States,* by Stephen Rose (New York: New Press, 1992). Special thanks to the magazine *Dollars and Sense* for their help.

SOURCE: SOCIAL STRATIFICATION IN THE UNITED STATES

### Distribution of Wealth by Wealth Holdings, 1988 in The United States of America

| Net Worth in $ | Population Share | Wealth Share |
|---|---|---|
| Negative | 11.1% | -0.6% |
| $0-5,000 | 15.1 | 0.3 |
| $5-10,000 | 6.2 | 0.5 |
| $10-25,000 | 11.5 | 2.1 |
| $25-50,000 | 13.0 | 5.2 |
| $50-100,000 | 16.7 | 13.1 |
| $100-250,000 | 17.5 | 30.0 |
| $250-500,000 | 6.0 | 22.2 |
| Over $500,000 | 2.8 | 27.2 |

# Job Gap

In most cities either a non-profit or governmental agency monitors the "job gap" — the gap between the number of those expected to work and the number of jobs available. Such statistics are a useful classroom tool.

In Milwaukee, for instance, the number of potential job seekers in January of 1994 was 44,540 while the number of jobs available was 5,212. Have students contact government or non-profit agencies agencies to find the job gap in your city or state.

Discussion questions include: What impact might such figures have on proposals to abolish welfare? How could a community generate those jobs that are necessary for full employment? Students could interview unemployed people, government officials, business people, and labor leaders to see what they think might be done to overcome the job gap.

**Additional questions**

• When there are so many unemployed people competing for so few jobs, how does this make people feel towards each other?

• How do employers take advantage of high unemployment to keep wages low? (See Organic Goodie Simulation, p. 88.) ☐

# Taking the Offensive Against Offensive Toys

### By Lenore Gordon

Inspired by an article from the Council on Interracial Books for Children, I took up the issue of biased toy packaging with my fifth grade class.

At the time I was teaching in a small private school in Brooklyn, N.Y. The class was racially mixed, with an equal number of boys and girls. Economically, students ranged from lower middle-class to upper middle-class, with a large number living with single working mothers.

Their consciousness about racism and sexism had been raised through studies of Native Americans, working people at their jobs and, on occasion, television commercials. Discussion of Studs Terkel's book *Working* had given them some insight into class issues. This had been furthered by their own interviews with working people.

Thus the group was primed for action when I brought up toys and the political implications of their packaging. Some of the questions I asked to stimulate this discussion included: If you're a boy, what kinds of presents have you gotten on holidays? What do people expect you to be like? What have girls gotten as presents? What are you expected to be like? How many girls have wanted trucks? How many boys have wanted dolls? Tell me about the TV commercials you've seen. What kinds of kids are they about?

The first products the children discussed were sneakers and jeans. When one child noted, "You wear Jordache and Pumas if you're poor;" other students added: "It's because of status;" "It's the only way to show you have something." Status, said one student, means "belonging — it means you're part of the group."

The students then discussed the manipulative techniques of corporations, including how advertisements try to make consumers think they need a product even if they can't afford it or how they make people think they have to "belong" to a larger group.

By the end of our discussion, we had begun to plan our next step: a visit to a local branch of the Toys-R-Us chain.

We created a checklist and I suggested that each child carry a clipboard with a copy. The list had such items as: Describe the picture on the package. Is it racist? Why? Is it sexist? Why? Is it classist? Why? What does the toy cost? Is it sturdy? Are people of color shown in the picture on the package? Is it a stereotypic picture? Do the kids on the package look real?

They were also asked to note the name of a toy, its manufacturer, and the firm's address.

When we arrived at the store, the students set to work enthusiastically. Some of the products they found to be the guiltiest were, of course, the kitchen toys (with pictures of little white girls), most science toys (only boys shown experimenting) and the sports equipment. I also found that although girls were being increasingly included on previously male-designated toys, the issue of racist packaging was barely being addressed.

When we returned to school, we discussed what we had seen and analyzed the students' checklists. Reporting on their experiences, they spoke of the noticeable absence of African Americans.

As part of this examination of toy packaging, I encouraged students to share their complaints with toy manufacturers. Following are samples from two of the letters written by the children.

"Dear Kenner:

"Your product, the X-Ray Stretch, is racist and sexist because your toy only has whites on the toy but no Blacks. The toy is sexist because there's a boy in it but not a girl. I advise you to change the appearance of this toy."

"Dear H-G Industries:

"One of your products [an archery set] is very badly stereotyped of a Native American. The facepaint, headdress and clothes are all stereotyped. Another thing, your toy is so badly built everything in the package is warped, so get it together and put together your toy."

The project helped make the children more aware of negative corporate mentality. They also felt more capable of judging that mentality and of identifying the tactics of some of the manufacturers. It is hoped they will be able to recognize similar tactics in other sectors of society.

Most important, they have become children who are less gullible targets of corporate advertising. ❑

*Lenore Gordon is a writer in the New York area.*

This article is adapted from *The Bulletin of the Council on Interracial Books for Children*, Vol. 12, #6.

> **We planned our next step: a visit to Toys-R-Us.**

# Forgiving My Father

By Justin Morris

I'd like to forgive you father,
but I don't know your heart.
Your face,
is it a mirror image of mine?

I'd like to forgive you father,
but I find your absence a fire
that your face might be able to extinguish.
I'd like to forgive you father, but my last name isn't
the same as yours
like it's supposed to be.
You rejected me, dad,
but can I sympathize for your ignorance?
For all the birthdays
you didn't send me a card,
for the Christmases
when I'd wake up,
and you weren't sitting by the tree waiting for me.
What about the summer nights
where prospects of you began to fade?
Fade like you did seventeen years go.
Out of my life.

I'd like to forgive you father,
but I don't know you.
And for that
I hate you.

Justin Morris is a student at Jefferson High School in Portland, Oregon.
(See p. 184 for teaching ideas.)

# The Day Sondra Took Over

## By Cynthia M. Ellwood

"If you write that big, you're never gonna be able to get them all up there," said Sondra, voicing her third critique of my teaching in five minutes. With that, I deposited the chalk in her hand.

"Take over," I said.

"Oh, my fault, Ms. Ellwood," she apologized.

"No, really, go for it. I want you to."

She looked doubtful, not sure whether she was being admonished.

"Try it. I think you'd be great."

After a minute or so of this back-and-forth, Sondra stood up, and I moved to a seat near the back of the room.

We had just read "Little Things are Big," by Jesús Colón, in my fifth hour American Ethnic Literature class. (See p. 102.) Set in New York during the 1950s, the short story is about a young, black Puerto Rican fighting an internal battle as he tries to decide whether he should offer to help a white woman loaded with luggage and children as she disembarks from the subway. "Courtesy is a characteristic of the Puerto Rican," the protagonist reports. "And here I was — a Puerto Rican — hours past midnight, a valise, two white children, and a white lady with a baby on her arm palpably needing someone to help her at least until she descended the long, concrete stairs." But he holds back, afraid that this white woman might misinterpret the intentions of a black man approaching her in a deserted subway so late at night. Later he is tortured by his choice: "I failed myself to myself," he muses. He vows that if he ever again faces such a situation, he will offer aid no matter how it may be received.

I asked each student to write down three questions for discussion and had just begun to list their questions on the board under two categories: "plot/fact questions" and "thought/opinion questions," when I handed Sondra the chalk.

Once up, Sondra took firm command of the class. She abandoned my approach. "Anthony, just tell me your best question," she said. Then rather than putting it on the board, she posed it to the class for immediate discussion. When it seemed as if a topic had been plumbed, she moved to the next student and asked again only for that student's best question. Whenever I tried to direct things, or other students tried to intervene, Sondra said firmly, "This is my class." She refused to recognize me unless I raised my hand like everyone else. At one point, when I forgot and simply spoke out my opinion, she did such a magnificent job of ignoring me that Ernesto took pity: "That's okay, Ms. Ellwood. Tell me what you want to say, and I'll say it," he offered magnanimously.

It was a fine discussion. We talked about what the author meant to convey, how the characters must have felt, whether it could happen today, where racism comes from, and both the obvious and subtle ways racial prejudice still affects our lives. We struggled with some tough questions. One student said he could do anything if he tried hard

> **How do students maintain hope if they see the world as troubled and even systematically unfair?**

enough, so racism wasn't an issue. "Well, you're just blaming a person that doesn't make it, then, just saying they didn't try hard enough when it might be because of racism," another countered. We agreed that it was important to believe in yourself and never give up. But we also agreed that inequality was real. Were these ideas contradictory? The students didn't reach consensus on that one, but I think we had a chance to talk and think hard about an issue that struck a deep chord.

As I listened and participated, I also learned. I was reminded that my students must hold fiercely to the conviction that they can "make it." The easy money of drug sales, the instant power of gang affiliation, the adoring neediness of a new baby are not trivial temptations if a young person — impatient to "become someone" as most teenagers are — has trouble believing the American dream. I've always tried to present them with examples of people who strove for their dreams, who acted heroically in everyday life, who fought oppression and pursued high ideals individually and collectively.

I've also encouraged students to critically examine our world and the problems we confront. Yet, while I'd always thought of this social critique as empowering, I realized as I listened to the discussion that day that for some of my students, such analysis might be feeding feelings of hopelessness and despair. The connection I made that day (or rather my students made for me) was subtle but important. In the future I'll try to confront this tension more directly: How do you maintain hope if you see the world as troubled and even systematically unfair? I'll be more careful to match our analysis of problems with an immediate exploration of the large and small steps people can take, and are taking, toward their solution.

That Monday in April was a triumph

for me. For while this penetrating, student-led discussion seemed almost to occur spontaneously, through some quirk of chemistry and circumstance, I had been trying to make this happen from the beginning of the year. (We were to study Mythology and Folklore the first semester, followed by American Ethnic Literature the second.) I had articulated three goals at the beginning of this course. First, I wanted my students to see themselves as learners, people who felt invested in and responsible for the learning (their own and others') in the classroom. Second, I wanted them to see literature as open to interpretation, and I hoped to train them to "unpack" a piece of literature. Third, I wanted them to learn to engage in "academic discourse," which I define briefly as arguing using evidence.

That day, my fifth hour seemed to fulfill all three goals as they had never done before. We had had many good discussions before, but never ones that were so clearly directed by the students themselves.

## No Accident

That the events that day were not simply happenstance set off by an interaction between Sondra and me was later reinforced when I formalized in my eighth hour the student leadership that had seemed to arise spontaneously in fifth hour. I explained that I wanted them to run this discussion and we appointed a student facilitator. The eighth hour discussion had a different rhythm and elaborated on different themes than in fifth hour. And without Sondra's commanding leadership, I had to exercise more self discipline to keep from controlling the discussion while still attempting to pose issues that might push students to dig deeper and think harder. But as in the earlier class, my eighth hour students willingly assumed responsibility for the discussion and, I felt, moved toward particularly thoughtful analyses of the short story and related themes in our lives. In the final months of the school year, both classes continued to build, albeit unevenly and imperfectly, on the abilities students showed that day.

Students need serious, open-ended questions.

Nor was this triumph the result of finally hitting upon the magic recipe, the perfect approach. I knew it couldn't have happened in the first month of class; we had all learned a lot to bring us to this point. I set about trying to analyze what exactly had worked to bring about the fulfillment of my goals, and how I might learn from it to become a better teacher.

## Laying the Groundwork: The First Semester

From the first day, I had attempted to train students in my three rules of "academic discourse." Whether you're discussing or writing, I said over and over, you must: 1) have a point (in an essay, this main point is called a thesis), 2) provide evidence to back it up, and 3) anchor your point (in discussion that usually meant drawing an explicit connection between your point and what had already been said; in an essay one often anchored one's thesis with reference to another written piece or to "common wisdom.") We had practiced these skills endlessly over the year and had made substantial progress before what I call "the day Sondra took over."

I had also constantly worked to confront students with serious, open-ended questions. As I see it, the main reason for studying literature is to discover more about humanity and oneself. And the main reason we learn to write is to be able to express our convictions powerfully. That means that moral controversies, searching questions, and even deeply personal dilemmas are not only admissible in my classroom, they are central. So I had attempted, with everything we studied, to bring these kinds of questions to the fore, and especially to forge a connection between the daily concerns of my students and age-old human questions, between their individual experiences and universal experience.

During the first semester, in Mythology and Folklore, we tried to identify the values implicit in Greek literature and compare Greek beliefs with our own views about fate, the role of women, family relationships, religion, right and wrong. We recalled how fantasies — myths — appeared to us as children and argued about whether children should be scared into obedience with threats of the boogie man, or taught to be good with the promise of presents from Santa. We identified archetypes — themes, symbols and story lines that come up again and again in the stories of cultures separated by time and distance — and tried to figure out why they recur.

As I look back, I can see that the groundwork we laid in the first semester and the first part of the second semester contributed to that moment in April when Sondra took over the class and my students began taking greater responsibility for their own learning. At the end of the first semester I had asked each student to evaluate the class in the form of an anonymous "letter to a friend" describing the course. While many letters complained that the course demanded too much writing, almost every letter noted that students were expected to think hard and formulate their own opinions. A typical comment was: "The fact that we are able to discuss our own point of view rather than always having to listen to the teacher's point of view. ... is a very positive and important part of this class." Another said simply, "She'll ask you your opinion whether you want to give it or not." A third student wrote, "You read stories to dig deep into what the characters are thinking and how they are alike and different from today's world."

As I reread these papers today, I see that by the end of the first semester we had not resolved the issue of who was responsible for the success of the class, the teacher or the students. Some students saw it as my responsibility to keep the class exciting at all times:

"But sometimes this class is so boring. Sometimes you have to pep us up or something. Like writing paragraphs — I hate it!"

Another at least recognized how demanding the teacher's role was:

"The most important aspect of all is the leader (or the teacher). She has to prepare herself for weeks in order to make the class interesting and not bore the whole class. What I'm trying to say is you need to have GANAS [Spanish for 'desire'] in order to make the class interesting."

One seemed possibly to be expressing ambivalence about whose responsibility the class was. This student wrote cryptically:

"I've learned that the teacher can influence how you act in class or what you learn in class is up to you."

## The Final Dilemma: Giving Students Responsibility

For all our circle discussions, essays, dramatizations, group work, freewrites, surveys, debates, mock "Oprah shows," more discussions, and more essays — and in spite of the tremendous progress we had made in the first semester and the beginning of the second — it was not until Sondra took over the class in April that I felt my goals were met. By late March, I had been feeling exhausted, and yet I felt I wasn't demanding enough of my students. It seemed like the burden of learning fell more heavily on me than on them! Students knew they were expected to articulate their views, but the responsibility for posing provocative questions and guiding the discussion to thoughtful conclusions seemed to fall entirely on my shoulders. I wrote in my journal during the March spring break:

"They [students] still don't get the purpose of academic discourse to the point of feeling truly invested in the process. They engage in it because they like me and want to please me, or because I've managed to awaken their interest by coming up with an angle that speaks to their concerns, or to get a good grade, or when they're feeling generally agreeable. But the class is still heavily teacher-propelled."

In my more cynical moments, I felt as if I were up there performing like a maniac to win their engagement or running myself ragged to contrive situations that led them to "discover meaning for themselves" only to have them view our analytic dialogues as "conversating," as a student put it once.

My friend Grace listened to my whining and then said simply, "Why did you participate in high school?" She was right. Somehow I hoped that I could teach my students to pick up a piece of literature and plumb it on their own, to find for themselves the universal themes, the ideas that speak to their experience — just for the pure joy of learning. Yet I didn't do that in high school, or even consistently in college. I participated to get a good grade, because I liked the teacher, because the teacher or a particular text raised issues I found interesting or useful.

## Finally: the Breakthrough

So how did it happen that one week later (the week after spring break), Sondra stepped to the front of the class, and I saw my students take more responsibility for raising questions and directing discussion? I think it happened, first, because we had laid the groundwork in previous months. Second, an article by Grant Wiggins entitled "Enabling Students to Be (Thoughtful) Workers" offered some useful suggestions at a key time. [Available through the Coalition for Essential Schools — see resource p. 199.] A friend showed me the article in February, and I went back to it over spring break as I pondered how to make my class less teacher-centered.

Wiggins says we should organize our courses — regardless of the subject area — around "essential questions." Instead of thinking about what content we want students to cover, we ought to identify large, overarching, higher-order questions which "go to the heart of the discipline" and which are open-ended enough to allow students to pursue their own answers. In this scheme, "the textbook, rather than providing the logic of the syllabus, becomes a reference book for posing and solving problems." I realized that Wiggins' "essential questions" were much like the questions I posed again and again to my students. I organized my courses around major themes or problems, which I presented at the beginning of every semester. And as we explored those themes I constantly confronted my students with open-ended questions designed to help them formulate their own understandings of the larger issues.

But I realized as I read Wiggins that I was asking most of the questions. Having students pose questions was part of my repertoire, something we did sometimes, the way I sometimes gave surveys to awaken their prior understanding of an issue or the way we sometimes staged debates to get students involved in articulating their opinions. Wiggins suggested that "students write down at least three questions for each lesson and reading." While students posing questions was an occasional part of my class, Wiggins was suggesting it should be a routine assignment for every reading.

Starting the first day after spring break, I asked students to write questions about everything we looked at in the class. (I found, incidentally, that grading these questions is not difficult. Students and I were clear on the criteria for a "good" question: it was one that was open-ended — having no right answer — meaty, and thought provoking. Such questions were easily recognizable, though not easy to produce. I gave C's for producing three relevant questions that showed a student had done the reading and A's when they produced two or more truly thought-provoking questions.) The following Monday we had our breakthrough, when Sondra took over the class.

## Qualifying Conclusions: When Students "Take Responsibility"

Of course, to say that Sondra "took over the class" that Monday in April or the students "took responsibility" for posing questions and running discussions from that day forward stretches the truth. In fact, I never once relinquished control over the class — even on the few occasions when I sat on the sidelines and steadfastly refused to take part in a discussion. Though we played at changing roles on that day and subsequently, I never stopped being the teacher and the authority.

Nor do I think giving up my authority is something worth striving for. I believe I have things to teach my students — I actively trained them to argue with evidence orally and in essay form. For example, I organized the course around themes which my experience tells me are "big ideas" they will encounter in college and adult life generally; I tracked down and introduced literature, essays, films, and other resources that I felt would be fertile ground for thought; and even as I sat in a discussion as "just another participant," I was constantly trying to pose questions and bring up issues that would focus the discussion and deepen students' thinking. I do, however, learn constantly from my students. They have helped me to see things from entirely new angles and have introduced questions that set me off on personal searches extending beyond the end of any particular school year. As I've learned about their views and experiences, the questions I pose to them and

At times, students are eager to assume control over their learning.

SUSAN LINA RUGGLES

the way I pose them have also changed.

At times students may assume full, responsible, eager control over their own learning. My experiences this year suggest that I should see such moments as goals and triumphs but not the absolute measure of success. My day-to-day job is to try to provide the training, skills, atmosphere, and conditions that will enable us to share the responsibility more and to change places from time to time — a job that remains exhausting.

We have not abandoned our roles as teacher and students. But I believe my students and I have learned more by changing the parameters of those roles. ☐

*Cynthia Ellwood is currently Director of Educational Services, Milwaukee Public Schools. This article was written when she taught English and Social Studies at South Division High School in Milwaukee. Students' names were changed in this article.*

For more information on "essential questions," consult the following two articles by Grant Wiggins:
• "Creating Thought Provoking Curriculum," *American Educator*, November 1987.
• "Mr. Sisyphys, Director of Curriculum: The Futility of Trying to Teach Everything of Importance," *Educational Leadership*, November 1989.

# Little Things Are Big

## By Jesús Colón

It was very late at night on the eve of Memorial Day. She came into the subway at the 34th Street Pennsylvania Station. I am still trying to remember how she managed to push herself in with a baby on her right arm, a valise in her left hand, and two children, a boy and girl about three and five years old, trailing after her. She was a nice looking white lady in her early twenties.

At Nevins Street, Brooklyn, we saw her preparing to get off at the the next station — Atlantic Avenue — which happened to be the place where I too had to get off. Just as it was a problem for her to get on, it was going to be a problem for her to get off the subway with two small children to be taken care of, a baby on her right arm and a medium sized valise in her left hand.

And there I was, also preparing to get off at Atlantic Avenue, with no bundles to take care of — not even the customary book under my arm without which I feel that I am not completely dressed.

As the train was entering the Atlantic Avenue station, some white man stood up from his seat and helped her out, placing the children on the long, deserted platform. There were only two adult persons on the long platform some time after midnight on the eve of last Memorial Day.

I could perceive the steep, long concrete stairs going down to the Long Island Railroad or into the street. Should I offer my help as the American white man did at the subway door placing the two children outside the subway car? Should I take care of the girl and the boy, take them by their hands until they reached the end of the steep long concrete stairs of the Atlantic Avenue station?

Courtesy is a characteristic of the Puerto Rican. And here I was — a Puerto Rican — hours past midnight, a valise, two white children, and a white lady with a baby on her arm palpably needing somebody to help her at least until she descended the long concrete stairs.

But how could I, a Negro and a Puerto Rican, approach this white lady who very likely might have preconceived prejudices against Negroes and everybody with foreign accents, in a deserted subway station very late at night?

## What Might Happen?

What would she say? What would be the first reaction of this white American woman, perhaps coming from a small town, with a valise, two children, and a baby on her right arm? Would she say: Yes, of course, you may help me. Or would she think that I was just trying to get too familiar? Or would she think worse than that perhaps? What would I do if she let out a scream as I went toward her to offer my help?

Was I misjudging her? So many slanders are written every day in the daily press against the Negroes and Puerto Ricans. I hesitated for a long, long minute. The ancestral manners that the most illiterate Puerto Rican passes on from father to son were struggling inside me. Here was I, way past midnight, face to face with a situation that could very well explode into an outburst of prejudices and chauvinistic conditioning of the "divide and rule" policy of present day society.

It was a long minute. I passed on by her as if I saw nothing. As if I was insensitive to her need. Like a rude animal walking on two legs, I just moved on half running by the long subway platform leaving the children and the valise and her with the baby on her arm. I took the steps of the long concrete stairs in twos until I reached the street above and the cold air slapped my warm face.

This is what racism and prejudice and chauvinism and official artificial divisions can do to people and a nation!

Perhaps the lady was not prejudiced after all. Or not prejudiced enough to scream at the coming of a Negro toward her in a solitary subway station a few hours past midnight.

If you were not that prejudiced, I failed you, dear lady. I know that there is a chance in a million that you will read these lines. I am willing to take that millionth chance. If you were not that prejudiced, I failed you, lady, I failed you, children. I failed myself to myself.

I buried my courtesy early on Memorial Day morning. But here is a promise that I make to myself here and now; if I am ever faced with an occasion like that again, I am going to offer my help regardless of how the offer is going to be received.

Then I will have my courtesy with me again. ❐

*Jesús Colón (1901-1974) was a social activist who wrote about the Puerto Rican community in New York.*

Reprinted with permission from International Publishers, New York from the book *A Puerto Rican in New York and Other Sketches*, 1982.

> How could I, a Negro and a Puerto Rican, approach this white lady in a deserted subway station very late at night?

# What Can Teachers Do About Sexual Harassment?

## By Ellen Bravo and Larry Miller

*Theresa was the only girl in the metalworking class. When a teacher asked her how things were going with the boys, Theresa replied, "Oh, it's much better. They don't grab my breasts and butt anymore. They just call me all those names."*

*Paula hated walking past Leon and his friends. They would grab themselves and say things like, "Come on, now, you know you want it." Some of her friends yelled comments back, but Paula never knew what to say.*

*Anton took the long way to class. He didn't want to pass a certain group of girls who always made fun of him for being a virgin.*

*The eighth grade girls didn't like the way the teacher would fondle their hair and then let his hand skim across their bodies. But because this had been going on for awhile, they were afraid to tell their parents. And they didn't know who to tell at school.*

These are just a few of the types of sexual harassment problems in our schools. Despite the headlines and well-publicized court cases, most administrators have focused little attention on the problem. But teachers don't have to wait for a directive that may be years in coming; we can take action right now in our classrooms.

Sexual harassment isn't the only problem kids face in school and for many, it's not the worst problem. But it's an area where a lot of confusion exists — confusion that's been cultivated by many people in authority who have trivialized the issue, criticized those who have raised it, and distorted proposed solutions.

Flirting should not be confused with harassment.

For high school students, the situation is further complicated by adolescence. If being preoccupied with sex makes someone a harasser, most teenagers would have to plead guilty. Where's the line between appropriate and inappropriate behavior — and who's drawing it?

Last year, when Larry Miller did a seven-day unit on sexual harassment, students afterward remarked that it was one of the highlights of the school year. He found that developing a unit on sexual harassment has several advantages:

• **The students love it**. Students repeatedly said throughout the year, "Why can't class always be as interesting?" Sexual harassment is also a subject on which students are eager to talk and have a great deal to say. What adolescent hasn't spent an inordinate amount of time contemplating the complexities of intimate relations?

• **The students need it**. Most students don't understand the issue of sexual harassment and have lots of misconceptions. They need guidance and support to help figure out what is and isn't appropriate behavior.

• **The students benefit from it**. The benefits occur on a number of different levels. First, a sexual harassment unit empowers those individual girls and boys who may have been harassed. (For boys, it's almost always for being gay or not "manly" enough.) Such students urgently need validation that harassment is wrong, that they're not crazy, and that they're not at fault. They need to hear that someone in authority cares about the problem and isn't blaming them or dismissing their pain.

Second, it makes clear that harassment is unacceptable behavior — thus helping to create a classroom culture in which students will have a stronger understanding that their rights will be respected and defended, regardless of whether they have ever been harassed. While it is essential to go beyond dealing with harassment on a classroom-by-classroom basis, individual discussions of the issue are often an essential first step (see article p. 106).

Third, it helps clear up confusion among boys who think they'll be in trouble for flirting or consensual joking. Larry found that while many boys initially felt hostile and suspicious during the unit (they feared the unit would demonize all boys and portray all girls as innocent victims), such attitudes changed when they found the focus was on inappropriate behavior and not on boys in general.

Fourth, it helps raise broader relationship and gender issues that the students need to talk about. One incident underscored this point to Larry. After the unit, a 16-year-old male student came up to him one day and asked to talk privately. It turned out the student had a common but simple biological question about sex — but had no adult male he felt comfortable talking to.

## A Good Curriculum

A good curriculum makes clear that while most harassers are male, most males are not harassers. It also encourages students to intervene when harassment occurs, to speak out not as champions of the "poor victims" but as people offended by such behavior.

At its minimum, the curriculum should have three goals. First, it must help the majority of students to understand why harassment is wrong. Second, it must help the harassers to stop their behavior. Third, in what is a more complex issue, it must address larger issues of gender stereotypes and power. Students need to understand that sexual harassment is part of a continuum of sexual misconduct that has to do with domination rather than sex. This takes the issue out of the battle-of-the-sexes mode and helps students better understand patterns of sexual discrimination.

It is also essential to deal with the perspective that those who challenge sexual harassment are merely whining "victims" rather than people with a legitimate anger. Some critics argue that sexual harassment awareness training contributes to a nation of "victims." Like any unit dealing with situations of oppression, the curriculum's purpose is not to create a sense of hopelessness but of understanding and power — the knowledge that each of us is important and deserves to be treated with dignity. We don't prevent or stop harassment by ignoring it any more than we do by condoning it. In fact, ignoring sexual harassment sends a powerful message that

no one cares. This "hidden curriculum" can leave girls with a sense of powerlessness and, in essence, teaches girls to accept sexual inequality.

## Teaching Techniques

Obviously, good teaching is central to the unit's success. Teachers can use a variety of techniques, from videos to role plays, small-group discussions, and student essays. It is useful to begin with a "safe" lesson idea that encourages students to share their feelings, such as an anonymous survey asking students both their definition of sexual harassment and whether they have ever been harassed.

It's a good idea to include at least one lesson plan that helps students distinguish between flirting and harassment. (See sample plan, p. 106). In helping students distinguish between the two, Larry found that two questions were essential: Was the behavior unwelcome? Did the behavior make the recipient feel uncomfortable? If the answer is "yes" to the questions, the line is usually crossed between flirting and harassment.

Role plays and scenarios are a particularly useful technique. In his unit,

# The Need for Districtwide Changes

Classroom lessons are the core of any sexual harassment policy. But classroom activities are not enough. To effectively combat sexual harassment, there must be school wide and district wide changes. All school and district staff should receive the training necessary to help create a school and district climate where sexual harassment is dealt with quickly and forcefully. Some of the essential components to help create such a climate include:

• **Commitment from the top**. A clear acknowledgment that sexual harassment is a problem and won't be tolerated.

• **Policy**. Procedures need to be clear and familiar. Information should be distributed to each student in a way that

will get their attention.

• **Definition**. The policy should describe, concisely and with specific examples, what sexual harassment is and what kinds of behavior are prohibited.

• **Complaint procedures**. Students and school personnel should be given several channels for reporting a complaint and a timetable for its handling. The policy should make clear that due process will be observed.

• **Discipline**. The policy should specify what the consequences are for engaging in prohibited behavior.

• **Protection**. Those reporting harassment need assurances that there will be no retaliation.

• **Confidentiality**. Every step should be taken to preserve confidentiality for

those involved. The procedures should include a telephone number students can call if they want to discuss the situation anonymously with a trained professional.

• **Investigations**. Impartial and well-trained investigators should be provided to pursue any formal complaints.

• **Education**. All students, teachers, and staff should receive training.

• **Healing**. Those who have been harassed may need access to trained professionals or a support group to help them heal.

• **Assessment**. Schools should monitor their progress and step up education and intervention if necessary. ❐

Larry took a male and a female student that he knew were mature enough to act out what was, from their own experiences, the difference between flirtation and harassment. For example, the young man would look the girl up and down, make comments such as, "Hey, you want some of this," or grab himself in his private parts. The girl would respond, "Go away, boy, I don't need that crap." It was clear from the class's response to the role plays that the students, whether or not they could articulate it, often knew the difference between flirting and harassment.

Scenarios, in which the teacher describes a situation and asks for students' responses, are a useful way to open up discussion. Larry developed the following activities and also used some from the resources listed on this page.

In one scenario, boys "rate" girls as they walk past them in the hallway. ("She's a 10"; "She's so ugly she'd be pretty if she were a dog."). During a discussion of such "ratings," some boys argued that rating girls can be a compliment. "It's just ugly girls who are offended," one said.

Some girls had a different view. "I don't care what I'm rated; it makes me uncomfortable," Betty replied. "I don't like it." Other girls backed her up and made the point that such ratings are degrading and make a woman feel less than a human being. Larry found that such conversations were much-needed. Whether or not every student took Betty's comments to heart, her point was made.

Another scenario focused on how boys "eye" girls. James, for instance, argued that he can look at anything he wants. "These are my eyes," he insisted. But another student responded, "If I feel disrespected, then you're out of order" — picking up on common student concern with "respect" as a key factor in determining what's right and wrong.

In doing such scenarios, it is important that at least one deal with the most evident form of harassment: the use of abusive words such as "bitch" and "whore." In the discussion following such a scenario in Larry's class, one female student reflected a common view that, "If a girl is not a 'whore' then she

should be tough enough not to be offended by these words."

Her view sparked a lively debate. A number of both young men and women shot back with comments such as, "We shouldn't have to put up with that kind of nonsense."

The power of the unit was most clear in the summary essays written by Larry's students. Many of the students came to clearly understand not only the difference between flirting and harassment, but the issue's importance.

Reflecting on flirting and harassment, Jamela wrote in her summary essay: "Flirting and sexual harassment are two different things. Flirting is when two people are joking and kidding around and none of them mind. But sexual harassment is when two people might be joking around and kidding around and one goes too far. Another form may be when two people are talking or playing and one of them touches the other in a way they don't like, or grabs the other in a way they don't like."

Jason, meanwhile, focused on the many responses to sexual harassment. Articulating a range of responses that most students were unaware of before the unit, he wrote, "Sometimes you can handle sexual harassment by ignoring it or asking the person to stop it, especially when it is name calling, rumors, light touching, or gestures. If it continues you need to go to someone in authority, either a teacher, parent, boss, or head of the department. If it still continues you need to keep taking action and not let them get away with it. Don't be afraid to talk to other students or co-workers about it. Perhaps it is happening to them too and you could build a better case against that person. Sexual harassment should be an important issue in all communities. Looking the other way and doing nothing about it is saying that sexual harassment is okay." ❑

*Ellen Bravo is executive director of 9to5, National Association of Working Women, and co-author of* The 9to5 Guide to Combating Sexual Harassment.

*Larry Miller teaches at Metropolitan High School for the Arts and Technology in Milwaukee.*

# Sexual Harassment Resources:

*Flirting or Hurting? A Teacher's Guide on Student-to-Student Sexual Harassment in Schools (Grade 6 through 12),* by Nan Stein and Lisa Sjostrom, published by The National Education Association (Washington, 1994). To order, contact Publications Department, The Center for Research on Women, Wellesley College, 106 Central St., Wellesley, MA 02181-8259. (617) 283-2510, fax (617) 283-2504, or NEA Professional Library, P.O. Box 509, West Haven, CT 06515. (800) 229-4200. Cost: $15.95 for NEA members, $19.95 for general public.

*Sexual Harassment in Schools,* a videotape produced for *Teacher TV* by NEA and The Learning Channel. Stock number A050-10119. $15 plus $2.50 per tape s&h. Available from the NEA Professional Library (see above).

*Sexual Harassment and Teens: A Program for Positive Change,* by Susan Strauss with Pamela Espeland, (Minneapolis: Free Spirit Publishing Inc., 1992). 400 First Ave. N., Suite 616, Minneapolis, MN 55401. (800) 735-7323.

"Hostile Hallways: The AAUW Survey on Sexual Harassment in America's Schools." 1993, $11.95 ($8.95 for AAUW members) plus $4 each s&h. AAUW Sales Office, P.O. Box 251, Annapolis Junction, MD 20701. (800) 225-9998 ext 246.

*Tune In To Your Rights: A Guide for Teenagers about Turning Off Sexual Harassment* (1985). Also available in Spanish, $3 includes s&h. Make checks out to the University of Michigan. Send to PEO, 1005 School of Education, University of Michigan, Ann Arbor, MI 48109. (313) 763-9910.

# Flirting vs. Sexual Harassment: Teaching the Difference

## By Nan Stein and Lisa Sjostrom

### Objectives:

To raise student awareness about the kinds of sexual harassment which take place all the time; to discern the fluid, subjective line between flirting and sexual harassment; to encourage open student discussion of a complicated topic.

### Preparation:

• Prepare three lists with headings and subheadings either on the blackboard or on big sheets of newsprint (these sheets may provide great reference points in later lessons). The titles of the first three lists should read "Verbal or Written," "Gestures," and "Physical." Under each heading write the two subheadings "Flirting" and "Harassment." During the discussion, anticipate creating a third subheading on each of the three lists titled "Depends." At this point, the three lists should be titled like this:

**Verbal or Written**
Flirting                    Harassment

**Gestures**
Flirting                    Harassment

**Physical**
Flirting                    Harassment

• Decide beforehand if you will allow students to use profanity or if they should speak in euphemisms. Another alternative is for students to write their answers on paper and hand these lists to you to decide what to record on the main lists.

• If possible, ask students to arrange their chairs in a circle.

• Decide upon the ground rules; e.g.,

1. Everyone must listen when someone is speaking.

2. Don't get personal by mentioning anyone's name when telling about a specific incident.

3. Ask students to determine other rules, such as "What's said here, stays here."

• Encourage younger students, in particular, to be in their most "mature" behavior mode.

### Introduction:

"This activity is pretty simple and fun. We're going to talk about the difference between flirting and sexual harassment. Before we begin, I want to state from the outset that we're not here to demonize or blame boys. Many of us may never be either targets of harassment or perpetrators. But all of us are *witnesses and bystanders* who see harassment happening, and we need to learn to say, "Hey, cut it out, that's not funny!" or "What would you do if this were your sister, your mom, or your brother?" So, we're not just trying to change boys and men. We're trying to change *all* of us — so we'll have the courage to actively respond when we see sexual harassment go on.

"You are the best anthropologists of your own culture — and 'subcultures' (cliques, who you 'hang' with). All the time you are observing other kids' behavior in school, and seeing how behaviors differ depending on where you are and whether there are adults around or not — in classrooms, locker rooms, the cafeteria, the parking lot, the hallways. In this discussion, I want you to draw upon what *you* already know and see. You are the experts and sophisticated 'critiquers' of your subcultures.

"In this exercise, we're going to talk about how you all interact with each other and what you observe, how you

make sense between what is sexual harassment and what is flirting ('hanging out,' 'getting to know someone').

"First we'll focus on verbal and written exchanges, such as comments and notes. Then we'll focus on gestures like winking, waving, and other ways you communicate without speaking or touching. Lastly we'll consider physical interactions. For each category, we'll talk about examples of flirting and then instances that cross the line into sexual harassment. I don't expect everyone to agree. What's most important is that we start talking. ... Can anyone give me an example of a comment or a note that's flirting and nice? ..."

### Activity:

• To avoid confusion, walk students through the lists one at a time.

• Write down student answers under the appropriate subheading.

• Encourage students to stay with specifics they know from a school setting and not stray to hypothetical or out-of-school situations.

• If one column isn't being addressed, ask students specific questions; e.g., "Can you give me examples of physical ways people flirt?"

• When students disagree upon the nature of a particular behavior or comment, ask them what they are basing their criteria upon and enter this under the heading "Depends." For example, perhaps the nature of a comment *depends* upon whether the speaker is a friend or a stranger, or upon their tone of voice. Write these dependent variables right on the three lists.

• If one behavior falls under both headings of "Flirting" and "Harassment," note this by drawing an arrow from one column to the other; e.g.,

### Verbal or Written

| Flirting | Harassment |
|----------|-----------|
| You look nice ➤ | nice ass |
| Like your hair | 'ho |

Depends on:
tone of voice
how they look at you

### Gestures

| Flirting | Harassment |
|----------|-----------|
| blowing kiss ➤ | grab crotch |
| wave | lip licking |

Depends on:
friend or stranger
how old they are
who else is around

### Physical

| Flirting | Harassment |
|----------|-----------|
| hug ➤ | pinch |
| holding hands | grabbing |

Depends on:
friend or stranger
where you are

**Questions to Raise Afterwards:**

After students have completed the activity, the following discussion questions can help them make sense of the lists.

• Why do people define sexual harassment differently?

• If sexual harassment is illegal, how come it goes on?

• Who allows sexual harassment to go on?

• What are some common forms of sexual harassment that often go unnoticed in schools?

• Do girls sexually harass other girls?

• Who harasses boys?

**Troubleshooting:**

Discussion often gets heated and students can raise many challenging questions. Here are some typical questions and scenarios, along with suggested responses.

1. Boys raise the argument that girls are asking to be harassed by the way they dress.

"All of our opinions about temptation are shaped by the times we live in. Did you know that in Puritanical New England in the 1600's if a woman wore a dress and her ankles or wrists showed, men would walk on the other side of the street and turn their eyes away in horror? They believed the Devil was tempting them."

"Sometimes we — both males and females — dress to look and feel good about ourselves. Yes, we may want attention, but that doesn't mean we want to be *harassed.*"

2. Students ask: "But how do we know which is which? We won't be able to say anything to one another!"

"We're figuring this out all the time — silently. You don't ever go up to someone and say, "Hi, can we flirt now?" This is why we need to keep talking and openly discussing our intentions, feelings, and interpretations of each other's words and behaviors."

3. Students ask about other hassles which don't fall under the category of sexual harassment.

• Crank calls: "Against the law. It is a crime under both state and federal laws for anyone to make obscene or harassing phone calls. Look in the front section of the telephone book — it's spelled out there, and tells you to call the phone company if these calls persist."

• Knocking books out of someone's hands: "Someone's provoking you, but it isn't sexual in nature, so it isn't covered by federal law. Of course, the school may have its own rules about student behavior, like rules against cheating and fighting. And remember, something doesn't have to be illegal for you to say 'This is making me uncomfortable!' or 'You're acting like a jerk!'"

• Being harassed by a family member at home: "Federal laws on sex discrimination and sexual harassment only apply to two places: one law covers school and school-sponsored events, and a second law covers the workplace. Of course, sexual assault at home or in the streets is just as serious. So speak up, say 'no,' tell someone you trust and keep telling until you find someone who believes you and will help you."

4. "Can a harasser get sued?"

"Yes and no. Under federal law Title IX, you bring a complaint against the school district and ask for monetary damages. Why? Because it's the school district's responsibility to enforce the rules and explain what's legal and illegal in school. Under law, the school district has to provide you with an environment that is safe and equal for learning for both girls and boys. So, the school district is responsible for maintaining a school climate and environment that is conducive to learning and one which allows everyone to participate without fear of sexual harassment. Though an individual cannot get sued under Title IX, if the person has done something that is also criminal (like assault), then the district attorney may choose to sue the individual in criminal court."

5. A student relates an incident of teen dating violence that occurred away from the school.

"Violence is a separate category from sexual harassment. Violence in teen relationships or domestic violence is a form of assault and is covered by criminal law. For that, you need to make a complaint through the police and the district attorney." ❑

*Nan Stein and Lisa Sjostrom are with the Center for Research on Women at Wellesley College, in Wellesley, MA.*

The above is adapted from *Flirting or Hurting? A Teacher's Guide on Student-to-Student Sexual Harassment in Schools (Grades 6 through 12),* published by the National Education Association (Washington, D.C., September 1994). [See resources p. 105]

> **Many of us may never be targets either of harassment or perpetrators. But all of us are witnesses and bystanders who see harassment happening.**

# Rayford's Song

## By Lawson Inada

Rayford's song was Rayford's song,
but it was not his alone, to own.

He had it, though, and kept it to himself
as we rowed-rowed-rowed the boat
through English country gardens
with all the whispering hope
we could muster, along with occasional
choruses of funiculi-funicula!

Weren't we a cheery lot —
comin' 'round the mountain
with Susanna, banjos on our knees,
rompin' through the leaves
of the third-grade music textbook.

Then Rayford Butler raised his hand.
For the first time, actually,
in all the weeks he had been in class,
and for the only time before he'd leave.
Yes, quiet Rayford, silent Rayford,
little Rayford, dark Rayford —
always in the same overalls —
that Rayford, Rayford Butler, raised his hand:

    "Miss Gordon, ma'am —
    we always singing your songs.
    Could I sing one of my own?"

Pause. We looked at one another;
we looked at Rayford Butler;
we looked up at Miss Gordon, who said:

    "Well, I suppose so, Rayford —
    if you insist. Go ahead.
    Just one song. Make it short."

And Rayford Butler stood up very straight,
and in his high voice, sang:

    "Suh-whing a-looow
    suh-wheeeet ah charr-ee-oohh,
    ah-comin' for to carr-ee
    meee ah-hooooome..."

Pause. Classroom, school, schoolyard,
neighborhood, the whole world
focusing on that one song, one voice
which had a light to it, making even
Miss Gordon's white hair shine
in the glory of it, glowing
in the radiance of the song.

Pause. Rayford Butler sat down.
And while the rest of us
may have been spellbound,
on Miss Gordon's face
was something like a smile,
or perhaps a frown:

    "Very good, Rayford.
    However, I must correct you:
    the word is 'chariot.'
    'Chariot.' And there is no
    such thing as a 'chario.'
    Do you understand me?"

    "But Miss Gordon..."

    "I said 'chariot, chariot.'
    Can you pronounce that for me?"

    "Yes, Miss Gordon. Chariot."

    "Very good, Rayford,
    Now, class, before we return
    to our book, would anyone else
    care to sing a song of their own?"

Our songs, our songs were there —
on tips of tongues, but stuck
in throats — songs of love,
fun, animals, and valor, songs
of other lands, in other languages,
but they just wouldn't come out.
Where did our voices go?

Rayford's song was Rayford's song,
but it was not his alone to own.

    "Well, then, class —
    let's turn our books to
    'Old Black Joe.'"

RETHINKING OUR CLASSROOMS

# Celebrating the Student's Voice

## By Linda Christensen

Lawson Inada, a Japanese-American poet and professor of literature at Southern Oregon College, came to our class last year. His visit was one of those lucky circumstances: the class was in the middle of a unit on the history of education and one of the poems he pulled from his new book *Legends from Camp* was about a classroom experience. When Lawson read "Rayford's Song" (see opposing page), we realized it was an opportunity for students to remember and explore their own history as students.

In "Rayford's Song," Inada remembers one of his classrooms in the 1930s in Fresno, a town in California's San Joaquin Valley where many people of African, Chinese, Filipino, Japanese, and Mexican descent worked in the fields and canneries. "Our classroom was filled with shades of brown," he recalls. "Our names were Rayford Butler, Consuela and Pedro Gonzales, Susie Chin, and Sam Shimabukuro. We were a mixture. The only white person in the room was our teacher. Our textbooks had pictures and stories about white kids named Dick and Jane and their dog, Spot. And the songs in our songbooks were about Old Susanah coming 'round the mountain and English gardens — songs we never heard in our neighborhood."

Some of the songs mentioned in the poem may not be familiar to today's students ("Old Black Joe" is a Stephen Foster song written in 1860 that evokes nostalgic memories of the days of slavery). Nonetheless, the poem evokes strong emotion in students because it speaks to the process that sometimes happens in schools of dampening our hopes and expectations. Many of us have experienced the loss of our voices, our songs, our stories. We've been told that we are not important, our people are not important, our gender is not important. Inada's poem dares to speak about that silencing.

Following are some ways a teacher might use the poem in class.

## Group poem

• Ask students to reread the poem and underline the words, lines, or phrases that strike them for some reason — perhaps because these seem important to the poem, maybe because they like the sound or because they can relate the line to something in their lives. (e.g., "Where did our voices go? ... I must correct you. ... One song. ... One voice.")

• Tell students that they are going to create an oral group poem with the words, phrases, or lines they've selected. Each student can say his/her addition to the oral poem when there is a pause. They might want to use some of the devices of poetry and song — repeating a line or word, echoing. Sometimes students like to experiment with the call and response more typical in sermons. Encourage students to call out lines or words to form the new poem, in what might be described as the literary equivalent of an improvisational musical composition. To give students the idea, have eight or ten students come in front of the room and experiment as an example.

Sometimes it takes a few times to get this going. Have patience. It's worth it. As students rewrite and reread the poem or any written text, they come to new understandings about the piece. Sometimes we have students begin singing "Swing Low, Sweet Chariot" as background to the poem — or play a recording.

## Reflections on the Poem

• Ask students to write for five or ten minutes about the poem; they might want to describe how the poem made them feel, their reactions to the poem, or memories that the poem evoked. There are no wrong answers.

• After students have written, begin the discussion. Some students might want to read their responses while others might want to use it as a springboard for their contribution to the class talk.

## Student Writing

• Inada speaks of schools silencing students, but he also speaks more broadly about whose lives are included in the curriculum and whose are excluded. Ask students to write about a time when their voices were silenced or they felt their history or stories were silenced or left out of the classroom. They might want to write this as a story or a poem.

## Read-Around/Collective Text

• Before students read their papers out loud, ask them to take notes on their classmates' papers. They might note how people felt about being silenced, who was silenced, who silenced them, and how they responded. After all the students have read who want to read, ask them to review their notes, think about the stories/poems and write a paragraph or two on the ideas that emerged from the stories. They might want to mention specific people's stories. See p. 186 for more information on how to use the read-around technique. ❏

*Linda Christensen (lchrist@aol.com) is language arts coordinator for Portland Public Schools and a* Rethinking Schools *editor.*

# Promoting Social Imagination Through Interior Monologues

## By Bill Bigelow and Linda Christensen

One of the most important aims of teaching is to prompt students to empathize with other human beings. This is no easy accomplishment in a society that pits people against each other, offers vastly greater or lesser amounts of privileges based on accidents of birth, and rewards exploitation with wealth and power. Empathy, or "social imagination," as Peter Johnson calls it in a recent issue of *The Reading Teacher*, allows students to connect to "the other" with whom, on the surface, they may appear to have little in common. A social imagination encourages students to construct a more profound "we" than daily life ordinarily permits. A social imagination prompts students to wonder about the social contexts that provoke hurtful behaviors, rather than simply to dismiss individuals as inherently "evil" or "greedy."

## Imagining Thoughts of Others

One teaching method we use to promote empathy, and return to unit after unit, is the interior monologue. An interior monologue is simply the imagined thoughts of a character in history, literature, or life at a specific point in time. After watching a film, reading a novel, short story, or essay, or performing improvisation skits, the class brainstorms particular key moments, turning points, or critical passages characters confronted. During a unit on the Vietnam War, we watch the documentary *Hearts and Minds*. The film (available in many video stores) weaves interviews with U.S. soldiers and Vietnamese with newsreel footage of the war and unexpected scenes of daily life in the United States. Student suggestions included writing from the points of view of an American pilot who has become critical of his role in the war, a North Vietnamese man whose entire family has been killed in a bombing raid, a Native American marine who was called "blanket ass" and "squaw" by commanding officers, and a Buddhist monk who solemnly lectures the United States on the futility of trying to conquer Vietnam, etc.

Sometimes students choose to write from the situations we brainstorm, sometimes they don't. The monologue technique gives structure to the assignment, but the freedom to write from anyone's point of view allows students to mold the piece to the contours of their lives and interests.

Jetta chose the point of view of a Vietnamese prostitute, and wrote in part:

"I sell my body because it's the only way to stay alive. They say my people are disgraceful, but they have disgraced us. ... We are forced to sell our bodies. ... but who forces them to pay, to strip the dignity from someone's daughter? Do they not have daughters at home? Do they not have mothers? Where did they learn this? What kind of place teaches this?"

Jetta embraces this woman as she explores the prostitute's feelings and consciousness and gives an imagined voice to her outrage.

In our classroom circle, students read their pieces aloud and give positive comments on each other's work. Listening to the collection of writings offers students an intimate portrait of the social consequences of the war. We feel, rather than observe from a distance. These portraits provide us a way to talk about the film without writing out typical discussion questions. The issues embedded in the text are viewed through a more personal lens. The different lives that students imagine and their different interpretations give us opportunities to explore the film or reading more thoroughly.

As is true anytime we wonder about other people's lives, our monologues are only guesses, at times marred by stereotype. But the very act of considering, "How might this person experience this situation?" develops an important "habit of the mind" and draws us closer together. We write the monologues along with our students and can testify at the startling insights and compassion that can arise. Usually, we — students and teachers — tap into our own well of pain, pride, sorrow, confusion, and joy. Although we may never have experienced war, we know the pain of losing a family member or friend; we have experienced the difficulty of making a tough decision. Likewise, we have felt joy. From these shared emotions we can construct a piece that allows us to attempt a momentary entrance into another person's life.

In our Literature and U.S. History class, we read "A Jury of Her Peers" by Susan Glaspell, a 1917 story about rural women's lives. In the story, Minnie Wright, who lives on an isolated farm, strangles her husband in desperate retaliation for his strangling her bird, the creature that brought her the only piece of joy in an otherwise bleak life. We suggested students might begin their monologue or poem with "Write that I ..." Maryanne assumes the persona of Minnie Wright and tries to imagine what in her life would lead her to commit such a horrid crime:

*Write that I was young,*
*tender like the gardenia blossom ...*

*I know that you think*
*I killed my husband,*
*my keeper, protector.*

*I stayed in that house, broken*
*chairs beneath me, husband on top*
*pushing his fury through me ...*

*Please don't forget the bird.*
*You must tell them about its voice.*
*It was strangled.*
*We were strangled.*

Interior monologues tap other people's pain, but they also tap people's hope. After watching *The Killing Floor*, about World War I Black migration to Chicago and union organizing in the stockyards, Debbie wrote an interior monologue from the point of view of Frank, a Black worker recently arrived from the South:

Startling insights can arise from interior monologues.

"I sit and listen to the unfamiliar air of music drifting in through my window. Crickets had made music in the South, but never in a tune like this one. I want Mattie to hear this new music. The sound of white men's feet on the dirt avoiding our black bodies on the sidewalk. Oh, to share the sounds of coins clinking together as I walk."

As students read their pieces aloud in the circle, we ask them to take notes on the "collective text" they create, to write about the common themes that emerge, or questions they're left with. Or we might pose a particular question for them to think about. For example, recently we finished watching the film, *Glory*, about a regiment of African-American soldiers who fought in the Civil War. We wrote a dictionary definition of the word "glory" on the board and asked students as they listened to each other's interior monologues to notice: "Where is the 'glory' in the film *Glory*?" Students' own writings and observations became different points of entry to explore the interesting contradictions in the film and the events it depicts. For example, Eugene wrote: "In our class reading it was commented

that there was mostly pain and not much glory. I think that their pain was their glory, the fact that they were willing to be martyrs. They were fighting for a freedom that they knew they would never have, because most of them would die in the war."

Empathy and sympathy are quite different. When Ghantel writes her *Color Purple* interior monologue from the point of view of Mr._____, Celie's uncaring husband, she shows empathy; she tries to imagine how he looks at the world and wonders what experiences made him who he is. But she's not sympathetic; she doesn't approve of his behavior. In fact, she detests him. Interior monologues, by encouraging students to empathize with other people, no matter how despicable, invite kids to probe for the social causes of human behavior. People are not inherently sexist or racist; and while interior monologues are not analytical panaceas, they can be useful tools in nurturing insight about why people think and act as they do.

In our experience, success with interior monologues depends on:

• Drawing on media or writing that is emotionally powerful.

• Brainstorming character and situation choices so most students can find an entry into the assignment.

• Allowing students the freedom to find their own passion — they might want to complete the assignment as a poem, a dialogue poem, from the point of view of an animal or an object (Minnie Wright's dead bird, for instance).

• Giving students the opportunity to read their pieces to the entire class.

• Using the collective text of students' writing to launch a discussion of the bigger picture.

Writing interior monologues won't necessarily have students hugging each other as they sing "We Shall Overcome," but they are a worthwhile piece in our attempt to construct a critical, multicultural curriculum. We want kids to think deeply about other people — why they do what they do, why they think what they think. We want students to care about each other and the world. Interior monologues are a good place to start. ❑

*Bill Bigelow teaches at Franklin High School in Portland, Oregon. Linda Christensen is language arts coordinator for Portland Public Schools. Both are* Rethinking Schools *editors.*

# Two Women

This poem was written by a working-class Chilean woman in 1973, shortly after Chile's socialist president, Salvador Allende, was overthrown. A U.S. missionary translated the work and brought it with her when she was forced to leave Chile. This is to be read by two people, one reading the bold-faced type and one reading the regular type.

**I am a woman.**
I am a woman.

**I am a woman born of a woman whose man owned a factory.**
I am a woman born of a woman whose man labored in a factory.

**I am a woman whose man wore silk suits, who constantly watched his weight.**
I am a woman whose man wore tattered clothing, whose heart was constantly strangled by hunger.

**I am a woman who watched two babies grow into beautiful children.**
I am a woman who watched two babies die because there was no milk.

**I am a woman who watched twins grow into popular college students with summers abroad.**
I am a woman who watched three children grow, but with bellies stretched from no food.

**But then there was a man;**
But then there was a man;

**And he talked about the peasants getting richer by my family getting poorer.**
And he told me of days that would be better, and he made the days better.

**We had to eat rice.**
We had rice.

**We had to eat beans!**
We had beans.

**My children were no longer given summer visas to Europe.**
My children no longer cried themselves to sleep.

**And I felt like a peasant.**
And I felt like a woman.

**A peasant with a dull, hard, unexciting life.**
Like a woman with a life that sometimes allowed a song.

**And I saw a man.**
And I saw a man.

**And together we began to plot with the hope of the return to freedom.**
I saw his heart begin to beat with hope of freedom, at last.

**Someday, the return to freedom.**
Someday freedom.

**And then,**
But then,

**One day,**
One day,

There were planes overhead and guns firing close by.
There were planes overhead and guns firing in the distance.

I gathered my children and went home.
I gathered my children and ran.

And the guns moved farther and farther away.
But the guns moved closer and closer.

And then, they announced that freedom had been restored!
And then they came, young boys really.

They came into my home along with my man.
They came and found my man.

Those men whose money was almost gone.
They found all of the men whose lives were almost their own.

And we all had drinks to celebrate.
And they shot them all.

The most wonderful martinis.
They shot my man.

And then they asked us to dance.
And they came for me.

Me.
For me, the woman.

And my sisters.
For my sisters.

And then they took us.
Then they took us,

They took us to dinner at a small, private club.
They stripped from us the dignity we had gained.

And they treated us to beef.
And then they raped us.

It was one course after another.
One after another they came after us.

We nearly burst we were so full.
Lunging, plunging — sisters bleeding, sisters dying.

It was magnificent to be free again!
It was hardly a relief to have survived.

The beans have almost disappeared now.
The beans have disappeared.

The rice — I've replaced it with chicken or steak.
The rice, I cannot find it.

And the parties continue night after night to make up for all the time wasted.
And my silent tears are joined once more by the midnight cries of my children.

And I feel like a woman again.
They say, I am a woman.

---

The period of rice and beans for the poor woman in the poem occurs after the election of the socialist, Salvador Allende, as president of Chile. Allende was elected in 1970. He was overthrown in a military coup in September 1973 after a long period of destabilization launched by the wealthy classes and supported by the U.S. government and U.S. corporations such as International Telephone and Telegraph. Along with thousands of others, Allende was killed by the military. The coup, under the leadership of Gen. Augusto Pinochet, launched a period of severe hardship for the working and peasant classes. Although Chile currently has a civilian government, the military is still the country's most powerful institution. (See p. 184 for lesson ideas.)

# Role Plays: Show, Don't Tell

## By Bill Bigelow

My lecture had put kids to sleep. As I looked out over the classroom, students' faces had that droopy, how-many-minutes-'til-the-bell-rings look. "But how can this be boring?" I silently protested. "We're talking about the Vietnam War." As students filed out of the classroom, I shook my head and pledged to find a way to ignite their interest. I was just a first-year teacher, but I knew there had to be a better approach.

Over the years, I've concluded that lectures have their place — but only when directly linked to activities that draw students into the intimacy of social dynamics. For me, the teaching strategy that most consistently enlightens and brings students to life is the role play. There are all kinds of role plays, but the best of these raise critical questions that require student initiative and creativity. At times students may roam the classroom, building alliances with other groups, or debating whether the U.S. government should recognize the independence of a united Vietnam at the end of World War II, or whether logging should be allowed in old-growth forests. A good role play invites students to enter the personas of contemporary or historical social groups to learn about issues in their characters' lives from the inside out.

I'm talking like the social studies teacher that I am, but role plays are valuable in just about every class — science, math, English — and at just about every grade level. Any time there is a division of opinion on an important issue, a role play can help students to understand the source of conflict and to imagine possible resolutions.

I start with a controversial contemporary or historical problem: Should the Cherokee people be uprooted and moved west of the Mississippi River?

> The teaching strategy that most consistently brings students to life is the role play.

Should the United States government build the Dalles Dam on the Columbia River? In a role play on the election of 1860: Do you favor banning slavery from the western territories? Should there be a Palestinian state? Should nuclear weapons be banned? Who is to blame for the 1968 massacre at My Lai? In a music class: Should rock'n'roll and rap be regulated by the government? In an English class, students might represent different community groups debating whether Standard English should be spoken at all times in school. In a science class, students might examine the ecological complexities of logging old-growth forests by role playing the interests of timber companies, loggers, and environmental activists, but also the salmon, owls, rivers, and trees themselves. Each group could propose answers to the question: Should logging be restricted?

### Developing a Role Play

Stage one is conceiving substantive questions like these. Stage two entails selecting groups that will give voice to a range of perspectives on a particular issue. For example, a role play on land reform in Central America divides students into five groups: tenant farmers, the management of an instant coffee factory owned by a U.S. company, landless peasants, urban unemployed workers, and coffee planters. In the role play, each group has a somewhat different perspective on whether there should be land reform, how much land should be involved, and who should receive it. As in real life, strategic alliances between various groups are possible, and in the course of the role play students usually discover these and work together. The vitality of a role play depends on insuring that actual social conflicts come to life in the classroom.

In a mock U.S. Constitutional Convention, I include roles for groups that weren't represented at the real convention. So instead of only lawyers, financiers, and plantation owners in attendance, I also invite poor farmers, workers, and enslaved African Americans. Students debate questions from each group's standpoint: whether to abolish slavery and/or the slave trade, whether to allow debt relief to farmers by permitting payment "in kind," and how political leaders should be chosen. This more representative assembly allows students to experience some of the underlying conflicts that were suppressed in the actual Constitutional Convention.

But a role play wouldn't work, or at least wouldn't work as well, if I simply said to students, "You play a poor farmer; you play a plantation owner." They'd have nothing to go on beyond their own preconceptions, often stereotypical, of farmers and plantation owners. So I have to do some research in order to provide students with information on the circumstances in different social groups' lives — circumstances that would contribute to shaping these groups' attitudes on a given issue. Students can do some of this work, of course, but my experience is that they need a base to work from. This is especially true because many of the groups I want to include in a role play have been written out of traditional history books. For example, it's not that easy to find information in a high school library on the problems of farmers after the American Revolution, or about the Unemployed Councils of the 1930s.

That said, involving students in researching different groups can sometimes make them more engaged in a role play. Earlier this year, in a somewhat different kind of role play, I told students that each of them would be representing members of the Cherokee Nation and that the U.S. government was proposing to move them off their land and relocate them hundreds of miles to the west. I provided a role sheet with some historical background, but before beginning the role play we spent time in the library researching the Cherokee in greater depth. In class, I played President Andrew Jackson at a gathering with the Cherokees. Although the meeting was imaginary, I read actual excerpts from Jackson's 1830 message to Congress on Indian Removal (*The Annals of America*, Encyclopedia Britannica, Vol. 5, pp. 418-421). After the speech, students pelted me with questions and criticisms based on their research. Following this exchange, their assignment was to write a critique of Jackson's speech.

## Role Plays and Learning

In this and other role plays, amidst the deal-making, arguing, and oratory, students absorb a tremendous amount of information. But they absorb it in a way that reveals underlying social conflict and solidarity, so they can make sense of that information. In large measure, the process itself is the product. To be effective, the results of a role play needn't repeat history. Indeed some of our best de-briefing sessions concentrate on discussing why students made different choices than did the actual social groups they portrayed. Role plays allow students to see that history is not inevitable, that had people understood their interests more clearly, or had they overcome prejudices that kept them from making alliances, events might

have turned out very differently. I want students to see themselves as social actors, to realize that what they do in the world matters — they are not simply objects to be thrown about by some remote process called History. When they succeed, role plays can help chip away at students' sense of pre-determination, their sense of powerlessness.

In a different version of the Cherokee Removal role play, I include plantation owners, Atlanta bankers, the Andrew Jackson Administration, and the Cherokee. In this, as in other role plays, the intent is never to suggest that all points of view are equally valid. Andrew Jackson and Southern plantation owners can't propose stripping the Cherokee and other Southeastern Indian nations of their homelands without resorting to racist arguments. The role play allows students to see that. It's essential that key interests in a particular issue be represented, not necessarily so students can hear "all points of view," but so they can dissect the relationship between people's social conditions and their ideas.

A final note: A role play aims at nurturing students' appreciation of why people in history and the world today think and behave as they do. But I never want students to sympathize with individuals who behaved in hurtful or exploitative ways, that is, to have some emotional identification or agreement with these people. In my experience, kids are able to make the distinction. This is especially so when in follow-up discussion we critique positions espoused by various groups in a role play, including their own.

In his book, *A People's History of*

Role plays are a useful tool to involve students in their learning.

the United States, Howard Zinn critiques traditional nationalistic approaches to history: "Nations are not communities and never have been. The history of any country, presented as the history of a family, conceals fierce conflicts of interest (sometimes exploding, most often repressed) between conquerors and conquered, masters and slaves, capitalists and workers, dominators and dominated in race and sex. And in such a world of conflict, a world of victims and executioners, it is the job of thinking people, as Albert Camus suggested, not to be on the side of the executioners." Role plays should bring that world of conflict to life in the classroom and allow students to explore the underlying premises of arguments and to choose: Which side am I on? ❑

*Bill Bigelow (bbpdx@aol.com) teaches at Franklin High School in Portland, Oregon and is a* Rethinking Schools *editor.*

# Suggestions for a Successful Role Play

**1.** Introduce the role play and give students a sense of why the class is participating, and what the general guidelines will be. Break students into groups, roughly equal in size. It's vital that the question(s) each group will address are clear and understood by all.

**2.** Allow students to connect with the roles they've been assigned. You might encourage students to read their roles aloud in their small groups. I usually ask students to answer questions in writing based on their role: "How do you make your living? Why do you put up with such rotten working conditions?" Or I might ask them to write interior monologues — their inner thoughts — about hopes and fears. Students can read these to each other in the small groups. Have each group make a placard so they can see who's who. You might interview students in front of the class or even bait them devil's-advocate fashion: "How do you really feel about that poor farmer in that group over there?" As mentioned earlier, be sure that students' roles are not too prescriptive. I've seen many role plays that tell students exactly who they are and what they think. What's left for the kids? Likewise, some role plays don't give students enough information to participate thoughtfully: "You are a Mexican farmer." That's not much to go on. Also, try not to mix up roles by having some economic and some moral, e.g., steel workers and liberals; steel workers may be liberals.

**3.** It's the students' show, but the teacher's participation is

> ## It's the students' show, but the teacher's participation is vital.

vital. I circulate in the classroom making sure that students understand their roles. I help them think of groups they might want to ally with. I also instigate turmoil: "Do you know what those middle class people are saying about you immigrants?" It makes for more lively exchanges.

**4.** Each role should include at least some information that other groups don't have. This requires students to teach and persuade one another. So they need an opportunity to meet. After they have read and considered their roles and positions on issues, I tell students to choose half of their group to be "travelling negotiators." The travellers may only meet and "wheel and deal" with non-travellers, to insure that the whole class is involved at any given time.

**5.** It's important that students have an opportunity to present their points of view and hear from the other groups. I often structure these gatherings as "community meetings" assembled to discuss the burning issue under consideration. As with the small group negotiation sessions, I encourage students to use the information in their roles in their presentations to teach others. I usually play a role myself, sometimes as a partisan. For

example, in a role play on whether "Mother Country" will grant independence to its Asian colony, "Laguna," I play the colonial governor and chair the assembly. I know some teachers will disagree, but in my experience, it hasn't been a great idea to have students actually run the meetings, as discussion is often heated and students will jump on each other for seeming to play favorites in whom they recognize. However, at times I'll conduct a meeting with a simplified version of Roberts' Rules of Order which offers students a good deal of say-so in the pacing of discussion. In some role plays, a major aim is to give students practice in making decisions without the presence of an authority figure. For example, a role play on the 1912 Lawrence, Massachusetts textile strike, asks students in a large group format to confront strategic and tactical issues on their own: "With thousands of workers out on strike, how will we make decisions? Should our commissaries feed non-striking workers?" In this role play, students simulate the euphoria and frustration that accompanies grassroots democracy.

**6.** It's essential to de-brief. No activity stands on its own. Before we discuss, I usually ask people to step out of their roles by asking them to write for a few minutes. I might ask them to speculate on what actually happened in history. Sometimes I'll ask them to critique their own positions to give them permission to distance themselves from the points of view they espoused in the role play debates. ❏

# Testing, Tracking, and Toeing the Line:

## A Role Play on the Origins of the Modern High School

### By Bill Bigelow

What we don't teach in school can be more important than what we do teach. When we fail to engage students in thinking critically about their own schooling, the hidden message is: Don't analyze the institutions that shape your lives; don't ask who benefits, who suffers and how it got to be this way; just shut up and do as you're told.

Several years ago, my partner Linda Christensen and I began teaching a unit on the history and sociology of schooling. In the unit, students wrote and shared stories about their own school lives — both good learning experiences as well as times they encountered unfairness or abuse. We invited students to probe the hidden curricula in their own classes, including ours, asking them to reflect on what they were learning about authority, bosses and democracy; solidarity and resistance, people's capacity to stand up for themselves and each other; knowledge, what kind is valued and where it comes from; and self respect. Our class travelled to a high school in a wealthy Portland suburb to compare the hidden curriculum there with that at Jefferson, a school serving a predominantly working class, African-American community.

### Roots of Modern Schooling

To explore some of the historical roots of the modern high school I wrote a role play that I hoped would allow students to question aspects of schooling they often take for granted, such as tracking ("ability grouping"), standardized testing, guidance counseling, student government, the flag salute, bells, required courses with patriotic themes, and extracurricular activities like athletics and the school newspaper. These now commonplace components of high school life were introduced in the early

> When we fail to engage students in thinking critically about their own schooling, the hidden message is: Don't analyze the institutions that shape your lives.

years of the twentieth century, a time of growing union militancy and radicalism, and large-scale immigration from southern and eastern Europe, accompanied by vastly increased high school enrollment.

### Class Stratification

Underlying the new reforms was a consensus among leading educators that social class stratification was here to stay, and that high schools should abandon a single academic curriculum for all students. Charles Eliot of Harvard, for example, argued that classes were "eternal," with an elite "guiding class" at the top and on the bottom, a "thick fundamental layer engaged in household work, agriculture, mining, quarrying, and forest work." Schools, the educational establishment concluded, must be "realistic" and train children for specific roles in the social

hierarchy. Intelligence testing would allegedly insure students' accurate placement in differentiated curricular tracks. Simultaneously, as one school board president complained, "Many educators have failed to face the big problem of teaching patriotism. ... We need to teach American children about American heroes and American ideals."

Instead of just lecturing about the profound changes in schools occurring in the early years of the century, I wanted students to encounter them as if they were members of different social classes and ethnic groups, learning of proposed reforms for the first time. Through argument and negotiation, students-as-different-social-groups would need to decide whether they supported the then-new reforms in public education.

In the activity, I portray a gung-ho superintendent, newly arrived in "Central City," determined to modernize — i.e., stratify and "Americanize"— the curriculum. Each student portrays an individual in one of five social groups: corporate executives, members of the Industrial Workers of the World (IWW), middle class people, Hungarian immigrants, and Black activists.

Everyone is posed a series of questions about their views on schooling and is invited to advise the superintendent at a community meeting. In preparation, each group has a chance to consult and build alliances with any of the others. Through participating in the role play I hoped students might see first-hand that the school reforms were not simply benign, value-free changes, but were deeply political, benefiting some people at the expense of others. (See also the section, "An explicit critique of tracking," in "Getting Off the Track: Stories from an Untracked Classroom," p. 63.)

## Role Play Instructions

**Materials Needed:** Enough for all students: copies of "Superintendent's Statement," "School Reform Meeting Questions," and "Sample Intelligence Test." Enough role sheets so that each student has a role. (pp.120-124)

**Procedure** (also see "Suggestions for a Successful Role Play," p. 116.):

1. Write on the board: Place: **"CENTRAL CITY, USA;"** Time: **"EARLY 1920S."** Also list the names of the five social groups. (Note: "Central City" represents numerous midwestern and Eastern U.S. cities; I set the role play in the early 1920s because this is when standardized testing took off, but the social and educational trends described in the role play began earlier, in the beginning years of the twentieth century.)

2. Divide the class into five groups, of roughly equal numbers. Distribute a different role sheet to students in each of the groups: i.e., all the members of one group portray Hungarian immigrants, etc. Ask students to read these carefully, and, in their role, to think about the kind of schooling they want for their children. Encourage them to mark important sections. After they've finished reading, you might ask them to write a brief interior monologue — their inner thoughts — on what kind of education they hope for their children; or they might write on their fears. Afterwards ask them to read these to others in their group. The goal here is simply to prompt students to internalize the information in their role sheets, and to encourage them to imagine these individuals as real people. Ask students to make placards or name cards indicating their social group.

3. Tell students that Central City has hired a new superintendent who is proposing a series of reforms in Central City high schools. To each student, hand out the "Superintendent's Statement" and the "School Reform Meeting Questions." As mentioned, the teacher plays the superintendent. Before my "speech," I generally ask a student to introduce me as Superintendent Quincy P. Aldrich or another similarly aristocratic sounding name. I read the

Immigrants at the turn of the century.

AUGUSTUS F. SHERMAN/AMERICAN MUSEUM OF IMMIGRATION

statement aloud, with a good dose of pomp, stopping along the way to emphasize a point and to make sure students understand each proposed reform. (Note that the four tracks — feeble-minded, dull, etc. — come from a quote by Lewis Terman of Stanford, who suggested that these categories of students would never change. I tell students that if they don't like those designations, perhaps they'd prefer the tracks suggested by Professor George Strayer of Teachers College: bright, slow, backward, and deficient. Clearly, I am hoping to provoke students by using these terms. For public consumption, the educational elite preferred designations such as college, general, commercial, and vocational.) I assure the gathering that all tracking will be based on scientific evidence and I have a sample test to prove it. Students always want to see the test, so at this point I distribute "Sample Intelligence Test," (developed by Lewis Terman, p. 121). "What does knowing the color of emeralds have to do with your intelligence?" an inquiring immigrant or Black activist might ask. I encourage students' critical ques-

tions, but don't respond to them all as I want to conserve their defiant energy for the community meeting.

After the superintendent's proposal on guidance counseling, I emphasize that this is especially important considering the increased number of females in school these days: "Why, suppose a girl were to score high on a science test. It would be senseless to place her in a chemistry class. There are few if any female chemists in the country. It would be more sound to place her in an advanced domestic science course, which will help prepare her for the actual challenges she'll face in her life."

After my presentation, I tell people that I don't want to argue about the reforms I've proposed, that right now all I want are questions about my speech, and later, in the community meeting, they'll have a chance to argue all they want. Generally, students in several of the groups will pay no attention to this plea and will argue anyway. Again, at this stage it's good to get their critical juices flowing, but not to exhaust their arguments.

4. In preparation for the community

meeting, in their small groups, students should discuss the "School Reform Meeting Questions" and, at least tentatively, decide what they think. These opinions may change based on their negotiations with other groups.

5. After they've had a while, probably 15 minutes or so, to discuss the questions, I say something like: "Choose half your group to be 'travelling negotiators.' These people will meet with individuals in other groups to discuss the questions. This is your chance to find people who agree with you about the superintendent's reforms, or to convince others. Remember, there is power in numbers; the more united you are in the community meeting, the more likely it is that the superintendent will be convinced — or forced — to agree with you. One rule: travellers can't meet with other travellers, otherwise people left sitting in their groups will be left out."

6. This is the part I enjoy the most. As students dart around the classroom arguing points and finding allies, I listen in (as teacher, not superintendent), sometimes prodding people to meet with other groups or raising points they may not have considered. There is no "correct" amount of time to give this phase, but I don't want students' enthusiasm to wane, so I call a halt before they're talked out, perhaps twenty minutes or so.

7. Students should return to their small groups to prepare a presentation, however informal, on the various questions. I ask each group to choose a member to write on the board their response to question #1, on the purpose of schooling.

8. I seat the entire class in a circle (people should remain seated with their social group, each indicated with a placard) and begin the meeting by asking each group to respond to the question on the purpose of schooling. Again, there is no right and wrong way to run the meeting. The aim is to encourage the most spirited and democratic participation possible. As superintendent, I'm able to provoke people, point out contradictions, and raise questions. By the way, sometime during the community meeting I remind them that this is

only an advisory meeting, that there is a school board, elected citywide, to decide educational policy. I'm just seeking "input." We wouldn't want to give students the false impression that all social groups affected by school reform actually had any say so.

9. After the meeting, it's important that students have a way to distance themselves from their roles so the debriefing discussion is not simply a continuation of the community meeting. Sometimes I ask students to write about who they think "won" in real life, and to think about how things work in our high school today, to get clues on whose vision of schooling prevailed. Students might write a critique of the superintendent's position or of the position of one of the groups, including their own. Alternatively, they might remain in character to write an interior monologue on how they feel about their child's future in Central City Schools. Afterwards they might read these to the class.

10. Discussion questions include:
• Who do you think "won" in real life?
• Which of the reforms do you think were adopted in U.S. schools?
• (If a majority of the groups opposed the superintendent's plan:) If most of you opposed the reforms, why were they put into effect? What power did the different social groups have?

What power didn't they have?
• Which of the alliances you built might not have happened in real life? Why not?
• Which of the superintendent's proposals do you see in our school today? (Note: When my partner, Linda Christensen, and I did this role play with our untracked Literature in U.S. History class this year, we noticed that students who had previously been in the top track "scholars" program recognized immediately that our school is tracked. Other students, the majority, who had not experienced life at the top were unaware of how stratified our school is. One girl said, "We're mixed in here. The immigrants must have won.")
• Draw students' attention to the five purposes of schooling on the board: Which of these do you personally find most appealing? Why?
• Which of these seems closest to the kind of schooling you've had? Which of these do you think guides the way our school is set up today?
• What did the "intelligence test" measure? What didn't it measure?
• If you haven't already done so, it might be valuable to have students write about their personal experiences with standardized testing and/or tracking. ❏

*Bill Bigelow (bbpdx@aol.com) teaches at Franklin High School in Portland, Oregon and is a* Rethinking Schools *editor.*

## Useful Background Materials

Some background materials I've found useful include: Paul Davis Chapman, *Schools as Sorters*, New York University Press, 1988, (especially Chapter 5: "The Use of Intelligence Tests in Schools: California Case Studies.") David Tyack, *The One Best System: A History of American Urban Education*, Harvard University Press, 1974. Joel Spring, *The American School, 1642-1985*, Longman, 1986, (especially Chapter 7: "Education and Human Capital.") Robert S. Lynd and Helen M. Lynd, *Middletown*, Harcourt, Brace, 1929, (especially part III: "Training the Young.") Jeannie Oakes, *Keeping Track: How Schools Structure Inequality*, Yale University Press, 1985, (Chapter 2, "Unlocking the Tradition.") Samuel Bowles and Herbert Gintis, *Schooling in Capitalist America*, Basic Books, 1976, (Chapters 5 and 6, "The Origins of Mass Public Education" and "Corporate Capital and Progressive Education.")

Thanks to Robert Lowe, Sarah McFarlane, and Deborah Menkart for their help with this article.

# Superintendent's Statement on Reforming the High Schools

I've inherited a nineteenth century school district in a twentieth century city. It's time for some changes. The following proposals are based on reforms that are sweeping the nation, reforms developed by the finest universities.

Up until now we've run pretty much on the "common school" system. We've assumed that all students are the same, that all should be trained to be President of the United States. Well, my friends, not all our students are going to be President. In 1890, when fewer than 10% of 14 to 17 year olds were in high school, this probably made sense. But by 1920 over a third of all teenagers were in high school, and not all these kids are well-served by such a difficult academic curriculum. Nor is our society as a whole well-served by such a system. As the revered Stanford educator, Lewis Terman, reminds us, we have both "gifted and defective" children in school and they need to be taught differently. It's too bad, but as Ellwood Cubberley, Dean of Education at Stanford points out, in our schools we have "many children of the foreign-born who have no aptitude for book learning, and many children of inferior mental qualities who do not profit by ordinary classroom procedure."

• Therefore, I propose segregating students into four tracks, each with a different curriculum: Track #1: Feeble minded; Track #2: Dull; Track #3: Average; and Track #4: Superior. This will allow us to adapt a given course of study to students' individual needs. As suggested by one California school administrator, the lower tracks will naturally train students for "definite hand occupations as opposed to brain occupations."

• There will be no guess work in placing students in different tracks. They will be placed scientifically, on the basis of test scores. A system of guidance counseling will assist students in the interpretation of test scores, and to help them plan a personally rewarding and socially useful occupation.

• Lots of the people entering Central City schools are immigrants. These immigrants are worrisome for a number of reasons. Instead of identifying themselves as Americans, they see themselves as Hungarians or Italians. Some of them identify with the working class against the owners, or even with radicals, people who want to overthrow our form of government. In order to insure that all children become loyal Americans I'm proposing the following: To encourage students to learn about democracy, all schools will have student councils, and every day all students will pledge allegiance to the flag. In all classes we will teach that our system of government is the best in the world. Through clubs, athletics, school assemblies, school newspapers, and the like, we will encourage students to identify not with their social class or radical group, but with their school. We will teach them to be patriotic to their country and patriotic to their school. ❑

# School Reform Meeting Questions

*Be prepared to explain the following in your presentation at the school reform community meeting.*

1. In one or two sentences, describe what you see as the purpose(s) of schooling.

2. Do you support the superintendent's plan for "tracking?" Why or why not? If you don't support the plan, how do you propose to deal with the variety of social backgrounds and skill levels in Central City high schools?

3. Do you support the superintendent's plan for increased testing and guidance counseling? Why or why not?

4. Do you support the superintendent's curricular and extra-curricular proposals? Why or why not? Do you have any other suggestions?

# MENTAL ABILITY TEST
## STANFORD UNIVERSITY    TEST 1    INFORMATION

Draw a line under the ONE word that makes the sentence true, as shown in the sample.

Sample.  Our first president was

    Adams    Jefferson    Lincoln    <u>Washington</u>

1. Coffee is a kind of
    bark    berry    leaf    root

2. Sirloin is a cut of
    beef    mutton    pork    veal

3. Gasoline comes from
    grains    petroleum    turpentine    seeds

4. Most exports go from
    Boston    San Francisco    New Orleans    New York

5. The number of pounds in a ton is
    1000    2000    3000    4000

6. Napolean was defeated at
    Leipzig    Paris    Verdun    Waterloo

7. Emeralds are usually
    blue    green    red    yellow

8. The optic nerve is for
    seeing    hearing    tasting    feeling

9. Larceny is a term used in
    medicine    theology    law    pedagogy

10. Sponges come from
    animals    farms    forests    mines

11. Confucius founded the religion of the
    Persians    Italians    Chinese    Indians

12. The larynx is in the
    abdomen    head    throat    shoulder

13. The piccolo is used in
    farming    music    photography    typewriting

14. The kilowatt measures
    rainfall    wind-power    electricity    water-power

15. The guillotine causes
    death    disease    fever    sickness

16. A character in *David Copperfield* is
    Sinbad    Uriah Heep    Rebecca    Hamlet

17. A windlass is used for
    boring    cutting    lifting    squeezing

18. A great law-giver of the Hebrews was
    Abraham    David    Moses    Saul

19. A six-sided figure is called a
    scholium    parallelogram    hexagon    trapezium

20. A meter is nearest in length to the
    inch    foot    yard    rod

(FROM PAUL DAVIS CHAPMAN, SCHOOLS AS SORTERS, NEW YORK UNIVERSITY PRESS, 1988.)

# Corporate Executive

You are an executive with a large and prosperous corporation. There are a lot of problems in the country, problems that pose serious challenges to public education. In your eyes, the schools have not been meeting these challenges very successfully. For example, before 1900, fewer than one out of every ten kids between the ages of 14 and 17 was enrolled in high school. This is a real problem because people not in school become juvenile delinquents, turn to crime or worse, join radical groups like the Industrial Workers of the World (IWW). And besides, there simply aren't enough jobs to go around for everyone who wants one.

Also, lots of those entering schools are immigrants. They don't speak much English and haven't learned anything of what it means to be an American. Instead of identifying themselves as Americans, these immigrants see themselves as Hungarians or Italians. Some identify with the working class against

the owners, or even see themselves as radicals. In Lawrence, Massachusetts, in 1912, a massive strike involving 30,000 workers — teenagers, men, women, almost all immigrants — led by IWW radicals, defeated the mill owners. What is this country coming to? You need to make sure that the children of immigrants identify themselves as loyal, responsible Americans — and that they don't identify with one social class against another.

Besides all the immigrants arriving in Central City, there are lots of people leaving the farms to come to the city. These immigrants and farmers aren't used to the factory ways of the city. They aren't used to being prompt, working by the clock, doing repetitive work, obeying orders from a boss, etc. — all skills and attitudes needed to succeed as a factory worker. Their children are not ready to meet the challenges of modern life. You want the schools to turn out good factory workers — but

also serve the needs of your children, who are certainly not going to be factory workers.

Up until now, the high schools in Central City have been "common schools" with one curriculum for all students. With few exceptions, everyone took the same subjects in the same classes: boys with girls, bright kids with dull kids. The problem is that in earlier times, very few people went to school, so if you had a high school diploma, it meant something – you could get a good job in the business world. These students tended to be from upper class or middle class families. But now, with all these farm kids and immigrants entering the schools, there's no way that all of them are going to get these high-paying jobs. You need to figure out a way for the school system to train the future bankers and the future factory hands in the same classrooms — or at least in the same schools. ❑

# Hungarian Immigrant

Let's get one thing straight: You didn't move to the United States to take anybody's job. At the turn of the century conditions were tremendously difficult in Hungary. You owned a little plot of land, but when wealthy farmers began buying machinery to harvest their crops, you simply couldn't compete. You could starve or move. When labor contractors began showing up, they promised good jobs and high wages if you would travel to the United States — a real land of milk and honey. The travelling conditions both in Europe, on the ship coming over, and within the United States were difficult beyond belief. But finally you arrived in Central City, home of Miller and Jones, a giant manufacturer of railroad cars.

Instead of milk and honey you found grease and grime. Even though in Hungary you were a skilled farmer,

here you were called "unskilled labor." Your pay was low, but at least work was steady — for awhile. But then you realized that you were guaranteed nothing. Often you'd work only six months out of the year and be laid off the rest of the time. Needless to say, during these periods there were no unemployment benefits. As an unskilled worker you had no security. At times your friends would not be hired back by Miller and Jones; younger, stronger workers would be hired to take their places. With no formal education, no access to additional training, and no big bank account, you have little hope of escaping this life of poverty.

There may be little hope for you, but there is hope for your children. In America, education is free. You've been told that a high school diploma guarantees a young person a decent job. Just because you are an unskilled laborer

doesn't mean that your children will suffer the same fate. They might be teachers, clerks, shopkeepers or even doctors or lawyers. That's why you will sacrifice anything to send your children to school. They will be in the same classes with the sons and daughters of bankers and businessmen, architects and artists. They will read the same books, write the same essays and solve the same equations. In school, rich and poor will mean nothing. Your children are smart. There will be no limit to what they can accomplish. You want them to learn to be Americans, but you are proud of your Hungarian culture and also want them to value that heritage. Your children learn quickly and already speak two languages. You have absolute confidence they will be able to thrive in high school and go on to get good jobs. ❑

*Planting, by Thomas Hart Benton*

During World War I many southern Blacks gave up sharecropping and moved north.

# Black Activist

You are a Black activist in Central City. Over the years you've worked with a number of organizations to promote civil rights and independence for Black people. Sometimes you've worked with groups that make alliances with whites, other times you've worked with Black-only organizations. You join with whomever you see as capable of effectively fighting racism in Central City and the country as a whole.

For years there weren't many Black people in Central City. Most Blacks came North during World War One. Conditions were horrible in Mississippi. Your family worked as sharecroppers there, growing cotton and a few vegetables. It seemed like you were always in debt to the white landlord. Everything you had to buy was expensive; but they paid you next to nothing for the crops you raised. Anyone who protested would be beaten or even killed. Blacks were denied the right to vote and the kids went to crummy schools. When people heard there were jobs up north, practically your whole county emptied out overnight.

But conditions in Central City have become increasingly difficult since the war. Perhaps the biggest problem is job discrimination. Employers hire Blacks in only the most dangerous, worst paid and dead-end jobs. Even when you have the skills and education that qualify you for good jobs, the jobs still go to white people. The Ku Klux Klan is a strong force in Central City. They want to make sure that Blacks stay poor and powerless and don't get too "uppity" and start demanding good jobs, better housing and decent schools.

You are especially concerned about the education of Black children. While schools are not formally segregated in Central City, you know that Black children are discriminated against. One recent study found that 50% of Black girls in Central City schools were classified as "retarded" and put in "special classes," whereas only 4% of native born whites were classified this way. For this you blame racist administrators and teachers.

Many school officials say that they want to teach children the skills they will need in "real life." They assume Blacks will continue to be janitors and maids and so want to teach you to be good — and happy — janitors and maids. But you want your children to get a good academic education so they can become anything they set their minds to. However, some people complain that this kind of education will only make Black children resentful. As one judge warned recently, education should not put "fool ideas of rising and equality into [Black] folks' heads, and [make] them discontent and unhappy." In your view, in an unjust society, education *should* make young people discontent. It should fill their heads with dreams of equality and give them the tools — reading, writing, knowledge of their history — that will allow them to make their dreams real.

You hope that the more education children have, the unhappier they will be with the racism in Central City and the larger society. A good education should help give children the skills to organize for a better, more just, society. What you want from the superintendent of schools in Central City, and the school system as a whole, is a commitment to fight racism. ❑

# IWW Member

You live in Central City, USA and are a member of the Industrial Workers of the World, a radical labor union. You're concerned about school because you care about children, but also because you see schools as a place where people learn about what is expected of them by society. You see changing the schools as part of a larger movement for changing the whole society.

Much is now different in America. The society is more and more divided between rich factory owners and workers who own nothing but their own ability to labor. As far as you in the IWW are concerned, the problems of working people will only begin to be solved when workers take over all the workplaces and run them together for the benefit of the whole society — not just for the private profit of the owners. As long as owners run industry for their own profit, there will be continual conflict between them and the workers they control. You believe that all wealth is produced by the workers, so all wealth should be controlled by the workers — what do owners produce?

Thus, the goal of the IWW is not only for higher wages or shorter hours, but to change the whole society. Workplaces and all of society should be run by the people who produce, the people who do the work. And schools should help people learn the skills to run the whole society.

In the IWW you don't believe in the idea of "follow the leader." Your goal is for every worker in the country to be a "leader." Recently, you read a speech by Eugene Debs, an IWW founder. Debs summed up the IWW belief:

*The average working [person] imagines that he must have a leader to look to; a guide to follow, right or wrong. ... You have depended too much on that leader and not enough on yourself. I don't want you to follow me. I want you to cultivate self-reliance. If I have the slightest capacity for leadership I can only give evidence of it by "leading" you to rely on yourselves.*

That's what democracy is all about as far as you're concerned: everyone a leader, a thinker, a participant — regardless of race, sex or class background. And that's what schools should promote for all the students, not just the ones from rich families. Schools should model a truly democratic, classless society. ❑

# Middle Class Person

You consider yourself "middle class" — maybe upper middle class. You manage a small variety "five and dime" store; your father was a clerk for a large machine shop in town. The changes going on in Central City make you nervous — not so much for yourself, but for your children.

When you were young, the common wisdom was that if you went to high school and you graduated, you were guaranteed a good solid middle class or business job. You might become a clerk or a factory superintendent, or go on to college to become a lawyer or a doctor. The ticket was high school graduation, and for the most part only the upper and middle classes went to high school. But now everything is changing. In the last twenty years or so the population of Central City has tripled. Quite a number of people are coming into town off the farms, but most of the newcomers are immigrants from overseas. These people, many of whom can't even speak English, think that in America the streets are lined with gold. Problem is, the immigrants think that the way to get some of that good American gold is to send their kids to high school.

Why is this a problem? Because there aren't enough good jobs to go around. A university did a survey recently. They asked high school kids what they wanted to be when they grew up. Just over 90% wanted to be some kind of professional person, clerk or business person; only 4% wanted to work in a factory. But in the real world, only about 18% of the jobs are those kind of decent middle class jobs. Over 60% are factory jobs or farmwork of some kind. You hate to think of yourself as selfish, but these statistics mean that there are going to be lots of people competing for the jobs that should belong to your children.

You know that in a fair competition your child would succeed. But what is happening now is that all these immigrant kids and farm kids who can barely read or write are crowding into the same classes. Soon, a high school diploma won't be worth anything. You want your child to read classic literature, take mathematics, write essays and research papers, learn the history of this great country and master the workings of our form of government. But all these slow learners are going to hold everyone back. And they are also disruptive, many of them juvenile delinquents.

The world is a different place. Today, good jobs require more education. You might even have to send your children to college. But what if they've had an inferior high school education because of all these rowdy newcomers? ❑

RICK REINHARD

# Rethinking Our Assumptions

Schools are often exhorted to be neutral and objective in their interactions with children. Yet schools have never been value-free. Politics, culture, and ideology shape all aspects of school life — from teachers' favoritism toward some students to unexamined premises guiding curriculum.

The writers in this chapter invite teachers to reflect on how they classify children, understand the sources of student failure, view history, and think about race, gender, and class.

# Expectations and 'At-Risk' Children: One Teacher's Perspective

By L. C. Clark

My principal and I have a fine working relationship. He has come to understand that I do not "do" Halloween (even as a child I never liked the holiday), and I never nag him about scheduling difficulties before 8:30 a.m. We share a common philosophy of education and know precisely why we come to work each morning — the kids! Generally, we are civil and never have "words" in the presence of others unless we are in the midst of a staff meeting where all those assembled have "lost it," know they have "lost it," and have every intention of forgetting what was said (or shouted) upon entering the local watering hole.

Yes, Mr. Smythe and I are doing quite well except for one thing. In my opinion, he does not hold the same expectations for my minority children, many of whom come from lower socio-economic backgrounds than most of the majority children. These children are often referred to as children "at-risk."

Before I continue, please understand that I do not believe this man is bigoted or lacking in respect for these children. On the contrary, I feel that his expectations come out of deep concern and caring for them. It is just that I see him as being so sensitive to the many difficulties and disasters which often occur in the children's home environments that he cannot accept the notion that even in the midst of crisis they have a responsibility to get an education, and we have a responsibility to expect them to go about acquiring one.

Though we do share a common philosophy of education, our particular methods of implementing our shared beliefs are quite different. I am of the opinion that his methodology, which focuses on assisting children in building self-esteem exclusively through the affective domain, manifests itself in lower expectations of the children. These lower expectations negatively influence the children's ability to grow intellectually and socially. In other words, he focuses on the idea that by being tolerant and understanding of their difficulties in the school setting, and not pushing too often or too hard, we can help them to develop higher self-esteem. I, on the other hand, assert that if children are firmly and continually encouraged to function in school by developing appropriate school behaviors to facilitate their learning, their self-esteem will rise because they will see themselves as learners, capable of functioning fully in an academic setting.

## Jamie's Story

I can illustrate our dilemma by describing an incident which transpired several months into the last school year.

Jamie, one of my 17 low-achieving math students, came running into class approximately five minutes after the

> Lower expectations negatively influence children's ability to grow intellectually and socially.

class began. I inquired as to his previous whereabouts. Jamie told me he had been in the administrative assistant's office trying to get out of losing his lunch recess for "roofing" a ball. I reminded him that math class began at 9:10 sharp, and it was to his benefit to be on time so as not to feel lost or confused during the class discussion of the day's topic.

I continued the lesson and watched as Jamie retrieved his book and a piece of paper. As various children came up to the chalkboard to solve problems, I noticed that Jamie was not writing. I walked over to him and asked if he had a pencil or needed a new one. He did not have a pencil, so I sent him over to a cabinet to get one.

Twenty-five minutes into the period, students were instructed to have a partner look over their homework before handing it in and going on to their next assignment. Jamie did not move. I went over to him and asked if there was a problem. He informed me that he had not done his homework. (Out of seven assignments due that week Jamie handed in two. Those two papers were completed because I sat with him during his study break as he worked independently.) I told Jamie to see me before reporting to his lunch recess with the administrative assistant. Then, I instructed him to go to one of the math stations to get a class assignment completed.

After school I related Jamie's behavior and performance to Mr. Smythe, hoping to get some feedback on how to get Jamie back on track in math. I reminded him that while Jamie had demonstrated good understanding of some number concepts and had done well with his basic facts (addition, subtraction, and multiplication through the sixes table), his overall rating was far below average and his progress was erratic.

Mr. Smythe stood in silence for a moment and then proceeded to tell me that it was possible that Jamie had had difficulty in class because of an incident which had occurred in his home last evening that required police involvement. I acknowledged his comment and waited for his input regarding alternatives for assisting Jamie with his learning. Neither of us spoke, and it dawned on me that what he had said about the previous evening was his response to my (and Jamie's) dilemma. It was somewhat unnerving, but I decided that the time had come for the issue of expectations to be addressed.

My question was: "How many times are we going to use the problems that happen at home to excuse ourselves from requiring Jamie to function as a learner in an academic setting?"

## "At Risk" of Not Being Taught

The "Jamie" story, one of many, has serious implications for teachers, administrators, and, most especially, students who are considered to be "at-risk." While I am sure there are some people in schools who do not believe all children can learn, I contend that the majority are in education because they know all children can learn, and they want to facilitate the process. However, I have observed that oversensitivity which manifests itself in repeated acceptance of children's problems while not addressing solutions involving academic concerns is inappropriate for several reasons.

First, it presumes that the problem is temporary. This can lull teachers and administrators into thinking that everything will be all right tomorrow (next week, next year). Some children are in dysfunctional families and it is highly unlikely that the conditions precipitating their difficulties will be relieved during their school years. However, this does not mean that parents are not to be notified or looked to for assistance when children do not behave appropriately.

For instance, in developing a plan to get Jamie to be more responsible about being prepared and on time for class, I contacted his grandmother. I explained Jamie's problem and how it was hurting him academically, then solicited her ideas for what I (and his other teachers, as well) could do to change his behavior. She told me that Jamie liked to watch television after dinner, and she would not allow him to watch T.V. if he did not "act right" in school. After sharing other possibilities, we agreed that whenever Jamie acted irresponsibly he would: (1) call home at the end of the school day to tell his grandmother of the accumulated time wasted due to being tardy or unprepared and (2) lose 30 minutes or more of viewing time depending on the accu-

# Teachers and Cultural Styles

## By Asa G. Hilliard III

I remain unconvinced that the explanation for the low performance of culturally different "minority" group students will be found by pursuing questions of cognitive or learning styles. I believe that the children, no matter what their style, are failing primarily because of systematic inequities in the delivery of whatever pedagogical approach the teachers claim to master — not because students cannot learn from teachers whose styles do not match their own.

There is a protocol of interactive behaviors of teachers who, for whatever reasons, have low expectations for students. Research in this area shows that teachers tend to:

• Demand less from low-expectation students ("lows") than from high-expectation students ("highs").

• Wait less time for lows to answer questions.

• Give lows the answer or call on someone else rather than try to improve the lows' response through repeating the question, providing clues, or asking a new question.

• Provide lows with inappropriate reinforcement by rewarding inappropriate behaviors or incorrect answers.

• Criticize lows more often than highs for failure.

• Fail to give feedback to lows' public responses.

• Pay less attention to lows and interact with them less frequently.

• Call on lows less often than highs to respond to questions.

• Seat lows farther away from the teacher than highs.

• Use more rapid pacing and less extended explanations or repetition of definitions and examples with highs than with lows.

• Accept more low-quality or more incorrect responses from low-expectation students.

• Interact with lows more privately than publicly.

• In administering or grading tests or assignments, give highs but not lows the benefit of the doubt in borderline cases.

• Give briefer and less informative feedback to the questions of lows than to those of highs.

• Use less intrusive instruction with highs than with lows, so that they have more opportunity to practice independently.

• When time is limited, use less effective and more time-consuming instructional methods with lows than with highs. ❐

*Asa G. Hilliard, III, is Professor of Urban Eduation at Georgia State University. He is co-author of* Saving the African American Child.

The above is an excerpt reprinted with permission of the National Education Association. Copyright © 1989 by the NEA.

IMPACT VISUALS/LOREN SANTOW

**Intended acts of compassion can lead to subtle racism toward 'at-risk' children.**

mulated time and frequency of offenses. By the end of the third marking period (early April), Jamie was occasionally late and unprepared, but he had come to understand that he had to take responsibility for his behavior and the consequences of his actions.

The second reason not addressing solutions is inappropriate is that not working on a solution with a child takes away his or her opportunity to develop positive ways to cope within the school, as well as outside of its walls, when problems arise. Case in point, Jamie often missed out on participating in extracurricular events, such as T-ball and softball, because he would fail to take the flyer home or forget to return the permission slip on time.

One day some other children were getting ready to go to an after school practice when Jamie became angry and started yelling. He confronted one of the boys, called him "stupid" and the softball team "dumb." I moved Jamie away from the boy, then asked him if he had received the same T-ball form at the same time as the other children. When he said he had, I told him to think about why he was not on the team. Jamie left to go home.

The following morning I asked Jamie if he now knew why he was not on the team. He was silent for awhile

and then admitted that he had forgotten to return the slip. I asked if he knew what he would do next time to make sure he got the chance to get on the team. He replied, "Put it (the slip) in my pocket and bring it back the next day." I suggested he apologize to the other boy. Jamie knew what his responsibility was and how to carry it out.

The final reason has to do with what I see as the primary tasks of a school — teaching and learning. It is my firm belief that when children, teachers, and administrators continually turn away from these fundamental tasks, the children, particularly those already deemed "at-risk," are placed in a cycle, the continuance of which is clearly detrimental to their individual lives and, in time, the society.

By adhering to a relativistic philosophy, educators in effect lock those considered to be "disadvantaged" or "at-risk" into the very situations from which education should free them. Intended acts of compassion result in outcomes which promote subtle racism. While I hold the position that expectations must reflect a belief in a child's ability to meet the established standards of an academic community, I am not advocating such a rigid adherence to any standard that the humanity of a child be sacrificed. Rather, I am insist-

ing that compassion be tempered with reason, so that a child deemed "at-risk" be allowed to fully develop and experience his or her power — intellectually, socially, and emotionally.

The issue of expectations which arose in my relationship with my principal has not been resolved and I must now address why it may not be for awhile, if ever. It is extremely difficult to bring the word "racism" into a discussion without creating either discomfort (which makes the dialogue hesitant and shallow) or dissension (which threatens to cut off dialogue completely). But, realizing that holding lower expectations for "at-risk" youngsters (even out of compassion) threatens their intellectual and social/emotional growth commands that the courage to acknowledge the real problem be found.

A relationship, whether personal or professional, reflects the degree of trust and respect between the individuals involved. I believe that between my principal and myself there exists a level of trust and respect that will advance the dialogue which needs to begin and hold the relationship intact even as we may stand against one another. ❐

*L.C. Clark is an elementary school teacher in New York state.*

# The Pigs: When Tracking Takes Its Toll

## By Molly Schwabe

*Sorting students into groups remains some teachers' response to perceived differences in children's abilities. Although Molly Schwabe's story highlights one parent's guile rather than a systemwide challenge to tracking, we include it as a poignant reminder of the potential lifelong consequences of so-called ability grouping. —editors*

"How was school, honey? Do you like your teacher? What are you learning?" I asked my daughter.

"School's fine. I like it. My teacher's nice," Katie beamed in reply.

I was so happy about Katie's attitude. Proud and expectant, knowing what a little wizard I had created, I waited anxiously for the school's affirmation. I imagined the first conference and how I would lower my head and modestly thank them for the compliments. Certainly they would soon discover the wonder of my pig-tailed six year old.

Katie was a mimic — she could mime almost anything, from applying pretend mascara to reading with expression. I had read religiously to Katie, and she loved it. She had a ready repartee of Mother Goose rhymes and could do all sorts of adorable tricks. Reading would be a snap, I thought.

For the next few weeks Katie continued to come home content and positive as she could be. She bubbled when I asked about the reading groups.

"What reading group are you in?" I casually asked.

"The Pigs," Katie proudly answered.

I was absolutely stunned. "What? Are you sure?"

"Yes," she squealed with sheer delight, "I'm a Pig!"

"What are the other groups?" I inquired.

"Oh, let's see, the Lions, the Tigers, and the Panthers."

"There must be other groups." I prayed silently, "Oh please, God, please let there be others — Worms, Sloths, Slugs ... something."

"No, that's all," she grinned, dashing my hopes.

Margot, one of Katie's friends, could rattle off the whole alphabet when she was only three, so I asked about Margot's group. Margot was a Panther. Christopher, whose parents both went "Back East" to school, was a Tiger.

"How about Darcy?" I asked. Darcy picked her nose, was rumored to have had head lice, and was very silly. Her mother never read to her, so I guessed she wouldn't be too successful in school.

Katie was jubilant. "Darcy's in my group. We're both Pigs!"

Then I was really sick. I asked about the readers. The Panthers and the Tigers were reading little stories. The Pigs were working on vowel sounds or letters. I started grabbing books off the shelves and asked Katie to read. She knew some of the words, others were total mysteries. To my surprise she couldn't, in fact, read as well as I had thought. Perhaps she wasn't a Panther; certainly, she was no Pig.

The next afternoon I visited the teacher. "Katie is terribly bored," I lied. She's beginning to hate school because she is miserable in her reading group. She's a great reader and should be reading real stories. I want her moved right away!"

Naturally the teacher was confused and surprised, but agreed to give her a chance in a new group. That evening

Tracking stigmatizes children.

Katie and I began Distar lessons. I timed, while Katie struggled with "mit, bit, sit, kit," over and over. Under duress, she could spout "mat, cat, sat, pat, hat," in less than 15 seconds.

Distar was discarded after a few evenings, but Katie remained in the top group. Eventually she was placed in the TAG Junior Great Book afterschool program, and today she's an avid reader. She's doing well in college and will be a junior at the University of Washington in the fall.

Downtown last weekend I ran into Darcy. She got her high school diploma only one year late and is hoping to land a practically permanent job in an all-night grocery. I often wonder what would have happened to Katie if I hadn't asked about the groups or had been too afraid to lie. ❒

*Molly Schwabe teaches English at Madison High School in Portland, Ore.*

# Seeing Color:
# A Review of *White Teacher*

## By Lisa Delpit

As a new teacher, I was delivering my first reading lesson to first-grade students in inner-city Philadelphia. I had practically memorized the publisher-provided lesson dialogue while practicing in front of a mirror the night before.

"Good morning, boys and girls. Today we're going to read a story about where we live, in the city." A small brown hand was raised. "Yes, Marti." Marti had been a kindergartner in the informal classroom where I completed student teaching.

"Teacher, how come you talkin' like a white person? You talkin' just like my momma talk when she get on the phone!"

Needless to say, the practiced lesson was put aside as we relaxed into my more typical informal and culturally familiar interaction patterns. And I was once again struck by the brilliant perception of six-year-olds.

This and other vignettes of my teaching career surfaced as I reread Vivian Gussin Paley's fascinating *White Teacher*. There was no stopping the flood of scenes of children, parents, and teachers, for Paley's writing is so vivid, so classroom-centered, so immediate that anyone who has ever taught — or ever thought about teaching — cannot help being drawn into the daily dramas she describes perfectly. *White Teacher*, originally published in 1979, was reissued in 1990, probably because Paley was awarded a prestigious MacArthur Foundation fellowship in 1989. She was the first classroom teacher so honored.

The book details Paley's development as she struggled to learn to teach diverse — particularly African-American children in her kindergarten classrooms. Her first teaching jobs were in the segregated schools of the South, where she became the school radical by telling everyone that she wanted an integrated class, that society forced her to teach only white children. When she moved back North, she found herself teaching white children in a white suburb. She had an occasional black student — one the child of the live-in maid of a prominent family, two others when the school board attempted some minor integration. And her encounters with these children caused Paley concern. One avoided looking at her and only responded to her questions with "Yes'm." Another, Fred, joined an aggressive group of six white kids. When the teachers came into Paley's room under various pretenses to, as Paley says, "check out the two black children," they all singled out Fred. "You've got your hands full with him." "Shouldn't he be in a special class?"

### Color Blindness

At the first faculty meeting Paley raised the issue that even though all the children in Fred's small group behaved as he did, teachers singled out Fred because of his color. After vigorous discussion, the faculty reached a consensus: "More than ever we must take care to ignore color. We must only look at behavior, and since a black child will be more prominent in a white classroom, we must bend over backward to see no color, hear no color, speak no color." Paley found herself confused by such directives when children themselves raised issues of color. In one instance a little white child told a little black girl that she looked like chocolate pudding. Was that an insult? Should Paley reprimand the white child? She found herself trapped not only by the school's position but by her own liberal upbringing: "We showed respect by completely ignoring black people as black people. Color blindness was the essence of the creed."

Insight came when Paley moved to a midwestern city and took a job at an integrated private school. Although most of the faculty and professional staff were white, about a third of the students were children of color. Early on she had a meeting with a black parent. "Mrs. Hawkins told me that in her children's previous school the teacher had said, 'There is no color difference in my classroom. All my children look alike to me.' 'What rot,' said Mrs. Hawkins. 'My children are black. They know they're black, and we want it recognized. It's a comfortable natural difference. At least it could be so, if you teachers learned to value differences more. What you value, you talk about.'"

Thus began the journey toward acknowledging and valuing differences. When Michelle, black and vivacious, pointed to a picture in a book and said she wished she looked like the pink-cheeked blond girl on the page, Paley recalls, "I could have easily ignored this. Maybe Juli Ann, white and plain, wished she looked like the girl in the book too ... But Michelle had a special, obvious reason. I knew I must say something. 'Michelle, I know how you feel. When I was little I also would have liked to look like this little girl. She doesn't look like anyone in my family, so I couldn't have looked like her. Sometimes, I wish I had smooth brown skin like yours. Then I could always be dark and pretty.' Michelle looked down at her skin. So did everyone else. I don't know what she was thinking. But I knew the feelings I had expressed were true, though I did not know it until I

Restructuring of schools must include restructuring interpersonal relationships.

spoke."

In Paley's chronicle of her development of learning from and with her students over five years, she encounters Steven's angry, "DON'T TALK TO ME. I don't have to listen to no white lady. ... Don't nobody white look at me. Don't talk to me. You stink. Fuckers!" Kenny didn't want to take off his jacket because the teacher might not like what his T-shirt said: "SUPERNIGGER, guardian of the oppressed." Clare, from a West Indian family, was in such unfamiliar cultural territory that she was almost diagnosed as retarded. Another Kenny, whose physical prowess and bravado were amazing as long as he was outside tumbling with his brothers, was so timid during school activities that he became speechless if required to perform some small task in front of the whole class.

It is important that this book has been reissued now. Never has there been so much talk about "restructuring" schools. While legislators, governors, and various "experts" debate the virtues of "site-based management," "merit pay," "choice," or "accountability schemes," there is little talk about the kind of "restructuring" that must happen before we can make any headway with education: the restructuring of interpersonal relationships. While the number of children of color in our public schools is rapidly rising, the number of teachers of color continues to decline. More than ever, white teachers will be teaching African-American children.

As a teacher-educator, I have worked with white students who will be tomorrow's teachers, and I have many African-American friends who have done the same. The attitude that Paley brought to her first black students — that to acknowledge their color would be to insult them — is prevalent among our young white people about to join the teaching profession. One of my teacher-education colleagues told me that Paley's book was the only book she had found that helped her students understand that to say you don't see color is to say you don't see children. Her students were then able to understand that people could be proud of their color and their differences and that the teacher could help this process.

## The Qualities of a Good Teacher

Paley exhibits other behavior and attitudes that I try to instill in future teachers. First and foremost, she is an observer of children. When something goes wrong with a child, she does not assume that the cause necessarily lies within the child. She looks to her own teaching and to her own lack of knowledge. She realizes that she probably misses much of the intelligence of the children who are from another culture. She points out that when a child who shares her own Jewish background makes comments about meat and dairy dishes, she receives instant messages about his or her intelligence. But when several black children tell her that "black people don't eat pig. Only white people eat pig," she is honest enough to say, "I think I am missing part of the picture presented by many black children by not being familiar with the context within which certain simple statements are made."

She also seeks to learn from adults who look like the children she teaches. Many white teachers, with the best of intentions, believe that they know what is best for all children. And because they view themselves as liberals, they believe that their behavior is above reproach. In Paley's words, "My luggage had 'liberal' ostentatiously plastered all over it, and I thought it unnecessary to see what was locked inside." Believing in their "rightness," some liberal white teachers do not seek the opinions of parents or teachers of color, and they even subtly discredit those opinions if offered. Paley, on the other hand, often sought the insights of the parents of her black students, and she worked with them to find solutions to problems. When teachers are teaching children who are different from themselves, they must call upon parents in a collaborative fashion if they are to learn who their students really are.

Paley also learned from an African-American woman who worked with her as a student teacher one year. Janet was an older woman and an exceptional teacher with lots of experience teaching in preschool. Paley watched how she handled situations and asked questions about her own performance. That Paley was different from most teachers can be verified by Janet's reaction to the rest of the staff, with whom she was withdrawn and silent. When Paley asked her about it, Janet said she didn't feel comfortable with most white teachers because "they either avoid talking about race like it was a plague, or else they look at me only when black kids are discussed as if the ghetto is the only thing I know anything about." White teachers can utilize culturally diverse colleagues as learning resources only if they respect them and their opinions — not a typical scenario in today's schools.

Paley's book and her approach to children have many strengths, and I could not hope for a more sensitive

> ## To say you don't see color is to say you don't see children.

white teacher of African-American children. Yet I worry. Paley asks, "How much does it matter if a child cannot identify ethnically or racially with a teacher? Does it matter at all? If the teacher accepts him and likes him as he really is, isn't that enough?" I suspect she and I might differ.

## Remaining Questions

I wonder whether so many of the African-American children in her classes would have expressed a desire to be white if their teacher had been black. I feel for Ayana when she and Rena were helping Paley put away blocks and Rena said, "White people tell lies." I surmise from other conversations in the book that several of Paley's black students have been exposed to the philosophies of the Nation of Islam and carried some of those discussions from home into the classroom. "That's right, they do tell lies," Ayana agreed. Paley asked, "Do all white people tell lies?" Paley continues: "Ayana read my face. 'Uh ... no. Not all white people.' She looked guiltily at Rena." Clearly Ayana must have been expending energy in this classroom determining what she could and could not say to this white teacher whom she loved and trusted. And this is an instance that Paley was aware of. In how may other situations in this class did Ayana and other black children have to spend time and energy working out the complexities of what was appropriate for a non-black audience?

By contrast, I recall the easiness with which Marti, in my opening vignette, could bring up race with me and the ease with which I could slip into our comfortable way of interacting. I also recall my understanding, apprecia-

tion, and suppressed laughter — and my white co-teacher's shock and hurt until we discussed the incident — when Doris, in perfect imitation of older black women, put her hands on her hips as my co-teacher was leading her to the "time-out" chair: Doris said, "You better take your hands off my clothes. People's mamas have to pay for their clothes!"

My own daughter is not yet two years old, but of course I have begun to think about what kind of school environment I want for her. After spending hours searching for black-oriented books and taking a brown felt-tip pen to white toy figures, I do not want her to come home, like many of my friends' children who have attended predominantly white preschools and kindergartens, and say that she's ugly because she's brown or that she wants long blond hair and blue eyes. I don't want her to spend much of her thinking power trying to figure out what she should or shouldn't say to a white teacher. In other words, when she is five years old, I want her to be nourished and nurtured as she would be at home. I don't want her to feel alien or different. I want her to believe that she and people who look like her are gorgeous, smart, and in charge of things. I strongly want her to be in an African-American environment. There will be time later to learn about differences, to learn to struggle in a sometimes hostile environment. But when she's five, I don't want her too far from home.

Paley praises the integrated kindergarten environment. But she does not have to worry about being a minority of color. In fact, she declined an offer to teach in an inner-city school because she didn't think she could handle being in the minority again, as she felt she had been in the South. Should we inflict such difficult status on our five-year-olds? ☐

*Lisa D. Delpit is a senior researcher at the Institute for Urban Research at Morgan State University in Baltimore, Md.*

"Seeing Color" originally appeared in the September/October 1990 issue of the *Hungry Mind Review*.

# Face the Facts: We're Not That Bad

By Felícitas Villanueva

*We're not talking about you!*
*Ooo, no SENOR, we're just having a chat.*
*And if we gave you a glance,*
*it's just what every human does.*
*Just because you can't understand,*
*it doesn't mean we're bad,*
*or that we're blurting your name!*
*We're sorry — DE VERDAD —*
*but it's not our fault, the truth is,*
*You BOLILLOS can't face the facts;*
*you're just pissed off, 'cause Spanish*
*you can't understand, and*
*if we speak English you still can't comprehend.*
*Again, I'd like you BOLILLOS to know:*
*I'm Latino from head to toe!*
*And Spanish is in my brains,*
*as well as English, but you AMIGO*
*in that brain, you only carry English,*
*that's about all!*

Felícitas Villanueva is a former student at South Division High School in Milwaukee. She wrote this poem while a student of *Rethinking Schools* founding co-editor Cynthia Ellwood. (See p. 184 for lesson ideas.)

# I Won't Learn From You!
## Confronting Student Resistance

### By Herbert Kohl

Years ago, one of my fifth-grade students told me that his grandfather Wilfredo wouldn't learn to speak English. He said that no matter how hard you tried to teach him, he ignored whatever words you tried to teach and forced you to speak to him in Spanish. When I got to know his grandfather I asked, in Spanish, whether I could teach him English and he told me unambiguously that he did not want to learn. He was frightened, he said, that his grandchildren would never learn Spanish if he gave in like the rest of the adults and spoke English with the children. Then, he said, they would not know who they were. At the end of our conversation he repeated adamantly that nothing could make him learn to speak English, that families and cultures could not survive if the children lost their parents' language, and, finally, that learning what others wanted you to learn can sometimes destroy you.

I discussed Wilfredo's reflections with several friends, and they interpreted his remarks as a cover-up of either his own fear of trying to learn English or his failure to do so. These explanations, however, show a lack of respect for Wilfredo's ability to judge what is appropriate learning for himself and his grandchildren. By attributing failure to Wilfredo and refusing to acknowledge the loss his family would experience through not knowing Spanish, they turned a cultural problem into a personal psychological problem: they turned willed refusal to learn into failure to learn.

I have encountered willed not-learning throughout my 30 years of teaching, and believe that such not-learning is often and disastrously mistaken for failure to learn or the inability to learn.

Learning how to not-learn is an in-

> **To agree to learn from a stranger who does not respect your integrity causes a major loss of self. The only alternative is to not-learn and reject their world.**

tellectual and social challenge; sometimes you have to work very hard at it. It consists of an active, often ingenious, willful rejection of even the most compassionate and well-designed teaching. Not-learning tends to take place when someone has to deal with unavoidable challenges to her or his personal and family loyalties, integrity, and identity. In such situations, there are forced choices and no apparent middle ground. To agree to learn from a stranger who does not respect your integrity causes a major loss of self. The only alternative is to not-learn and reject their world.

### The Lessons of San Antonio

I remember visiting some teacher friends in San Antonio, Texas, about 15 years ago. I was there trying to help in their struggles to eliminate anti-Latino racism in the public schools in the barrios. There were very few Latino teach-

ers and no Latino administrators in barrio schools in the parts of San Antonio where my friends worked. Many of the administrators were Anglo, retired military personnel from the San Antonio air force base who had hostile, imperialist attitudes towards the children they taught and the communities they served.

In one junior high I was invited to observe a history class by a teacher who admitted that he needed help with this particular group of students, all of whom were Latino. The teacher gave me a copy of his textbook, and I sat in the back of the room and followed the lesson for the day, which was entitled, "The first people to settle Texas." The teacher asked for someone to volunteer to read and no one responded. Most of the students were slumped down in their desks and none of them looked directly at the teacher. Some gazed off into space, others exchanged glimpses and grimaces. The teacher didn't ask for attention and started to read the text himself. It went something like, "The first people to settle Texas arrived from New England and the South in ...." Two boys in the back put their hands in their eyes, there were a few giggles and some murmuring. One hand shot up and that student blurted out, "What are we, animals or something?" The teacher's response was, "What does that have to do with the text?" Then he decided to abandon the lesson, introduced me as a visiting teacher who would substitute for the rest of the period and left the room.

I don't know if he planned to do that all along and set me up to fail with the students just as he did, or if his anger at being observed overcame him and he decided to dump the whole thing on me. Whatever the motivation, he left the room, and I was there with the students.

I went up front and reread the sentence from the book and asked the class to raise their hands if they believed what I had just read. A few of them became alert, though they looked at me suspiciously as I continued, "This is lies, nonsense. In fact, I think the textbook is racist and an insult to everyone in this room." Everyone woke up and the same student who had asked the teacher about animal life turned to me and asked, "You mean that?" I said I did, and then he interrupted and said, "Well, there's more than that book that's racist around here."

I said that it was obvious that the textbook was racist, it was there for everyone to read, but wondered how they detected racism in their teachers. The class launched into a serious and sophisticated discussion of the way in which racism manifests itself in their everyday lives at school. And they described the stance they took in order to resist that racism and yet not be thrown out of school. It amounted to nothing less than full-blown and cooperative not-learning. They accepted the failing grades it produced in exchange for the passive defense of their personal and cultural integrity. This was a class of school failures, and perhaps, I believed then and still believe, the repository for the positive leadership and intelligence of their generation.

Until we learn to distinguish not-learning from failure and respect the truth behind this massive rejection of schooling by students from poor and oppressed communities, it will not be possible to solve the major problems of education in the United States today. Risk-taking is at the heart of teaching well. That means that teachers will have to not-learn the ways of loyalty to the system and to speak out for, as the traditional African-American song goes, the concept that everyone has a right to the tree of life. We must give up looking at resistant students as failures and turn a critical eye towards this wealthy society and the schools that it supports.

No amount of educational research, no development of techniques or materials, no special programs or compensatory services, no restructuring or retraining of teachers will make any fun-

**Student resistance must not be confused with inability to learn.**

SUSAN LINA RUGGLES

damental difference until we concede that for many students, the only sane alternative to not-learning is the acknowledgement and direct confrontation of oppression — social, sexual, and economic — both in school and in society. Education built on accepting that hard truth about our society can break through not-learning and lead students and teachers together, not to the solution of problems but to direct intelligent engagement in the struggles that might lead to solutions. ❑

*Herbert Kohl is author of* 36 Children. *This essay is dedicated to the memory of Betty Rawls and the struggle for justice. Excerpted from the book* I Won't Learn from You and Other Thoughts on Creative Maladjustment *(The New Press, New York, 1994.)*

> We must give up looking at resistant students as failures and turn a critical eye towards this wealthy society and the schools that it supports.

# Rebellion Against the North Side

By Naomi Shihab Nye

There will be no monograms on our skulls.
You who are training your daughters to check for the words
"Calvin Klein" before they look to see if there are pockets
are giving them no hands to put in those pockets.

You are giving them eyes that will find nothing solid in stones.
No comfort in rough land, nameless sheep trails.
No answers from things which do not speak.

Since when do children sketch dreams with price tags attached?
Don't tell me they were born this way.
We were all born like empty fields.
What we are now shows what has been planted.

Will you remind them there were people
who hemmed their days with thick-spun wool
and wore them till they fell apart?

Think of darkness hugging the houses,
caring nothing for the material of our pajamas.
Think of the delicate mesh of neckbones
when you clasp the golden chains.
These words the world rains back and forth
are temporary as clouds.
Clouds? Tell your children to look up.
The sky is the only store worth shopping in
for anything as long as a life.

*Naomi Shihab Nye, winner of the National Poetry Series in 1982 for her book* Hugging the Jukebox, *currently lives and writes in San Antonio, Texas. (See p. 184 for lesson ideas.)*

# The Politics of Children's Literature
## What's Wrong with the Rosa Parks Myth

### By Herbert Kohl

Issues of racism and direct confrontation between African-American and European-American people in the United States are usually considered too sensitive to be dealt with directly in the elementary school classroom. When African Americans and European Americans are involved in confrontation in children's texts, the situation is routinely described as a problem between individuals that can be worked out on a personal basis. In the few cases where racism is addressed as a social problem, there has to be a happy ending.

This is most readily apparent in the biographical treatment of Rosa Parks, one of the two names that most children associate with the civil rights movement, the other being Martin Luther King Jr.

The image of "Rosa Parks the Tired" exists on the level of a national cultural icon. Dozens of children's books and textbooks present the same version of what might be called "Rosa Parks and the Montgomery Bus Boycott." This version can be synthesized as follows:

*Rosa Parks was a poor seamstress. She lived in Montgomery, Alabama, during the 1950s. In those days there was still segregation in parts of the United States. That meant that African Americans and European Americans were not allowed to use the same public facilities such as restaurants or swimming pools. It also meant that whenever the city buses were crowded, African Americans had to give up seats in front to European Americans and move to the back of the bus.*

*One day on her way home from work Rosa was tired and sat down in the front of the bus. As the bus got crowded she was asked to give up her seat to a European-American man, and she*

*refused. The bus driver told her she had to go to the back of the bus, and she still refused to move. It was a hot day, she was tired and angry, and she became very stubborn.*

*The driver called a policeman who arrested Rosa.*

*When other African Americans in Montgomery heard this, they became angry too, so they decided to refuse to ride the buses until everyone was allowed to ride together. They boycotted the buses.*

*The boycott, which was led by Martin Luther King Jr., succeeded. Now African Americans and European Americans can ride the buses together in Montgomery.*

*Rosa Parks was a very brave person.*

This story seems innocent enough. Rosa Parks is treated with respect, and the African-American community is given credit for running the boycott and winning the struggle. On closer examination, however, this version reveals some distressing characteristics that serve to turn a carefully planned movement for social change into a spontaneous outburst based upon frustration and anger.

The following annotations on the previous summary suggest that we need a new story, one not only more in line

> The image of "Rosa Parks the Tired" exists on the level of a national cultural icon.

with the truth but one that shows the organizational skills and determination of the African-American community in Montgomery and the role of the bus boycott in the larger struggle to desegregate Montgomery and the South.

### The Annotated "Rosa Was Tired"

*1. Rosa Parks was a poor seamstress. She lived in Montgomery, Alabama, during the 1950s.*

Rosa Parks was one of the first women in Montgomery to join the National Association for the Advancement of Colored People and was its secretary for years. At the NAACP she worked with chapter president E.D. Nixon, who was also vice president of the Brotherhood of Sleeping Car Porters. Parks learned about union struggles from him. She also worked with the youth division of the NAACP, and she took a youth NAACP group to visit the Freedom Train when it came to Montgomery in 1954. The train, which carried the originals of the U.S. Constitution and the Declaration of Independence, was traveling around the United States promoting the virtues of democracy. Since its visit was a federal project, access to the exhibits could not be segregated. Parks took advantage of that fact to visit the train. There, she and the members of the youth group mingled freely with European Americans who were also looking at the documents. This overt act of crossing the boundaries of segregation did not endear Parks to the Montgomery political and social establishment.

Parks' work as a seamstress in a large department store was secondary to her community work. In addition, as she says in an interview in *My Soul is Rested*, she had almost a life history of "being rebellious against being mistreated because of my color." She was well known to African-American leaders in Montgomery for her opposition to segregation, her leadership abilities, and her moral strength. Since the 1954 *Brown vs Board of Education* decision, she had been working to desegregate the Montgomery schools. She had also attended an interracial meeting at the Highlander Folk School in Tennessee a few months before the boycott. Highlander was known throughout the South as a radical education center that was overtly planning for the total desegregation of the South. At that meeting, which dealt with plans for school desegregation, Parks indicated that she intended to participate in other attempts to break down the barriers of segregation. To call Rosa Parks a poor tired seamstress and not talk about her role as a community leader is to turn an organized struggle for freedom into a personal act of frustration. It is a thorough misrepresentation of the Civil Rights Movement in Montgomery and an insult to Parks as well.

## Children and the Reality of Racism

*2. In those days there was still segregation in parts of the United States. That meant that African Americans and European Americans were not allowed to use the same public facilities.*

The existence of legalized segregation in the South during the 1950s is integral to the story of the Montgomery bus boycott, yet it is an embarrassment to many school people and difficult to explain to children without accounting for the moral corruption of the majority of the European-American community in the South.

Locating segregation in the past is a way of avoiding dealing with its current manifestations and implying that racism is no longer a major problem.

Describing segregation passively ("There was still segregation" instead of "European Americans segregated facilities so that African Americans couldn't use them") also ignores the issue of legalized segregation, even though Parks was arrested for a viola-

Signs like this appeared in buses in the South in the days of Jim Crow.

tion of the Alabama law that required segregation in public facilities. It doesn't talk overtly about racism. And it refers to "parts" of the United States, softening the tone and muddying the reference to the South.

I've raised the question of how to expose children to the reality of segregation and racism to a number of educators, both African-American and European-American. Most of the European-American and a few of the African-American educators felt that young children do not need to be exposed to the violent history of segregation. They worried about the effects such exposure would have on race relations in their classrooms and especially about provoking rage on the part of African-American students. The other educators felt that, given the resurgence of overt racism in the United States, allowing rage and anger to come out was the only way African-American and European-

American children could work toward a common life. They felt that conflict was a positive thing that could be healing when confronted directly and that avoiding the horrors of racism was just another way of perpetuating them. I agree with this second group.

## Segregated Sections

*3. Whenever the city buses were crowded, African Americans had to give up seats in front to European Americans and move to the back of the bus.*

Actually, African-Americans were never allowed to sit in the front of the bus in the South in those days. The front seats were reserved for European-Americans. Between five and ten rows back the "colored" section began. When the front filled up, African-Americans seated in the "colored" section had to give up their seats and move toward the back of the bus. Thus, for example, an elderly African American would have to give up his or her seat to a European-American teenager at the peril of being arrested.

## On Dignity and History

*4. One day on her way home from work Rosa was tired and sat down in the front of the bus.*

Parks did not sit in the front of the bus. She sat in the front row of the "colored" section. When the bus got crowded she refused to give up her seat in the "colored" section to a European-American. It is important to point this out as it indicates quite clearly that it was not her intent, initially, to break the segregation laws.

At this point the story lapses into the familiar and refers to Rosa Parks as "Rosa." The question of whether to use the first name for historical characters in a factual story is complicated. One argument is that young children will more readily identify with characters presented in a personalized and familiar way. However, given that it was a sanctioned social practice in the South during the time of the story for European-Americans to call African-American adults by their first names as a way of reinforcing the African-Americans' inferior status (African-Americans could never call European-Americans by their first names without breaking the social code of segregation), it seems unwise to use that practice in the story.

In addition, it's reasonable to assume that Parks was not any more tired on that one day than on other days. She worked at an exhausting full-time job and was also active full time in the community. To emphasize her being tired is another way of saying that her defiance was an accidental result of her fatigue and consequent short temper. Rage, however, is not a one-day thing, and Parks acted with full knowledge of what she was doing.

## Civil Disobedience, Not Mere Stubborness

*5. As the bus got crowded she was asked to give up her seat to a European-*

*American man, and she refused. The bus driver told her she had to go to the back of the bus, and she still refused to move. It was a hot day, she was tired and angry, and she became very stubborn. The driver called a policeman who arrested Rosa.*

This is the way that Parks, in her book *My Soul is Rested,* described her experiences with buses:

"I had problems with bus drivers over the years because I didn't see fit to pay my money into the front and then go to the back. Sometimes bus drivers wouldn't permit me to get on the bus, and I had been evicted from the bus. But, as I say, there had been incidents over the years. One of the things that made this [incident] ... get so much publicity was the fact that the police were called in and I was placed under arrest. See, if I had just been evicted from the bus and he hadn't placed me under arrest or had any charges brought against me, it probably could have been just another incident."

In the book *Voices of Freedom* by Henry Hampton and Steve Fayer, Parks describes that day in the following way:

"On December 1, 1955, I had finished my day's work as a tailor's assistant in the Montgomery Fair Department Store and I was on my way home. There was one vacant seat on the Cleve-

land Avenue bus, which I took, alongside a man and two women across the aisle. There were still a few vacant seats in the white section in the front, of course. We went to the next stop without being disturbed. On the third, the front seats were occupied and this one man, a white man, was standing. The driver asked us to stand up and let him have those seats, and when none of us moved at his first words, he said, 'You all make it light on yourselves and let me have those seats.' And the man who was sitting next to the window stood up, and I made room for him to pass by me. The two women across the aisle stood up and moved out.

"When the driver saw me still sitting, he asked if I was going to stand up and I said, 'No, I'm not.'

"And he said, 'Well, if you don't stand up, I'm going to call the police and have you arrested.'

"I said, 'You may do that.'

"He did get off the bus, and I still stayed where I was. Two policemen came on the bus. One of the policemen asked me if the bus driver had asked me to stand and I said yes.

"He said, 'Why don't you stand up?'

"And I asked him, 'Why do you push us around?'

"He said 'I do not know, but the law is the law and you're under arrest.'"

In 1955, Rosa Parks was arrested in Montgomery for refusing to give up her seat on a bus to a white person.

Mere anger and stubbornness could not account for the clear resolve with which Parks acted. She knew what she was doing, understood the consequences, and was prepared to confront segregation head-on at whatever sacrifice she had to make.

## Planned Resistance

*6. When other African Americans in Montgomery heard this, they became angry too, so they decided to refuse to ride the buses until everyone was allowed to ride together. They boycotted the buses.*

The connection between Parks' arrest and the boycott is a mystery in most accounts of what happened in Montgomery. Community support for the boycott is portrayed as being instantaneous and miraculously effective the very day after Parks was arrested. Things don't happen that way, and it is an insult to the intelligence and courage of the African-American community in Montgomery to turn their planned resistance to segregation into a spontaneous emotional response. The actual situation was more interesting and complex. Not only had Parks defied the bus segregation laws in the past, according to E.D. Nixon, in the three months preceding her arrest at least three other African-American people had been arrested in Montgomery for refusing to give up their bus seats to European-American people. In each case, Nixon and other people in leadership positions in the African-American community in Montgomery investigated the background of the person arrested. They were looking for someone who had the respect of the community and the strength to deal with the racist police force as well as all of the publicity that would result from being at the center of a court challenge.

This leads to the most important point left out in popularized accounts of the Montgomery bus boycott. Community leaders had long considered a boycott as a tactic to achieve racial justice. Of particular importance in this discussion was an African-American women's organization in Montgomery called the Women's Political Council

> The Rosa Parks story opens the possibility of all children identifying themselves as activists.

(WPC). It was headed by Jo Ann Gibson Robinson, a professor of English at Alabama State University in Montgomery, an African-American university. In 1949, Gibson was put off a bus in Montgomery for refusing to move to the back of an almost empty bus. She and other women resolved to do something about bus segregation.

The boycott was an event waiting to take place, and that is why it could be mobilized over a single weekend. Parks' arrest brought it about because she was part of the African-American leadership in Montgomery and was trusted not to cave in under the pressure everyone knew she would be exposed to, not the least of which would be threats to her life.

This story of collective decision-making, willed risk, and coordinated action is more dramatic than the story of an angry individual who sparked a demonstration; it is one that has more to teach children who themselves may one day have to organize and act collectively against oppressive forces.

## King's Role

*7. The boycott, which was led by Martin Luther King, Jr., succeeded. Now African Americans and European Americans can ride the buses together in Montgomery. Rosa Parks was a very brave person.*

The boycott was planned by the WPC, E.D. Nixon and others in Montgomery. Martin Luther King, Jr. was a new member of the community. He had just taken over the Dexter Avenue Baptist Church, and when Nixon told him that Parks' arrest was just what every-

body was waiting for to kick off a bus boycott and assault the institution of segregation, King was at first reluctant. However, the community people chose him to lead, and he accepted their call. The boycott lasted 381 inconvenient days, something not usually mentioned in children's books. It did succeed and was one of the events that sparked the entire civil rights movement. People who had been planning an overt attack on segregation for years took that victory as a sign that the time was ripe even though the people involved in the Montgomery boycott did not themselves anticipate such a result.

## Concluding Thoughts

What remains then, is to retitle the story. The revised version is still about Rosa Parks, but it is also about the African-American people of Montgomery, Alabama. It takes the usual, individualized version of the Rosa Parks' tale and puts it in the context of a coherent, community-based social struggle. This does not diminish Parks in any way. It places her, however, in the midst of a consciously planned movement for social change, and reminds me of the freedom song "We Shall Not Be Moved," for it was precisely Parks' and the community's refusal to be moved that made the boycott possible.

When the story of the Montgomery bus boycott is told merely as a tale of a single heroic person, it leaves children hanging. Not everyone is a hero or heroine. Of course, the idea that only special people can create change is useful if you want to prevent mass movements and keep change from happening. Not every child can be a Rosa Parks, but everyone can imagine herself or himself as a participant in the boycott. As a tale of a social movement and a community effort to overthrow injustice, the Rosa Parks story opens the possibility of every child identifying herself or himself as an activist, as someone who can help make justice happen. ❐

*Herbert Kohl is an educator and author of numerous books. His most recent is* I Won't Learn from You and Other Thoughts on Creative Maladjustment *(The New Press, New York, 1994).*

# The Funeral of Martin Luther King, Jr.

By Nikki Giovanni

*His headstone said*
*FREE AT LAST, FREE AT LAST*
*But death is a slave's freedom*
*We seek the freedom of free men*
*And the construction of a world*
*Where Martin Luther King could have lived and*
*preached non-violence*

*ATLANTA*
*4-9-'68*

Since the 1960s, Nikki Giovanni, a poet, essayist, and children's book author, has been active in expressing the need for Black awareness and unity. (See p. 184 for lesson ideas.)

# Whose Standard?
# Teaching Standard English

### By Linda Christensen

When I was in the ninth grade, Mrs. Delaney, my English teacher wanted to demonstrate the correct and incorrect ways to pronounce the English language. She asked Helen Draper, whose father owned several clothing stores in town, to stand and say "lawyer." Then she asked me, whose father owned a bar, to stand and say "lawyer." Everyone burst into laughter at my pronunciation.

What did Mrs. Delaney accomplish? Did she make me pronounce lawyer correctly? No. I say attorney. I never say lawyer. In fact, I've found substitutes for every word my tongue can't get around and for all the rules I can't remember.

For years I've played word cop on myself. I stop what I'm saying to think, "Objective or subjective case? Do I need I or me here? Hmmm. There's a lay coming up. What word can I substitute for it? Recline?"

And I've studied this stuff. After all, I've been an English teacher for almost 20 years. I've gone through all of the Warriner's workbook exercises. I even found a lie/lay computer program and kept it in my head until I needed it in speech and became confused again.

Thanks to Mrs. Delaney I learned early on that in our society language classifies me. Generosity, warmth, kindness, intelligence, good humor aren't enough — we need to speak correctly to make it. Mrs. Delaney taught me that the "melting pot" was an illusion. The real version of the melting pot is that people of diverse backgrounds are mixed together and when they come out they're supposed to look like Vanna White and sound like Dan Rather. The only diversity we celebrate is tacos and chop suey at the mall.

## Unlearning "Inferiority"

It wasn't until a few years ago that I realized grammar was an indication of class and cultural background in the United States and that there is a bias against people who do not use language "correctly." Even the terminology "standard" and "nonstandard" reflects that one is less than the other. English teachers are urged to "correct" students who speak or write in their home language. A friend of mine, whose ancestors came over on the Mayflower, never studied any of the grammar texts I keep by my side, but she can spot all of my errors because she grew up in a home where Standard English was spoken.

And I didn't, so I've trained myself to play language cop. The problem is that every time I pause, I stop the momentum of my thinking. I'm no longer pursuing content, no longer engaged in trying to persuade or entertain or clarify. Instead I'm pulling Warriner's or Mrs.

> **Students must be taught to hold their own voices sacred, to ignore the teachers who have made them feel that what they've said is wrong or bad or stupid.**

Delaney out of my head and trying to figure out how to say something.

"Ah, but this is good," you might say. "You have the rules and Mrs. Delaney to go back to. This is what our students need."

But it doesn't happen that way. I try to remember the rule or the catchy phrase that is supposed to etch the rule in my mind forever like "people never get laid," but I'm still not sure if I used it correctly. These side trips cost a lot of velocity in my logic.

Over the years my English teachers pointed out all of my errors — the usage errors I inherited from my mother's Bandon, Oregon dialect, the spelling errors I overlooked, the fancy words I used incorrectly. They did this in good faith, in the same way, years later, I "corrected" my students' "errors" because I wanted them to know the rules. They were keys to a secret and wealthier society and I wanted them to be prepared to enter, just as my teachers wanted to help me.

And we should help kids. It would be misleading to suggest that people in our society will value my thoughts or my students' thoughts as readily in our home languages as in the "cash language" as Jesse Jackson calls it. Students need to know where to find help, and they need to understand what changes might be necessary, but they need to learn in a context that doesn't say, "The way you said this is wrong."

## When Fear Interferes

English teachers must know when to correct and how to correct — and I use that word uneasily. Take Fred, for example. Fred entered my freshman class last year unwilling to write. Every day during writing time I'd find

Fred doodling pictures of *Playboy* bunnies. When I sat down and asked him why he didn't write, he said he couldn't.

I explained to him that in this class his writing couldn't be wrong because we were just practicing our writing until we found a piece we wanted to polish, in the same way that he practiced football every day after school, but only played games on Fridays. His resistance lasted for a couple of weeks. Around him, other students struggled with their writing, shared it with the class on occasion and heard positive comments. Certainly the writing of his fellow students was not intimidating.

On October 1st, after reading the story, "Raymond's Run" by Toni Cade Bambara, about trusting people in our lives, Fred wrote for the first time:

*I remember my next door neighbor trusted me with some money that she owed my grandmother. She owed my grandmother about 25 dollars.*

Fred didn't make a lot of errors. In this first piece of writing it looked like he had basic punctuation figured out. He didn't misspell any words. And he certainly didn't make any usage errors. Based on this sample, he appeared to be a competent writer.

However, the biggest problem with Fred's writing was the fact that he didn't make mistakes. This piece demonstrates his discomfort with writing. He wasn't taking any risks. Just as I avoid lawyer and lay, he wrote to avoid errors instead of writing to communicate or think on paper.

When more attention is paid to the way something is written or said than to what is said, students' words and thoughts become devalued. Students learn to be silent, to give as few words as possible for teacher criticism.

## Valuing What We Know

Students must be taught to hold their own voices sacred, to ignore the teachers who have made them feel that what they've said is wrong or bad or stupid. Students must be taught how to listen to the knowledge they've stored up, but which they are seldom asked to relate.

Too often students feel alienated in schools. Knowledge is foreign. It's

Students need to find their own voices.

about other people in other times. At a conference I attended recently, a young woman whose mother was Puerto Rican and whose father was Haitian said, "I went through school wondering if anyone like me had ever done anything worthwhile or important. We kept reading and hearing about all of these famous people. I remember thinking, 'Don't we have anyone?' I walked out of the school that day feeling tiny, invisible, unimportant."

As teachers, we have daily opportunities to affirm that our students' lives and language are unique and important. We do that in the selections of literature we read, in the history we choose to teach, and we do it by giving legitimacy to our students' lives as a content worthy of study.

One way to encourage the reluctant writers who have been silenced and the not-so-reluctant writers who have found a safe and sterile voice is to encourage them to recount their experiences. I sometimes recruit former students to share their writing and their wisdom as a way of underscoring the importance of the voices and stories of teenagers. Rochelle, a student in my senior writing class, brought in a few of her stories and poems to read to my freshmen. Rochelle, like Zora Neale

Hurston, blends her home language with Standard English in most pieces. She read the following piece to open up a discussion about how kids are sometimes treated as servants in their homes, but also to demonstrate the necessity of using the language she hears in her family to develop characters:

*"I'm tired of washing dishes. Seems like every time our family gets together, they just got to eat and bring their millions of kids over to our house. And then we got to wash the dishes."*

*I listened sympathetically as my little sister mumbled these words.*

*"And how come we can't have ribs like the grownups? After all, ain't we grown?"*

*"Lord," I prayed, "seal her lips while the blood is still running warm in her veins."*

*Her bottom lip protruded farther and farther as she dipped each plate in the soapy water, then rinsed each side with cold water (about a two second process) until she felt the majority of suds were off.*

*"One minute we lazy women that can't keep the living room half clean. The next minute we just kids and gotta eat some funky chicken while they eat ribs."*

A sense of community encourages students to share their writing.

*... Suddenly it was quiet. All except my little sister who was still talking. I strained to hear a laugh or joke from the adults in the living room, a hint that all were well, full and ready to go home. Everyone was still sitting in their same spots, not making a move to leave.*

*"You ought to be thankful you got a choice."*

*Uh-oh. Now she got Aunt Macy started. ...*

After reading her work, Rochelle talked about listening to her family and friends tell their stories. She urged the freshmen to relate the tales of their own lives — the times they were caught doing something forbidden, the times they got stuck with the dishes, the funny/sad events that made their freshman year memorable. When Rochelle left, students wrote more easily. Some. Some were afraid of the stories because as Rance said, "It takes heart to tell the truth about your life."

But eventually they write. They write stories. They write poems. They write letters. They write essays. They learn how to switch in and out of the language of the powerful as Rochelle does so effortlessly in her "Tired of Chicken" piece.

## Sharing Lessons

And after we write, we listen to each other's stories in our read-around circle where everyone has the opportunity to share, to be heard, to learn that knowledge can be gained by examining our lives. (See "read-arounds" page 186.) In the circle, we discover that many young women encounter sexual harassment, we learn that store clerks follow black students, especially males, more frequently than they follow white students, we find that many of our parents drink or use drugs, we learn that many of us are kept awake by the crack houses in our neighborhood.

Before we share, students often understand these incidents individually. They feel there's something wrong with them. If they were smarter, prettier, stronger, these things wouldn't have happened to them. When they hear other students' stories, they begin to realize that many of their problems aren't caused by a character defect. For example, in Literature in U.S. History,

the class I teach with Bill Bigelow, a young man shared a passionate story about life with his mother, who is a lesbian. He loved her, but felt embarrassed to bring his friends home. He was afraid his peers would think he was gay or reject him if they knew about his mother. After he read, the class was silent. Some students cried. One young woman told him that her father was gay and she'd experienced similar difficulties, but hadn't had the courage to tell people about it. She thanked him. Another student confided that his uncle had died from AIDS the year before. What had been a secret shame became an opportunity for students to discuss sexual diversity more openly. Students who were rigidly opposed to the idea of homosexuality gained insights into their own homophobia — especially when presented with the personal revelations from their classmates. Those with homosexual relatives found new allies with whom they could continue their discussion and find support.

Sharing also provides a "collective text" for us to examine the social roots of problems more closely: Where do men/women develop the ideas that women are sexual objects? Where do they learn that it's OK for men to follow women or make suggestive remarks? Where is it written that it's the woman's fault if a man leers at her? How did these roles develop? Who gains from them? Who loses? How could we make it different? Our lives become a window to examine society.

## Learning the "Standard" Without Humiliation

But the lessons can't stop there. Fred can write better now. He and his classmates can feel comfortable and safe sharing their lives or discussing literature and the world. They can even understand that they need to ask "Who benefits?" to get a better perspective on a problem. But still when they leave my class or this school, some people will judge them by how their subjects and verbs line up.

So I teach Fred the rules. It's the language of power in this country, and I would be cheating him if I pretended otherwise. I teach him this more effectively than Mrs. Delaney taught me because I don't humiliate him or put down his language. I'm also more effective because I don't rely on textbook drills; I use the text of Fred's writing. But I also teach Fred what Mrs. Delaney left out.

I teach Fred that language, like tracking, functions as part of a gatekeeping system in our country. Who gets managerial jobs, who works at banks and who works at fast food restaurants, who gets into what college and who gets into college at all, are decisions linked to the ability to use Standard English. So how do we teach kids to write with honesty and passion about their world and get them to study the rules of the cash language? We go back to our study of society. We ask: Who made the rules that govern how we speak and write? Did Ninh's family and Fred's family and LaShonda's family all sit down together and decide on these rules? Who already talks like this and writes like this? Who has to learn how to change the way they talk and write? Why?

We make up our own tests that speakers of Standard English would find difficult. We read articles, stories, poems written in Standard English and those written in home language. We listen to videotapes of people speaking. Most kids like the sound of their home language better. They like the energy, the poetry, and the rhythm of the language. We determine when and why people shift. We talk about why it might be necessary to learn Standard English.

Asking my students to memorize the rules without asking who makes the

---

# Language Prison

All day words
run past my tongue

words tumble and fall
and you catch
the wrong ones
and count them back to me

All day I watch
my tongue

for words
that slip
down the slope of my
neighborhood

words that separate
me from you

words that you catch
and hold against me

All day I watch
for words misshapen
or bent
around my too thick tongue

run-down at the heel words
thin soled words

words that slip
from my tongue

words that tell of mops
and beer
and bent backs

words that shape my world
against a different map
than yours

All day I watch my tongue
for words

*—Linda Christensen*

---

rules, who enforces the rules, who benefits from the rules, who loses from the rules, who uses the rules to keep some in and keep others out, legitimates a social system that devalues my students' knowledge and language. Teaching the rules without reflection also underscores that it's OK for others — "authorities" — to dictate something as fundamental and as personal as the way they speak. Further, the study of Standard English without critique encourages students to believe that if they fail, it is because they are not smart enough or didn't work hard enough. They learn to blame themselves. If they get poor SAT scores, low grades on term papers or essays because of language errors, fail teacher entrance exams, they will internalize the blame; they will believe they did not succeed because they are inferior instead of questioning the standard of measurement and those making the standards.

We must teach our students how to match subjects and verbs, how to pronounce lawyer, because they are the ones without power and, for the moment, have to use the language of the powerful to be heard. But, in addition, we need to equip them to question an educational system that devalues their life and their knowledge. If we don't, we condition them to a pedagogy of consumption where they will consume the knowledge, priorities, and products that have been decided and manufactured without them in mind.

It took me years to undo what Mrs. Delaney did to me. Years to discover that what I said was more important than how I said it. Years to understand that my words, my family's words, weren't wrong, weren't bad — they were just the words of the working class. For too long, I felt inferior when I spoke. I knew the voice of my childhood crept out, and I confused that with ignorance. It wasn't. I just didn't belong to the group who made the rules. I was an outsider, a foreigner in their world. My students won't be. ❑

*Linda Christensen (lchrist@aol.com) is language arts coordinator for Portland Public Schools and a* Rethinking Schools *editor.*

Reprinted from the *English Journal* with permission of the author.

# Thoughts on Teaching Native American Literature

By Joseph Bruchac

My own first experiences in teaching American Indian literature came after three years in West Africa. I returned to the United States in 1969 and found myself at Skidmore College near my home town of Greenfield Center, New York, an instructor with little chance of tenure who had been given a job because there was a last-minute opening at the school.

That was okay with me. My main objective had been to come home to my Abenaki grandfather in whose house I'd been raised. He lived only three miles east from the college, an easy ride on a bicycle through the hills and backroads at the edge of the Kaydeross Range. As I rode from the dawn towards the west, I passed fields which had been filled with Mohawk corn, and within my line of sight to the north were the mountains and the old, still hidden burial places of some of my own ancestors. The road passed a stone's throw from samp mortars worn deep into bedrock where corn and acorns had been ground into flour for thousands of years. Just south of that road were streams where my grandfather and I caught trout and said words of thanks to the fish spirits.

Somehow, being home made it easier to be a "low man on the academic totem pole" — one of *their* favorite images, no irony intended — teaching freshman composition and little else. It was in 1970 that the first Native American literature course was taught at Skidmore, during their one-month winter term. I wasn't allowed to teach it, though by then I was being allowed to teach a single course in Black Literature. "Topics in American Indian Literature" was taught by a senior faculty member who used a lot of work from anthropologists and a little contemporary Indian writing. He used Kroeber's *The Inland Whale*, some creation stories, threw in a few poems by poets who were Indian. He tried his best and he consulted with me — with apologies.

"You ought to be teaching this, Joseph, but you know how it is."

"Totem pole?" I said.

He nodded, without irony. "You understand."

Along the way he set up a reading. One of those who spoke was Harry W. Paige, whose book, *Songs of the Teton Sioux*, had been his Ph.D. thesis at the State University of New York at Albany for his doctorate in English — the first doctorate in English from SUNY/Albany. Harry's book wasn't bad, and it was a result of a lot of time spent among the Teton Sioux. He gave his talk, followed by Duane McGinnis (not yet Niatum) and myself. Duane, a Klallam poet and editor, had been invited to campus to talk to that special one-time-only Native American literature course and I was, after all, of Indian descent and had published a few things here and there. In the audience that night was William Fenton, whose lifetime of study of the Iroquois was evidenced by many books and articles and the emeritus chair of anthropology at the same SUNY/Albany that gave Paige his degree.

In fact, I'm pretty sure Bill Fenton was there for Paige — not for Duane and myself. After the readings and talk, the question and answer session got around to such things as vocables in traditional songs — "nonsense words," as Fenton put it — and storytelling traditions. "There are," Fenton said, "no more traditional Iroquois storytellers. I knew the last one and he died some years ago." There was some disagreement that night, and I leave it to your imagination as to which two people were the most vocal in their disagreeing.

## My Own Directions

I begin at Skidmore and with those details because I feel it sets the scene for my own directions as a writer of Native American literature and a teacher of the literature of Native Americans. Those details also lend themselves well to some points I'd like to make about teaching Native American literature. First, however, another story.

Not long ago, I was invited to do a storytelling program at a college in Vermont. While there, I had dinner with several people who have been teaching Native American literature in college. Our conversation was an illuminating one for me, because it pointed out how widespread the teaching of Native American literature is becoming and just how needed are some directions in HOW and WHAT to teach in such courses. One of the people said that he was having a hard time finding texts. Another said that he was using Frederick Turner's 1973 volume *The Portable Native American Reader* and beginning with Creation myths, but that he had some misgivings about the accuracy of the translations, though he didn't know enough to know for sure how good they were. The third teacher of Native American literature mentioned taking a course in how to teach Native American literature from a certain professor. Someone else at the table knew that professor and mentioned that when she taught Native American lit-

Literature grows out of tradition and culture.

erature as a visiting professor at their school, the few Native American students on campus had signed up for the course but all dropped it because they found something objectionable about it. No one knew what.

## A Lot of Listening

I do a lot of listening in such conversations. Partly because I was raised to listen and partly because when academic conversations start, it isn't that easy to break into them. Even when people ask you a direct question, they often try to answer it themselves before you can open your mouth. So I waited. These people I was having dinner with were good folks and their interest and their concerns were very real. *When you're ready to listen*, I thought. *When it is quiet enough.* And when it was quiet enough, I began to say a few words about how I have approached the teaching of Native American literature. And unless you've lost patience by now with my slow developing style, you're about to read some of those words.

When we speak about Native American literature today, it is, in many ways, like speaking of African literature. More accurately, it is how speaking about African literature would be if we were living in an Africa which had lost 90% of its population in the last 500 years and was being run as a single united continent by European colonials. As is the case with Africa, when we speak of "Native American Literature," of "American Indian Literature" or (as they say in Canada) "Native Literature," we are speaking of many literatures, especially when we refer to that work which comes from what might loosely be called (though there were, in fact, a number of writing and mnemonic recording systems in North America) "Oral Tradition." Just as Zulu oral poetry from southern Africa is very different from the traditions of the griots of Mali in the northwest of Africa, the Haudenosaunee (as the "Iroquois" call themselves) epic of the founding of their Great League of Peace is not at all like the deer songs of the Yaqui.

When you approach the totality of "Native American Literature," you are confronted by an incredibly vast body of work. It comes out of, in just the area now called the continental United States, more than 400 different languages and distinct cultures. It is thousands of years old. Yet, without any special preparation, without any real grounding in the cultures which produced those many literatures, without any familiarity with the languages from which they were translated (seldom by native speakers and all too often translated in very slipshod and inappropriate ways), teachers on the university and even high school level are expected to teach this "Native American Literature." Not only that, most of those teachers have never visited a Native American community or spoken with a single Native American. It is, to say the least, daunting. To put it another way, as one of my friends and teachers, a Pueblo elder known to the world as "Swift Eagle," said, "It's dumb!"

The first full-fledged Native American literature course I taught was in a maximum security prison. I was, by then, no longer in Skidmore's English Department. My terminal contract had been terminated. Other job opportunities in other parts of America had been possible, but I wasn't about to leave my native soil again. Eventually, I'd been rehired by Skidmore's external degree program to develop and direct a college program at Great Meadow Correctional Facility. I stayed with that job for eight years. In addition to being an administrator, I taught a course now and then. African Literature, Black Literature, and finally, in 1975, Introduction to Native American Literature.

If I'd had my druthers, I would have begun any Native American literature course not in the classroom, but in the woods. (That would have been *just fine* insofar as the men in my class at Great Meadow went. They understood what I meant, but that got almost as big a laugh from them as the proposed course in Astronomy at the prison that was nixed by the Deputy Superintendent in charge of Security when the professor said that field trips outside at night would be necessary). It was important, I told that class, to have a sense of the American earth, of the land and the people as one.

I divided the syllabus into four directions and focused on the literary traditions of one particular Native nation from each corner of the continent. To the east, we looked at the People of the Long House, the Haudenosaunee. We began with poems written in English by Maurice Kenny and Peter Blue Cloud before turning to the epic story of the Founding of the Great League, listening to recordings of Mohawk social dance songs as we did so. To the south, we began with poems of Leslie Silko and Simon Ortiz and we read Silko's *Ceremony* and Momaday's *House Made of Dawn* in the context of the healing traditions of Navajo and Pueblo cultures. To the north, we looked at James Welch's novel *Winter in the Blood*. To the west, we focussed on translations of Lakota and Cheyenne traditional songs while we read Lance Henson's poetry. Again, as with the Iroquois material, we listened to the music of the people, including not just grass dance songs, but also Floyd Westerman singing "Custer Died for Your Sins." We looked at maps of America (and allowing any maps into

the prison was a major struggle), and we talked about history, from east to west, from north to south. It was one of the best classes I'd ever taught, and I still have some of the papers written by those men.

## Four Simple Directions

Although there have been other courses in Native American literature that I have taught since then — in seminar courses for senior citizens, at Hamilton College and at the State University of New York at Albany — and a great deal of new Native American work and work about Native American literature has come into print, I have not really changed my approach to teaching Native American literature. There are four simple directions that I follow (in addition to those cardinal ones) and I would suggest them as applicable for others who wish to teach Native American literature.

1. Clearly define what you mean by "Native American Literature." Remember the breadth and diversity of what we call "American Indian." Remember that we are referring, in fact, to many nations within this nation; to many literatures, literatures which each come

> When you approach the totality of "Native American Literature," you are confronted by an incredibly vast body of work coming out of hundreds of languages and cultures.

from a national identity and a strong sense of place. You might make a good case that contemporary Native American writing in English is one continuous literary body, but when you look at the influence of the old traditions and then look at those traditions themselves, you recognize that you're seeing just the tip of the iceberg.

To my mind, it is best to teach introductory courses focusing on the work written in English, to think of these courses as only the beginning and to hope for both the knowledgeable instructors and the opportunity for schools to offer more advanced studies — a course in Haudenosaunee Literature 301 or Momaday 405 — just as we offer introductory courses in British Literature and then give our advanced students a chance to study the Victorians or Shakespeare.

2. Teach the work in context. The Native American view of life as reflected in literature (whether in English or originally in an earlier native language) is holistic. Remember that if you are teaching Native American literature well, you are not just teaching literature, you are also teaching culture. To understand the work — or to begin to understand it — it must be seen as it was *used*. The word is regarded as alive, not just syllables and symbols. An understanding, for example, of the traditional Navajo Night Chant is impossible without knowing the place of the Night Chant in the practices of healing, without recognizing that it is only one part of an event which involves the participation of dozens or even hundreds of individuals, that it is meant to be sung in a certain place at a certain time, and that the making of a sand painting depicting a particular event in Navajo mythology is intimately connected to it. Similarly, it is difficult to teach a modern work such as Silko's *Ceremony* without some awareness of the place and purpose of similar healing and storytelling traditions among the Pueblo people.

3. Pay attention to continuance. Be aware of the strong connections in all Native American writing between what the western world calls "past" and "present." I am not just talking about

the awareness of literary tradition — though that works at least in part as an analogy — but of something more than that. Many of the native languages deal with "time" in a very different way than does English. Similarly, the time sense of many contemporary Native American novels can seem strange, circuitous, even circular. Continuance is an important word for me in dealing with Native American writing. I stress this continuance by constantly linking contemporary Native writers to their roots, to their people and their places, their traditions.

4. Be wary of work in translation. My own approach is, for introductory courses at least, to place the strongest emphasis on contemporary work written in English and to use a few *carefully* selected translations from the old traditions in direct relation to those newer writings. A great many stories, songs, ceremonies, and the like which can be found in books are flawed in many ways. In some cases, the translations are bowdlerized or inaccurate. Imagine what it would be like if Shakespeare's plays had been written in Lakota and we only knew his work in English through a single translation of *Othello* done by an 18th century puritanical and racist Baptist missionary with a tin ear who transcribed the play from a verbal recounting of it by a slightly senile octogenarian who never liked the theater that much. From my own knowledge of certain Native American languages and some of the translations that have been foisted off as legitimate, I can assure you that I am not exaggerating the injustices that have been done. In some cases, in fact, rather than translations, the so-called myths and legends that we find in any number of places are sometimes made up from the whole cloth — oft involving a tragic love between a boy from one tribe and a girl from another and either a lover's leap or a canoe going over whatever high waterfall is handy to the translator's fevered imagination.

Another point about work in translation to keep in mind is that some things which have been recorded or translated have been recorded or translated without the permission of the na-

tive people who own that work. Much of Native America's traditional culture is *living* in the strongest sense of that word. Revealing that culture to the uninitiated is sacrilegious. A good teacher of Native American literature needs to know enough to be able to know which works need to be shown special respect. I cannot emphasize that word *respect* strongly enough. In some cases it may even mean NOT discussing something. That is a hard direction for people with the western mindset to follow, that western mindset which says "Tell it all, show it all, explain it all." I feel that those with that mindset would be better off avoiding the teaching of Native American literature.

## Sense of Sound

When using Native American literature in translation, it is safest to use work which has been translated by Native scholars themselves. Alfonso Ortiz and J.N.B. Hewitt are two examples. There are also a number of ethnologists whose reputations and whose relations with the people whose work they translated are quite reputable. Dennis Tedlock and Frances Densmore represent some of the best in contemporary and early 20th century work. I also like to have access to both the English translation and the original language. Then,

even a non-native speaker can have some sense of the sound and rhythms as they were meant to be. But, again, show respect. Walk slowly. *Listen* to Native people.

Native American literature, as we now have the chance to offer it, is more than just an extra area, more than just a little diversity for the curriculum. It is the literature of a continent (of two continents, in fact, but I'll confine myself to the area north of Mexico for now), and it is a literature continually growing, being created and rediscovered. It is said that when Columbus touched onto the island of Hispaniola he didn't know where he really was. He didn't have, you might say, a good sense of direction. I certainly hope that future teachers of Native American literature will at least avoid that mistake of a European coming into contact with something new. I hope they will see where they are, see which way is south, which way is west, which way is north, and which way to look if they want to see the light of dawn. □

*Joseph Bruchac is a poet, storyteller, teacher, author, and co-editor of* Keepers of the Earth: Native American Stories *and* Environmental Activities for Children.

The above article originally appeared in *SAIL, Studies in American Indian Literature*, Spring 1991. Reprinted with permission of the author.

# Why Students Should Study History
## An Interview with Howard Zinn

*The following is condensed from an interview with Howard Zinn, author of* A People's History of the United States. *He was interviewed by Barbara Miner of* Rethinking Schools.

### Why should students study history?

I started studying history with one view in mind: to look for answers to the issues and problems I saw in the world about me. By the time I went to college I had worked in a shipyard, had been in the Air Force, had been in a war. I came to history asking questions about war and peace, about wealth and poverty, about racial division.

Sure, there's a certain interest in inspecting the past and it can be fun, sort of like a detective story. I can make an argument for knowledge for its own sake as something that can add to your life. But while that's good, it is small in relation to the very large objective of trying to understand and do something about the issues that face us in the world today.

Students should be encouraged to go into history in order to come out of it, and should be discouraged from going into history and getting lost in it, as some historians do.

### What do you see as some of the major problems in how U.S. history has been taught in this country?

One major problem has been the intense focus on U.S. history in isolation from the world. This is a problem that all nations have, their nationalistic focus on their own history, and it goes to absurd lengths. Some states in this country even require a year-long course in the history of that state.

But even if you are willing to see the United States in relation to world history, you face the problem that we have not looked at the world in an equitable way. We have concentrated on the Western world, in fact on Western Europe. I remember coming into my first class in Spelman College in Atlanta in 1956 and finding that there was no required course in black history, or Asian or African history, but there was a required course in the history of England. And there on the board was this chart of the Tudors and the Stuarts, the dynasties of England.

For the United States, emphasis has been particularly glaring in terms of Latin America, which is that part of the world closest to us and with which we've had the most to do economically and politically.

Another glaring problem has been the emphasis in teaching American history through the eyes of the important and powerful people, through the Presidents, the Congress, the Supreme Court, the generals, the industrialists. History textbooks don't say, "We are going to tell the story of the Mexican War from the standpoint of the generals," but when they tell us it was a great military victory, that's exactly what they are doing.

### Taking that as an example, if one were to have a more inclusive view of the war with Mexico, what would be some of the themes and perspectives one would include?

The Mexican War is an example of how one event raises so many issues. You'd have to see the war first of all as more than a military action. So often the history of war is dominated by the story of battles, and this is a way of diverting attention from the political factors behind a war. It's possible to concentrate upon the battles of the Mexican War and just to talk about the triumphant march into Mexico City, and not talk about the relationship of the Mexican War to slavery and to the acquisition of territories which might possibly be slave territories.

Another thing that is neglected in the Mexican War is the viewpoint of the ordinary soldiers. The soldiers who had volunteered for the Mexican War — you didn't need a draft because so many people in the working classes were so destitute that they would join the military on the promise of a little bit of pay and mustering out money and a little bit of prestige — the volunteers went into it not really knowing the bloodshed it would involve. And then so many of them deserted. For example, seven regiments of General Winfield Scott deserted on the road to Mexico City.

You should tell the story of the Massachusetts volunteers who went into the Mexican War. Half of them died, and the half who returned were invited to a homecoming party and when a commanding officer got up to address the gathering, they booed him off the platform.

I think it's a good idea also to do something which isn't done anywhere so far as I know in histories in any country, and that is: tell the story of the war from the standpoint of the other side, of "the enemy." To tell the story of the Mexican War from the standpoint of the Mexicans means to ask: How did they feel about having 40% of their territory taken away from them as a result of the war? How did they view the incident that President Polk used as a reason for

Birmingham, Ala., 1963: Demonstrators attacked by the force of water powerful enough to rip bark from trees.

the beginning of the war? Did it look real or manufactured to them?

You'd also have to talk about the people in the United States who protested against the war. That would be the time to bring up Henry Thoreau and his essay, "Civil Disobedience."

You'd have to look at Congress and how it behaved. You'd have to look at Abraham Lincoln, who was in the House of Representatives during the Mexican War. You'd learn a lot about politicians and politics because you'd see that Abraham Lincoln on the one hand spoke up against the war, but on the other hand voted to give money to finance the war. This is so important because this is something that is repeated again and again in American history: the feeble opposition in Congress to presidential wars, and then the voting of funds for whatever war the President has initiated.

[For a student activity on the Mexican War, see page 158.]

## How do you prevent history lessons from becoming a recitation of dates and battles and Congresspersons and Presidents?

You can take any incident in American history and enrich it and find parallels with today. One important thing is not to concentrate on chronological order, but to go back and forth and find similarities and analogies.

You should ask students if anything in a particular historical event reminds them of something they read in the newspapers or see on television about the world today. When you press students to make connections, to abstract from the uniqueness of a particular his-

torical event and find something it has in common with another event — then history becomes alive, not just past but present.

And, of course, you must raise the controversial questions and ask students, "Was it right for us to take Mexican territory? Should we be proud of that, should we celebrate that?" History teachers often think they must avoid judgments of right and wrong because, after all, those are matters of subjective opinions, those are issues on which students will disagree and teachers will disagree.

But it's the areas of disagreement that are the most important. Questions of right and wrong and justice are exactly the questions that should be raised all the time. When students are asked, "Is this right, is this wrong?" then it becomes interesting, then they can have a debate — especially if they learn that there's no simple, absolute, agreed-upon, universal answer. It's not like giving them multiple choice questions where they are right or wrong. I think that's a tremendous advance in their understanding of what education is.

Teachers must also address the problem that people have been mis-educated to become dependent on government, to think that their supreme act as citizens is to go to the polls and vote every two years or four years. That's where the history of social movements comes in. Teachers should dwell on Shay's Rebellion, on colonial rebellions, on the abolitionist movement, on the populist movement, on the labor movement, and so on, and make sure these social movements don't get lost in the overall story of presidents and Congresses and Supreme Courts. Emphasizing social and protest movements in the making of history gives students a feeling that they as citizens are the most important actors in history.

Students, for example, should learn that during the Depression there were strikes and demonstrations all over the country. And it was that turmoil and protest that created the atmosphere in which Roosevelt and Congress passed Social Security and unemployment insurance and housing subsidies and so on.

### How can teachers foster critical thinking so that students don't merely memorize a new, albeit more progressive, set of facts?

Substituting one indoctrination for another is a danger and it's very hard to deal with. After all, the teacher, no matter how hard she or he tries, is the dominant figure in the classroom and has the power of authority and of grades. It's easy for the teacher to fall into the trap of bullying students into accepting one set of facts or ideas. It takes hard work and delicate dealings with students to overcome that.

The way I've tried to deal with that problem is to make it clear to the students that when we study history we are dealing with controversial issues with no one, absolute, god-like answer.

And that I, as a teacher, have my opinion and they can have their opinions, and that I, as a teacher, will try to present as much information as I can but that I may leave out information. I try to make them understand that while there are experts on facts, on little things, on the big issues, on the controversies and the issues of right and wrong and justice, there are no experts and their opinion is as good as mine.

### But how do you then foster a sense of justice and avoid the trap of relativity that, "Well, some people say this and some people say that"?

I find such relativity especially true on the college level, where there's a great tendency to indecisiveness. People are unwilling to take a stand on a moral issue because, well, there's this side and there's that side.

I deal with this by example. I never simply present both sides and leave it at that. I take a stand. If I'm dealing with Columbus, I say, look, there are these people who say that we shouldn't judge Columbus by the standards of the 20th century. But my view is that basic moral standards are not different for the 20th century or the 15th century.

I don't simply lay history out on a platter and say, "I don't care what you choose, they're both valid." I let them know, "No, I care what you choose; I don't think they're both valid. But you don't have to agree with me." I want them to know that if people don't take a stand the world will remain unchanged, and who wants that?

### Are there specific ways that teachers can foster an antiracist perspective?

To a great extent, this moral objective is not considered in teaching history. I think people have to be given the facts of slavery, the facts of racial segregation, the facts of government complicity in racial segregation, the facts of the fight for equality. But that is not enough.

I think students need to be aroused emotionally on the issue of equality.

They have to try to feel what it was like, to be a slave, to be jammed into slave ships, to be separated from your family. Novels, poems, autobiographies, memoirs, the reminiscences of ex-slaves, the letters that slaves wrote, the writings of Frederick Douglass — I think they have to be introduced as much as possible. Students should learn the words of people themselves, to feel their anger, their indignation.

In general, I don't think there has been enough use of literature in history. People should read Richard Wright's *Black Boy*; they should read the poems of Countee Cullen; they should read the novels of Alice Walker, the poems of Langston Hughes, Lorraine Hansbury's *A Raisin in the Sun*. These writings have an emotional impact that can't be found in an ordinary recitation of history.

It is especially important that students learn about the relationship of the United States government to slavery and race.

It's very easy to fall into the view that slavery and racial segregation were a southern problem. The federal government is very often exempted from responsibility for the problem, and is presented as a benign force helping black people on the road to equality. In our time, students are taught how Eisenhower sent his troops to Little Rock, Ark., and Kennedy sent troops to Oxford, Miss., and Congress passed civil rights laws.

Yet the federal government is very often an obstacle to resolving those problems of race, and when it enters it comes in late in the picture. Abraham Lincoln was not the initiator of the movement against slavery but a follower of a movement that had developed for 30 years by the time he became president in 1860; it was the anti-slavery movement that was the major force creating the atmosphere in which emancipation took place following the Civil War. And it was the President and Congress and the Supreme Court that ignored the 13th, 14th, and 15th Amendments after they were passed. In the 1960s it wasn't Johnson and Kennedy who were the leaders and initiators of the movement for race equality, but it was black people.

In addition to focusing on social movements and having a more consciously anti-racist perspective, what are some other thematic ways in which the teaching of history must change?

I think the issue of class and class conflict needs to be addressed more honestly because it is ignored in traditional nationalist history. This is true not just of the United States but of other countries. Nationhood is a cover for extreme conflicts among classes in society, in our country, from its founding, from the making of the Constitution. Too often, there's a tendency to overlook these conflicts, and concentrate on the creation of a national identity.

How does a teacher deal with the intersection of race, class, and gender in terms of U.S. history, in particular that the white working-class has often been complicit, consciously or unconsciously, in some very unforgivable actions?

The complicity of poor white people in racism, the complicity of males in sexism, is a very important issue. It seems to me that complicity can't be understood without showing the intense hardships that poor white people faced in this country, making it easier for them to look for scapegoats for their condition. You have to recognize the problems of white working people in order to understand why they turn racist, because they aren't born racist.

When discussing the Civil War, teachers should point out that only a small percentage of the white population of the South owned slaves. The rest of the white population was poor and they were driven to support slavery and to be racist by the messages of those who controlled society — that they would be better off if the Negroes were put in a lower position, and that those calling for black equality were threat-

Demonstration in support of women's rights during the height of the women's movement in the 1970s.

ening the lives of these ordinary white people.

In the history of labor struggles, you should show how blacks and whites were used against one another, how white workers would go out on strike and then black people, desperate themselves for jobs, would be brought in to replace the white workers, how all-white craft unions excluded black workers, and how all this creates murderously intense racial antagonisms. So the class and race issues are very much intertwined, as is the gender issue.

One of the ways of giving some satisfaction to men who are themselves exploited is to make them masters in their own household. So they may be humiliated on the job, but they come back home and humiliate their wives and their children. There's a wonderful short story by a black woman writer, Ann Petry, "Like a Winding Sheet" that should be required reading in school. It's about a black man who is humiliated on the job and comes home and, on the flimsiest of reasons, beats his

wife. The story is told in such a way as to make you really understand the pent-up anger that explodes inside a family as a result of what happens out in the world. In all these instances of racial and sexual mistreatment, it is important for students to understand that the roots of such hostility are social, environmental, situational, and are not an inevitability of human nature. It is also important to show how these antagonisms so divide people from one another as to make it difficult for them to solve their common problems in united action.

How can we explain the roots of this complicity in racism and sexism by white working class people without falling into the trap of condoning it?

That's always a problem: how do you explain something without justifying it? That issue, as a theoretical issue, needs to be explained because it's a common confusion. You need to make the point again and again that trying to understand why people do something is not the same as justifying it. And you need to give specific historical examples of that problem, or, as I suggested, literary examples.

**How can you teach white students to take an anti-racist perspective that isn't based merely on guilt over the things that white people have done to people of color?**

If such a perspective is based only on guilt, it doesn't have a secure foundation. It has to be based on empathy and on self-interest, on an understanding that the divisions between black and white have not just resulted in the exploitation of black people, even though they've been the greatest victims, but have prevented whites and blacks from getting together to bring about the social change that would benefit them all. Showing the self-interest is also important in order to avoid the patronizing view of feeling sorry for someone, of giving somebody equality because you feel guilty about what has been done to them.

At the same time, to approach the issue merely on the basis of self-interest would be wrong, because people should learn to empathize with other people even where there is no visible, immediate self-interest.

**In response to concerns about multiculturalism, there's more lip service to include events and perspectives affecting women and people of color. But often it's presented as more facts and people to learn, without any fundamental change in perspective. What would be the approach of a truly anti-racist, multicultural perspective in U.S. history?**

I've noticed this problem in some of the new textbooks, which obviously are trying to respond to the need for a multicultural approach. What I find is a bland eclecticism where everything has equal weight. You add more facts, you add more continents, you add more cultures, you add more people. But then it becomes a confusing melange in which you've added a lot of different elements but without any real emphasis on what had previously been omitted. You're left with a kind of unemotional, cold combination salad.

You need the equivalent of affirmative action in education. What affirmative action does is to say, look, things have been slanted one way for a long time. We're going to pay special attention to this person or to this group of people because they have been left out for so long.

People ask me why in my book, *A People's History of the United States*, I did not simply take the things that I put in and add them to the orthodox approaches so, as they put it, the book

> **History teachers often think they must avoid judgments of right and wrong because, after all, those are matters of subjective opinions. But it's the areas of disagreement that are the most important.**

would be better balanced. But there's a way in which this so-called balance leaves people nowhere, with no moral sensibility, no firm convictions, no outrage, no indignation, no energy to go anywhere.

I think it is important to pay special attention to the history of black people, of Indians, of women, in a way that highlights not only the facts but the emotional intensity of such issues.

**Is it possible for history to be objective?**

Objectivity is neither possible nor desirable.

It's not possible because all history is subjective, all history represents a point of view. History is always a selection from an infinite number of facts and everybody makes the selection differently, based on their values and what they think is important. Since it's not possible to be objective, you should be honest about that.

Objectivity is not desirable because if we want to have an effect on the world, we need to emphasize those things which will make students more active citizens and more moral people.

**One of the problems for high school history teachers is they may have five periods and 30 kids in each class, and before you know it they're dealing with 150 students. What types of projects and approaches can they use?**

The most important thing is to get students to do independent reading and research. Tell the students, "Pick something that interests you, pick out a person that interests you." Your job as teacher is to present them with a wide spectrum of events and people, and not just the usual heroes of history but all sorts of people or incidents that they may never have heard of but that might intrigue them. I find that when students have a research project of their own they can get excited about it — especially if they are allowed to choose from a complex set of possibilities.

**How can a progressive teacher promote a radical perspective within a bureaucratic, conservative institution? Teachers sometimes either push the limits so far that they alienate their colleagues or get fired, or they're so afraid that they tone down what they really think. How can a teacher resolve this dilemma?**

The problem certainly exists on the college and university level — people want to get tenure, they want to keep teaching, they want to get promoted, they want to get salary raises, and so there are all these economic punishments if they do something that looks outlandish and radical and different. But I've always believed that the main problem with college and university teachers has been self-censorship. I suspect that the same thing is true in the high schools, although you have to be more sympathetic with high school teachers because they operate in a much more repressive atmosphere. I've seen again and again where college and university teachers don't really have a problem in, for instance, using my *People's History* in their classrooms, but high school teachers always have a problem. They can't get it officially adopted, they have to get permission, they have to photocopy parts of it themselves in order to pass it out to the students, they have to worry about parents complaining, about what the head of the department or the principal or the school superintendent will say.

But I still believe, based on a lot of contact with high school teachers over the past few years, that while there's a danger of becoming overly assertive and insensitive to how others might view you, the most common behavior is timidity. Teachers withdraw and use the real fact of outside control as an excuse for teaching in the orthodox way.

Teachers need to take risks. The problem is how to minimize those risks.

One important way is to make sure that you present material in class making it clear that it is subjective, that it is controversial, that you are not laying down the law for students. Another important thing is to be extremely tolerant of students who disagree with your views, or students who express racist or sexist ideas. I don't mean tolerant in the sense of not challenging such ideas, but tolerant in the sense of treating them as human beings. It's important to develop a reputation that you don't give kids poor grades on the basis of their disagreements with you. You need to create an atmosphere of freedom in the classroom.

It's also important to talk with other teachers to gain support and encouragement, to organize. Where there are teachers unions, those are logical places for teachers to support and defend one another. Where there are not teachers unions, teachers should always think how they can organize and create a collective strength.

**Teachers don't always know where to get those other perspectives. Do you have any tips?**

The orthodox perspective is easy to get. But once teachers begin to look for other perspectives, once they start out on that road, they will quickly be led from one thing to another to another.

**So it's not as daunting as people might think?**

No. It's all there. It's in the library. ❏

*Howard Zinn has taught history and political science at Spelman College in Atlanta and at Boston University. He is the author of* A People's History of the United States, The Politics of History, Declarations of Independence *and other works.*

Picket sign from a protest in 1941 during a time of heightened labor unrest, when Walt Disney fired union organizers on his art staff.

# History Book Resources

## By Howard Zinn

Aptheker, Herbert (editor) (1990). *A Documentary History of the Negro People of the United States, Vols. 1 - 4*. Citadel Press. An extremely valuable, I am tempted to say indispensable, collection, not at all dry, as are some documentaries.

Brown, Dee (editor) (1971). *Bury My Heart at Wounded Knee*. Holt, Rinehart & Winston. A moving collection of statements and recollections by American Indians which gives you *their* point of view in a vivid, passionate way.

Chomsky, Noam (1992). *Year 501*. South End Press. Here, the nation's most distinguished intellectual rebel gives us huge amounts of information about recent American foreign policy, and puts it into historical perspective, going back to the Columbus era.

Drinnon, Richard (1990). *Facing West*. Schocken. A brilliantly written account of imperial expansion by the United States, not just on the American continent against the Indians, but overseas in the Philippines and in Vietnam.

Foner, Eric (1988). *Reconstruction: America's Unfinished Revolution*. Harper & Row. A rich, vivid, epic-like narrative of those extraordinary years 1863 to 1877, by one of the leading "new historians."

Hampton, Henry, and Steve Fayer, with Sarah Flynn (editor) (1990). *Voices of Freedom*. Bantam. An oral history of the black movement for civil rights, from the 1950s to the 1980s, much of its material coming out of the research done for the TV documentary, *Eyes on the Prize*.

Hofstadter, Richard (1974). *The American Political Tradition*. Vintage. A classic of American history, beautifully written, an iconoclastic view of American political leaders, including Jefferson, Jackson, Lincoln, Wilson, and the two Roosevelts, suggesting more consensus than difference at the top of the political hierarchy.

Hope Franklin, John (1974). *From Slavery to Freedom*. Knopf. The classic overview of Afro-American history by the nation's leading black historian.

Lerner, Gerda (editor) (1977). *Black Women in White America: A Documentary History*. Random House. A rare glimpse into the lives, the minds, the spirits of that doubly oppressed group, ranging from slavery to our time, a wonderful sourcebook.

Lerner, Gerda (editor) (1977). *The Female Experience: An American Documentary*. Bobbs-Merrill. A marvelous collection of the writings of women throughout U.S. history, dealing with childhood, marriage, housework, old age, education, industrial work, politics, and sexual freedom.

Lynd, Staughton (editor) (1966). *Nonviolence in America*. Bobbs-Merrill. A valuable examination of the ideas, in their own words, of early Quaker dissidents, abolitionists, anarchists, progressives, conscientious objectors, trade unionists, civil rights workers, and pacifists, from the colonial period to the 1960s.

Martínez, Elizabeth (editor) (1991). *500 años del pueblo chicano: 500 Years of Chicano History*. Albuquerque: Southwest Organizing Project. Marvelous photos but also an exciting, bilingual text loaded with valuable history.

Nash, Gary (1970). *Red, White and Black: The Peoples of Early America*. Prentice Hall. A pioneering work of "multi-culturalism" dealing with racial interactions in the colonial period.

Takaki, Ronald (1993). *A Different Mirror*. Little, Brown & Company. A splendid, comprehensive look at the role ethnic minorities have played in American history. Eloquent, powerful, meticulously researched.

Takaki, Ronald (1989). *Strangers from a Distant Shore*. Penguin. Gives us what has been glaringly missing from our traditional histories, the story of Asian Americans, from the early years of the republic through the dramatic and tragic experiences of Chinese and Japanese immigrants, to the recent arrival of refugees from Southeast Asia.

Yellen, Samuel (1974). *American Labor Struggles*. Pathfinder. This brings to life the great labor conflicts of American history, from the railroad strikes of 1877 to the San Francisco general strike of 1934.

Young, Marilyn (1991). *The Vietnam Wars, 1945-1990*. Harper Collins. A superb history of U.S. involvement in Vietnam.

• • • • • • • • • •

*Editors note: Don't forget Zinn's* A People's History of the United States *(1981), Harper and Row.* ❐

> Once teachers begin to look for other perspectives, they will quickly be led from one thing to another.

# In Memory of Crossing the Columbia

By Elizabeth Woody
for Charlotte Edwards Pitt and Charlotte Agnes Pitt

*My board and my blanket were Navajo,*
*but my bed is inside the River.*
*In the beads of remembrance,*
*I am her body in my father's hands.*
*She gave me her eyes*
*and the warmth of basalt.*
*The vertebrae of her back,*
*my breastplate, the sturdy*
*belly of mountainside.*
*"Pahtu," he whispered in her language.*
*She is the mountain of change.*
*She is the mountain of women*
*who have lain as volcanoes*
*before men.*
*Red, as the women much loved,*
*she twisted like silvery chinook*
*beyond his reach.*
*Dancing the Woman-Salmon dance,*
*there is not much time to waste.*

Elizabeth Woody ( Warm Springs Wasco/Navajo) has two new books **Seven Hands, Seven Hearts: Prose and Poetry** and **Luminaries of the Humble**. (For lesson ideas, see p. 184.)

# Students as Textbook Detectives

## By Bill Bigelow and Bob Peterson

Many school districts rely on basal textbook series for basic curricula in social studies, science, math and other subjects. Such texts have many problems, but one thing they do offer is an opportunity for teachers and students to uncover bias. We include the lesson described below as an example of teaching critical literacy — offering students some tools to question the basic assumptions of the material they read, to "talk back" to their texts.

Grade Level 5 - 12

### Procedure:

1. For background information on the causes and consequences of the U.S. war with Mexico, see Howard Zinn's *A People's History of the United States* (Chapter 8: "We Take Nothing by Conquest, Thank God,") and Ronald Takaki's *A Different Mirror* (Chapter 7: "Foreigners in Their Native Land.") Also see the interview with Howard Zinn on pp. 150-155. Useful first-person accounts of participants can be found in Milton Meltzer's *Bound for the Rio Grande*. As a follow-up activity you might use Henry David Thoreau's essay "On Civil Disobedience."

2. If possible, share with students excerpts of these books — representing perspectives not found in traditional basal texts. The more background students have on the war with Mexico, the more easily they will be able to complete the assignment. However, this is also a useful introductory activity that can alert students to issues of point of view and bias.

3. Distribute to students the selection from Macmillan's, *United States and Its Neighbors*, a fifth grade text. Note that this is the book's entire section on the Mexican War. Also distribute to students the "Thinking Deeply" questions. (As an alternative to using the excerpt provided, ask students to use their own textbooks, or distribute several different texts so they can compare coverage.)

4. Divide students into small groups and ask them to read the textbook excerpt, discuss the questions and answer them in writing.

5. Bring students back together to share their insights. Be sure to ask the bigger "why" questions, such as:

• Why do you think this textbook leaves out important information?

• Why do you think some school districts use textbooks that present such an incomplete story?

• Why is it important when textbooks fail to tell students about individuals and movements in history that opposed government policies?

Also ask:

• How do you think books like these affect the way students think about wars the United States has been involved in?

• How do the books affect the way students view the world today, for example, "illegal" immigration from Mexico to the United States? (Our students are often surprised to learn that Texas, California, New Mexico, Arizona, etc. were once Mexican territory, and were acquired by the United States through deceit and invasion. For some, this puts the legitimacy of the border and the issue of so-called illegal aliens in a new light.)

• In the Macmillan text, the entire section on the Mexican American War consists of six paragraphs. What message does that send to readers about the importance of this period to people in the United States and Mexico?

6. Allow students to act on what they find. They might write letters to a textbook company or a school district textbook selection committee, re-write sections of the text or write critiques to be left in the book for the following year's students, and/or lead workshops with other students and young children about the biases they have uncovered.

**Note:** While the "Thinking Deeply" questions here are aimed at critiquing representations of the U.S. War with Mexico, this format can be used with virtually any textbook account of any historical period, or with children's literature. For example, in examining stories or descriptions of the "discovery" of America, elementary students could be asked: How many times does Columbus talk? How many times do we get to know what he is thinking? How many times do the Native people have names? How many times do the Native people talk? How many times do we get to know what the Native people are thinking? etc. Or on the high school level, students might be encouraged to ask: What kinds of things do you learn about Columbus, his background, why he's sailing west, what he wants, etc.? What do you learn about the Taino people he encounters in the Caribbean? Whom does the book get you to root for and how does it accomplish that? (For example, are the books horrified at the treament of the Tainos or thrilled that Columbus makes it to the "New World"?).

### Thinking Deeply

1. What do you learn about the *causes* for the war with Mexico? What *doesn't* the book tell you about the causes?

2. What does the textbook tell about the many American citizens who opposed U.S. involvement in the war?

3. What does the textbook include about the lives and thoughts of African Americans, Mexicans, or women?

4. If everything that a student knew about the U.S. War with Mexico came from this textbook, do you suppose they'd think the war was right or wrong? Explain. ❑

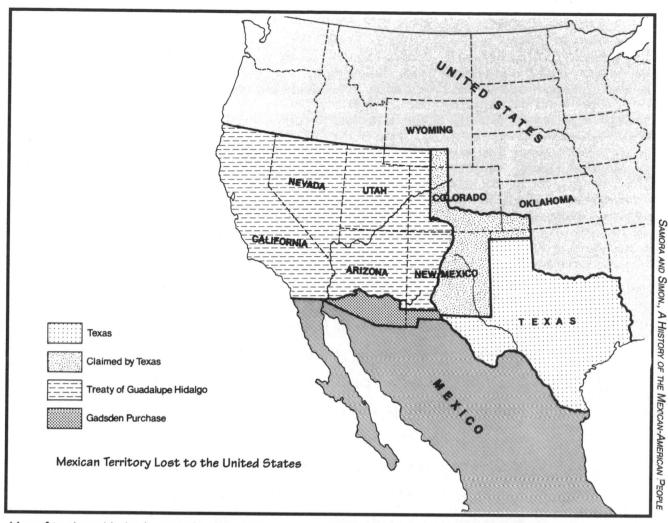

SAMORA AND SIMON, A HISTORY OF THE MEXICAN-AMERICAN PEOPLE

**Legend:**
- Texas
- Claimed by Texas
- Treaty of Guadalupe Hidalgo
- Gadsden Purchase

**Mexican Territory Lost to the United States**

Map of territory Mexico lost to the United States — a map not included in the Macmillan textbook.

# War with Mexico

While the Mormons were settling in Utah, the United States went to war with Mexico. The war began on the border between Texas and Mexico. Americans claimed the border was the **Rio Grande**. Mexicans said the border was farther north and east at the Nueces River.

In January 1846, President **James K. Polk** sent 1,500 troops down to the Rio Grande. They camped in an area claimed by both countries. When a Mexican army appeared across the river, a battle of bands broke out. The Americans played "The Star-Spangled Banner" and "Yankee Doodle." The Mexicans answered with patriotic songs of Mexico.

It was not long before songs gave way to battle sounds. Fighting broke out along the Rio Grande. Then, in May, the United States declared war on Mexico.

American troops marched into Mexico in the summer of 1846. Many soldiers never came home. Some died in battle. More died of disease. Even so, spirits were high. Americans bragged that "We may be killed, but we can't be whipped."

The war ended in 1847 when American troops captured Mexico City, the capital of Mexico. The final battle took place at an old fort called Chapultepec Castle. One hundred students from a Mexican military school joined the fighting. *Los Niños,* or "the boys," died defending their country.

Early in 1848 the two countries signed a peace treaty. A treaty is a formal agreement. According to the treaty, Mexico was forced to give up about half of its territory. That land is now Arizona, Nevada, Utah, California, and parts of New Mexico, Colorado, and Wyoming. In return the United States paid Mexico $15 million. ☐

From *United States and its Neighbors,* Macmillan, 1990, p. 380.

# To The Young Who Want to Die

By Gwendolyn Brooks

Sit down. Inhale. Exhale.
The gun will wait. The lake will wait.
The tall gall in the small seductive vial
will wait will wait:
will wait a week:   will wait through April.
You do not have to die this certain day.
Death will abide, will pamper your postponement.
I assure you death will wait. Death has
a lot of time. Death can
attend to you tomorrow. Or next week. Death is
just down the street; is most obliging neighbor;
can meet you any moment.

You need not die today.
Stay here — through pout or pain or peskiness.
Stay here. See what the news is going to be  tomorrow.

Graves grow no green that you can use.
Remember, green's your color. You are Spring.

Gwendolyn Brooks is one of the foremost African-American poets in this country. She
was the first African American to win the Pulitzer Prize for poetry, in 1950. (See p. 184 for lesson ideas.)

EARL DOTTER

# Beyond the Classroom

No classroom is an island. Teachers soon become painfully aware of how factors beyond the classroom limit what they can accomplish with their students.

Overcrowded classes, tracking, crumbling social services, social inequality, and the isolation of teachers themselves all undermine effective education.

As the writers in this chapter argue, reform-minded teachers must complement their efforts inside their classrooms with alliances to transform the schools, districts, and communities they work in.

# Why We Need to Go Beyond the Classroom

By Stan Karp

School power comes in many pieces. Those of us who teach have daily opportunities to shape classroom life in ways that reflect a vision of social justice and equality. Whether it's developing curriculum that includes the real lives of our students, encouraging young people to examine issues of race, class, and gender as they build academic competence, or organizing activities that promote cooperative skills and spirit, classroom teachers can often find ways to promote social justice despite the institutional agendas and bureaucratic practices imposed upon us.

But what if we stop at the classroom door? What if we see our role as teachers only in terms of classroom practice? Is our job essentially to create "safe spaces" inside an often ineffective and oppressive educational system? Can we sustain ourselves for years as committed professionals by focusing simply on the 30, 60, or 150 students for whom we assume direct responsibility each September? What about other arenas of educational activity beyond our classrooms: schoolwide change, community and districtwide education politics, teacher unionism, and national education reform? What do these have to do with next week's lesson plans?

One fundamental answer is that teachers will never really succeed until conditions of teaching and learning improve dramatically. We need more resources, better training and support, smaller classes, more effective partnerships with the communities we serve, and, especially in poorer areas, a vision of social change that can replace poverty and despair with progress and hope. We need effective responses to violence, racism, drug addiction, family crisis and the many other problems that surface daily in our classrooms. Teachers will have to help address these problems as surely as our students have to study and do their homework to achieve their individual academic goals.

Whether the issue is vouchers, funding, multiculturalism, testing, or tracking, schools have become public battlegrounds for competing social and political agendas. The voices of grassroots teachers, parents, and students are essential if education reform is going to make schools more effective, more equitable, and more democratic institutions. If we don't help to change our schools from the bottom up, we will have them changed for us from the top down.

Educational activism is also crucial to finding the allies we need. It is naive to believe that we can transform our schools and our students' lives by ourselves. While we can admire and strive to emulate teachers who through hard work and commitment manage to perform classroom "magic," the real hope for educational transformation does not lie in the development of isolated "superteachers," but in the reorganization of school life. We need better, more collaborative relations with our colleagues and the space to nurture those possibilities. We need better, more cooperative relations with parents and communities, particularly where cultural and racial differences exist. And we need better and more democratic practices in our schools, our unions, and our districts which can only come with contacts and activism beyond our classroom boundaries.

Finally, critical teachers need to move beyond the classroom because to do otherwise would undercut the very efforts we make each day. If we recognize that effective education requires students to bring their real lives into the classrooms, and to take what they learn back to their homes and neighborhoods in the form of new understandings and new behavior, how can teachers not do the same? Critical teaching should not merely be an abstraction or academic formula for classroom "experimentation." It should be a strategy for educational organizing that changes lives, including our own.

Teachers who find these arguments compelling still face tough practical questions beginning with "where to put the lever?" Fortunately the current ferment around education has widened the space for all sorts of initiatives. Each of the possibilities discussed below offers teachers the potential for creating

> Critical teaching should not merely be an academic formula for classroom "experimentation." It should be a strategy for educational organizing that changes lives, including our own.

change, making allies, and expanding horizons.

## Site-based Management

Site-based management and shared decision-making reforms (which invest varying degrees of authority in school-based councils of teachers, administrators, parents and even students) hold considerable possibilities for change. While there is an air of trendiness surrounding it, site-based reform does have the potential to be more than another fad. It's currently on the agenda because there is a near-universal recognition that the system as it now functions cannot satisfy the varied constituencies who look to schools to meet competing needs. Site-based reform draws on both corporate strategies for boosting productivity by promoting joint labor/management collaboration, and the more democratic traditions of U.S. schools as local institutions that should be subject to community control.

At its best, site-based reform can open a credible process for replacing hierarchical and bureaucratic forms of school governance with more representative and democratic structures. Where site councils are given real power and resources, parents, teachers and others in the school community can make significant decisions about budget priorities, curricula, and school policies in ways that can nourish community/school/teacher collaboration. They can become places where members of a school community try to reconcile different perspectives and priorities, and learn to build mutual trust and respect over the long term.

At its worst, however, site-based reform can become simply another bureaucratic layer in a system that doesn't work. It can consume valuable time and energy in a seemingly endless cycle of unproductive meetings. Instead of representative bodies, site councils can be empty shells dominated by administrative appointees, or bodies that marginalize parents (or classroom teachers) in ways that promote old antagonisms rather than new alliances. They can also become pawns in a cynical process of imposing austerity,

breaking union power, or otherwise administering policies of educational retrenchment rather than reform. (Much as African-American mayors have gained access to political power only to find themselves compelled to oversee disinvestment and decay in urban areas.)

Whether or not a particular site-based project is worth a teacher's investment of time and energy probably depends on the answers to several questions: Has the council been created in response to a top-down directive or is it the product of grassroots, union, or community action? Does the site council have direct control over resources or policies that can substantially impact on the school? Is site-based reform ac-

companied by a transfer of resources from central office to individual schools? Is the site council a place where teachers and parents really have a chance to engage in dialogue and form alliances? Will participation expand useful contacts with parents and colleagues? Is the process characterized by an increase in communication, access to information, and debate by key constituencies? Is site-based reform accompanied by a tangible investment in the time and training needed to make it work? Have the criteria and timelines for evaluating site-based projects been set bureaucratically or determined by the councils themselves? Is there building-wide or districtwide discussion of how such reform will change the roles

of all concerned, or is it being grafted onto existing structures?

Site-based reform is definitely not a "quick fix," but given time, resources, and a staff committed to the process it can succeed. Daniel Webster Accelerated School in San Francisco, Calif., an elementary school with a culturally diverse, largely low-income population of about 350 students, used site-based governance reform to guide basic restructuring of the school program. They created many subcommittees connected to a central steering committee, and, through rescheduling and having the principal teach phys-ed. classes, time was created for the committees to meet each week during the school day. With high levels of parent participation, the school used this process to implement a thematic, language-rich curriculum that emphasized "active and inter-active learning, discussion, problem-solving and research." Within five years, student achievement showed significant improvement.

Districtwide site-based reform is now underway in such large problem-plagued urban systems as Chicago and Philadelphia. In Chicago, local councils of parents, teachers, and community members have been created to direct each of the city's more than 500 schools. In Philadelphia, site-based reform has been used to help break down many of the city's huge comprehensive high schools into smaller, theme-based "charter" schools. Neither of these ambitious reform efforts suggests that site-based management is a panacea that can miraculously compensate for deeply-rooted educational problems, years of neglect, or inadequate funding. But they do indicate that site-based governance reform can play an important role in mobilizing teachers and parents to re-invest in school communities, particularly in areas where the existing bureaucracies have been exhausted by failure.

Teachers in schools where site reforms are underway can participate in a variety of ways: serving on the council itself, organizing a subcommittee to ensure that a re-examination of instructional practices is part of the reform process, organizing initiatives with parents, or turning the school newsletter or the faculty room bulletin board into a lively source of resources, information, and debate. The key is to seize upon a school's encounter with site-based decision-making as an opportunity to re-think and re-examine all aspects of school life.

## School Restructuring and Districtwide Initiatives

While site-based reform of school governance offers one possible road to change, there are many others. In-school restructuring projects can encourage teachers to rethink areas like curriculum, scheduling, and staff collaboration and move away from the traditional factory-model school towards child-centered learning environments that promote critical teaching. Small steps can lead to bigger ones. For example, social studies or language arts teachers might look for ways to move away from textbook-driven chronological surveys of American history or literature to more inter-disciplinary, thematically-based approaches (including, for example, investigations of students' own family pasts, or the cultural and literary history of the local community). This, in turn, could lead to consider-

> Too often, progressive teachers abstain from union activity, lumping the union with the administration as "them." But teachers unions are *our* organizations, or at any rate, they should be.

ation of how to reschedule the school day to permit larger blocs of learning time, team-teaching, or common prep time for staff. Taken further, teachers might develop proposals for "schools within schools" organized around specific curriculum themes or instructional philosophies. The key is to recognize that particular styles of classroom practice reflect, in large measure, a school's assumptions about what curriculum should include, about how teachers should collaborate, and how teaching and learning should be assessed. Raising questions in one area inevitably opens debate in others. By clearly identifying the policies, resources, and structures necessary to support critical teaching in the classroom, teachers can initiate a buildingwide process of change.

The same is true at the district level. Teachers in Milwaukee, for example, began by questioning the district's heavy reliance on basal readers. They formed a Reading Textbook Adoption Committee which challenged both the bureaucratic process by which textbook selections had been made, and the curriculum implications of relying heavily on basals (i.e., fragmented skills drills, rigid workbook sequences, etc.). They succeeded in winning support for a whole language alternative, including formation of a Whole Language Teachers Council with district support, staff development, and alternative materials. The number of teachers using whole language approaches in Milwaukee public schools rose ten-fold.

Wherever possible, critical teachers need to act on the broader implications of their classroom innovations. The public debate over how best to teach reading in Milwaukee schools was followed by an even more basic debate over curriculum reform. (See p.168) In Montclair, NJ, English teachers in the high school initiated an untracked course that began a communitywide debate on ability grouping. (See p. 176). Schoolwide or even districtwide debates about curriculum, tracking policies, assessment, or other educational issues are readily influenced by a few well-informed, committed teachers. Successful efforts can both reshape an individual teaching situation and redirect district policy.

## Teachers Unions

Teachers unions offer another maze of opportunities and obstacles for classroom teachers looking to effect change. Like public schools themselves, teachers unions are both deeply flawed institutions, and, at the same time, indispensable to hopes for educational democracy and justice. Labor unions in general, and teachers unions in particular, have won essential rights and better salaries for those they represent. In most school systems, unions serve as some check on the arbitrary power of the politicized bureaucracies that manage school districts. More significantly, they are an important reservoir of collective strength and resources that need to be protected from a variety of anti-labor crusades in education today, including privatization, voucher schemes, and legal restrictions on organizing and the right to strike.

Unfortunately, however, in too many cases teachers unions have become bureaucratic partners in the management of failing school systems. Like other labor organizations, they often suffer from undemocratic and uninspiring internal practices which demobilize and fragment their memberships instead of enlisting them in creative campaigns for better schools. And like most other social institutions, they have been deformed by the persistence of racism and sexism which has at times crippled their ability to respond effectively to complex issues such as affirmative action vs. seniority rights, the need to close the gap between communities of color and predominantly white professional staffs, and the building of parent-teacher partnerships.

Teachers unions have too often adopted short-sighted and defensive perspectives on key reform issues. They are typically driven by narrowly conceived salary and contract concerns at the expense of a broader vision of educational justice and change. As a result they often pit the short-term interests of their members against the long-term interests of schools and the communi-

Teachers demonstrate against for-profit schools in Baltimore.

MARYLAND STATE TEACHERS FEDERATION

ties they serve. Ultimately this undercuts their ability to respond to the current educational crisis and weakens public support for both unions and schools. Whether the issue is helping ineffective teachers, prioritizing scarce resources, including community and parent concerns in contract talks, or otherwise facilitating the transformation of existing school systems, teachers unions have too often acted like they were incapable of a creative initiative or new idea and committed to the most narrow defense of existing arrangements. The consequences can be devastating for both school systems and teachers. In Chicago and New York, reforms to increase community and parent power had to be instituted, to a large extent, against union opposition, weakening the reforms in both cases. Elsewhere unions have intransigently refused to address the issue of "bad teachers," thereby helping to magnify and sensationalize what in actuality is a marginal issue, while at the same time failing to address the dismal state of teacher training and in-school support.

But some of the responsibility for the failure of teachers unions is our own. Too often progressive-minded teachers abstain from union activity, lumping the union with the administration as "them." But teachers unions are *our* organizations, or at any rate, they should be; and while it would be naive to ignore the obstacles that bureaucratized unions can place in the path of

rank and file activism, it is self-defeating to surrender in advance.

Many locals are starved for the participation of committed members. Others may be genuinely committed to the interests of teachers and kids but have no awareness of critical perspectives or alternative strategies. Moreover, it's not necessary to pursue the possibilities of union activism by starting with a frontal attack on the leadership. Most teachers unions have a variety of committees and forums that offer possibilities for initiative and debate. A teacher looking for connections with other colleagues and potential allies should definitely consider becoming a building delegate, reviving a moribund instructional committee, organizing a classroom discussion caucus, or proposing a union-sponsored community forum on some hot educational issue. Even if a year or two of union work leads you to conclude that the space for change in your local is limited, you're likely to have made valuable contacts, and positioned yourself and others for a broader challenge to the union status quo as the education crisis deepens and more unions find business-as-usual strategies unequal to the tasks before them.

## Teacher Study Groups

A major reason for critical teachers to look beyond the classroom is to break out of the confining isolation they often face. Most school cultures are not very supportive of critical thought, change, or even collaboration among staff. Starting a teachers study group can be a way of finding allies to sustain committed teaching over the long haul. A teachers group might begin as an informal after-school social hour where teachers trade stories, resources, and ideas. To encourage discussion beyond the "gripe session stage" (a chronic tendency among teachers), it's often helpful to pick a specific topic like tracking, assessment, or discipline, read a background article, and then talk about the issue's impact on your own school and classrooms. Once a group establishes some cohesion and continuity, it can address more difficult issues such as multicultural relations among teachers and students, or differing parent-teacher perspectives. It may be useful to invite outside participants for frank conversations about sensitive issues often avoided in typical "in-service" programs.

Discussion or study groups have a variety of attractions for teachers looking to move beyond the classroom.

They're flexible, and can set their own agendas and pace without interference. If the interest in one school is insufficient to sustain a group, teachers from several schools can begin coalescing a local network of progressive educators. They can draw on a variety of national resources and networks for ideas and support, (See resources, p. 199), and can develop into a safe space for critical reflection and mutual support not often available elsewhere.

Eventually, discussion and study will hopefully lead to action, public discussion, and local campaigns to improve schools. After several years, a Portland, Ore., teachers study group moved from discussion to taking initiatives through the union's education reform committee and, later, to developing a public citywide school reform document in response to ongoing budget crises. With public attention increasingly focused on education, a local teachers group (or a combined teacher/parent/community group) has the potential to evolve into an important grassroots institution. One person posting a sign on the faculty bulletin board, or approaching a few colleagues, can

initiate a low-risk strategy that can pay big dividends.

## Local, State, and National Education Activism

The opportunities discussed above can each be used to promote social justice in education, and at the same time sustain individual teachers in their daily efforts in the classroom. But there are many key educational issues that will be determined, not primarily inside local schools and classrooms, but in the larger context of community, state, and national politics. These include the fate of voucher plans, which threaten to divert public funds to private schools, and privatization schemes, which propose disinvesting in the very concept of public education and turning over schools to private managers.

It also includes legal battles now underway in more than 20 states over school funding inequities which reproduce society's racial and class divisions, create a patchwork of rich schools and poor schools, and breed crippling inequality. And it includes the imposition of state and national testing standards which bureaucratically drive school curricula and limit teacher autonomy in the classroom, often in ways that hinder effective instructional practices. Teachers need to be informed about these issues and where possible, join efforts to resolve them in positive ways.

In the final analysis, however, what's important is not that classroom teachers assume an impossible burden of individual responsibility for solving all the social and educational problems that affect their classrooms. What matters is that they see the connections between those classrooms and the society around them, and realize that efforts to apply critical teaching are tied to broader efforts to promote democracy and equality in society. If teachers can find ways to link the two, they will strengthen both. ❐

*Stan Karp (StanKarp@aol.com) has been a high school teacher in Paterson, NJ for over 25 years and is a* Rethinking Schools *editor.*

---

# 10 Things You Can Do Beyond Your Classroom

1. Serve on a local school council
2. Become active in your union
3. Breathe new life into a standing union/school committee (e.g., instruction, community outreach, curriculum)
4. Organize a teachers study or discussion group
5. Join the National Coalition of Education Activists
6. Help distribute *Rethinking Schools*
7. Join a local community organization with an interest in schools (e.g., the NAACP, a local neighborhood coalition)
8. Investigate and publicize tracking policies in your school
9. Flood your faculty room with provocative materials about critical teaching
10. Investigate and publicize education funding policies in your state

**For related resources, organizations and periodicals, see pp. 197-201.**

# Gurl

By Mary Blalock

From Adam's rib
it's prophesied
I came,
but that's his story.

I'm walking on my own

down these streets
with a stop sign on every
corner,
takin' my time.
I've got no place to go 'cept
forward.

Down these highways without
a road map,
down these sidewalks,
where the cracks want to

break my mother's back,
where the city is crowded.

I'm walking on my own.

I'm not on a Stairmaster,
and I won't wait for an eleva-
tor.
I'm taking the fire escape
to the top floor.

If I want to,
I'll walk all around the world,
taking the long way
or the shortcuts,
'cross countries and through
oceans.
I won't be swimming.
I'll walk
on my own.

Mary Blalock wrote "Gurl" when she was a senior at Jefferson High School
in Portland, Oregon, 1994.

# Forging Curriculum Reform Throughout a District

By David Levine

In 1991, Milwaukee Public School parent and volunteer Helen Dixon was asked to serve on the district's K-12 Curriculum Summer Committee. She agreed with strong misgivings, wondering, "Is this going to be another set of meetings where we just end up spinning our wheels?"

Her apprehensions were shared by many of the 80 parents, teachers, and administrators asked to spend three weeks charting a course for curricular reform within the Milwaukee Public Schools. MPS has a long history of promising reforms lost somewhere on the road to implementation.

But after three weeks of intense, difficult, and at times exhilarating work, she and her colleagues had produced a document and a momentum that gave a strong boost to reform within Milwaukee's public schools. Dixon told a Milwaukee School Board committee, "As the process went on and I saw and felt the sense of dedication and commitment of everyone, I thought there is no way our work will be denied success." Phil Foster, a Social Studies teacher at Milwaukee Tech, echoed these sentiments at the same hearing, "I've been in the system since 1967 and the K-12 curriculum reform is probably the most exciting thing that's happened during my teaching career."

Not surprisingly, implementation has proven to be a complex, arduous, and piecemeal process. Yet the initiative which this committee was part of has led to some real steps forward, and provides important insights to urban districts interested in overhauling their curriculum. Three key lessons emerge from the Milwaukee experience:

1) District curricular goals should be broad guidelines rather than detailed recipes which risk straitjacketing teach-ers or being ignored by them.

2) The goals should be defined and modified through democratic discussions among teachers, parents, community members, and school officials.

3) Districtwide curricular plans should focus on practical ways to insure that equity and academic rigor are pursued as complementary objectives.

The focus of the Summer Committee's work was a 30-page document entitled "Moving Forward with K-12 Teaching and Learning: A Working Model." A marked departure from the highly detailed "curriculum cookbooks" that line a thousand dusty shelves, this report crisply articulates ten Teaching and Learning Goals to guide all K-12 teaching. Each goal is further defined by age-appropriate

> Traditional curriculum development has often been driven by textbook companies and controlled by central office administrators. But curriculum reform will only be effective if it comes from the bottom up.

"Performance Indicators" which describe specific abilities students are to develop. These indicators are broadly stated and limited in number to "allow schools to exercise creative initiative and flexibility."

## A New Vision of Curriculum

The goals and indicators are guided by an innovative perspective. Curriculum has traditionally been seen as "content," which is separate from "teaching methods." Many people think of curriculum in static terms, as textbooks, lists of goals and objectives, or computer programs. By contrast the K-12 Report defines curriculum as what we teach, how we teach, and the entire learning environment that surrounds the child. This conception gives prime importance to the vision each teacher brings to her students. Grace Thomsen, a social studies teacher at South Division High School, comments, "What's exciting and promising about this approach is that it's challenging us to reshuffle what we have in our heads and really think about what we want our kids to be able to do."

Traditional curriculum development has often been driven by textbook companies and controlled by central office administrators. But curriculum reform will only be effective if it comes from the bottom up. The K-12 Curriculum Report therefore recommends that curriculum development be based on the grassroots involvement of parents, teachers, and students.

## A New Model for Change

As the committee members struggled to produce a new curricular framework, they were continuing a process which reflected a new approach to curricular decision-making. Hundreds of teacher-delegates and scores of parents were brought together during the 1990-1991 school year to create draft learning goals for the Summer Curriculum Committee to develop and refine. Cynthia Ellwood, who coordinated the spring and summer work and is now MPS Director of Education, explains why she deemed it so important to involve many people in the change process. "Improving teaching and learning is a challenge we have to tackle together. Good teaching is incredibly demanding. You not only need a strong command of the subject matter, you have to make complex judgments about how to motivate students and help them to understand. You really have to be able to get inside a student's head or thirty students' heads and figure out how they're seeing things. It's a lot like parenting and there are no easy answers; every interaction is a judgment call. You have to know when to encourage and when to demand, how to be firm and caring at the same time. What examples and questions can you pose so that a student will really understand? And what works with one student will not necessarily work with the next, just as parents find their children have different strengths and personalities."

Ellwood says curriculum reform mandated from the top down will never produce teachers who can make these complex professional judgments on behalf of children. "There's no way good teaching will ever come from a script. If we want change we've got to have a process that asks people to think, and there have to be opportunities for people to learn from each other about the children whose education we share responsibility for. I think teachers and administrators have a lot to learn from parents, for example. And since the kids we teach come from diverse backgrounds, we've got to talk seriously to adults from backgrounds different from our own if we hope to understand and educate all kids."

During the early sessions, committee members focused on essential educational questions: What is critical thinking? Why is multicultural education crucial? What kinds of assessment best measure learning? As the work of the committee unfolded, the facilitators carefully orchestrated a variety of experiences. Committee members met most often by developmental level: primary, intermediate, middle school, and high school. But these meetings were balanced by other kinds of groupings: teams which included teachers from all four developmental levels, separate caucuses of parents, teachers, and administrators, discipline-specific meetings, and sessions of the entire committee. This fluid reliance on different kinds of groups meant committee members were constantly considering new perspectives and sharing their ideas with new people.

The skillful interweaving of groups was accompanied by leadership which encouraged the open expression of differing views. Rose Guajardo, principal at Kagel Elementary, notes "What I liked about the whole thing was that you could speak your mind freely. You could disagree with someone and give your reasons why. Everyone had a chance to speak and give their ideas. We valued and respected everyone's input."

One of the most important features of the committee's work is that parents were able to play a crucial part. By insisting that educational jargon be kept to a minimum, and that parents be paid as consultants, the committee organizers were able to insure their full involvement.

### New Priorities

Perhaps the most striking feature of the K-12 document is the high priority it gives to building a curriculum which

## Teaching and Learning Goals in Milwaukee

Following are the 10 Teaching and Learning Goals included in *Moving Forward with K-12,* the report of the curriculum reform committee in the Milwaukee Public Schools.

1. Students will project anti-racist, anti-biased attitudes through their participation in a multi-lingual, multi-ethnic, culturally diverse curriculum.

2. Students will participate and gain knowledge in all the arts (visual arts, dance, theater, literature, music), developing personal vehicles for self-expression reinforced in an integrated curriculum.

3. Students will demonstrate positive attitudes towards life, living, and learning through an understanding and respect of self and others.

4. Students will make responsible decisions, solve problems, and think critically.

5. Students will demonstrate responsible citizenship and an understanding of global interdependence.

6. Students will use technological resources capably, actively, and responsibly.

7. Students will think logically and abstractly, applying mathematical and scientific principles of inquiry to solve problems, create new solutions, and communicate new ideas and relationships to real world experiences.

8. Students will communicate knowledge, ideas, thoughts, feelings, concepts, opinions, and needs effectively and creatively using varied modes of expression.

9. Students will learn strategies to cope with the challenges of daily living and will establish practices which promote health, fitness, and safety.

10. Students will set short and long-term goals, will develop an awareness of career opportunities, and will be motivated to actualize their potential. □

Curriculum reform: a key component in improving classrooms.

celebrates diversity and is explicitly anti-racist. While such goals commonly adorn the mission statements of urban school systems, here they are fleshed out in a manner designed to make them a reality in every classroom. The report stipulates: "Students will project anti-racist, anti-biased attitudes through their participation in a multilingual, multiethnic, culturally diverse curriculum." This goal is complemented by developmentally appropriate performance indicators for each age level. For example, middle school students are expected to:

• Develop an activity unit that charts the history and contributions of different ethnic groups in the world society.

• Describe/demonstrate how customs, values, and traditions help form the culture of a society.

• Use tools and resources to analyze and assess ethnic components that express the basic tenets of a culture.

• Participate in second language activities based on their language experience.

These objectives challenge teachers to treat the cultural background of each child as a valuable source of ideas, themes, experiences, and self-esteem. Olalekan Benson, a teacher at Lloyd Street Elementary School, explains "We're telling the teacher — look for the richness in your classroom as far as the diversity of culture and build on it. Use it to help your children grow. Use it to help them work together. Use it to enrich yourself and your students."

## Will It Work?

During the three years since the K-12 report was adopted, the system has struggled with mixed success to implement it. Bright spots include a de-tracking ninth grade algebra project, and the innovative work of four systemwide teachers councils: a Humanities Council at the high school level, the Multicultural Council at the middle and elementary school levels, and the elementary Whole Language and Ungraded Primary Councils, all now coordinated by a recently formed Council of Councils.

But the reform initiative has had to contend with many obstacles: long-standing reliance on standardized testing, staff resistance to new styles of teaching, lack of adequate preparation time, and pupil/teacher ratios which remain unfavorable to innovative approaches. Dedicated teachers must put in long evening and weekend hours to feel adequately prepared. Their efforts at cooperative planning with colleagues must be squeezed into hurried hallway consultations, discussions over lunch, or faculty meetings already jammed with too many agenda items. The interdisciplinary, project-oriented thrust of the recommendations is hampered at the high school level by the rigid division of the school day into 48 minute slices. Old habits and organizational structures have proven stubbornly resistant to change.

As MPS travels farther down the path of reform, and encounters the inevitable setbacks, frustrations, and barriers, it is important that insistence for progress be tempered by commitment to a long-term process. The new forms of learning, organization, and collegiality our schools need will take time to develop. But if members of the MPS community are willing to settle in for the long haul, there is good reason to share Helen Dixon's view that "These wheels have started moving, with the involvement of parents, teachers, and administrators we will be seeing progress instead of just speaking progress." ❏

*David Levine, an editor of* Rethinking Schools, *is currently in graduate school in the Department of Educational Policy Studies at the University of Wisconsin, Madison.*

# Why Standardized Tests Are Bad

By Terry Meier

No phenomenon poses a greater threat to educational equity, and ultimately to the quality of education in this country, than the escalating use of standardized achievement tests.

Fueled by public concern that schools are less rigorous than they used to be, standardized tests are increasingly prescribed as the "get tough" medicine needed to return excellence to our classrooms. Across the country, standardized tests are now routinely used to determine how and when students advance, from first grade through graduate school.

Standardized tests, which are notorious for their discriminatory effect on students of color, clearly threaten whatever small measures of educational equity have been won in recent decades. What is less obvious is that standardized tests threaten the educational experience of all children. The threat is so great, in fact, that standardized testing should be abolished.

It is estimated that a student will take more than 30 standardized tests by the time he or she graduates from high school. Because standardized tests are a constant reality in students' lives, it is essential that parents understand the biases and limitations of such tests. Yet, as in so many other educational areas, parents are often excluded from the debate because they are deemed unable to understand the issue's complexity.

Tests are called "standardized" when the same test is given under similar conditions to large groups of students, whether districtwide, statewide, or nationwide. Most standardized tests ask multiple-choice questions and are corrected by a computer which recognizes only one "right" answer.

Decades of research have documented the biases in standardized tests, with students of color bearing the brunt

Standardized testing narrows opportunity for students of color.

*Earl Dotter/American Labor Ed. Center*

of that discrimination. Across age groups, standardized tests discriminate against low-income students and students of color. While girls tend to do better on standardized tests at an early age, by high school and college their scores are on average below those of males, according to FairTest, a national group based in Cambridge, Mass., that lobbies against the growing use of standardized tests.

Advocates of testing argue that standardized achievement tests do not create inequities within schools, they merely reflect pre-existing inequities. According to this argument, children of color and low-income students tend to perform less well on standardized tests because they receive an inferior education.

Two false assumptions support this view. One is that standardized tests are a valid measure of excellence. The second is that standardized tests can be used to improve education, especially

for low-income students and students of color.

## No Real Connection to Excellence

Standardized achievement tests tend to focus on mechanical, lower-order skills and to reward students' rapid recognition of factual information. For example, standardized reading tests for young children stress phonics and the recognition of individual words. Research on learning to read, however, has shown the importance of integrating oral language, writing, reading, and spelling in a meaningful context that emphasizes children understanding what they read, not merely sounding out words. Similarly, research on teaching math stresses the importance of young children learning concepts through first-hand experience, while achievement tests for young children define math as knowing one's numbers.

Thus teachers face the dilemma of providing instruction that they know fosters a student's understanding, versus drilling students in isolated skills and facts that will help them do well on standardized tests.

It's not that students don't need to work on isolated skills sometimes, especially when they're first learning to read and write. But such work is only a means to the larger end of applying those skills in a meaningful context. Removed from context as they are on standardized tests, such skills are meaningless. Held up as a measure of achievement, they become mistaken for what is most important instead of what is ultimately trivial.

There is little, if any, connection between quality instruction and standardized test performance. Consider, for example, a successful high school English class in which students learn to write thoughtful, original essays in clear, concise language about topics they genuinely care about and that draw on their experiences. Assume that the teacher taught students to edit their work so that grammatical errors were rare.

Yet what does the American College Testing (ACT) Program test? Whether a student knows if the word "pioneered" is preferable to "started up by," or if "prove to be" is preferable to "come to be," or if "reach my destination" is preferable to "get there."

On one recent ACT test — which along with the SAT is a key determinant of who attends college — students were asked whether the italicized selection in "my thoughts were *irresistibly sucked* toward the moment when ..." should be replaced by *pulled helplessly, uncontrollably drawn,* or *propelled mercilessly.* (These examples are taken from a study by researcher Mary Hoover.)

How could anyone argue that such questions test effective writing skills or analytical thinking? In fact, one could well argue that a student who preferred "started up by" to "pioneered" might be a better writer than the student who chose the "correct" answer because she chose the clearest, most easily understood words to communicate her ideas.

The point is that the choice is sty-

## Standardized tests neither measure excellence nor foster it in our schools. So why the emphasis on such tests?

listic, dependent upon what one is trying to say and to whom. Removed from real life, the choice is meaningless. It reveals nothing about a student's competence in reading and writing.

Consider another example, from a standardized reading achievement test where the child was asked to determine the "right" answer in the following selection:

"Father said: 'Once there was a land where boys and girls never grew up. They were always growing.' What was Father telling?

The truth___ A lie___ A story___"

Any of these could be the "right" answer. If the father were speaking metaphorically, referring to mental and not physical growth, he could be telling the truth. It could also be a lie, for in blackspeech the word "lie" can also mean a joke or a story. And, of course, its initial "once" signals the conventions of fiction/fairy tales. (Hoover, Politzer, and Taylor, 1987, p. 91)

Standardized tests also ignore the skills and abilities needed to function in a complex, pluralistic society — such as the ability to work collectively in various social and cultural contexts, to adjust to change, to understand the perspectives of others, to persevere, to motivate, to solve problems in a real-life context, to lead, to value moral integrity and social commitment. As Harvard psychologist Howard Gardner points out, "there are hundreds and hundreds of ways to succeed, and many different abilities that will help you get there."

It is tragic that at the time when many developmental psychologists stress a broad and complex conception of intelligence and ability, and when one needs multiple talents to function effectively in the world, we have come to define excellence in our schools within the narrow parameters of what can be measured by standardized tests. When we use standardized tests to decide who gets to go to the "best" high school or college, we may actually be discriminating against those students with the greatest potential to contribute to society.

## Excluding Diversity

It is naive to assume that we can solve the problems confronting society without embracing the perspectives and diverse skills and abilities represented in our multicultural population. Yet the continued reliance on standardized testing perpetuates a narrow definition of excellence that excludes diversity.

Standardized achievement tests thus potentially sound the death knell of diversity in our schools. They silence a cross-cultural dialogue that has barely begun, not only in the field of education, but in every area of academic, professional, and political life.

This article focuses on the overwhelmingly discriminatory effects of standardized tests on students of color. It is also well documented that tests such as the SAT and the ACT discriminate against women and working-class students.

In every ethnic and racial group, females score much lower on the SAT than males. African-American and Latina women face a double jeopardy due to the test's racial and gender discrimination. On the 1988 SAT, for example, African-American women scored on average 724 points compared to an average of 965 for white males, according to FairTest. At the same time, white women score higher on average than male students of color, with the exception of Asian- and Pacific-American students.

Similarly, there is a direct relationship between family income and SAT scores. In 1988, students whose annual family income was more than $70,000 scored an average 992, with figures declining for each income group to an average score of 781 for students with annual family income under $10,000. Further, upper-income students are also more likely to afford the $600 "coaching" courses that can raise student scores by as much as 100 points.

It is inarguable that students of color are often ill-served in our schools. But given that standardized tests bear little, if any, relationship to substantive learning, it makes no sense to assume that improving the educational experience of students of color will necessarily affect their test scores. What *is* clear is that in many schools, the opposite tends to occur. As teachers have come under increasing pressure to raise test scores, the quality of education the students receive has declined. In too many classrooms, test content dictates curriculum.

In some cases, abilities and skills not measured on achievement tests have been removed from the curriculum altogether. According to FairTest, when Virginia's state minimum competency tests decided to include only the multiplication and division of fractions several years ago, some teachers in the state stopped teaching students how to add and subtract fractions. Similarly, Deborah Meier, a public school principal in Manhattan, reports that when one New York City test eliminated items on synonyms and antonyms, these were also eliminated from the curriculum.

In some states, matching curriculum with the content of standardized achievement tests has become a systemwide mandate. FairTest reports that school systems in at least 13 states have attempted to "align" their curriculum with standardized tests so that students do not spend hours studying materials upon which they will never be tested, regardless of the value or benefits which could be derived from that effort.

Pressure on teachers and administrators to standardize curriculum in order to raise test scores can be intense. One 1987 report by researcher John Weiss, for instance, found that in 1985 the superintendent of schools in St. Louis fired 60 teachers and principals because their students didn't improve their scores sufficiently on standardized multiple-choice tests.

## Tests as a Sorting System

Clearly, standardized tests neither measure excellence nor foster it in our schools. So why the emphasis on such tests?

The fundamental reason is that the tests provide a seemingly objective basis upon which to allocate limited educational resources — to decide who gets into the best classes, high schools, or colleges. To that end, test items are deliberately selected so as to maximize differences between high and low scorers. By design, only some people will do well on the tests.

There can be little doubt that if a large percentage of white middle class students performed poorly on standardized tests, the test results would be viewed as invalid and discriminatory. There is no similar concern for students of color, despite some 25 years of extensive documentation of cultural bias in standardized testing.

According to one study, one-third of the items in typical reading achievement tests are prejudiced against those speaking non-standard English. For example, they require students of color to distinguish between words, removed from context, which are often homonyms (sound alike) in their everyday oral speech patterns, such as had/hat and right/rat for African-American dialect speakers or this/these and tag/tack for Spanish dominant speakers (Examples taken from Hoover, Politzer and Taylor, 1987). Despite considerable research indicating that phonological distinctions like these do not necessarily affect reading comprehension when the words appear in meaningful context, such distinctions are used on standardized tests to help measure minority children's reading level.

Dialect items place African-American and bilingual speakers at a major disadvantage compared to native standard English speakers, who do not have to waste energy sorting out the differences between two language systems. Even if the stated intent of dialect-prejudiced items were to determine whether or not students of color had mastered standard English conventions (which it is not), such items would not provide valid information about how these students use language in a real-life context as opposed to the highly stressful conditions involved in taking a test.

Distinctions which involve dialect or language don't just discriminate against individual students of color, however. They discriminate against excellence. They turn what is a plus in a multicultural society — the ability to speak more than one dialect or language and thus communicate across a variety of social and cultural contexts — into

a negative.

Researchers have also criticized the use of questions which assume cultural values and/or experiences which may not be shared by members of minority communities. On the vocabulary subtest of a standardized reading achievement test, for example, students are directed to choose the best synonym for *inequality* from among the following items: absence, foreign, difference, similarity, poor. Researchers Hoover, Politzer, and Taylor note that "of the responses, all except 'absence' and 'similarity' could be 'correct' in cultures in which students are aware that difference, poverty, and foreignness are associated with inequality."

## Class and Cultural Biases

Similarly John Weiss found in his study that questions which appear on forms of the Scholastic Aptitude Test necessitated familiarity with such upper-income pursuits as polo, golfing, tennis, minuets, pirouettes, property taxes, melodeons, and horseback riding. Again, even leaving aside the issue of cultural bias, what does knowledge of these activities have to do with scholastic aptitude?

There is some research which indicates that minority children do much better on test items whose content relates to familiar cultural experience. Statistician A.P. Schmidt found, for example, that on a reading comprehension passage about life-style changes in Mexican-American families, Mexican-American students scored significantly higher than they did on reading comprehension passages whose content was less related to their lives. Similarly, researcher Darlene Williams found that the I.Q. scores of Black students rose when test items included pictures of Black people and of events related to Black culture.

Doubtless, many people would strongly object to the proposal that standardized tests be revised so as to include a sizeable body of content specifically related to minority cultural experiences on the grounds that this would place middle class white students at a disadvantage. After all, why should they be expected to know anything about minority experience?

Yet aren't minority students placed at an even greater disadvantage when standardized tests reflect little or nothing about their cultural experience, while for middle class white students almost everything on the test is familiar cultural terrain? There is some common ground on tests, to be sure. But middle class white students have to struggle far less often than minority students to make meaning out of test items which take for granted experiences they've never had and which have absolutely nothing to do with ability.

Is it ability or cultural experience that is being measured, for example, on the following item from the Scholastic Aptitude Test:

RUNNER : MARATHON
(A) envoy : embassy
(B) martyr : massacre
(C) oarsman: regatta
(D) horse : stable

In this example, it is marathons and regattas which a student must be familiar with to prove her fitness for college. At the other end of the educational ladder, it's piano lessons, airplane trips, zoo excursions, musical recitals, museums, daddies who read story books, farm animals, historical sites, and friendly policemen.

The advantages which middle class white students have on standardized tests extend beyond the linguistic features and the content of test items, however. There is good reason to believe that the test-taking situation itself is experienced very differently by majority and minority students. Test-taking is a skill which many middle class students are very good at because they tend to receive extensive practice in answering "test questions" from the time they first learn to to speak.

Numerous studies of language socialization in white middle class communities indicate that the largest percentage of questions addressed to pre-schoolers by mothers and other primary caregivers consists of simply structured questions to which the questioner already has the answer — e.g., "How many eyes do you have?" "What color is this dolly's dress?" "How many fin-

gers is mommy holding up?" The purpose of such questions is not for the questioner to gain information, but for the child to *display* information, for which she is typically rewarded with extensive non-verbal and verbal praise.

When reading stories to pre-school children, many middle-class parents often intersperse their reading with questions which focus the child's attention on noting and recalling specific details of the text (e.g., " *Now,* how many balls is the little boy holding?" "What is the bird doing?") Perhaps the most important "lesson" which pre-schoolers learn as a result of such interactions is how one is expected to communicate about, and respond to, text.

Research indicates that many working class and minority children come to school with very different values and assumptions about what constitutes meaningful communication. In a 1983 study, Shirley Brice Heath found that in the working-class Black community where she spent 11 years studying language socialization, children were almost never asked questions to which the adult or older child already knew the answer. According to Heath's data, the most prevalent type of question addressed to pre-schoolers in this community was the "analogy question," calling for an open-ended response drawn from the child's experience (e.g., "What do you think you are?" to a child crawling under the furniture). Other frequently asked questions were "story starters" (e.g., "Did you see Maggie's dog yesterday?") and accusations (e.g., "What's that all over your face?") Children were also asked questions to which only they knew the answer (e.g., "What do you want?"). But very seldom were they asked test-type questions, the assumption being, why would you ask someone something you already know the answer to?

Reading was also often perceived differently, according to Heath. It tended to be a social event in which listeners, young and old, were free to throw in comments or to elaborate on some connection with their personal experience, rather than a context for testing children's reading comprehension or teaching appropriate school be-

Standardized tests often measure a narrow range of skills.

haviors. People in this community were admired for their ability to tell a good story, draw insightful analogies, or present an interesting and unique point of view, rather than for their ability to display information or show off knowledge for its own sake.

Research in other communities corroborated Heath's findings. Many working-class and minority children grow up in communities where little value is placed upon asking children to display information for its own sake and where "stating the obvious," or "saying what everyone knows" is not encouraged because it is perceived as having no meaningful communicative purpose. Thus, for many working-class and minority students, the testing situation violates deeply held assumptions and values about the nature and purpose of communication.

Communicative style — including how one interprets the meaning of what another says, how one frames questions and structures answers, notions about what is worth talking about — is learned early in life and is deeply tied to one's personal and cultural identity. To suggest that members of minority communities change the way in which they interact with their children so that they will be better prepared to take tests in school is really to ask that they surrender part of their cultural identity.

Those who argue that it is possible to make standardized tests less discriminatory by removing their cultural bias seriously underestimate the enormity of their task. What is a "culture-fair" test in a multicultural society? And who could design such a test? The truth is that any knowledge worth having is inextricably linked to culture and to context — and thus can't be reduced to measurement on a standardized test.

In the final analysis, the most fundamental question to be answered about standardized testing is not why students of color tend to perform less well than white students, or even what can be done about it. Rather, the fundamental question is what is wrong with a society which allocates its educational resources on the basis of tests which not only fail to measure excellence, but which discriminate against the vast majority of its minority population? ❑

*Terry Meier is an associate professor in the graduate school at Wheelock College in Boston.*

### References

Delpit, Lisa (1988). "The Silenced Dialogue: Power and Pedagogy." *The Harvard Educational Review*, Vol. 58, No. 3.

Heath, Shirley Brice, (1983). *Ways With Words: Language, Life, and Work in Communities and Classrooms.* New York: Cambridge University Press.

Hoover, Mary R., Robert L. Politzer, and Orlando Taylor (1987). "Bias in Reading Tests for Black Language Speakers: A Socio-linguistic Perspective." *The Negro Educational Review*, Volume 38, Nos. 2-3.

Hoover, Mary R. (1981). "Bias in Composition Tests with Suggestions for a Culturally Appropriate Assessment Technique." In M. F. Whiteman (ed.), *Writing: The Nature, Development, and Teaching of Written Communication.* Hillsdale: Lawrence Erlbaum Associates.

Scollon, Ron and Suzanne B.K. Scollon (1981). *Narrative, Literacy and Face in Interethnic Communication.* Roy O. Freedle (Ed.) Norwood, NJ: Ablex Publishing.

Schmidt, A. P. (1986). "Unexpected Differential Item Performance of Hispanic Examinees on the SAT-Verbal, Forms 3FSAOS and 3GSAOS." Unpublished statistical report of the Educational Testing Service.

Smith, G. Pritchy, (1986). "Unresolved Issues and New Developments in Teacher Competency Testing." *Urban Educator*, Fall, 1986.

Weiss, John G. (1987). "It's Time to Examine the Examiners." *The Negro Educational Review*, Volume 38, Nos. 2-3.

Williams, Darlene (1979). "Black English and the Stanford-Binet of Intelligence," Stanford, CA: Stanford University School of Education, Ph.D. Thesis, 1979.

# Detracking Montclair High

## By Stan Karp

Dr. Bernadette Anand, chair of the English Department at Montclair High School in New Jersey, had become convinced by both research and experience that detracking was overdue. To her, the sorting system which separated English students into three distinct levels served no one's long-term educational interests and reinforced the racial polarization that was a growing concern within the school and the community.

With the Social Studies Department, Dr. Anand developed the idea for a "World Cultures and Literature" course that would encourage both detracking and multicultural reform. The course presented diverse cultural and literary perspectives to a racially balanced, heterogeneous group of freshmen in a cooperative learning setting. World Cultures was a clear success. Students gave it rave reviews, and academic achievement was encouraging during a two-year pilot program.

Based on this record, the English Department proposed replacing the entire freshman English program with the untracked World Literature course. (Since the Social Studies Department wasn't ready to do the same, World Cultures reverted to the English-only World Literature). The Department unanimously endorsed the proposal, as did the "School Review" committee of parents and community residents.

As the plan worked its way up the administrative review ladder, objections were raised by the district's principals committee, which thought college-anxious parents would balk at the elimination of "high-level" sections whose weighted grades were worth more in calculating class rankings and grade point averages. The committee recommended that the new course be taught at "the most challenging level" and be given the same weighted grades. The English Department had wanted to move away from competitive course rankings altogether. It was also reconsidering the very mix of lectures, tests, and teacher-centered instructional practices that rewarded one narrow range of abilities in the typical high-level course. On the other hand, the Department was also trying to raise academic expectations across the board, and the principals' suggestion would constitute some defense against inevitable accusations that detracking meant diluting standards. The English Department accepted the recommendation and the revised proposal went before the Board. It quickly became a hot public issue.

### 'There goes the neighborhood.'

Every fear, real and imagined, that parents had about the educational program and social climate in the high school seemed to translate into a different objection. Parents of high-tracked achievers denounced the plan as a leveling formula for mediocrity. "Do not lower the top to make it look equal," one wrote to the local paper. More than a few were convinced that mixed ability grouping, by definition, meant lower standards. In fact, academic standards were being raised for the majority of freshmen, who before had been put in the lower tracks, but years of tracking had created a close association between academic rigor and academic segregation. Many had come to see advanced course placements as a privilege reserved for the few, and they responded to the implications of detracking with the educational equivalent of "there goes the neighborhood."

Some complained that the alternative assessment features of the proposal were "vague and non-measurable," and would "erode the chances of pursuing academic excellence in the system." They dismissed the collaborative learning and multicultural aspects of the new curriculum as "feel-good education."

While teachers in the high school were re-examining traditional curriculum and instructional practices, many parents who felt well served by those practices wanted them retained.

Montclair's Board of Education was also under pressure to reject or weaken the proposal, as whispers of "white flight" from the high school circulated throughout the town, and passionate attacks on the plan filled the local paper. Board meetings took on an increasingly contentious character, with opposing speakers and steadily growing audiences that, at first, appeared in the majority to oppose the change.

But a multiracial group of residents, including public school educators, academics, political activists, African-American parent advocates and others began to rally behind the plan. To them it was a small first step toward addressing tracking and racial polarization at the high school. This group feared long-term negative implications if such a relatively modest plan was defeated. It was important to demonstrate that a strong constituency for educational change existed within the community, and that the consequences of *not* moving ahead with detracking and multicultural reform were at least as serious as the problems of potential resistance to such reforms.

### Educational Civil Rights

Supporters also made it clear that tracking was indeed an issue of educational civil rights. Leaflets laid out in stark statistical terms the racial imbalance in level placements. (In 1992, for example, the top track in freshman English had 13 black students and 63 whites, while the lowest track had 72 blacks and just 7 whites. This in a student body of 1500 that was about 50% African-American). Speakers at Board meetings presented the formidable research case against tracking, documenting its negative impact on the overwhelming number of minority students in the lower tracks. African-American parents and students who felt personally victimized by tracking expressed their anger and pain. Students who had taken the World Cultures course were among the most eloquent, speaking to the ways tracking impoverishes the educational experience of the more academically successful by narrowing their experience and making their lives in public school less democratic. "Just because we're all in the high school doesn't mean we're learning from each other," one senior said.

These appeals to racial equity and the emotional testimony from students were hard for the opposition to respond to and went a long way toward dominating the debate. Invariably, opponents of the plan resented having the racial implications of tracking raised at all. Ability-grouping, they insisted, was an "educational" not a "political" issue. Many parents, particularly privileged white parents, found it almost impossible to see academic tracking, backed up by "objective" test scores and years of institutional legitimacy, for what it is: a self-fulfilling policy of educational discrimination. In the long run, the hard job of changing such attitudes falls to classroom teachers who, with schoolwide support, need to successfully demonstrate that mixed grouping can improve outcomes and enrich educational experience for all students.

After months of heated debate, the school board voted 4-3 to endorse the proposal. In September, 1994, about 400 freshmen filled 17 sections of World Literature. By juggling programs and schedules, racial and gender balance was attained and class size held to 22 (well below the district average). A special Writers' Room, staffed by over 30 community volunteers trained in writing process methods, was opened to support the new course. The seven freshman teachers had prepared extensively over the summer, designing an ambitious assessment plan. Student writing portfolios were maintained, including work that demonstrated knowledge of the writing process, specific types of literary and reflective essays,

*Skold Photographs*

**To be successful, untracking must involve students.**

and assignments dictated by the proficiencies of a new state test. Progress in collaborative learning was monitored by a series of classroom videotapes taken at the beginning, middle, and end of the school year. End of course questionnaires were completed by parents and students, and a representative sampling of materials was turned over to a committee of education professionals to evaluate the first year's progress.

## Community Organizing Project

The Montclair proposal incorporates many features necessary for a successful detracking effort, yet it still faces formidable obstacles. Outside of World Literature, the rest of the high school remains tracked, academically and socially driven by competitive rankings and advanced placement agendas. While some in the high school hope the course will be the first step towards general detracking, others are intent on containing or even reversing the change. Moreover, no single course can reverse long-standing trends towards educational inequity and racial division. It is important to frame broader initiatives around issues of tracking and racial polarization that will shift the spotlight away from this one course to a more comprehensive approach.

Long-term success will also depend on mobilizing those parents and students who have traditionally been steered towards the bottom of the academic ladder. Students themselves need to be more directly involved in such policy discussions. The core of African-American activists who helped campaign for the freshman plan recognizes a need to continue emphasizing the civil rights implications of detracking, and to keep raising educational expectations and demands.

As the Montclair example suggests, detracking is not simply a matter of administrative declarations or paper policies. To succeed, it requires innovations in curriculum, instruction, assessment practices, and school-community relations. At times, it is as much a community organizing project as an educational one, and calls for a broad-based campaign of education, activism and public policy debate. In the final analysis, detracking is about making schools more democratic institutions. As long as schools have economic, social, and class forces pulling them in decidedly different directions, debates over tracking will continue to raise fundamental questions about who our schools should serve and how. ☐

*Stan Karp (StanKarp@aol.com) has been a high school teacher in Paterson, NJ for over 25 years and is a* Rethinking Schools *editor.*

# Tracking: Why Schools Need to Take Another Route

By Jeannie Oakes

Few widespread schooling practices are as controversial as ability grouping and tracking. On one side of the issue, many educators and parents assert that when schools group by ability, teachers are better able to target individual needs and students will learn more. Some link tracking to our national security and economic well-being, contending that the top students need special grooming to be leaders in science, government, and business.

On the other side, growing numbers of school professionals and parents oppose tracking because they believe it locks most students into classes where they are stereotyped as "less able," and where they have fewer opportunities to learn. Many express particular concern about tracking's effects on poor and minority students, who are placed in low-ability groups more often than other students and are less likely to be found in programs for gifted students or in college preparatory tracks.

These opposing opinions and re-

> **Students who are placed in high-ability groups have access to far richer schooling experiences than other students.**

search findings may, at first, appear puzzling and contradictory. But further examination sheds light on both sides of the argument and may help point the way out of the tracking quandary. There is growing evidence that as policymakers and educators become disenchanted with tracking, they may not need to throw out the baby (possible benefits to the top students) with the bathwater (likely disadvantages to the rest). Alternative strategies, while not simple to implement, promise to help schools reach their goal of providing high-quality, relevant education to all students.

## Tracking's Consequences

One fact about tracking is unequivocal: tracking leads to substantial differences in the day-to-day learning experiences students have at school. Moreover, the nature of these differences suggests that students who are placed in high-ability groups have access to far richer schooling experiences than other students. This finding helps explain, at least in part, why it is that tracking sometimes seems to "work" for high-ability students and not for others. It also provides clues about what needs to be changed.

For example, in John Goodlad's national study of schools, reported in the book *A Place Called School*, students in high-ability English classes were more likely to be taught classic and modern literature, provided instruction in expository writing and library research, and expected to learn vocabulary that would eventually boost their scores on college entrance exams. In these classes, critical thinking and problem-solving skills seemed to emerge

from the high quality of the course content. Few low-ability classes, on the other hand, were taught these topics and skills. Students in the latter classes learned basic reading skills taught mostly by workbooks, kits, and easy-to-read stories. Learning tasks consisted most often of memorizing and repeating answers back to the teacher. Since so much of importance was omitted from their curriculum, students in these low-ability classes were likely to have little contact with the knowledge and skills that would allow them to move into higher classes or to be successful if they got there.

Of course, these differences are not restricted to English classes. Similar patterns have been observed in secondary math, science, and social studies classes and in ability-grouped elementary classes — fewer topics, a far more restricted range of topics, and less depth of coverage in remedial and "typical" classes.

## Uneven Opportunities

Perhaps as important as students' access to knowledge are critical instructional conditions in their classrooms, that is, the quantity of time spent on learning and the quality of the teaching. In both respects, high-ability classes tend to have better instruction. A number of studies have found that top-track classes spend more class time on learning activities and less on discipline, socializing, or class routines. Higher-ability students are expected to spend more time doing homework. Their teachers tend to be more enthusiastic, to make instructions clearer, and to use strong criticism or ridicule less frequently than teachers of low-ability classes. Classroom tasks are often better organized, and students are given a greater variety of things to do. These differences in learning opportunities point to fundamental and ironic school inequities. Students who need more time to learn appear to get less; those who have the most difficulty learning seem to have fewer of the best teachers.

Other important differences have been noted in the classroom atmosphere. Most teachers realize that for students, feeling comfortable in class is more than just a nice addition to learning. They also know that when teachers and students trust one another, class time and energy are freed up for teaching and learning. On the other hand, without a positive classroom climate, students spend considerable energy interfering with the teacher's agenda, and teachers must spend more of their time and energy just trying to maintain control. When classes are tracked, important differences in these climate dimensions appear.

In low-ability classes, for example, teachers seem to be less encouraging and more punitive, placing more emphasis on discipline and behavior and less on academic learning. Compared to teachers in high-ability classes, they seem to be more concerned about getting students to follow directions, be on time, and sit quietly. Students in low-ability classes more often feel excluded from class activities and tend to find their classmates unfriendly. Their classes are more often interrupted by problems and arguing, while students in higher-ability classes seem to be much more involved in their classwork. When they're not being disruptive, students in low-ability classes are often apathetic. The reason for this may be that because they're more likely to fail, they risk more by trying. Where these differences are found, students in lower-ability classes have classroom environments that are less conducive to learning than do their peers in upper-level classes.

What about average kids? The quality of classes for average students usually falls somewhere between the high- and low-class extremes. Some interest-

"PRIVILEGED CLASS, MIDDLE CLASS, OR BORN LOSER?"

JOEL PETT/PHI DELTA KAPPAN

ing examples of the experiences of average students were found in a study of American high schools reported in the book *The Shopping Mall High School*. The researchers found that the proliferation of classes and special programs for students at the extremes — students with high abilities or with handicaps — had the effect of making students in the middle "unspecial" and guaranteeing that they were taught in quite "unspecial" ways. For example, in average classes, many teachers expected relatively little of students. They established set routines of lecturing and doing worksheets, held time and workload demands (both in class and for homework) to a minimum, accepted and sometimes even encouraged distractions, and rarely asked students to think deeply or critically. When classes are conducted in this way, average students, too, are deprived of the best that schools have to offer.

Taken together, these typical differences begin to suggest why tracking can and often does work well for top students. Start by providing the best teachers, a concentration of the most successful students and sometimes even the lowest class size. Add special resources, a sense of superior academic "mission,"

perhaps a parent support group, and these students will get the best education in town. In fact, studies that control for instructional differences — providing identical curriculum and instruction to both tracked and mixed groups of students — typically find that high-ability students do equally well in either setting. The fact that students are tracked seems less important than that they have the other instructional advantages that seem to come along with classes that are highly able. It's ironic that when other, less able students are offered similar advantages, they also seem to benefit. No wonder we find a "rich get richer and poor get poorer" pattern of outcomes from tracking. It seems that tracking is both a response to significant differences among students and an ongoing contribution to those differences.

## Tracking Alternatives

Creating constructive alternatives to tracking presents technical as well as political problems. Despite promising research findings about heterogeneous grouping, little is likely to be accomplished by simply mixing students up. To be effective, alternatives will probably require fundamental changes. There may be a need for changes in the types of knowledge that children are expected to acquire, in the social organization of schools and classrooms, and in student evaluation.

Perhaps the most important and difficult task for those who would change tracking is to confront deeply held beliefs, such as the belief that academic ability is fixed very early and is largely unchangeable or that achievement differences can be largely accounted for by differences in ability.

Recent work of cognitive psychologists suggests, for example, that academic ability is not unchangeable but developmental and grows throughout childhood. As children interact with their environment, they acquire cognitive abilities. Especially important are studies showing that cognitive abilities can be taught, and that even students who begin school with less developed abilities can learn. Other work suggests that what we conventionally consider "low" ability may not be as limiting as we generally think. The achievement gaps we observe among students of differing abilities are exacerbated by the failure of classrooms to provide all students with the time, opportunities, and resources they need to learn.

Prevailing beliefs about the limits of ability are critical. Unless teachers and administrators believe and expect all students to learn well, they will be unlikely to create school and classroom conditions where students believe in their own ability and exert the effort it takes to succeed.

## Curriculum Rich with Meaning

In classrooms where the curriculum consists of a sequence of topics and skills that require prerequisite knowledge and skill mastery, mixing students who have different skills is difficult. Students do differ from one another, and the most striking differences among them might be in the speed at which they master sequentially presented skills. Unless students are similar in learning "speed," such a curriculum raises horrendous problems of pacing. Some students are ready to race ahead, but others lag behind. Enrichment for the quicker students often becomes make-work; reteaching becomes a chore; being retaught can be humiliating for the slower students.

Heterogeneous groups of students will probably do best in classrooms where the curriculum content is challenging, complex, related to real life and — most of all — rich with meaning. When curriculum is organized around the central themes of a subject area rather than around disconnected topics and skills, all students stand the greatest chance of enhancing their intellectual development. Students need not be held back from ideas because of skill differences; rather they can acquire skills as they become ready. Moreover, classroom knowledge that remains connected to its larger context is much easier for students to understand and use. Finally, when students grapple with complex problems, solutions have to be compatible with so many ideas that two people rarely come up with identical solutions. While right answers certainly have their place, with a concept-based curriculum there are opportunities for multiple right answers and multiple routes to success.

Some rules of thumb can help teachers judge whether the lessons they plan are likely to help students of all ability levels succeed. First, lessons will probably be most successful if they require active learning tasks rather than passive ones, and if they have students working together rather than alone. Second, learning tasks are probably most helpful when they are full of complications and when they require multiple abilities — thinking, discussing, writing, and visualizing — to accomplish. Third, learning tasks will suit most students if they are modeled on complex and challenging "real world" problem-solving. These guidelines keep the curriculum from drifting too far into the highly technical and abstract world of "school" knowledge and too far away from "the real thing."

Some ways of organizing classrooms are more conducive to student learning than others. In the standard classroom, instruction is characterized by:

• Competitive whole-group instruction.

• Lecturing as the prevailing teaching strategy.

• Common assignments.

• Uniform due dates and tests.

• A single set of standards of com-

Cooperative learning can help provide alternatives to tracking.

SUSAN LINA RUGGLES

petence and criteria for grades.

Usually students work alone, silently. They occasionally get a chance to articulate, explain, offer reasons, and try to be convincing about what they are learning.

If students of all abilities are to benefit from being taught together, classrooms will probably need to be organized far differently, providing a diversity of tasks and interactions with few "public" comparisons of students' ability. A vast amount of classroom research has identified many of the necessary academic and social conditions needed for students to work together productively. With cooperative learning strategies, for example, students can exchange ideas and help in small groups. Frequently they will work at separate but interrelated tasks. Teachers can function like conductors, getting things started and keeping them moving along, providing information and resources, coordinating the buzz of activity taking place. Such classrooms present a variety of paths to success, and when such classes are skillfully orchestrated, any one student's strengths — or weaknesses — are seldom held up to the class for display, comparison, or embarrassment.

While group work is no panacea, the advantages are considerable. Teachers cannot simply tell students to move their chairs and work together, however. Without the gradual development of students' skills and the careful design of lessons to take advantage of those skills, group work may not be an improvement over working alone. But when teachers are skillful, there is considerable evidence that even the very best students make stronger intellectual gains while working with students of varying skill levels than when they work alone.

## Evaluation that Supports Learning

In many classrooms the evidence of students' capability is a matter of public record. Grades and progress are prominently posted: letters, numbers, stars, smiley faces, race horses, and halos — along with sad faces, zeros,

and the ever present blanks. Performance scores are read aloud or distributed by other students. Even the results of aptitude, achievement, and other types of standardized tests get out when scores are read, carelessly left available, or shared voluntarily by students. Most public displays are well-enough meant: good work shown as a matter of pride, intended to motivate and provide examples for others. But too often they are convenient and irresistible opportunities for comparison. Similarly, conventional grades and standardized test scores are easily summed up into measures of a student's overall worth. They become raw materials for a consensus that develops in classrooms about who is a good student and who isn't.

## Student Evaluation

To be successful, heterogeneous classrooms probably need to lean toward placing students more in charge of their own evaluation — checking their own understanding and asking for and providing feedback. This is what happens naturally when students are engaged in complex tasks and have lots of interaction.

This doesn't imply that teachers abandon their evaluation responsibilities. For teachers, evaluation might involve more private, individual questions, such as, "What did she learn?" rather than "How did she compare with others?" When evaluations are more formalized, they probably need to be "student-referenced" and criterion-referenced; that is, they should compare what a student knows after instruction with what he or she knew before. Grades or points can then be based on improvement or on progress toward a learning goal. Personalized grading of this sort respects the complex interrelationship between evaluation and students' self-concepts. It helps to put students in charge of their learning and to make them willing to put forth the considerable effort it takes to be a good student.

While difficult to implement, such changes in curriculum, instruction, and evaluation are not terribly incompatible with elementary schooling. But they do

crash head on into the standard practices of middle and high schools, where grouping, teaching, and evaluation policies are firmly grounded in the notions of sorting, standardization, and competition. Additionally, secondary educators are constrained from making changes by the experience of students in earlier grades.

Typically, low-track high school students have been in low-ability groups and remedial programs since elementary school. The gap between them and more successful students has grown wider — not only in achievement but in attitudes toward school and toward their own ability to succeed. By the time students reach secondary school, track-related achievement and attitude differences are often well established. These differences undoubtedly limit the alternatives to tracking that might be attempted. Consequently, alternatives will be most effective if they begin early. Junior high is probably too late — and first grade is probably not too early.

Obviously, the kinds of changes likely to promote high-quality learning for all students in heterogeneous classrooms go far beyond mere fine tuning of current practice. These changes also require fundamental changes in the structure of schooling and teachers' work. Finally, as with most major reform initiatives, teacher professionalism is central to successful tracking alternatives. Working with their communities, school staffs can design changes that are compatible with school goals and also politically manageable. But unless teachers have the time and the autonomy to deliberate about, develop, and experiment with fundamental changes in school organization and classroom practices, alternatives to tracking are unlikely to be intelligently conceived, enthusiastically endorsed, or successfully implemented. □

*Jeannie Oakes is a social scientist with the RAND Corporation in Santa Monica, Calif.*

The above is adapted from her book, *Keeping Track: How Schools Structure Inequality* (Yale University Press, 1985).

# Lineage

By Margaret Walker


*My grandmothers were strong.*
*They followed plows and bent to toil.*
*They moved through fields sowing seed.*
*They touched the earth and grain grew.*
*They were full of sturdiness and singing.*
*My grandmothers were strong.*

*My grandmothers are full of memories*
*Smelling of soap and onions and wet clay*
*With veins rolling roughly over quick hands*
*They have many clean words to say.*
*My grandmothers were strong.*
*Why am I not as they?*

Margaret Walker was one of the youngest African-American poets to publish a full volume of poetry. She won the Yale Younger Poet award in 1942 for her book *For My People*, her master's thesis at the University of Iowa.
(See page 184 for lesson ideas.)

RICK REINHARD

# Teaching Guide/Resources

We can thoroughly "rethink our classrooms," but if we lack resources, we'll be less effective in turning our ideas into reality. In this chapter we offer lists of quality materials helpful to any teacher interested in promoting social justice. Do not be misled when we indicate that certain materials are oriented to age groups other than those you work with. High school students can benefit greatly from looking at books intended for younger children, while teachers can adapt more sophisticated materials for use with children in the lower grades.

We also include a teaching guide that offers ideas on how to use the poems throughout this book.

# Poetry Teaching Guide

## By Linda Christensen

Poetry is by turns playful, respectful, angry, and political. Because poetry is so closely related to music, it provides students an easy slide into writing. Advice? Leave the critic at the door until students feel connected and comfortable. After each assignment, ask students to circle up their desks and read-around their poems. (Sometimes cookies and milk make these special occasions — even in a high school classroom.)

### Family Poems

*Lineage*, p. 182; *My Father Was a Musician*, p. 73; *Forgiving My Father*, p. 97.

Family poems are a way for students to bring their homes and their lives into the classroom. They also provide an opportunity for students to praise a loved one — a mother, father, brother, aunt, grandparent, or someone who has played that role in their lives. Parent relationships are rarely easy, so allowing students a range of choices is helpful. Sometimes students have angry feelings that need to be expressed as well. "Forgiving My Father" might not praise a family member, but it is a legitimate expression of anger.

Beginning poets often write "ghost poems" — vague poems full of abstractions about their love for their mother, friend, or pet. This poetry assignment forces them to become concrete by describing details from photographs, clothing their ghosts.

1. A few days before this activity tell students that they will be writing about a person in their family. (Be sensitive to the fact that some students may not have a traditional two-parent family. Talk about how families might have different formations.) Encourage students to bring some pictures from home. The pictures should include family members they might want to write about. Some students will forget the pictures, but they can still write using the questions below as prompts.

2. As a warm-up, ask students to share their pictures in pairs or in small groups, depending on the size and comfort level of the class. This sharing will happen anyway; initiate it before the activity so it won't interrupt while students are writing.

3. Have students read the three poetry selections out loud. Sometimes it helps if you read the poetry first — read with passion, then ask a student to read it again. Point out details: Walker indicates the kind of work her grandmothers did, the details about their hands, "smelling of soap and wet clay." Try to get them to note that she uses the sense of smell as well as the sense of sight. Watson uses sound. You might point out her use of language — "halting only to mend a chord or two." We don't literally mend music, but her words allow us to see her father going back over a musical passage.

4. Encourage students to remember details about their person. Ask: What do you remember them doing? Gardening? Cooking? Painting? Polishing the car? Fishing? Was there a certain dress, hat, shirt, style of pants that makes you remember them? Did they have any habits? Did they play with their glasses, smoke a pipe, burn the biscuits? Did they repeat sayings?

5. When their "pump is primed," turn off the lights or find some kind of signal to break from brainstorming to writing. It helps if you write too.

### Praise Poems

*My Hair Is Long*, p. 29; *what the mirror said*, p. 66

Many poets find it necessary to praise themselves because the standards of beauty in the dominant culture are European-American or set by the fashion industry. For example, Lucille Clifton and Maya Angelou praise big women — going against the norm of beauty that holds thinness as the standard. Writing praise poems gives students a positive way to look at themselves, but these poems also speak against the negative portrayals too often associated with their neighborhood, race, gender, nationality, size, school. Follow the guidelines for the parent poem, but ask students to write praise poems about themselves.

1. Ask students to think of something about themselves, their school, community, or culture that deserves praise, but may not receive it. Ask a few students to share ideas so they can help shake loose ideas for classmates.

2. Read "My Hair Is Long" out loud and have students look at the poet's list of comparisons. Ask what they could compare their hair to, their eyes, lips, and so on. They might have their own pictures to look at while writing. (Poems and photos make a wonderful bulletin board.)

3. Older students like the sassy tone of Clifton's poem. They could look in mirrors and begin their poems, "what the mirror says." Sometimes students feel awkward praising themselves, but may find one attribute to praise.

### Ballad/Story Poems

*Ballad of the Landlord*, p. 39; *Face the Facts*, p. 133; *To the Young Who Want to Die*, p. 160

These are angry poems. They shout; there are no pretty pansies waiting to be picked here. These poems break students' stereotypes that poetry has to be about "lovely" things. You might want to do these poems one at a time over the year or as a group. "Face the Facts" could be used while studying the politics of language, where students "talk back" to people who put down their "home language." (See p. 142.) "Ballad of the Landlord" could be used in a unit on homelessness and economics.

1. Ask students to read the poems out loud. These make for dramatic reading. You might give them to students to read in advance so they can practice. These poems are even better if students can memorize and act them out.

2. After each poem is read, ask for reactions. What's going on in the poems? Ask someone to summarize the "story" of the poem. Ask who the poet is talking to. You might even ask how these poems differ from "typical" poems.

3. Ask students to make two columns on their paper. (It helps to model this on the board or overhead.) At the top of one column write: People Who Make Me Angry; at the top of the other write: Things That Make Me Angry. You might write down a few items under each category to get them started.

4. Ask them to circle one or two of the topics. Some students may be able to write their poems at this point. Others might need to get more details. Have them write it first as a letter. They can put the name of the person at the beginning, "Dear Aunt Macy" or "Dear Joe Camel" or "Dear Budget Cutters," then write why they are angry. Encourage them to tell the story. "I am angry because ..."

5. Encourage or demonstrate how to cut a paragraph down to a poem by lining it out and picking out their best lines or details for the poem. Sometimes it helps to work with a partner.

## Ancestor/Heritage Poems

*To My People With Retinitis Pigmentosa*, p. 54; *In Memory of Crossing the Columbia*, p. 157; *Lineage*, p. 182

Students belong to many intersecting communities: family, school, region, race, nationality, sports, and as Jim Jackson demonstrates, even the community of people who share medical history. This poetry lesson invites students to talk about their particular history. It's especially powerful during a unit on families or autobiography.

(See pp. 30, 50.) Because of the repetition and strong first line, Margaret Walker's poem "For My People," which is widely anthologized, provides an excellent model for this assignment.

1. Begin by asking students to describe all of the communities they belong to. Then ask them to list those communities. Model this on the board with your own diverse memberships. Students might share their lists as a way of expanding ideas.

2. Ask for volunteers to read the poetry aloud. Read the poems through at least twice.

3. After each poem, talk about it. What community did this writer talk about? Do they have a sense of why heritage is important to the poet? Note the strong imagery in Elizabeth Woody's description of her heritage. She recalls the location as well as her ties to her Navajo ancestors.

4. Ask students to choose one of the communities they listed and list some ideas about it. Some students who belong to more than one racial group may choose to write about that. Robert Smith, a senior at Jefferson High School, wrote: "What are you if you're not black and you're not white?/ I am both, so how could I choose just one?/ ... I am not a blank space between black and white .../I am a black man who has never touched the sands of Africa./I am a European looking for riches./ I am a slave stripped away from his home .../I

am the red faces who walked the Trail of Tears./ I am my mother's father whose face is covered by a white hood. I am the German soldier who spilled my Jewish blood./ I am the South African Republic that beat my black grandmother. ..."

## Advertising Poems

*Love's Gonna Get Us (Material Love)*, p. 49; *Dream Voyage*, p. 79; *Rebellion Against the North Side*, p. 136

As Bertolt Brecht said, "Art is not a mirror held up to reality, but a hammer with which to shape it." Students don't need to confine their poems to reflecting the world, they can also write to critique it or change it as Damon Turner, Naomi Nye, and Eve Merriam do in their poetry. This assignment is excellent during a study of advertising.

1. Engage students in a critical examination of advertising. (See pp. 80 - 85.)

2. Ask students to read the three poems. (Before reading Turner's, tell them that this was written in 1991, so some of the sports stars and clothing might be different.) Talk with students about the poems. What is Eve Merriam's message? How is she trying to reshape people's minds? What is Damon Turner's message? To whom is his poem directed?

3. Students might cut out ads from slick magazines or just brainstorm com-

# How to Do Read-arounds

In *Rethinking Our Classrooms* we've talked a lot about students sharing their lives, but they need a safe space to start. Most students love to share their writing. Reading aloud in class is a conversation, a gossip session, a chance to socialize in a teacher-approved way. Unfortunately, too many students arrive with bruises from the red pen, so when we begin the year, it's necessary to build their confidence:

1. Seat the students in a circle — or the nearest approximation. Students should not have their backs to each other. This way they can see each other and be seen as they read. The attention will be focused on the reader.

2. Distribute as many blank strips of paper as there are students in the class. Students will write a compliment to each classmate.

3. Students write each reader's name on the paper. So if Vonda volunteers to read her paper first, everyone in the class writes Vonda's name on their strip. (This is also a way for students to learn their classmates' names.)

4. Tell students they must respond with a positive comment to each writer. As they listen, they should think about what they like about the piece. Tell them by listening and using what works in their classmates' writing, they will improve their own. Write a list of ways to respond on the board: **Respond to the writer's style of writing.** What do you like about how the piece was written? Do you like the rhyme? The repeating lines? The humor? (Later, these points can change, particularly if you are focusing on a specific skill — like introductions, transitions, evidence, imagery.) **Respond to the writer's content.** What did the writer say that you liked? **Respond by sharing a memory that surfaced for you.** Did you have a similar experience? Did this remind you of something from your life? **As the writer reads, write down lines, ideas, words or phrases that you like. Remember: you must compliment the writer.**

5. As students write each compliment, tell them to sign their slip so the writer knows who praised them.

6. Ask for a few volunteers to share their praise with the writer. This is slow at first, so try modeling it. This is an opportunity to teach writing: point out dialogue, description, attention to detail.

7. Tell students to look at the writer and give that person the compliment. Usually, students will look at the teacher and say what they liked about the student's piece. Establish early on that all dialogue in the class does not funnel through the teacher.

8. If the class does not immediately respond, try giving points for positive oral comments. In my classes where defiance is a badge of honor, I give points. The points allow some people a "cover" for giving positive feedback: "I just do it for the points." Whether they actually do it for the points or not, their compliments contribute to a positive classroom climate.

9. After everyone has read, ask students to hand out their compliment strips to each other. (This is usually chaotic, but it's another way for students to identify who's who in the class.) ❐

---

### Poetry Guide continued

mercials together. Students may choose one genre of ads — Turner wrote about how advertisers use sports stars to seduce youngsters into buying athletic gear for everyday wear. Or they may choose to write about advertising or another issue that arouses their passion.

4. Encourage students to think of an audience for their poems as Turner did.

### Dialogue Poems

*Honeybees,* p. 42; *Childbirth*, p. 61; *Two Women,* p. 112

Dialogue poems are effective to use where controversy or different opinions might arise: plantation owner and slave, Hiroshima bomb victim and an Enola Gay pilot. But the poem can also point out similarities between people who might not appear to have much in common on the surface: for example, a Salvadoran immigrant and an African American whose family migrated from the South. The dialogue poem also works with literature. While studying *Grapes of Wrath,* for example, students could write a dialogue between the machines pushing over homes and the families forced off their lands. (See pp. 30, 40, 44, 58, 93, 110.)

1. Before class starts, choose two students to prepare for a dramatic reading the next day. Assign one student the bold-faced part, the other student the part that is not in bold-face type.

2. Read the poem as a dialogue. To convey the power of the poem, the student readers can stand in opposite corners of the room and, in full voice, recite the lines back and forth.

3. Distribute copies of the poem to the entire class. If you are using "Two Women," provide students some background information about Chile to explain the references in the poem.

4. Elicit response to the poem. Discuss what makes it so powerful. Point out the subtle differences in lines — how even the addition of one or two words underscores the deep inequality of the two women's lives: "We had to eat rice" — "We had rice."

5. Brainstorm possible topics as a group. Think about what the different pairs might say. In partners or alone, write dialogue poems based on the content studied in class. ❐

# Videos with a Conscience

## By Bill Bigelow and Linda Christensen

In Portland, we have a network of informal video lending libraries. Teachers call each other to locate videos that can offer our classes an added dimension of humanity and immediacy — "What do you have on South Africa/the women's movement/Vietnam?" It's not unusual to discover a wonderful resource, totally new to us, that has been in someone's curriculum for years.

Different videos lend themselves to different teaching strategies. We've found announcing the assignment before viewing helps keep students focused and better prepares them for post-viewing discussion. Here are a few of the activities we've initiated using some of the "videos with a conscience" listed here.

**Interior Monologue.** With students, we brainstorm the dilemmas or choices faced by various characters in a movie: Frank, in *The Killing Floor*, when he decides to cross the picket line set up by white union members; Danny, in *Matewan,* when company thugs threaten to kill him if he reveals their plans; Breaker Morant, when he is convicted of war crimes; Molly, in *A World Apart*, when her mother is "detained" by South African police; etc. Students then write a character's interior monologue — that individual's thoughts and feelings during a particular event. Afterwards, in a circle, we encourage students to read their pieces and suggest that they take notes on a particular question. For example, with *A World Apart*, students can reflect on how people in South Africa maintained their hope in the face of such enormous injustice. The question or questions posed allow students to draw additional insights from the group portrait of the collected interior monologues.

A scene from *We Shall Overcome*, available from California Newsreel.

CALIFORNIA NEWSREEL.

**Poetry.** Instead of, or in addition to, interior monologues, students can be encouraged to write poems. Our student Mira wrote, "Poetry made history come to life. When we wrote after (the film) *Hearts and Minds,* I was there. I was a soldier. I identified with what was going on. I felt their feelings. I got more involved. This wasn't just history. This was life. Poetry helped me examine why the war happened because I got inside the people who witnessed it." In *Hearts and Minds*, we asked students to note powerful images or quotes from the people interviewed. Afterwards, students shared a number of these and we distributed a sheet of film quotes that we'd collected. We then offered a series of poems to suggest different struc-

tures students might borrow. Several of these were from Yusef Komunyakaa's *Dien Cai Dau*, and some Vietnamese poems from the anthology *Of Quiet Courage.*

We followed the read-around of students' pieces with a discussion of the issues raised. The result was a much higher degree of student empathy than had we simply discussed the film without writing, or assigned the writing without giving students a chance to hear each other's pieces.

**Critique.** With films like *The Santa Fe Trail* or cartoons like *Peter Pan, Beauty and the Beast,* or *The Little Mermaid*, we distribute the following "critical viewing" questions for students to

Laundry workers on strike in *Union Maids*, by New Day Films.

think about:

1. **Who makes decisions?**
2. **Who follows orders?**
3. **Who speaks?**
4. **Who is silent?**
5. **What causes conflict and how is it solved?**
6. **What role does money and/or material possessions play in the story/history?**
7. **What roles are women, men, people of color, the differently abled, working class people, and the poor given?**
8. **Why do you think the video contains the biases that it does? Who benefits and who suffers from the images and values promoted in this video?**

The last question is a difficult one, but it's important that as we teach students critical skills, we encourage them to think about the deeper "Why?" questions, encourage them to push beyond simply *describing* what may be wrong with a given piece of media. In this instance, raising the question is more important than arriving at the "correct" answer. After viewing, we may discuss the film based on these questions or we might encourage them to write from their observations. Using their notes, drawing on experiences in their own lives, and incorporating insights from readings, students can write critical essays. Another possibility is to allow students to reconstruct a given story from a more equitable, more multicultural standpoint.

**Trial.** A number of the films included here deal with violations of human rights, discrimination, and bigotry: homophobia and anti-gay violence in *The Times of Harvey Milk*; the unprovoked murder of Black Panthers Fred Hampton and Mark Clark in *Eyes on the Prize;* poverty and repression in Guatemala and the U. S. in *El Norte*; and the massacre of civilians in *Remember My Lai*. Determining "guilt" can encourage students to reflect on complex ethical, political, and historical questions. For example, in *Remember My Lai*, we divide the class into five groups representing Lt. Calley, U. S. soldiers who carried out Calley's orders to shoot civilians, Lt. Calley's superior officers, the Vietnamese National Liberation Front, and the "system," as represented by U. S. corporate and government leaders. They all stand accused of the murder of innocent civilians at My Lai, and each group gets an indictment listing charges against them. The two of us portray the prosecution team. Each "defendant" is prosecuted and argues against the charges, at times pointing an accusing finger at one or more of the other groups. Stepping out of their roles, students assign amounts of guilt or innocence to each group. Who's responsible: The ones who pulled the triggers? The ones who gave the orders? The ones who sent them there in the first place?

## Videos with a Conscience

The following is a list of some videos we've found useful. Unless otherwise noted, the films are available in video stores (though sometimes it requires a bit of hunting) and are appropriate for high school age, and in many cases middle school age, students. Encourage your district to buy worthwhile documentaries like the ones included here.

***Killing Us Softly* (30 min.) (and *Still Killing Us Softly*)**

A funny and shocking look at the

images of women (and to a lesser extent, men) in advertising. The format — researcher Jean Kilbourne commenting on slides — is a simple one, but students find the film gripping and enlightening. *Still Killing Us Softly* updates the earlier *Killing Us Softly* (1979), and has a more astute and comprehensive narration. Unfortunately, it's a bit too wordy and students may not get as much as they do from the earlier version. (Cambridge Films.)

### Advertising Alcohol: Calling the Shots (30 min.)

Unfortunately, this is more a "talking heads" video than it ought to be. Nonetheless, presenter Jean Kilbourne offers a compelling critique of the deadly intersection of the advertising and alcohol industries. (Cambridge Films.)

### Breaker Morant (approx. 115 min.)

A feature film about the Australian role in the Boer War in South Africa. However, the issues it raises allow us to use it during a unit on Vietnam. Three Australians are tried for war crimes against white Afrikaner civilians. The film poses questions about the culpability of individuals caught in an evil enterprise of "empire building."

### Defending Our Lives (30 min.)

Winner of an Academy Award for Best Short Documentary, this is a gripping examination of domestic violence and women who kill their batterers. Domestic violence is the leading cause of injury to women in America — more than muggings, rapes, and car accidents combined. Several women tell their tales of stalking, beatings, and rape. What rescues students from despair is seeing women in the film who have organized in groups like Battered Women Fighting Back! Students responded to the video with tears and personal stories. (Cambridge Films.)

### Modern Times (85 min.)

We use only the first twenty minutes of this Chaplin classic in a unit on the history of work and workers. It's a wonderful resource to discuss the psychological effects of assembly line

work. In one hilarious scene, Chaplin as the Little Tramp is assaulted by an automatic eating machine being tested by the company in an attempt to make the workday more efficient. Also useful to prompt students to reflect on how the structure of the workplace affects workers' relationships with each other.

### Santa Fe Trail (approx. 100 min.)

Without question this is a video without a conscience. Starring Errol Flynn, Ronald Reagan and Olivia de Haviland, this 1940 film slanders the Abolition movement and John Brown. Errol Flynn, as the future Confederate general, Jeb Stuart, is the good guy who throughout the film maintains that the South will solve its problems if only left alone to work them out. We use the film during a unit on U.S. slavery and slave resistance to encourage students to critique the ways the media can manipulate history.

### Thousand Pieces of Gold (105 min.)

This feature film is a generally decent adaptation of Ruthann Lum McCunn's novel about Lalu Nathoy, a Chinese-American pioneer woman. Set in the 1870s on the West Coast, *Thousand Pieces of Gold* subtly compares Lalu's situation and the legal status of Chinese Americans with the enslavement of African Americans. We combine the video with the novel, some pieces from *The Big Aiiieeee!*, *The Forbidden Stitch*, and *Making Waves: An Anthology of Writings By and About Asian American Women*.

### Hearts and Minds (112 min.)

This powerful Academy Award winning documentary about the war in Vietnam is a metaphorical collage of interviews, battle footage, and daily life. Students need a good deal of background about the war prior to viewing, but if they're prepared, it can be an extraordinarily valuable resource. Some of the scenes and individuals are unforgettable, as our students, years later, will testify. Note: A scene in a Saigon brothel is sexually explicit. The filmmakers included it in part to explore the war's effect on Vietnamese women, as well as U.S. soldiers' attitudes towards

these women. (Takes some hunting, but it's available in video stores.)

### The Times of Harvey Milk (90 min.)

A sad but inspirational look at the life and death of San Francisco Supervisor Harvey Milk and at the gay rights movement. This is a good film to begin to chip away at students' homophobia. It's personal, funny, sad, and infuriating. Students will likely note the parallels to the Rodney King verdict and riots, as Milk's admitted assassin is convicted of a lesser charge and spends only a little over five years in prison. (October Films.)

### El Norte (approx. 140 min.)

Long, but useful in exploring the causes of Central American, particularly Guatemalan, immigration to the United States. *El Norte* tells the story of a brother and sister forced to flee repression, their journey northward and their experiences after arrival. Somewhat unrealistic and sappy in places, but also poetic and visually stunning, it is a worthwhile portrayal of some of the tribulations of Central American refugees.

### Union Maids (55 min.) and Seeing Red (100 min.)

Two documentaries, both nominated for Academy Awards, from filmmakers Jim Klein and Julia Reichert. With interviews, music and archival footage, *Union Maids* tells the story of three women who helped build industrial unions in the 1930s and 1940s. The three are great storytellers. It's lively history, a must-use. With more characters, but with the same humor and drama, *Seeing Red* chronicles the rise and fall of the U.S. Communist Party. It's hard to imagine teaching about the McCarthy period without using this film. (New Day Films)

### The Killing Floor (118 min.)

Two African-American men migrate from the country to Chicago during World War I and land jobs in a packing house. They respond very differently to the challenges presented. The film deals forthrightly and pretty effectively with racism in the workplace and the union and ends with the 1919 riots and their aftermath.

### Matewan (100 min.)

John Sayles' feature film about a strike in a mining town in Appalachia. Mine owners bring in black workers in an attempt to break the strike. Can Italian immigrants, white Appalachians, and African Americans work together? Should they even bother to try? A powerful and well-crafted film. (The short essay "Why Matewan?" from John Sayles' book, *Thinking in Pictures: The Making of the Movie Matewan*, can also be used in class.)

### Remember My Lai (60 min.)

About the My Lai massacre, this is an extraordinary documentary that first aired as a PBS "Frontline." This is much more complex and morally riveting than a simple retelling of what happened. Interviewed are participants, both U.S. and Vietnamese. Significantly, and rarely mentioned, some Americans disobeyed orders that day. Who they were and what they did is included here. (Check libraries — not available from PBS.)

### We Shall Overcome (60 min.)

This inspiring film follows the development of the song that became the anthem of the Civil Rights Movement. It combines archival footage with music and interviews, and invites students to feel themselves part of the "We" in *We Shall Overcome*. A good resource for teaching the Civil Rights Movement and/or the role of song in social change. (We've seen this in video stores; also available from California Newsreel.)

### The Good Fight (approx. 90 min.)

A personal and engaging documentary about the men and women who joined the U.S. Abraham Lincoln Brigade to fight on behalf of the Republic during the Spanish Civil War. We first used this film in 1987, the year Ben Linder was killed by the Contras in Nicaragua. Linder's death raised questions about the rights and responsibilities of U.S. citizens in responding to injustice around the world. The film is also useful in a study of the Spanish Civil War, a conflict that in many respects set the stage for World War II. (First Run/Icarus Films.)

### Eyes on the Prize: Fighting Back: 1957-1962 and Eyes on the Prize: A Nation of Law? 1968-1971 (60 min. each)

The entire PBS *Eyes on the Prize* series on the history of the Civil Rights Movement is worthwhile. These two episodes are especially dramatic: the first recounts the struggle to desegregate Central High School in Little Rock and the University of Mississippi; the second covers the police murder of Chicago Black Panther leader Fred Hampton, and the Attica Prison uprising in New York state. *Fighting Back* is a compelling mix of documentary footage and candid interviews with participants. Students are particularly moved by the stories of the youngsters who volunteered to integrate Central High, and amazed and outraged at the vicious resistance they encountered.

In 1969, FBI chief J. Edgar Hoover labeled the Black Panther Party the number one threat to the internal security of the United States. The FBI called the Panthers' free breakfast for children program a "nefarious activity." *A Nation of Law?* is a troubling video about established authority's concept of "order" and the measures it will take to preserve that order. (PBS Video.)

### A World Apart (114 min.)

A feature film based on the life of white South African Ruth First, a member of the then-outlawed African National Congress. Especially effective with middle and high school students because the events are seen largely through the eyes of First's daughter, who appears to be about twelve. Some background is necessary, but the film effectively explores the terrain of government repression, the risks of political activism, and the toll on the life of one family. So many of the commercial films on South Africa have white protagonists (*A Dry White Season* and *Cry Freedom*, for example) but given that limitation, we think this may be the best of them.

### Peter Pan, The Little Mermaid, Beauty and the Beast, Popeye, Snow White . . .

These and other children's cartoon stories are useful in prompting students of all ages to think about social messages imparted in different media. Because no student feels that a cartoon is over his or her head, it's a student-friendly medium to help kids develop critical thinking skills. See "Critique," pp. 187-188.

### Series: African American Perspective Series

This collection of valuable videos includes, among others, *In Black and White*, profiles of African-American authors; *Miles of Smiles*, about the first Black trade union; and *Color Adjustment*, a study of African-American images on TV. (California Newsreel.)

## Sources for Videos

**California Newsreel,**
www.newsreel.org, 415-284-7800
**Cambridge Documentary Films,**
www.cambridgedocumentaryfilms.org, 617-354-3677
**Deep Dish TV Network,**
www.deepdishtv.org,
212-473-8933
   Distributes alternative documentaries to cable stations. Ask for a program schedule.
**First Run/Icarus Films,**
www.frif.com, 718-488-8900
**Focus Features,**
www.focusfeatures.com,
212-539-4000
**National Asian American Telecommunications Asociation,**
www.naatanet.org
**New Day Films,**
www.newday.com, 201-652-6590
**PBS Video,** www.shoppbs.org,
800-328-7271
**Turning Tide Productions,**
www.turningtide.com,
800-557-6414
**Viewing Race,** www.viewingrace.org, 212-274-8080
   Independent films/videos on race and diversity.
**Witness,** www.witness.org
   Video and technology to fight for human rights.
**Women Make Movies,**
www.wmm.com

# Books to Empower Young People

The books listed below have children or young people as the protagonists fighting for social justice. We suggest you read the whole bibliography because the categories overlap. We also suggest that books for the youngest children, e.g., picture books, can be used successfully with older students.

## Abolitionist Movement/ Underground Railroad

Armstrong, Jennifer, *Steal Away ... to Freedom* (New York: Scholastic, 1992). A tale of two girls — one white and one black — escaping on the Underground Railroad. Told from each girl's perspective. Gr. 5/up.

Clark, Margaret Goff, *Freedom Crossing* (New York: Scholastic, 1991). Young people working on the Underground Railroad. Gr. 5/up.

Hansen, Joyce, *The Captive* (New York: Scholastic, 1993). Inspired by the true story "The Life of Olaudah Equiano or Gustavus Vass, the African," Hansen writes from the perspective of a young African kidnapped and brought to New England who struggles to return to his homeland. Gr. 5/up.

Hansen, Joyce, *Which Way Freedom?* (New York: Walker, 1986). An ALA Notable Book. Obi, a young slave during the Civil War, is determined to escape from his terrible plantation life and fight for freedom. Obi ends up joining the Union army. Gr. 6/up.

Lyons, Mary, *Letters from a Slave Girl* (New York: Scribners, 1992). Harriet Jacobs is born into slavery. Following the death of her mistress, a promise to be freed goes unfulfilled and young Harriet finally escapes slavery. She is forced to live seven years in a cramped

attic waiting for a chance to go North. She communicates with family members through letters describing her ordeal. Gr. 6/up.

Meadowcraft, Enid La Monte, *By Secret Railway* (New York: Scholastic, 1972). Historical adventure about a white boy and a black boy working in the Underground Railroad. Traditional sex roles are displayed throughout the book and could be the basis of some anti-sexist discussion. Gr. 5/up.

Sterne, Emma Gedlers, *The Slave Ship* (New York: Scholastic, 1953). A fictionalized account of the slave rebellion on the *Amistad* ship led by Cinque. Gr. 5/up.

Smucker, Barbara, *Underground to Canada* (New York: Puffin Books, 1977). A story of escape from slavery by two African-American girls. Author draws on activities of two Abolitionists, Alexander M. Ross of Canada and Levi Coffin of Ohio. Gr. 6/up.

Turner, Glennette Tilley, *Running for Our Lives* (New York: Holiday House, 1994). A young boy helps his family make a long and dangerous trek on the underground railroad from Missouri to Canada. Gr. 5/up.

## Anti-Nazi Struggle

Gallaz, Christopher and Roberto Innocenti, *Rose Blanche* (Mankato, MN: Creative Education, 1985). Translated from Italian by Martha Coventry and Richard Graglia. During World War II a young girl shows courage in the face of injustice when she takes food to the prisoners of a concentration camp. Picture book.

Lowry, Lois, *Number the Stars* (New York: Dell Publishing, 1989). Ten year old Annemarie Johansen embarks on a dangerous mission to save her friend in Nazi-occupied Denmark. Gr. 5/up.

McSwigan, Marie, *Snow Treasure* (New York: Scholastic Paperback, 1942). A moving story — the truthfulness of which is in question — of how Norwegian children courageously outwitted the Nazis. Gr. 4/up.

Orlev, Uri, *The Island on Bird Street* (Boston: Houghton Mifflin, 1984). Translated from Hebrew by Hillel Halkin. A young Jewish boy is left alone in a fictionalized Warsaw-type ghetto and must draw on his own resources to survive. The horror of war is described for children without blood-curdling details. The story ends with a gun in the boy's hand. Gr. 5/up.

Serrailler, Ian, *Escape from Warsaw* (New York: Scholastic, 1972). An intense and moving story of four Polish children in WWII Europe. Gr. 5/up.

Yolen, Jane, *The Devil's Arithmetic* (New York: Trumpet, 1988). A young girl is transfered back to a Polish village to face the Nazi soldiers who come to take them to the concentration camps. Gr. 5/up.

## Anti-prejudice

Bannerji, Himani, *Coloured Pictures* (Toronto, Ont.: Sister Vision, Black Women and Women of Color Press, 1991). Sujata, a 13-year-old South Asian Canadian Sikh, and her friends confront racism in her classroom and her community. Gr. 5/up.

Garcia, Maria, *The Adventures of Connie and Diego* (Emeryville, CA: Children's Book Press, 1986). Tired of being laughed at because they are different, a pair of multicolored twins run away to ask the animals where they truly belong. An interesting twist on prejudice against multi-racial children. Spanish/English. Gr. 2/up.

Greene, Bette, *The Drowning of Stephan Jones* (New York: Bantam, 1991). Sixteen-year-old Carla Wayland confronts her boyfriend's anti-gay prejudice. When her boyfriend's harassment of a gay couple leads to a drowning, she must decide which side she is on when her boyfriend goes on trial. Gr. 7/up.

Tran, Khanh Tuyet, *The Little Weaver of Thai-Yen Village* (Emeryville, CA: Children's Book Press, 1986). A young Vietnamese girl wounded in the war struggles to maintain her cultural identity while adjusting to life in America. Vietnamese/English. Gr. 3/up.

## African-American Struggles

Coles, Robert, illus. by George Ford, *The Story of Ruby Bridges* (New York: Scholastic, 1995). This picture book tells the story of six-year-old Ruby Bridges, the first Black child to attend an all-white elementary school, and how she deals with the hatred and prejudice she encounters. Kindergarten/up.

Meyer, Carolyn, *White Lilacs* (New York: Harcourt Brace, 1993). The 1921 story of a teenage girl and her family who struggle against an effort by white leaders to move the entire African-

American town of "Freedom," Texas. Based on a true story. Gr. 5/up.

Moore, Yvette, *Freedom Songs* ( New York: Puffin, 1991). Fourteen year old Sheryl traveling from Brooklyn to the South is awakened to the racist segregation and gets involved with her uncle who is working in the Civil Rights Movement. Gr. 5/up.

Taylor, Mildred, *Let the Circle be Unbroken* (New York: Bantam, 1981). Cassie Logan and her family confront all forms of racism in this powerful sequel to *Roll of Thunder, Hear My Cry*. Gr. 6/up.

## Asian Struggles

Crew, Linda, *Children of the River* (New York: Dell, 1991). 13-year-old Sundara fled the Khmer Rouge. Four years later, she struggles to fit in at her Oregon high school, fighting racial prejudice. Gr. 5/up.

Dejong, Meindert, *The House of Sixty Fathers* (New York: Harper Trophy, 1984). Pictures by Maurice Sendak. Tien Pao is alone in Japanese-occupied Chinese territory. He embarks on a long and dangerous journey in search of his home and family. Gr. 4/up.

Hasbudak, Zeynep & Brian Simons, *Zeynep: That really happened to me ...* (London: Panther House, 1986). Available in English and Turkish. The story

of the deportation of a Turkish girl and her and her friends' struggle to prevent it. Gr. 3/up.

Houston, Jeanne Wakatsuki and James D. Houston, *Farewell to Manzanar* (New York: Bantam, 1983). Seen through the eyes of a child, the story of a Japanese-American family's four years at Manzanar internment camp during WWII. Gr. 6/up.

Uchida, Yoshiko, *Journey Home* (New York: Macmillan Children's Group, 1992). The struggle of Yuki and her Japanese-American family after they were released from the WWII concentration camps in the USA. Gr. 4/up.

Watkins, Yoko Kawashima, *So Far From the Bamboo Grove* (New York: Lothrop, 1986). An ALA Notable Book. Despite the hardships she endures with her mother and sister while escaping Korea during WWII, Yoko's story is ultimately one of determination, survival, and love. Yoko survives despite poverty and violence. Gr. 5/up.

Yep, Laurence, *Dragon's Gate* (New York: Harper Collins, 1993). A Chinese youth comes to America to build the transcontinental railroad. He meets intolerable conditions and works with others to overcome them. Gr. 5/up.

Yep, Laurence, *The Star Fisher* (New York: Scholastic, 1991). Chinese-American, Joan Lee and her family are traveling across the U.S. in 1927 and confront racism upon their arrival in West Virginia. She's going to fight to stay. Gr. 5/up.

## Economic Justice Struggles

Hunt, L.C., ed., *The Boy Who Could Sing Pictures* ( New York: Holt and Company, 1973). A medieval tale where the King keeps all the riches and builds a huge army. A child uses his special ability to mobilize the poor people to challenge the King. Gr. 2-6.

Kurusa, *La calle es libre (The Streets Are Free)* (Spanish version: New York: Bilingual Publications, Co., 1966; English version: Scarsborough, Ont.: Firefly Books, 1981). A wonderful story about how a group of children in a Caracas slum struggle to get a park. Beautiful illustrations. Gr. 3/up.

Mathis, Sharon Bell, *Sidewalk Story* (New York: Puffin, 1986). 9-year-old Lilly Etta feels awful when her best friend's family is evicted, so she does something about it. Good for units on homelessness. Gr. 3/up.

Paterson, Katherine, *Lyddie* (Brandon, FL: Trumpet Club, 1991). A teenage farm girl becomes a mill worker in Lowell, Massachusetts, in the mid-1800s and must decide if she will fight for better working conditions. Gr. 5/up.

Taylor, Mildred, *Roll of Thunder, Hear My Cry* (New York: Bantam Books, 1976). A Newberry Award-winning novel about blacks surviving in the South during the Depression. Nine-year old Cassie Logan is the main character. Gr. 6/up.

## Environmental Struggles

Collier, James Lincoln, *When the Stars Begin to Fall* (New York: Delacorte Press, 1986). Angry and frustrated that his family is considered "poor white trash," 14-year-old Harry defies his father and attempts to prove that a factory is polluting their small Adirondack community. Gr. 5/up.

George, Jean Craighead, *Who Really Killed Cock Robin?* (New York: Dutton, 1971). George is an outstanding naturalist, biologist, and activist, and his weaving of these concerns into a mystery novel is skillful. A robin is dead — what really killed the bird, something in the environment or ...? Two children find out through shrewd detective work. Gr. 5/up.

George, Jean Craighead, *The Missing 'Gator of Gumbo Limbo, An Ecological Mystery* (New York: Harper Trophy, 1992). The author of *Julie of the Wolves* writes a mystery involving Liza and her mother who are homeless and live in the Everglades. Gr. 4/up.

Rose, Deborah Lee, *The People Who Hugged The Trees: An Environmental Folk Tale* (Niwot, CO: Roberts Rinehart, Inc., 1990). Illustrated by Birgitta Säflund. A classic folktale of Rajasthan, India, where a young girl, Amrita, led a struggle against a warrior prince who ordered that the forest be cut down. Gr. 1/up.

Zak, Monica, *Save My Rainforest*, illus. Bengt-Arne Runnerström (Volcano, CA: Volcano Press, 1992). Also available in Spanish under the title *Salvan mi selva*, 1987. Eight-year-old Omar Castillo visits the endangered Lacandona Rainforest of Southern Mexico with his father and then starts a campaign to save it, including a talk with the Mexican president and a demonstration in Mexico City's main square. Gr. 2/up.

## Haitian Struggles

Temple, Frances, *Taste of Salt: a Story of Modern Haiti* (New York: Orchard, 1992). Two young Haitians become active in the fight for justice in Haiti. Young Djo, hospitalized after a terrorist bombing, moves into an orphanage because his mother can't afford to keep him. He becomes politically active until he is kidnapped to work in the sugarcane plantations of the Dominican Republic. His dramatic escape brings him back to Haiti to get reinvolved in the dangerous political battle. Gr. 7/up.

## Latino Struggles

Anzaldua, Gloria, *Friends from the Other Side* (Emeryville, CA: Children's Book Press, 1993). Having crossed the Rio Grande into Texas with his mother, Joaquin receives help and friendship from Prietita, a brave Mexican-American girl. Spanish/English. Gr. 4/up.

Mohr, Nicholasa, *Felita* (New York: Bantam, 1989). Illustrated by Ray Cruz. Eight-year old Felita struggles to survive amid discrimination and other problems when her family moves to a new neighborhood. Gr. 4/up.

Picó, Fernando, illus. by María Antonia Ordóñez, *The Red Comb* (Mahwah, NJ: BridgeWater Books, 1994). This brightly illustrated book tells the story of a young girl in rural Puerto Rico in the mid-1800s, and how she enlists the help of her elderly neighbor to protect a runaway slave. Gr. 2/up.

Taylor, Theodore, *The Maldonado Miracle* (New York: Avon Books, 1973). The story of a Mexican boy who illegally comes into the USA to find his father. Gr. 6/up.

Vasquez, Ely Patricia Martinez, *The Story of Ana* (Pasadena, CA: Hope Publishers, 1985). The story of a girl from El Salvador and her flight to the USA. Spanish/English. Gr. 3/up.

## Native American Struggles

Banks, Sara, *Remember My Name* (Niwot, CO: Roberts Rinehart Co., 1993). Eleven-year-old Annie Rising Fawn is a Cherokee Indian who must struggle to survive during the Indian Removal of 1838. Gr. 4/up.

Le Sueur, Meridel, *Sparrow Hawk* (Duluth, MN: Holy Cow! Press, 1987). Story of two boys who experience the joy of discovery and the tragedy of swift change at the time of the Black Hawk War. Gr. 5/up.

O'Dell, Scott and Elizabeth Hall, *Thunder Rolling in the Mountains* (Boston: Houghton Mifflin, 1992). Through the eyes of Chief Joseph's daughter, the reader shares every twist in this classic tale of cruelty, heroism, and betrayal. Gr. 5/up.

Paul, Paula G., *Dance With Me, Gods* (New York: E.P. Dutton, 1982). A fictionalized account of a young Pueblo boy's participation in the Pueblo rebellion of August 10, 1680, against Spanish colonialists of what is now New Mexico. Pakatu is caught between his friendship with a Spanish priest and his people's desire for self-determination. Based on true accounts of written history by Spaniards and oral history by Pueblo Indians. Gr. 5/up.

Thomasma, Kenneth, *Kunu: Escape on the Missouri* (Jackson, WY: Grandview Publishing, 1989). Illustrated by Craig Fleuter. Kunu and his grandfather attempt to return to their homeland in Minnesota after approximately 2,000 Winnebago Indian people were forcibly removed from their land in an order signed by President Lincoln. Gr. 5/up.

## Peace Struggles

Boyd, Candy Dawson, *Charlie Pippin* (New York: Puffin Book, 1988). Charlie, an African-American 11-year-old girl, gets in trouble for setting up an illegal store in her school. But her real trouble revolves around understanding her Vietnam War veteran father. When she sets up a "War and Peace" committee in school she begins to understand lots of things. Gr. 5/up.

Coerr, Eleanor, *Sadako and the Thousand Paper Cranes* (New York: Dell, 1977). A true story about an 11-year old Japanese girl who dies because of the radiation poisoning she suffered 9 years earlier in the bombing of Hiroshima. The story shows her spirit and strength. Gr. 3/up.

Dolphin, Laurie, *Oasis of Peace* (New York: Scholastic, 1993). Provides an insightful look at a unique community in Israel, Nev Shalom/Wahat al-Salam. Its purpose is to promote peace and harmony between Arabs and Jews. Includes Hebrew and Arab language. Kinder./up.

Langton, Jane, *The Fragile Flag* (New York: Harper & Row, 1984). A modern-day fantasy where a group of children lead a massive march on the White House to stop the new "Peace Missile." A great read-aloud book for a classroom. Gr. 5/up.

Pirtle, Sarah, *An Outbreak of Peace* (Philadelphia: New Society Publishers, 1987). Children plan to enlist an entire New England town in declaring "an outbreak of peace." Gr. 4/up.

Rostkowski, Margaret, *After the Dancing Days* (New York: Harper, 1986). ALA Notable Book. As she makes friends with two wounded soldiers at a veterans' hospital and learns the real cause of her uncle's death in WWI, Annie discovers that war is not the exciting, heroic venture she thought it was. Annie's empowerment comes through her loss of innocence and her determination to work with the wounded. She doesn't fight for peace, but she understands the horrors of war. Gr. 9/up.

Vigna, Judith, *Nobody Wants a Nuclear War* (San Francisco: Albert Whitman, 1986). A girl who fears the possibility of nuclear war learns what she can do to prevent such a tragedy. Gr. 1/up.

Wahl, Jan, *How the Children Stopped the Wars* (Berkeley: Farrar, 1993). A fable in the Middle Ages in which a children's crusade stops all war. Gr. 4/up.

Wondriska, William, *John John Twilliger* (New York: Holt & Winston, 1966). A fantasy story in the village of Merry-All in which a little boy defeats an evil Machine Gun man. Gr. 2/up.

## South African Struggles

Gordan, Sheila, *The Middle of Somewhere: A Story of South Africa* (New York: Bantam Books, 1992). A family struggles against the relocation of their village by the South African government. Gr. 5/up.

Gordan, Sheila, *Waiting for the Rain* (Brandon, FL: Trumpet, 1989). Two life-long friends on opposite sides of apartheid, Tengo and Frikkie come of age amidst the oppressive conditions of South Africa. Gr. 5/up.

Naidoo, Beverly, *Chain of Fire* (New York: HarperCollins, 1993). Fifteen-year-old Naledi and her friends struggle to prevent the white South African government from relocating their entire vil-

lage. A sequel to *Journey to Jo'Burg*. Gr. 4/up.

Naidoo, Beverly, *Journey to Jo'Burg: A South African Story* (New York: Scholastic, 1985). Thirteen-year-old Naledi must make a harrowing journey with her younger brother into Johannesburg to fetch her mother, as their baby brother is dying. Gr. 3/up.

Sacks, Margaret, *Beyond Safe Boundaries* (New York: Puffin, 1989). A white girl comes of age in South Africa in the 1960s as her older sister joins a secret group opposed to apartheid. Gr. 6/up.

## Free Speech/Human Rights

Schami, Rafik, *A Hand Full of Stars* (New York: Puffin, 1990). A first-person account of a teenage boy who keeps a journal and becomes increasingly angry with the repressive Syrian government, which arrests and tortures his father. The boy embarks on a dangerous mission of publishing an underground newspaper. Gr. 6/up.

UNICEF, *A Children's Chorus: Celebrating the 30th Anniversary of the Universal Declaration of the Rights of the Child* (New York: E.P. Dutton, 1989). Beautifully illustrated book summarizes the 1959 Declaration of the Rights of the Child which speaks to issues of nutrition, housing, recreation and medical services as well as freedom from discrimination, special attention for the handicapped, and the right to be treated equally. Gr. 3/up.

## Women's Movement

Oneal, Zibby, *A Long Way to Go: A Story of Women's Right to Vote* (New York: Puffin Books, 1990). The suffragist movement from the perspective of children. Gr. 3/up.

Hoffman, Mary, *Amazing Grace* (New York: Dial Books, 1991). With the help of her mother and grandmother, Grace overcomes her classmates' objections to a girl being cast as Peter Pan in their school play. ❐

# Non-fiction Books for Children on Movements for Social Justice

The books listed below are non-fiction and in limited ways help children understand the breadth and strength of past and contemporary social movements. Although we have designated them for children, older students will benefit greatly from reading them and critiquing their shortcomings. We have also listed several books that are "how to" manuals for social activism. These, too, can be helpful if used critically.

## Asian

Chin, Steven, *When Justice Failed: The Fred Korematsu Story* (Austin: Steck Vaughn Co., 1993). Part of *Stories of America* series. Explains the Japanese internment during WWII and the struggle against it. Gr. 3/up.

## Native American

Ortiz, Simon, *The People Shall Continue* (Emeryville, CA: Children's Book Press, 1987). Illustrated by Sharol Graves. An epic story of Native American peoples, extending from the creation to present, a "teaching story" of destruction, fighting back, and survival. Highly recommended. Gr. 3/up. (Write for catalog as they publish many good books: Children's Book Press, 6400 Hollis St #4, Emeryville, CA 94608.)

## Latino

Catharine de Ruiz, Dana and Richard Larios, *La Causa: the Migrant Farmworkers' Story* (Austin: Steck Vaughn Co., 1993). Part of *Stories of America* series. Gr. 3/up.

Martínez, Elizabeth, ed., *500 años del pueblo chicano/500 Years of Chicano History* (Albuquerque: SouthWest Organizing Project, 1992). Bilingual pictorial history of the Chicano people. Gr. 6/up.

Samora, Julian and Patricia Vandel Simon, *A History of the Mexican-American People* (South Bend: University of Notre Dame Press, 1993). A useful overview spanning from the arrival

1910 march for women's right to vote.

of the Spaniards to current events. Gr. 6/up.

## Women

Ash, Maureen, *The Story of The Women's Movement* (Chicago: Children's Press, 1989). Good basic introduction for children. Gr. 3/up.

Sullivan, George, *The Day the Women Got the Vote: A Photo History of the Women's Rights Movement* (New York: Scholastic, 1994). Excellent photos. Gr. 3/up.

Stein, R. Conrad, *The Story of the Nineteenth Amendment* (Chicago: Children's Press, 1982). Story of the women's suffrage movement. Gr. 2/up.

## Labor Movement

Cahn, William, *A Pictorial History of American Labor* (New York: Crown Publishers, 1975). Oversized reference book accessible to all ages of children. Gr. 5/up.

Meltzer, Milton, *Bread and Roses: The Struggle of American Labor, 1865-1915* (New York: Vintage, 1973). The best short work for students on early U.S. labor struggles. Gr. 6/up.

Meltzer, Milton, *Cheap Raw Material: How Our Youngest Workers Are Exploited and Abused* (New York: Viking, 1994). A highly readable account of child labor throughout history. Gr. 6/up.

## Civil Rights Movement

Hughes, Langston, and Milton Meltzer, *A Pictorial History of the Negro in America* (New York: Crown, 1963). Valuable for children of all ages.

Kelso, Richard, *Days of Courage: The Little Rock Story* (Austin: Steck-Vaughn Co., 1993). Part of a series of non-fiction children's books edited by Alex Haley, this book describes the struggle by high school students to integrate Little Rock Central High School. Gr. 4/up.

Kent, Deborah, *The Freedom Riders* (Chicago: Children's Press, 1993). A description of the movement of young people who fought to end segregation in our nation's bus system. Wonderful photos. Gr. 3/up.

Levine, Ellen, *Freedom's Children* (New York: Putnam, 1993). A well-written description of thirty different young people who participated in the Civil Rights Movement, serving time in jail, attending previously all white schools, and participating in marches. Black and white photos, chronology, bibliography and index. Gr. 7/up.

Rochelle, Belinda, *Witness to Freedom: Young People Who Fought for Civil Rights* (Woodland Park, CO: Lodestar Books, 1993). An overview of the Civil Rights Movement focusing on nine young people who participated in different parts of it. Includes photos and index. Gr. 4/up.

Webb, Sheyann and Rachel West Nelson, *Selma, Lord Selma: Girlhood Memories of the Civil Rights Days* (Tuscaloosa: University of Alabama Press, 1980). An excellent account of the Civil Rights Movement from two children who were active in it. Gr. 5/up.

McKissack, Patricia and Fredrick, *The Civil Rights Movement in America* (Chicago: Children's Press, 1987). A conventional, but useful, history with lots of good illustrations. Gr. 7/up.

One of the "Little Rock Nine" trying to enter high school in 1957.

UPI/BETTMANN

Myers, Walter Dean, *Now is Your Time! The African-American Struggle for Freedom* (New York: Scholastic, 1993). A fine overview of the struggle against slavery in the 19th century. Brief chapters on 20th century struggles are not as satisfactory. Gr. 7/up.

## Organizing Manuals

Hoose, Phillip, *It's Our World Too: Stories of Young People Who are Making a Difference* (New York: Little Brown and Co., 1993). Accounts of young people (mainly in their teens) who have worked for social justice on issues ranging from sexism in high schools to organizing a campaign against racist grafitti. Includes short intro on young activists throughout history. Gr. 6/up.

Lesko, Wendy, *No Kidding Around! America's Youngest Activists Are Changing Our World and You Can Too* (Information USA: 1-800-879-6862.) Examples of student activism. Gr. 7/up.

Lewis, Barbara, *Kids with Courage, True Stories About Young People Making a Difference* (Minneapolis: Free Spirit Publishing, 1992). An anthology of true stories of kids fighting crime and working for democracy and social justice. Also available: *A Teacher's Guide to Kids with Courage*, which includes questions and addresses for children to write. Gr. 6/up.

Lewis, Barbara, *The Kid's Guide to Social Action: How to Solve the Social Problems You Choose — and Turn Creative Thinking into Positive Action* (Minneapolis: Free Spirit Publishing, 1991). A useful handbook offering tips and sample formats for letters to the editor, petitions, etc. Environmentally oriented. List of contact organizations includes everything from the Republican Party to the People's Anti-war Mobilization. Gr. 7/up.

Milne, Teddy, *Kids Who Have Made a Difference* (Northampton, MA: Pittenbruach Press, 1989). 34 short descriptions of kids who have made a difference. Gr. 4/up.

Terrell, Ruth Harris, *A Kids Guide to How to Stop the Violence* (New York: Avon Books, 1992). An easy to understand explanation of many forms of violence that affect children, and ideas on what they can do about it. Includes glossary and index. Gr. 4/up. ❏

# Curricula to Promote Equity and Justice

The following curricula should be in every school's professional library. An asterisk* indicates that the resource is available from Teaching for Change (see page 200).

*Anti-Bias Curriculum: Tools for Empowering Young Children*, Louise Derman-Sparks and the A.B.C. Task Force. National Association for the Education of Young Children, 1989. www.naeyc.org Perhaps the best book for the early child/primary level on how to teach about all forms of bias and what to do about it.

*Beyond Heroes and Holidays: A Practical Guide to K-12 Anti-Racist, Multicultural Education and Staff Development,* Enid Lee, Deborah Menkart, and Margo Okazawa-Rey, eds. Teaching for Change, 2002. A 432-page treasury that includes lesson plans and staff development activities, as well as critical examinations of controversial school issues such as bilingual education and tracking. Contains an extensive guide to teaching and learning resources and many helpful Internet sites.

*Caribbean Connections,* Catherine Sunshine, ed., Teaching for Change/EPICA, 1991. Stories, interviews, songs, drama, and oral histories, accompanied by lesson plans for secondary language arts and social studies. Puerto Rico, Jamaica, Haiti, Moving North, Overview of Regional History.

*Colonialism in the Americas: A Critical Look* and *Colonialism in Asia: A Critical Look,* Susan Gage, VIDEA, 1991. Through dialogue and cartoons, each book traces the development of colonialism and its legacy.

*Flirting or Hurting? A Teacher's Guide on Student-to-Student Sexual Harassment in Schools (Grades 6 through 12),* Nan Stein and Lisa Sjostrom, NEA Professional Library, 1994. Order from Center for Research on Women, Wellesley College, Wellesley, MA 02181, 617-283-2510; or NEA Professional Library, 800-229-4200. An excellent curriculum with stories and role plays.

*How to Tell the Difference: A Guide for Evaluating Children's Books for Anti-Indian Bias*, Beverly Slapin, Doris Seale, and Rosemary Gonzalez, Oyate, 1996. Excellent activities to prompt critical thinking around Native American issues.

*Keepers of the Earth: Native American Stories and Environmental Activities for Children*, Michael J. Caduto and Joseph Bruchac, Fulcrum Inc., 1988. Features a collection of North American Indian stories and related hands-on activities designed to inspire children. An interdisciplinary approach to teaching about the earth and Native American cultures. Also *Keepers of the Earth Teacher Guide*.

*Multicultural Mathematics*, Claudia Zaslavsky, J. Weston Walch, 1993. Creative and useful math activities. Includes some excellent lessons to prompt critical thinking around issues of tobacco consumption.

*Multicultural Voices in Contemporary Literature: A Resource Guide for Teachers*, Frances Ann Day, Heinemann, 1994. Short biographies of 39 authors and illustrators from 20 different cultures, with a bibliography of their writings. Also contains suggestions for classroom use.

*Open Minds to Equality: A Sourcebook of Learning Activities to Promote Race, Sex, Class, and Age Equity*, Nancy Schniedewind and Ellen Davidson, Prentice Hall, 1998. This activity-packed guide for grades 3-8 does an excellent job addressing controversial topics. Also by Schniedewind and Davidson is *Cooperative Learning, Cooperative Lives: A Sourcebook for Learning Activities for Building a Peaceful World*, W.C. Brown, 1987.

*The Power in Our Hands: A Curriculum on the History of Work and Workers in the United States,* Bill Bigelow and Norm Diamond, Monthly Review, 1988. Role plays and writing activities help students explore issues about work and social change. An essential curriculum for any school-to-work program.

*Putting the Movement Back into Civil Rights Teaching*, Deborah Menkart, Alana D. Murray, and Jenice L. View, eds., Teaching for Change and the Poverty and Race Research Action Council, 2004. This book provides lessons and articles on how to go beyond a "heroes" approach to teaching about the Civil Rights Movement. It includes interactive and interdisciplinary lessons, readings, writings, photographs, illustrations, and interviews.

*Reading, Writing, and Rising Up: Teaching About Social Justice and the Power of the Written Word,* Linda Christensen, Rethinking Schools, 2000. "My students walk out the school door into a social emergency," Linda Christensen writes. "I believe that writing is a basic skill that will help them both understand that emergency and work to change it." This practical, inspirational book offers essays, lesson plans, and a remarkable collection of student writing, all rooted in language arts teaching for justice.

*Rethinking Columbus*, 2nd edition, revised, Bill Bigelow and Bob Peterson, eds., Rethinking Schools, 1998. This 196-page book includes 80 articles, poems, historical documents, resources, and classroom activities to teach about indigenous rights and American history.

*Rethinking Globalization: Teaching for Justice in an Unjust World,* Bill Bigelow and Bob Peterson, eds., Rethinking Schools, 2002. This comprehensive 402-page book helps teachers raise critical issues with students in grades 4-12 about the increasing globalization of the world's economies and infrastructures, and the many different impacts this trend has on our planet and those who live here. *Rethinking Globalization* offers an extensive collection of readings and source material on critical global issues, plus teaching ideas,

Continued on next page

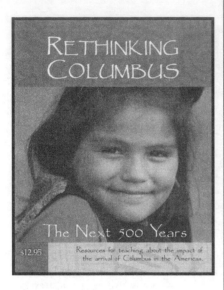

RETHINKING COLUMBUS

The Next 500 Years

$12.95    Resources for teaching about the impact of the arrival of Columbus in the Americas.

## Curricula

**(continued from previous page)**

lesson plans, and resources for classroom teachers.

*Rethinking Our Classrooms, Volume 2: Teaching for Equity and Justice,* Bill Bigelow, Brenda Harvey, Stan Karp, Larry Miller, eds., Rethinking Schools, 2001. This companion to *Rethinking Our Classrooms, Volume 1* presents a rich new collection of from-the-classroom articles, curriculum ideas, lesson plans, poetry, and resources — all grounded in the realities of school life.

*Strangers in Their Own Country: A Curriculum on South Africa*, Bill Bigelow, Africa World Press, 1985. Dated, but excellent historical background and useful lesson models.

*Through Indian Eyes: The Native Experience in Books for Children,* Beverly Slapin and Doris Seale, eds., Oyate, 1998. An excellent resource for elementary classroom teachers and librarians. Articles, stories, poetry, and in-depth reviews of books dealing with Native Americans. ❑

# Anthologies:

## For Older Students:

*African American Literature* (Austin: Holt, Rinehart, and Winston, 1992). Outstanding selections of historical and contemporary literature. The writing assignments provoke students to examine their own lives.

Annas, Pamela J., and Robert C. Rosen, eds., *Literature and Society: an Introduction to Fiction, Poetry, Drama, Nonfiction* (Engelwood, N.J.: Prentice Hall, 1990). An extensive reader organized around various themes. Includes useful teaching guide and helpful suggestions for use in the classroom.

*King, Laurie, ed., *Hear My Voice: A Multicultural Anthology of Literature from the United States* (Menlo Park, CA: Addison Wesley, 1991). This collection includes literature and writing assignments. A former teacher, King has a good feel for selecting and providing assignments that work well with students.

## For Younger Students:

Ada, Alma Flor, Violet J. Harris, and Lee Bennet Hopkins, eds., *A Chorus of Cultures: Developing Literacy Through Multicultural Poetry* (Carmel: Hampton-Brown Books, 1993). An excellent collection that includes many student-written examples.

*Brody, Ed, et al., eds., *Spinning Tales Weaving Hope: Stories of Peace, Justice and the Environment* (Philadelphia: New Society Publishers, 1992). Stories from around the world.

*Harris, Violet J. and Christopher Harris, eds., *Teaching Multicultural Literature in Grades K-8* (Norwood, MA: Christopher Gordon, 1992). Excellent essays and extensive bibliographies on many racial groups. Well annotated.

Sullivan, Charles, ed., *Children of Promise: African-American Literature and Art for Young People* (New York: Abrams, 1991). Beautiful artwork and inspiring collection of poetry. Useful for students of all ages. ❑

---

# Maps and Posters

*Peters Projection World Map* presents all countries according to their true size. *A New View of the World* by Ward Kaiser is a handbook on the Peters map. Map: $20. Available from Northern Sun Merchandising, 2916 E. Lake St., Minneapolis, MN 55406. www.northernsun.com, 612-729-2001.

Asante, Molefi K. and Mark T. Mattson, *Historical and Cultural Atlas of African Americans* (MacMillan, 1992). Excellent reference book.

Waldman, Carl, *Atlas of the North American Indian* (Facts on File, 1989). Maps and illus. by Molly Braun. $16.95.

*Turnabout Map of the Americas* presents South America on the top and North America on the bottom. Available in English, Spanish, or Portuguese. $7.95. Available from Laguna Sales, 4015 Orme St., Palo Alto, CA 94306. 415-494-2717.

A variety of progressive posters are available from these sources: Syracuse Cultural Workers, www.syrcultural workers.com, 315-474-1132; Donnelly/Colt, www.donnellycolt.com, 860-455-9621; Northern Sun Merchandising, www.northernsun.com; and Northland Poster Collective,www.north landposter.com, 800-627-3082.

A collection of 84 maps and charts on Native-American history is available from Historic Indian Pub., c/o Bruce Roberts, 676 DeSoto St., Salt Lake City, UT 84103. 801-359-0306; fax 801-533-9379.

*Women of Hope* Poster Series by the Bread and Roses Cultural Project. Four series: African-American, Latina, Asian-American, and Native-American/Hawaiian. All consist of 12 beautiful photos and paintings and a study guide. ❑

*Available from Teaching for Change.

# Organizations and Periodicals

### Adbusters Media Information
www.adbusters.org; 1243 W. 7th Avenue, Vancouver, BC V6H 1B7; 604-736-9401

Publishes *Adbusters,* a provocative bimonthly magazine. A fun-to-read critique of media and advertising. Excellent website that includes spoof cartoons that generate class discussion.

### Center for Law and Education
www.cleweb.org; 1875 Connecticut Avenue NW, Suite 510, Washington, DC 20009; 202-986-3000

An excellent source for information on federal education legislation and policy.

### Defense for Children International
www.dci-is.org

A secular, international organization working for the rights of children throughout the world. Excellent web resources.

### *Dollars & Sense*
www.dollarsandsense.org; 740 Cambridge Street, Cambridge, MA 02141; 617-876-2434

6 issues/year. Provides easy to understand articles on the economy from a critical perspective.

### Facing History and Ourselves
www.facing.org; 16 Hurd Road, Brookline, MA 02146; 617-232-1595

An education project that targets hatred, prejudice, racism, and indifference by focusing on teaching students about the Holocaust. Resources, workshops, and newsletter.

### Fairness & Accuracy In Reporting
www.fair.org; 130 W. 25th Street, New York, NY 10001; 212-633-6700

Excellent national media watch group. Publishes *Extra!,* an indispensible journal of media criticism. Articles useful in classroom.

### Food First
www.foodfirst.org; 398 60th Street, Oakland, CA 94618; 510-654-4400

Educational materials on the roots of hunger and global inequality.

### The Gay, Lesbian and Straight Education Network (GLSEN)
www.glsen.org; 121 W. 27th Street, Suite 804, New York, NY 10001; 212-727-0135

An excellent provider of resources, lesson plans, and materials to teach against bullying and homophobia. Good for teachers and students alike.

### *Green Teacher*
www.greenteacher.com; 2045 Niagara Falls Blvd., U-7 Niagara Falls, NY 14304; 416-960-1244

Quarterly. Emphasizes hands-on environmental education.

### *In These Times*
www.itt.org

A biweekly magazine of news, opinion, and culture, committed to extending political and economic democracy and to opposing the tyranny of the marketplace over human values.

### National Association for the Education of Young Children
www.naeyc.org; 1509 16th Street NW, Washington, DC 20036; 800-424-2460

Publishes *Young Children* and other useful materials.

### National Center for Fair and Open Testing (FairTest)
www.fairtest.org; 342 Broadway, Cambridge, MA 02139; 617-864-4810

See especially *FairTest Examiner,* a quarterly newsletter on assessment issues.

### National Coalition of Education Activists (NCEA)
www.edactivists.org; 1420 Walnut Street, Philadelphia, PA 19102; 215-735-2418

Activist group of parents and teachers working on anti-racist education projects including tracking, standardized testing, and class size. Quarterly newsletter and annual conference.

### *New Internationalist*
www.newint.org; PO Box 1062, Niagara Falls, NY, 14304; 905-946-0407

Reports on issues of world poverty and inequality. Articles reproducible for students. 11 issues/year.

### *NACLA Report on the Americas*
www.nacla.org; 38 Greene Street, 4th Floor, New York, NY 10013; 646-613-1440

Detailed analyses on Latin-American and Caribbean issues. 6 issues/year.

### *The Nation*
www.thenation.com; 33 Irving Place, New York, NY 10003

Weekly. Important articles on world and national events from a progressive perspective.

### National Women's History Project,
www.nwhp.org; 3343 Industrial Drive, Suite 4, Santa Rosa, CA 95403; 707-636-2888

The project has a variety of K-12 curriculum materials, and also holds workshops and training seminars.

### *Our Schools, Our Selves*
5502 Atlantic Street, Halifax, NS BCH 9Z9; 416-463-6978

Bimonthly journal on educational issues, focusing on Canada.

### OYATE
www.oyate.org; 2702 Mathews Street, Berkeley, CA 94702; 510-848-6700

Organization focusing on histories of indigenous people of the Americas. Evaluation of texts, distribution of materials.

## Organizations and Periodicals

(continued from previous page)

### Philadelphia Public School Notebook
www.thenotebook.org; 215-951-0330 ext. 107

A quarterly newspaper that reports on issues of school reform and social justice in the Philadelphia area.

### Radical Teacher
www.radicalteacher.org; PO Box 382616, Cambridge, MA 02238

Quarterly magazine with many valuable articles and teaching ideas from a critical standpoint.

### Resource Center of the Americas
www.americas.org; 317 17th Avenue SE, Minneapolis, MN 55414; 612-627-9445

Distributes excellent curricula on Central and Latin American issues.

### Rethinking Schools
www.rethinkingschools.org; 1001 E. Keefe Avenue, Milwaukee, WI 53212; 800-669-4192

Publishes quarterly magazine with articles on social justice teaching and educational policy. Also publishers valuable books on critical teaching.

### Teachers and Writers Collaborative
www.twc.org; 5 Union Square West, New York, NY 10003

Offers ideas and strategies for teaching writing, poetry, and fiction. Publishes *Teachers and Writers* magazine. 6 issues/year. Also has an online bookstore with hard-to-get teaching and writing books.

### Teaching for Change
www.teachingforchange.org; PO Box 73038, Washington, DC 20056; 800-763-9131

The best catalog of multicultural curricular resources.

### Teaching Tolerance
www.tolerance.org; 400 Washington Ave., Montgomery, AL 36104

Mailed twice a year to teachers at no charge, this magazine has a range of popularly written articles and a useful resource section. Published by Southern Poverty Law Center which also offers videos, CDs, and curriculum on the Civil Rights Movement and hate and

prejudice reduction. Small grants to teachers are also available from the center.

### U.S. Committee for UNICEF
www.unicefusa.org; Education Department, 333 E. 38th St., New York, NY 10016; 212-922-2510

Publishes a variety of materials on world poverty and development. Has a free-loan video service.

### VIDEA
www.videa.ca

Resources and lessons on global issues appropriate for all age levels.

### Wilmington College Peace Resource Center
www.wilmington.edu/manila/peace/home.html

Distributes wide selection of peace and justice videos and materials.

### Z Magazine
www.zmag.org; 18 Millfield Street, Woods Hole, MA 02543

Detailed articles on current events from a critical perspective. 11 issues/year.☐

# Books on History, Policy, and Educational Theory

*At the risk of neglecting dozens of books, we include here a few of the volumes that have helped shape our social and pedagogical analysis.*

Apple, Michael, *Ideology and Curriculum* (New York: Routledge, 1990). An evaluation of the politics of curriculum — how the structure and content of schooling is profoundly undemocratic. A tough read, but worthwhile.

American Social History Project, *Who Built America?* in two volumes (New York: Pantheon Books, 1992). The central focus of this history is the changing nature of work in America.

Banks, James A., *Teaching Strategies for Ethnic Studies,* 5th edition (Boston: Allyn and Bacon, 1991). A readable summary of the histories of the main ethnic groups in the U.S. along with teaching ideas.

*Christensen, Linda and Stan Karp, eds., *Rethinking School Reform: Views from the Classroom* (Milwaukee: Rethinking Schools, 2003). This anthology puts classrooms and teaching at the center of the debate over how to improve public schools, providing a primer on a broad range of pressing issues, including school vouchers and funding, multiculturalism, standards and testing, teacher unions, bilingual education, and federal education policy.

*Delpit, Lisa, *Other People's Children: White Teachers, Students of Color, and Other Cultural Conflicts in the Classroom* (New York: The New Press, 1995). An eloquent, thought-provoking book that is a must-read for white educators in urban classrooms.

Freire, Paulo, *Pedagogy of the Oppressed* (New York: Continuum, 1970). The classic work on critical teaching. Not a quick read, but an essential text.

Galeano, Eduardo, *Open Veins of Latin America: Five Centuries of the Pillage of a Continent* (Monthly Review Press, 1998). A well-documented indictment of U.S. corporate and governmental policy towards Latin America by one of the world's most renowned writers.

Gould, Stephen Jay, *The Mismeasure of Man* (New York: Norton, 1981). A devastating critique of efforts to "measure" intelligence. Particularly useful in rethinking today's assessment tools.

hooks, bell, *Talking Back: Thinking Feminist, Thinking Black* (Boston: South End Press, 1989). Sharply argued critical essays on life in America. Emphasizes the intersection of race, class, and gender oppression.

*Horton, Myles, Judith Kohl, and Herbert Kohl, *The Long Haul: An Autobiography* (New York: Anchor, 1990). An inspiring look at the founder of the Highlander School. Everyone has something to learn from Horton's vision of teaching and learning.

*Lee, Enid, *Letters to Marcia: A Teacher's Guide to Anti-Racist Education* (Toronto: Cross Cultural Communications, 1989). Very practical teaching ideas that challenge conventional modes of thought.

*Loewen, James, *Lies My Teacher Told Me: Everything Your American History Textbook Got Wrong* (New York: The New Press, 1995). Survey and analysis of 12 leading high school textbooks that documents inaccuracies and omissions.

*Lowe, Robert and Barbara Miner, eds., *Selling Out Our Schools: Vouchers, Markets, and the Future of Public Education* (Milwaukee: Rethinking Schools, 1996). A popularly written primer, with a special section on the right-wing education agenda. Available from Rethinking Schools.

McCracken, Janet Brown, *Valuing Diversity: The Primary Years* (Washington, DC: NAEYC, 1993). This is one of the few books on multiculturalism that offers both practical suggestions for classroom activities and strategies to challenge one's own thinking.

*Peterson, Bob and Michael Charney, eds., *Transforming Teacher Unions: Fighting for Better Schools and Social Justice* (Milwaukee: Rethinking Schools, 1999). This stimulating anthology looks at exemplary practices of teacher unions from the local to the national level. The 25 articles weave together issues of teacher unionism, classroom reform, working with local communities, and social justice.

*Swope, Kathy and Barbara Miner, eds., *Failing Our Kids: Why the Testing Craze Won't Fix Our Schools* (Milwaukee: Rethinking Schools, 2000). This anthology includes more than 50 articles that provide a compelling critique of standardized tests and also outline alternative ways to assess how well our children are learning.

*Perry, Theresa and Lisa Delpit, eds., *The Real Ebonics Debate: Power, Language, and the Education of African-American Children* (Milwaukee: Rethinking Schools, 1998). Some of our most important educators, linguists, and writers — as well as teachers and students reporting from the field — examine the lessons of the Ebonics controversy and unravel complexities of the issue that have never been widely acknowledged.

*Nieto, Sonia, *Affirming Diversity: The Sociopolitical Context of Multicultural Education* (New York: Longman, 2000). Offers a research-based rationale for multicultural education and examines how personal, social, political, cultural, and educational factors interact to affect student success.

Oakes, Jeannie, *Keeping Track: How Schools Structure Inequality* (New Haven, CT: Yale University Press, 1985). A classic work revealing how tracking hurts all students, not just the ones in lower tracks.

*Perry, Theresa and James Fraser, eds., *Freedom's Plow: Teaching in the Multicultural Classroom* (New York: Routledge, 1993). A collection of articles that outlines the role of multicultural education in a society that professes to be democratic.

*Shannon, Patrick, ed., *Becoming Political: Readings and Writings in the Politics of Literacy Education* (Portsmouth, NH: Heinemann, 1992). Explains how race, social class, gender, and language play roles in affirming or marginalizing different student groups.

Shor, Ira and Paulo Freire, *A Pedagogy for Liberation: Dialogue on Transforming Education* (Granby, MA: Bergin and Garvey, 1987). Provocative conversations, with great relevance for classroom teachers. Highly recommended.

*Smitherman, Geneva, *Talkin' and Testifyin': The Language of Black America* (Boston: Houghton Mifflin, 1977). A good background resource for people who want to understand standard Black English.

*Takaki, Ronald, *A Different Mirror* (New York: Little Brown, 1993). A multicultural history of the United States. Takaki shows how the conflicts and connections between different groups have shaped society. Excellent background for teachers, with some parts accessible by high schoolers.

*Zinn, Howard, *A People's History of the United States* (New York: Harper and Row, 1999). The best single-volume history of the United States; no teacher should be without a copy. Some sections readable by high school students. ❏

# Poetry Credits

**"Lions,"** by Langston Hughes. Reprinted by permission of the Yale Collection of American Literature, Beinecke Rare Book and Manuscript Library, Yale University. By permission of Alfred A. Knopf, Inc.

**"Ode to My Socks,"** by Pablo Neruda. Reprinted by permission of University of California Press. *Selected Odes of Pablo Neruda,* trans./ed. Margaret Saye Peden. Copyright © 1990 Regents of the University of California, Fundación Pablo Neruda.

**"My Hair is Long,"** by Loyen Redhawk Gali. Reprinted by permission of the author.

**"Ballad of the Landlord,"** by Langston Hughes. Reprinted by permission of Alfred A. Knopf, Inc. Copyright © 1951 by Langston Hughes. Copyright renewed 1979 by George Houston Bass.

**"Honeybees,"** by Paul Fleischman. *Joyful Noise: Poems for Two Voices,* HarperCollins, New York, 1988. Reprinted by permission of HarperCollins Children's Books.

**"Love's Gonna Get Us (Material Love),"** by Damon Turner, student at Jefferson High School. From *Rites of Passage,* Jefferson High School Literary Magazine, Portland, Ore., 1991-1992. Reprinted by permision of the author.

**"what the mirror said,"** by Lucille Clifton. *two-headed woman.* Copyright © 1980 University of Massachusetts Press. Reprinted by permission of Curtis Brown, Ltd.

**"My Father Was a Musician,"** by Dyan Watson, student at Jefferson High School. From *Rites of Passage,* Jefferson High School Literary Magazine, Portland, Ore., 1990-1991. Reprinted by permission of the author.

**"Dream Voyage to the Center of the Subway,"** by Eve Merriam. From *Finding a Poem,* Copyright © 1970 by Eve Merriam. Reprinted by permission of Marian Reiner.

**"Questions from a Worker Who Reads,"** by Bertolt Brecht. *Bertolt Brecht Poems, 1913-1956* (1987). Reprinted by permission of the publisher, Routledge, New York and the Brecht Estate.

**"Forgiving My Father,"** by Justin Morris. From *Rites of Passage,* Jefferson High School Literary Magazine, Portland, Ore., 1994-95. Reprinted by permission of the author.

**"Rayford's Song,"** by Lawson Inada. *Legends from Camp,* Coffee House Press, Minneapolis, 1992. Reprinted by permission of the author.

**"Face the Facts: We're Not that Bad,"** by Felícitas Villanueva, student at South Division High School, Milwaukee, WI, 1988. Reprinted by permission of the author.

**"Rebellion Against the North Side,"** by Naomi Shahib Nye. *Hugging the Jukebox,* Breitenbush, Portland, 1984. Reprinted by permission of the author.

**"The Funeral of Martin Luther King, Jr.,"** by Nikki Giovanni. *Black Feeling, Black Talk, Black Judgement* (1971). Copyright © 1968, 1970 by Nikki Giovanni. Reprinted by permission of William Morrow and Co., New York.

**"In Memory of Crossing the Columbia,"** by Elizabeth Woody. *Seven Hands, Seven Hearts: Prose and Poetry.* Eighth Mountain Press, Portland, Oregon, 1994. Reprinted by permission of the author.

**"Gurl,"** by Mary Blalock, student at Jefferson High School. From *Rites of Passage,* Jefferson High School Literary Magazine, Portland, Ore., 1993-1994. Reprinted by permission of the author.

**"To the Young Who Want to Die,"** by Gwendolyn Brooks. *The Near Johannesburg Boy.* Third World Press, Chicago, 1987. Reprinted with permission.

**"Lineage,"** by Margaret Walker. *This is My Century: New and Collected Poems,* Copyright © 1989 by Margaret Walker. Reprinted by permission of the University of Georgia Press, Athens, Georgia. ❑

# Reprints from Rethinking Schools

The following articles originally appeared in *Rethinking Schools*. Back issues and subscriptions are available from Rethinking Schools, 1001 E. Keefe Ave., Milwaukee, WI 53212-1710, 414-964-9646.

"Unlearning the Myths That Bind Us," by Linda Christensen.

"Taking Multicultural, Anti-racist Education Seriously, an interview with Enid Lee."

"Race and Respect Among Young Children," by Rita Tenorio.

"Teaching for Social Justice: One Teacher's Journey," by Bob Peterson.

"The Challenge of Classroom Discipline," by Bob Peterson.

"Getting Off the Track," by Bill Bigelow.

"My Mom's Job Is Important," by Matt Witt.

"There's More to Heroes Than He-Man," by Marcie Osinsky.

"Looking Pretty: Waiting for the Prince," by Lila Johnson.

"The Day Sondra Took Over," by Cynthia Ellwood.

"Promoting Social Imagination," by Bill Bigelow and Linda Christensen.

"Expectations and 'At-Risk' Children," by L.C. Clark.

"The Pigs," by Molly Schwabe.

"The Politics of Children's Literature," by Herb Kohl.

"Why Students Should Study History, an interview with Howard Zinn."

"Why We Need to Go Beyond the Classroom," by Stan Karp.

"Forging Curriculum Reform Throughout a District," by David Levine.

"Why Standardized Tests Are Bad," by Terry Meier.

"Detracking Montclair High," by Stan Karp.

"Videos with a Conscience," by Bill Bigelow and Linda Christensen.

"Books to Empower Young People," by Bob Peterson. ❑

# INDEX

## A

**activism,**
student, 30-33; 35-38; 40-41; 47; 55; 191-195;
social investigation and changemaking, 62-63;
teacher, 30-33; 35-38; 40-41; 48; 162-167.

**African Americans,** *see also Civil Rights Movement;*
as anti-tracking activists, 176-177;
*Glory* (film), 111;
*The Color Purple* (film), 111;
Rosa Parks, 137-140.

**anthologies,** 201.

**anti-racist education,** 4; 19-22; 170; *see also multicultural education, racism, stereotypes;*
compared to multicultural education, 19;
implementation of, 20;
slavery, 152;
teaching resources, 22.

**Asian Americans,**
immigration, 44-48;
students, 44-48.

**assessment,** *see also testing;*
grades and equity, 64-65;
in untracked classes, 59;
181.

**"at-risk" students,** 126-128.

## B

**bibliographies,** *see resource lists*

**Bigelow, Bill,** 58-65; 88-90; 110-111; 114-124; 158-159; 187-190.

**black migration,** 111.

**Bravo, Ellen,** 103-105.

**Brecht, Bertolt,** 91.

**Brooks, Gwendolyn,** 125; 160.

**Bruchac, Joseph,** 146-149.

**bureaucracy,**
and site-based management, 163;
in teacher unions, 165.

## C

**cartoons,** 8-9;
student critique of, 83; 187; 190.

**Central America,** 40-41.

**child labor,**
teaching about, 70-71.

**children's literature,** 191-195;
African-American struggles, 191-192;
anti-fascism, 191;
anti-prejudice, 191-192;
anti-slavery, 191;
Asian struggles, 192;
"Cinderella," African-American versions, 10;
civil rights, 192-193;
economics, 193;
environment, 193;
freedom of speech, 195;
Haitian, 193;
Latino(a), 193-194;
Native American, 194;
peace movement, 194-195;
social justice movements, 196;
South Africa, 195;
"The Three Little Pigs," 11;
women's movement, 195.

**Christensen, Linda,** 8-13; 16; 50-55; 56-57; 109; 110-111; 142-145; 184-186; 187-190.

**civil disobedience,** 139-140.

**Civil Rights Movement,** 137-140;
*see also African Americans;*
Montgomery bus boycott, 140.

**Clark, L.C.,** 126-128.

**classroom community,** 46-48;
building, 50-55; 62; 74;
creating a safe space for sharing, 186.

**classroom organization,** 34-35.

**Clifton, Lucille,** 66.

**cognitive research,**
and tracking, 180.

**Colón, Jesús,** 102.

**colorblindness,** 24; 130-131.

**commercialism,** 49.

**Constitutional Convention role play,** 114.

**Council on Interracial Books for Children,** 14-15; 21.

**critical literacy,** 56.
how to teach, 158-159.

**curricula,**
to promote equity and justice, 197.

**curriculum reform,** 117-124; 168-170;
obstacles to, 170.

## D

**Davidson, Ellen,** 75.

**Delpit, Lisa,** 130-132.

**dialogue journal,** 8.

**Diamond, Norm,** 88-90.

**dictionary skills**
and racism in language lesson, 75.

**discipline,** 34-39;
and coaching, 56-57;
and name-calling, 56-57;
and rules, 34-35.

**distribution of resources (world),** 92-93.

**districtwide reform,** 164; *see also restructuring.*

**diversity,** *see also multicultural education;*
and standardized tests, 172-173.

**Dorfman, Ariel,** 8.

## E

**economics,** 94.

**Ellwood, Cynthia,** 98.

**expectations,** 126-128; 129; 134-135.

## F

**Fairness and Accuracy in Reporting (FAIR),** 84.

**Fleischman, Paul,** 42-43.

**flirting,** 106-107; *see also sexual harassment.*

**folktales,** 74.

## G

**Gall, Loyen Redhawk,** 29.

**games,**
to combat bias among young children, 68-69;
math, 78.

**gangs,** 50-52.

**gender roles,** 14.

**Giovanni, Nikki,** 141.

**Goodlad, John,**
and tracking research, 178.

**Gordon, Lenore,** 86.

## H

**harassment,** *see also sexual harassment;*
techniques to counter, 26.

**Hilliard III, Asa G.,** 127.

**Hersh, Susan,** 92-93.

**Hispanics,** *see Latino(a)s*

**history,**
Douglass, Frederick, 63;
immigrants, 45-46;
immigration, 158;
Mexican War, 150-151; 158-159;
resources, 156;
slavery, 61-62; 152;
teaching about sexism, 153;
teaching about racism, 153;
and objectivity, 154;
West Coast longshore strike, 59-60;

# INDEX

Zinn, Howard, interview with, 150-155.
**homophobia,** 86-87; 144-145.
**homosexuality,** 37-38; 144-145.
**Hughes, Langston,** 6; 39.

**I**

**immigration,** 53; 117-124; 158; anti-immigrant sentiment, 44-48.
**Inada, Lawson Fusao,** 108.
**Industrial Workers of the World (IWW) role play,** 124.
**interior monologues,** 187; and teaching history, 60-61.

**J**

**jobs,** *see work.*
**Johnson, Lila,** 83.

**K**

**Karp, Stan,** 82; 162-167; 176-177.
**kindergarten,** 24-28.
**King, Martin Luther, Jr.,** 140; 141.
**Kohl, Herbert,** 134-135; 137-140.

**L**

**language arts,** standard English, 142-145; writing support, 177.
**Latino(a)s,** 134-135; in children's literature, 193-194; Mexican immigration, 158; Puerto Ricans, 102.
**learning styles,** 127; *see also multiple intelligences.*
**Lee, Enid,** 19-22.
**Levine, David,** 168.
**libraries,** researching bias, 85.
**"Little Things Are Big" (story),** Jesús Colón, 102.
**"Looking Pretty, Waiting for the Prince" (student prose),** 83.
**low expectations,** 126-128; 129.

**M**

**maps,** 200.
**mathematics,** 94; games of chance and skill, 78; geometry, 77; math literacy resources, 85; measurement, 77; media bias lessons, 84-85;

numbers in foreign languages, 76; symbols, 76-77; teaching ideas, 76-78.
**Meier, Terry,** 171.
**Merriam, Eve,** 182.
**Mexican War,** 150-151; 158-159.
**Miller, Karen,** 44-48.
**Miller, Larry,** 103-105.
**multicultural education,** 4; 19-22; and anti-racist education, 19; definition of, 19; implementation of, 20; 170; 176.
**multiple intelligences,** 172; *see also learning styles.*
**myths,** and folklore, 100; and stereotyping, 8-13.

**N**

**Native Americans,** 36; and anti-racist education, 20; Cherokee removal role play, 115; creation myths, 146; literature, 146-149; oral traditions, 147.
**Neruda, Pablo,** 16; 17-18.
**newspapers,** researching bias in, 84.
**No T.V. Week,** 80.
**Nye, Naomi Shihab,** 136.

**O**

**Oakes, Jeannie,** 178-181.
**oral history,** 74.
**organizations,** 198-199.
**Osinsky, Marcie,** 74.

**P**

**Paley, Vivian Gussin,** 130-132.
**parents,** 74; 169; disagreement with reforms, 176; and work, 70-72.
**parent involvement,** 127-128; 129; 168-170; 176; and No T.V. Week, 80; and site-based management, 163; and story sharing, 74.
**Parks, Rosa,** 137-140.
**periodicals,** 198-199.
**Peterson, Bob,** 30-33; 34; 35-38; 39; 40-41; 80-81; 84-85; 92-93; 158-159; 191-195.
**poems,**

"Ballad of the Landlord," Langston Hughes, 39; "Dream Voyage to the Center of the Subway," Eve Merriam, 182; "Face the Facts: We're Not that Bad," Felícitas Villanueva, 133; "Forgiving My Father," Justin Morris, 97; "Funeral of Martin Luther King, Jr., The," Nikki Giovanni, 141; "Gurl," Mary Blalock, 67; "Honeybees," Paul Fleischman, 42-43; "In Memory of Crossing the Columbia," Elizabeth Woody, 157; "Lions," Langston Hughes, 6; "My Father Was a Musician," Dyan Watson, 73; "My Hair Is Long," Loyen Redhawk Gali, 29; "Ode to My Socks (Oda a los calcetines)," Pablo Neruda, 17-18; "Questions from a Worker Who Reads," Bertolt Brecht, 91; "Rayford's Song," Lawson Fusao Inada, 108; "Rebellion Against the North Side," Naomi Shihab Nye, 136; "To the Young Who Want to Die," Gwendolyn Brooks, 160; "Two Women," anonymous, 112-113; "What the Mirror Said," Lucille Clifton, 66.
**poetry,** credits, 202; lessons, 16; 109; teaching guide, 184-186.
**policy,** books on, 200.
**posters,** 200.
**poverty,** 92-93.
**pre-kindergarten children,** 68-69.
**Puerto Ricans,** 102; culture, 98.

**R**

**racism,** 102; *see also anti-racist education;* in children's literature, 14-15; dignity, 139;

RETHINKING OUR CLASSROOMS

# INDEX

and guilt, 21-22; 154;
and language lesson, 75;
in language, 14;
and teaching, 134-135;
and textbooks, 14-15; 134-135;
and toys, 95;
and tracking, 176-177;
and white students, 154;
and working class whites, 153-154;
and young children, 24-28.

**read-arounds,** 186.

**reading,** 129.

**resource lists,** 48; 69; 81; 85; 94; 105; 156;
anthologies, 201;
books for children on movements for social justice, 196;
books to empower young people, 191-195;
curricula to promote equity and justice, 197;
educational books on theory and practice, 200;
maps and posters, 200;
organizations and periodicals, 198-199;
videos, 187-190.

**restructuring,** 131; 164-165;
*see also districtwide reform.*
and standardized tests, 173.

**role plays,** 88-90; 114-124;
implementation of, 116;
and teaching history, 59-61;
West Coast longshore strike, 59-60.

## S

**Schniedewind, Nancy,** 75.

**Schwabe, Molly,** 129.

**schoolwide themes,** 27.

**school reform,** 121; 162-166;
role play, 117-124;

**segregation,** 137-140; 152.

**sexism,** 10-13; 111; 188;
and toys, 95.

**sexual harassment,** 103-105; 106-107; *see also flirting;*
resources, 105;
school policy on, 104;
victimization, 104.

**Shakespeare, William,** 149.

**simulation,** 88-90.

**Sjostrom, Lisa,** 106-107.

**slavery,** 61-62; 152.

**site-based management,** 163-164; *see also restructuring.*

**standardized testing,** 171-175.

**standard English,**
teaching of, 142-145.

**Stein, Nan,** 106-107.

**stereotypes,** 8-9; *see also anti-racist education;*
in cartoons, 83;
and children's literature, 11; 14-15; 36;
and games to combat bias among young children, 68-69.
and gender roles, 10;
in media, 85;
and Native Americans, 10;
using pictures to combat, 68-69.
and young children, 27-28.

**storytelling,** 74.

**student prose and poetry,** 29; 49; 52-55; 61; 73; 83; 133, 143-144.

**student responsibility,** 100.

## T

**teacher neutrality,** 40-41.

**teacher study groups,** 165-167.

**teacher unions,** 165.

**television,** 80-82;
alternative activities, 80;
and children's viewing habits, 80-81;
critiquing, 81;
critiquing commercials, 49; 82;
and elementary children, 32;
and gender roles, 9; 37;
lesson ideas, 80-83;
No T.V. resources, 81;
and young children, 25.

**Tenorio, Rita,** 24-28.

**testing,**
ACT, 172;
SAT, 172;
and class and cultural biases, 174-175;
standardized testing, 171-175;
and tracking, 173.

**textbooks,**
student critique of, 158-159.

**theory,**
books on, 200.

**tokenism,**
in children's literature, 14.

**toys,** 95.

**tracking,** 129; 178-181;
alternatives to, 58-65; 179-181;
and average students, 179;

consequences of, 178;
detracking efforts, 176-177;
and heterogeneous grouping, 180;
and high-ability students, 179;
and low-ability classes, 179;
and racism, 176-177;
student critiques of, 63-64;
and student evaluation, 181;
and uneven opportunities, 178-179.

**Turner, Damon,** 49.

## U

**unions,** *see teacher unions.*

## V

**videos,**
African Americans, 190;
Asian Americans, 189;
cartoons, 190;
civil rights, 189;
fascism, 189;
gay rights, 189;
immigration, 189;
labor, 189;
Latino(a)s, 189;
Native Americans, 190;
South Africa, 190;
Vietnam, 189;
women, 188.

**Vietnam War,** 110.

**Villanueva, Felícitas,** 133.

**violence,** 50-52; 107.

## W

**Walker, Margaret,** 133.

**Watson, Dyan,** 73.

***White Teacher* (book),** Vivian Gussin Paley, 130-132.

**whole language,**
and anti-racist education, 24-28.

**Wiggins, Grant,** 100.

**Witt, Matt,** 70-72.

**Wolpert, Ellen,** 11; 68-69.

**women's lives,** 10-13; 110-111; 188.

**Woody, Elizabeth,** 157.

**work,** 70-72.
and job segregation, 71;
why study? 70.

## Z

**Zaslavsky, Claudia,** 76-77.

**Zinn, Howard,** 150-155.

# THE NEW TEACHER BOOK

### Finding Purpose, Balance, and Hope During Your First Years in the Classroom

Teaching is a lifelong challenge, but the first few years in the classroom are typically among a teacher's hardest.

This collection of writings and reflections — some by new teachers, others by veterans with decades of experience to share — offers practical guidance on how to effectively navigate the school system, how to form rewarding professional relationships with colleagues, and how to connect in meaningful ways with students and families from all cultures and backgrounds.

*The New Teacher Book* will help new teachers from kindergarten through high school to sustain the passion and ideals that led them to teaching, and channel that energy into the day-to-day reality of working in a school.

September 2004 • Paperback • 248 pages • ISBN 0-942961-45-5

## Only $14.95!

Plus shipping and handling

U.S. shipping and handling is 15% of the subtotal (minimum charge $4.00). Canadian shipping and handling is 25% of the subtotal (minimum charge $5.00).

*"The New Teacher Book* puts to rest the false dichotomy between academic excellence and teaching for social justice. It is highly motivating for new teachers and inspirational for us 'old' teachers, who will be reminded of the joy, activism, and caring with which we began teaching."

— Jill Moss Greenberg, Executive Director, National Association for Multicultural Education (NAME)

ORDER ONLINE: www.rethinkingschools.org

CALL TOLL-FREE: 1-800-669-4192 • OR USE THE ORDER FORM ON PAGE 215

# RETHINKING GLOBALIZATION
## TEACHING FOR JUSTICE IN AN UNJUST WORLD

Edited by Bill Bigelow and Bob Peterson

**GLOBALIZATION.** The word speaks to our growing interconnectedness. American teenagers wearing sneakers made in China. South Americans watching US television shows. Internet messages flashing across continents. But this is only a partial view of our "global village." We are connected, but in very unequal ways – ways that pose dire threats to the health of the planet.

*Rethinking Globalization* alerts readers to the challenges we face – and also spotlights the enormous courage and creativity of people working to set things right. This essential resource includes role plays, interviews, poetry, stories, background readings, hands-on teaching tools, and much more.

## ONLY $18.95 EACH!
Plus shipping and handling

U.S. shipping and handling costs are 15% of the total. Minimum s&h charge of $4.
Canadian shipping and handling costs are 25% of the total. Minimum s&h charge of $5.

March, 2002/Paperback/400 pages/ISBN 0-942961-28-5

---

*"Rethinking Globalization is an invaluable resource for educators, youth organizers, and those of us who seek to move our world toward hope and justice in a time of privatization, greed, and despair. This book dares to educate youth about global economic and racial relations, insisting always on our collective responsibility to know, to organize, and to resist exploitation."*

Michelle Fine
Professor, Graduate Center, City University of New York

---

**ORDER ONLINE: www.rethinkingschools.org**
**CALL TOLL-FREE: 1-800-669-4192 ▪ OR USE ORDER FORM ON PAGE 215**

# Reading, Writing, and Rising Up:

Teaching About Social Justice and the Power of the Written Word

## by Linda Christensen

"My students walk out the school door into a social emergency," Linda Christensen writes. "They are in the center of it. I believe that writing is a basic skill that will help them both understand that emergency and work to change it."

This practical, inspirational book offers essays, lesson plans, and a remarkable collection of student writing, all rooted in an unwavering focus on language arts teaching for justice. An excellent resource for colleagues, staff development, teacher education, and school libraries.

2000 • Paperback • 196 pp. • ISBN 0-942961-25-0

## Only $12.95!

Plus shipping and handling*

* U.S. shipping and handling costs are 15% of the total.
Minimum s&h charge of $4.00.
Canadian shipping and handling costs are 25% of the total.
Minimum s&h charge of $5.00.
For other international orders, contact our office for additional shipping costs.
Payment in U.S. dollars only.

**SECURE ONLINE ORDERING:**
**www.rethinkingschools.org**

**CALL TOLL-FREE: 1-800-669-4192**
**Monday - Friday, 8am - 9pm (ET)**

**OR USE ORDER FORM ON PAGE 215**

*Visa and MasterCard accepted.*

**CALL 1-800-669-4192 FOR A <u>FREE</u> CATALOG OF ALL OUR MATERIALS.**

"At long last we have a book that both shows and tells how to teach students to produce not only "pretty words and adept dialogue," but "searing analysis." This profound work of emancipatory pedagogy brings together theory, classroom practice, personal narrative, and student work. Linda Christensen is a talented, brilliant teacher, who has distilled her 24 years with students in a rainbow classroom into a major accomplishment."

— Geneva Smitherman, University Distinguished Professor, Michigan State University; author of <u>Talkin' That Talk: Language, Culture, and Education in African America.</u>

RETHINKING COLUMBUS
The Next 500 Years

**RETHINKING COLUMBUS
The Next 500 Years**

edited by
**Bill Bigelow and
Bob Peterson**

## Only $12.95!
Plus shipping and handling

**SHIPPING AND HANDLING**
USA: 15% of the total. Minimum $4.00.
Canada: 25% of the total. Minimum $5.00.

1998 / Paperback / 192 pages
ISBN 0-942961-20-X

"Since its first publication, *Rethinking Columbus* has been a valuable resource. This is truly a book that deserves (and needs) to be in every school library."
Joseph Bruchac (Abenaki)
author of numerous award-winning books for children

"Even richer material, a marvelous compendium ... an exciting treasure for teachers and students."
Howard Zinn
author of *A People's History of the United States*

*Rethinking Columbus* has changed the way schools teach about the "discovery of America." This greatly expanded new edition has over 100 pages of new material including the exciting classroom-tested role play, The Trial of Columbus, Thanksgiving Day materials, updated resource listings, and much more. Over 80 essays, poems, interviews, historical vignettes, and lesson plans re-evaluate the myth of Columbus — right up to the present day. Packed with useful teaching ideas for kindergarten through college.

*Rethinking Columbus* draws together a rich chorus of multicultural voices that will help replace murky legends with a more honest, inquisitive sense of who we are and why we are here — and help us celebrate the courageous struggles and lasting wisdom of indigenous peoples.

- *many short articles*
- *classroom materials*
- *handouts*
- *lesson plans*
- *poems*
- *reviews*
- *resources*
- *websites*
- *and much more*

# RETHINKING OUR CLASSROOMS
## Volume 2

This companion volume to the bestselling *Rethinking Our Classrooms: Teaching for Equity and Justice* is packed with articles about teaching, as well as curriculum ideas, lesson plans, poetry, and resources — all grounded in the realities of the classroom. This is an essential book for every educator who seeks to pair concerns for social justice with academic achievement.

*2001/Paperback/244 pages/ISBN 0-942961-27-7*

## ONLY $12.95 EACH!
Plus shipping and handling*

\* U.S. shipping and handling costs are 15% of the total. Minimum s&h charge of $4.00. Canadian shipping and handling costs are 25% of the total. Minimum s&h charge of $5.00.

RETHINKING OUR CLASSROOMS

Teaching for Equity and Justice

VOLUME 2

A RETHINKING SCHOOLS PUBLICATION

$12.95

**SECURE ONLINE ORDERING:**
www.rethinkingschools.org

**FAX:** 802-864-7626

**CALL TOLL-FREE:** 1-800-669-4192
Monday - Friday, 8am - 9pm (ET)

**USE ORDER FORM ON PAGE 215**

Visa, MasterCard and Purchase Orders accepted.

*"Brimming with respect for the intelligence and integrity of teachers as well as for students of all ages, this second volume of Rethinking Our Classrooms continues in the same proud tradition as its predecessor. In its pages, teachers will find hope, energy, and renewal."*

Sonia Nieto, Professor of Language, Literacy, and Culture at the School of Education, University of Massachusetts.

CALL 1-800-669-4192 FOR A <u>FREE</u> CATALOG OF ALL OUR MATERIALS.

## Combined Set of *Rethinking Our Classrooms* and *Rethinking Our Classrooms, Volume 2* for only $19.95

Widely used in teacher education and staff development programs, this two volume set of *Rethinking Our Classrooms* is packed with useful teaching ideas for kindergarten through college.
ISBN for Set: 0-942962-36-6 • $19.95/set, plus shipping and handling.

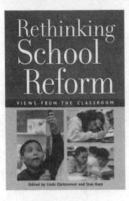
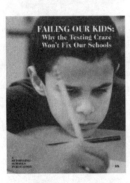

# ORDER FORM

Name _____

Address _____

City _____ State _____ Zip _____

Phone(day) _____

Phone(evening) _____

## Method of payment

❏ Check or Money Order made out to
   Rethinking Schools
❏ Purchase Order
❏ MasterCard   ❏ Visa

Credit Card Number:

_____

Expiration Date: _____

Authorized Signature:

_____

## Mail to:

**RETHINKING SCHOOLS**
**P.O. Box 2222**
**Williston, VT 05495**

**Call toll-free: 1-800-669-4192**
**Monday - Friday 8am - 9pm (ET)**

**FAX: 802-864-7626**
**E-Mail: rts.order@aidcvt.com**

**Secure online ordering at**
**www.rethinkingschools.org**

**Visa, MC and purchase orders**
**accepted.**

**\* Shipping and handling costs** for books in the
U.S. are 15% of the subtotal. (Minimum $4.00.)
Shipping and handling costs for books to Canada
are 25% of the subtotal. (Minimum $5.00.)
Contact for other international shipping costs.
All payments in U.S. dollars. Subscriptions
already include shipping and handling.

Discounts are available for quantity orders for
schools, school districts and nonprofit organizations.
Call 414-964-9646 or email rsmike@execpc.com
Bookstores and distributors call for special rates.

## Books/Booklets

Title _____

___ Number of copies x $_____ (Unit price)   $_____

Title _____

___ Number of copies x $_____ (Unit price)   $_____

Title _____

___ Number of copies x $_____ (Unit price)   $_____

Title _____

___ Number of copies x $_____ (Unit price)   $_____

Title _____

___ Number of copies x $_____ (Unit price)   $_____

*Books/Booklets Subtotal*   $_____

*Shipping and Handling \**   $_____
(Minimum $4.00 for U.S.)
(Minimum $5.00 for Canada)

## Subscriptions

❏ Two-year subscription: $29.95          $_____
   (Save over $9.00 off the cover price!)
❏ One-year subscription: $17.95          $_____

   Subscriptions to Canada and Mexico,
   add $5 per year.                        $_____

   All other international subscriptions,
   add $10 per year.                       $_____
❏ Sample copy: $5                         $_____
❏ Send me information about
   bulk subscriptions.

*Subscription Subtotal*   $_____

## TOTAL ENCLOSED   $_____

2BROC7

RETHINKING OUR CLASSROOMS

# If you liked Rethinking Our Classrooms, then Rethinking Schools is for you.

*Rethinking Schools* is an independent, quarterly magazine published by the same people who brought you *Rethinking Our Classrooms.* Each issue includes:

- Ideas to improve classroom teaching.
- Listings of valuable resources.
- Analyses of critical issues.

All of this and more, written by educators who understand the realities of the classroom.

## Subscribe today!

**Rethinking Schools**
P.O. Box 2222
Williston, VT 05495
802-862-0095
Toll-free: 1-800-669-4192
FAX: 802-864-7626
E-mail: rts.orders@aidcvt.com

**Secure online ordering at:**
www.rethinkingschools.org

*"Rethinking Schools is
a terrific publication."*
Jonathan Kozol
author of Savage Inequalities

## BUSINESS REPLY MAIL
FIRST-CLASS MAIL PERMIT NO 2222 WILLISTON VT

POSTAGE WILL BE PAID BY ADDRESSEE

RETHINKING SCHOOLS
PO BOX 2222
WILLISTON VT  05495-9940

---

*"Rethinking Schools is
a terrific publication."*
Jonathan Kozol
author of Savage Inequalities

## BUSINESS REPLY MAIL
FIRST-CLASS MAIL PERMIT NO 2222 WILLISTON VT

POSTAGE WILL BE PAID BY ADDRESSEE

RETHINKING SCHOOLS
PO BOX 2222
WILLISTON VT  05495-9940

---

*"Rethinking Schools is
a terrific publication."*
Jonathan Kozol
author of Savage Inequalities

## BUSINESS REPLY MAIL
FIRST-CLASS MAIL PERMIT NO 2222 WILLISTON VT

POSTAGE WILL BE PAID BY ADDRESSEE

RETHINKING SCHOOLS
PO BOX 2222
WILLISTON VT  05495-9940